12/10/97
NYPL

DEC

THE COMING OF THE SPANISH CIVIL WAR

THE COMING OF THE SPANISH CIVIL WAR

*Reform, Reaction and Revolution
in the Second Republic*

Paul Preston

METHUEN
London and New York

First published in 1978 by
The Macmillan Press Ltd

First published as a University Paperback in 1983 by
Methuen & Co. Ltd
11 New Fetter Lane, London EC4P 4EE

Published in the USA by
Methuen & Co.
in association with Methuen, Inc.
733 Third Avenue, New York, NY 10017

Printed in Great Britain at the
University Press, Cambridge

British Library Cataloguing in Publication Data
Preston, Paul
    The coming of the Spanish Civil War.
    1. Spain – Politics and government – 1886–1937
    2. Spain – Politics and government – 1931–1939
    I. Title
    946.08   DP243

    ISBN 0-416-35720-2 (University paperback 806)

Library of Congress Cataloging in Publication Data
Preston, Paul.
    The coming of the Spanish Civil War.

    (University paperbacks; 806)
    Reprint. Originally published: London: Macmillan,
1978.
    Bibliography: p.
    Includes index.
    1. Spain – Politics and government – 1931–1939.
2. Spain – Social conditions.   3. Socialism – Spain –
History – 20th century.   4. Right and left (Political
science)   5. Spain – History – Civil War, 1936–1939 –
Causes.   I. Title.

[DP255.P73 1983]   946.081   83-5405
ISBN 0-416-35720-2 (pbk.)

Contents

List of Abbreviations

Political parties, trade unions, etc.

ACNP   Asociación Católica Nacional de Propagandistas – the political wing of Catholic Action.

ASM   Agrupación Socialista Madrileña – the Madrid section of the PSOE.

CEDA   Confederación Española de Derechas Autónomas – the Spanish Confederation of Autonomous Rightist Groups, the largest political grouping of the legalist Right.

CNCA   Confederación Nacional Católico-Agraria – a conservative, Catholic, smallholders' organisation which provided much mass support for the CEDA.

CNT   Confederación Nacional del Trabajo – anarcho-syndicalist trade union.

DRV   Derecha Regional Valenciana – the Valencian section of the CEDA.

FAI   Federación Anarquista Ibérica – the insurrectionary vanguard of the anarchist movement.

FJS   Federación de Juventudes Socialistas – PSOE youth movement, which amalgamated with the Communist youth in April 1936 to form the JSU.

FNTT   Federación Nacional de Trabajadores de la Tierra – landworkers' section of the UGT.

JAP   Juventud de Acción Popular – the youth movement of the CEDA.

JSU   Juventudes Socialistas Unificadas – the joint Socialist–Communist youth movement.

PCE   Partido Comunista de España – the Moscow-oriented Communist party.

POUM   Partido Obrero de Unificación Marxista – the group of left communist dissidents from the BOC and the Izquierda Comunista who joined forces in late 1935 to create a revolutionary alternative to the PSOE and the PCE.

PSOE   Partido Socialista Obrero Español – the Spanish Workers' Socialist Party.

SMA   Sindicato Minero Asturiano – the Asturian miners' section
           of the UGT.
UGT   Unión General de Trabajadores – the trade union organisa-
           tion of the Socialist movement.

Sources

BUGT   *Boletín de la Unión General de Trabajadores de España.*
DSC   *Diario de las sesiones de Cortes,* December 1933 to July
           1936.
DSCC   *Diario de sesiones de las Cortes Constituyentes.*

Preface

During the Second Republic, the parliamentary parties of the Left introduced a series of reforms which fundamentally challenged the social and economic structure prevailing in Spain before 1931. The activities of both the legalist and the so-called 'catastrophist' Right between 1931 and 1939 were primarily a response to these reforming ambitions of the Left. The right-wing victory in the civil war paved the way for General Franco's re-establishment after 1939 of the traditional social order. This book is an examination of the part played by the Socialist party in mounting the reformist challenge, of the determined resistance to reform put up by the political representatives of the landed and industrial oligarchies, and of the effects of the consequent conflict on the Socialist movement and on the democratic regime in Spain.

The Socialists constituted the most important single group on the Spanish Left throughout the 1920s and the 1930s. They were more decisive than their bourgeois Republican allies, both in terms of numerical strength and of their commitment to fundamental social reform. Moreover, as the largest parliamentary party of the Left, they had greater potential efficacy within the democratic system than their more revolutionary rivals. The desultory insurrectionism of the anarchists and the numerical insignificance of both orthodox and dissident Communists deprived all of them of serious possibilities of combating the state apparatus and implanting their view of society. Nevertheless, the theoretical criticisms and the activities of these groups form the background against which the Socialists' drift from reformism to an apparent revolutionism is assessed.

The Socialist role in the Second Republic is examined in the light of two main factors, party ideology and rank-and-file aspirations. Given that the PSOE was a self-proclaimed marxist party, the policies adopted by its leaders were often the consequence of their ideological interpretation of contemporary political and economic development in Spain. At the same time, since the Republic was inaugurated at a time of acute economic crisis and the 1930s saw a massive influx into the Socialist movement of the rural proletariat most affected by that crisis, much party policy is only meaningful in terms of pressures emanating from the base.

These two poles of Socialist activity were naturally conditioned by the stout resistance to change organised by the parties of the Right. Accordingly, the book's second main theme is the legalist Right's attempts first to block reforms and later to introduce a corporative state as a long-term solution to the leftist challenge. In fact, the principal argument of the book is that the most central conflict of the Second Republic, and the main cause of the civil war, was the struggle between the PSOE and the legalist Right, particularly the CEDA, to impose their respective views of social organisation on Spain by means of their control of the apparatus of the state. Both the Socialists and the legalist Right felt at the time that theirs was the crucial battle. They were each confident that the activities of the extremists of Right and Left could be dealt with by the forces of order. What each feared far more was that the other would be able to use legal means to give the Republic a legislative content which would damage the material interests of its followers.

In a predominantly agrarian society, both leftist and rightist considerations of social organisation centred on the land. Rural labourers constituted by far the largest single occupational group within the Socialist union, the UGT. The political formations of the legalist Right, the CEDA, the Agrarians and, to a lesser extent, the Radicals, received finance from and defended the interests of the landed upper classes. They also sought their mass support largely among smallholders. Inevitably, then, this study is concerned to a large degree with the class struggle in agricultural areas and its impact on national politics through the PSOE and the CEDA. Other socially conflictive sectors, especially mining, are also considered in some detail.

The book begins with a chapter on the ideological and tactical development of the Socialist movement between 1917 and 1931. Its purpose is to clarify the unspoken assumptions behind the behaviour of the three main Socialist factions when under pressure during the Second Republic. Chapters two and three deal with the period 1931–3 and examine separately the activities of the legalist Right and of the Socialists in that period. During those years, both groups were elaborating their stance towards the regime and towards each other : the legalist Right moving from a defensive obstructionism to an active determination to establish the corporative state; the Socialists moving from an optimistic reformism to a tentative and rhetorical revolutionism in response to the Right's success in blocking reform. Chapter four brings both groups together and deals with their constant interaction and growing hostility from the right-wing electoral victory of November 1933 to the leftist insurrection of October 1934. In those eleven months, the CEDA under Gil Robles revealed its determination to protect the pre-1931 social order by introducing an authoritarian corporative state. In reply, the Socialists tried to preserve the progressive character of the Republican regime by threats of revolution, which they hoped never to have to fulfil.

The October 1934 rising and its defeat conditioned the tactics of both the Right and the Socialists until the end of 1935. The Socialists were forced to withdraw from organized politics. Chapter five deals with the major internal dissensions and theoretical adjustments suffered by the Socialist leadership from the moment of defeat until the creation of the Popular Front electoral coalition. Chapter six examines the attempts of the CEDA to proceed slowly towards the authoritarian state, in an awareness of the proletarian resistance to such a state revealed in October 1934. The highly skilful strategy employed by the CEDA leader, Gil Robles, was undermined when a tactical miscalculation at the end of 1935 led to the calling of elections. The final chapter deals with the consequences of those Popular Front elections. A leftist victory ended the Right's chances of legally establishing the corporative state and the defence of the threatened social order passed to more violent groups. The Socialists, because of their own internal differences, did not add their strength to the government. Thus, when the bitterness of social conflict spilled over into a partly provoked break-down of law and order, the Socialists were not in a position from which to take effective steps against the rightist resort to a military coup.

Day-to-day violence and the escalation of social hatred are central to the subject of this book. Constant clashes between the forces of order and the rural and urban proletariat were the long drawn-out prelude to a savage civil war. Yet the origin of the conflict has to be sought not in extremist attempts to overthrow society but in reformist efforts to ameliorate the daily living conditions of the most wretched members of society. The implication is clear. The achievements of reformist socialism at a time of economic crisis are as likely as all-out revolutionism to provoke attempts to impose a fascist or corporative state. This is not only revealing with regard to Spain in the 1930s, but also illuminating about the tragedy of Allende's Popular Unity in Chile. Moreover, it highlights the problems facing the Left today in Italy and once more in Spain, as well as illustrating the reasons for the adoption in those countries of 'Eurocommunist' policies. The lessons of Spain and Chile have suggested that the road to reform must be via alliances with the parties of the centre. The failure of the reformist experiment in the Spanish Republic raises crucial questions about the future of 'Eurocommunism'. It is an experience that still has a sombre contemporary relevance.

*   *   *

In preparing this book, I lived for over three years in Spain as well as making many shorter visits. Not surprisingly, given the open-heartedness of Spaniards in general, I incurred a number of debts of gratitude and would like therefore to express my appreciation here.

Many hours of conversation with two participants in the events described helped me to comprehend the daily brutality of Spanish rural life in the thirties. Miguel González Inestal was, and is, one of the libertarian movement's greatest experts on the land question. The late Ignacio Arenillas de Chaves, Marqués de Gracia Real, was a monarchist landowner from Salamanca who was to be defending lawyer at the trial of Julián Besteiro in 1939. Both of them were more generous with time and information than an untried foreign historian could ever have expected.

Two Spanish scholars and friends helped me not to see Spain through English eyes. Jerónimo Gonzalo Rubio has been for many years unstinting with ideas, hospitality and friendship. Joaquín Romero Maura deepened my sense of Spanish history and taught me much about scholarship in general. Without wishing to implicate them as accomplices in this book's shortcomings, I thank them both for their contribution to it.

Special thanks are due to Martin Blinkhorn, Norman Cooper and Frances Lannon who, at various times, went to considerable trouble to read and comment on the text. I also benefited from the suggestions and criticisms of the following friends and colleagues: Juan-José Castillo, Elías Díaz, Juan-Pablo Fusi, Juan García Durán, Gabriel Jackson, Joe Harrison, Edward Malefakis, José Montero Gibert and Angel Viñas.

A number of senior colleagues were generous in their support. Christopher Seton-Watson supervised with unfailing patience the doctoral thesis on which this book is based. Hugh Thomas was kind with books and advice in the early days of my research. Herbert R. Southworth made available to me the unrivalled resources of his library and his knowledge of the Spanish Right. Professors E. A. Bayne, Alistair Hennessy, James Joll and Victor Kiernan gave welcome advice and encouragement.

Had it not been for the kindly prodding of Professor Robert F. Leslie, this study might never have seen the light of day. Nevertheless, neither he nor anyone else mentioned above can be held responsible for any of the judgements or errors contained therein.

Queen Mary College   June 1977

1 The Origins of the Socialist Schism: 1917–31

In the continuing debate on the origins of the Spanish Civil War it has become commonplace for major responsibility to be attributed to the Socialist Party, the PSOE (Partido Socialista Obrero Español). Whether or not the PSOE was responsible for the breakdown of the Second Republic, it certainly had a crucial role to play therein. As the biggest party of the Left, the PSOE provided three ministers in the reforming governments of 1931–3 and the backbone of their parliamentary support. During the period of Centre–Right dominance from 1933 to 1935, the Socialists were the only major opposition force, both in parliament and in the street, and even took part in a major insurrection in 1934. From the so-called Popular Front elections of February 1936 until the outbreak of war in July of that year, the Socialists, yet again the biggest party, were the arbiters of Republican politics. Referring to the 1934 insurrection, one scholar has gone so far as to state that, 'given that the future of the Republic depended on the Socialist movement and the Catholic party, it is important to recognise that it was the former and not the latter which abandoned democratic methods and appealed to violence'.[1]

This appeal to violence was the most obvious symptom of a growing radicalisation of the PSOE which began in 1933 as a result of disillusion with the paucity of the Republic's reforming achievement; of fear that a less militant line would lead Spanish Socialists to share the fate of their German and Austrian comrades; and of a major reassessment of the ideology and tactics of the party. The radicalisation or 'bolshevisation', as its advocates called it, was never complete and was advanced only at the cost of the most bitter polemic within the party. In fact, it was the continuing struggle for power within that virtually paralysed the more moderate groups of the party and prevented them from contributing to the defence of the Republic when it was under threat in the spring of 1936. It is presumably to this fact that Salvador de Madariaga refers in declaring that 'what made the Spanish Civil War inevitable was the Civil War within the Socialist Party'.[2]

The origins of the radicalisation of the Socialists have never been satisfactorily explained. The same is true of its extremely close relationship with contemporary political developments within the Republic and outside Spain. Clearly, until this has been done, it is premature to reach final conclusions about 'responsibilities' for the coming of the Civil War. Nevertheless, it remains true that even militants of the PSOE, and not only those who took the moderate side in the polemic, have been harsh in their later judgements of the attempts to 'bolshevise' the party.[3] In the case of the moderates, this is not difficult to explain. Apart from an understandable resentment of the personal attacks to which they were subject, as long standing militants they also opposed what they saw as an attack on the traditions of the party, which were anything but extreme. In the case of the repentant bolshevisers, it is also not difficult to explain their change of heart. One of the results of the 'bolshevisation' was that large sections of the PSOE fell under the influence of the Communist Party, whose behaviour during the Civil War left a legacy of great bitterness among its erstwhile republican allies. In the aftermath of defeat, they clearly regretted the part they had played in helping the Communists to prominence. In fact, neither of these critical stances substantiates the view of Madariaga, although both help to explain why such a view has been widely accepted as an explanation of the outbreak of hostilities in 1936.

The radicalisation remains to be explained, not least because it made the Spanish Socialist party unique in Europe at a time when most socialist movements were evolving towards ever more moderate positions. The contrast was even greater in relation to the PSOE's own past history of deeply rooted reformism and its lack of a tradition of theoretical Marxism.[4] The party never broke away from its origins among the working-class aristocracy of Madrid printers. Pablo Iglesias, its founder, never gave his party much in the way of independent theory. *Pablismo*, as his ideas were later termed by Trotskyist critics, was always more preoccupied with cleaning up existing politics than with the class struggle, adopting an austere and monkish tone which made the party seem to at least one observer like a brotherhood of moralists. In fact, *pablismo* was a mixture of revolutionary ideology and reformist tactics, which, given the party's numerical weakness, was for Iglesias the only realistic alternative to either destruction or clandestinity. Julián Besteiro, his successor as party leader, also felt that austerity and aloofness were the only viable tactics in the corrupt politics of the restoration era.[5] Thus, after the tragic week of 1909, the PSOE joined with Republican forces in what was virtually a civil-rights campaign. In 1914, even though Spain was not involved in the hostilities, the PSOE leadership failed to take the opportunity to condemn the war and followed the French lead in breaking international solidarity, much to the chagrin of several groups within the party.

The aspirations of the reformist leadership were, until the 1930s, focused on the need to replace the discredited monarchy with a popular republic and hardly at all concerned with notions of social revolution and class struggle. Indeed, *El Socialista*, the party newspaper, at first ignored the Russian revolution, then roundly declared it to be a sad deviation from Russia's real duty – the defeat of Germany.[6] Leaving aside the poverty of the party's Marxism, its lack of revolutionary fervour was partly the result of the fact that, from the PSOE's foundation in 1879 to the boom of the Great War, prices and wages remained relatively stable – albeit among the highest prices and lowest wages in Europe. Perhaps as a partial consequence of that stability, the Spanish working class remained largely demobilised.[7] In 1914 those circumstances began to change. Spain's position as a non-belligerent allowed her to assume the role of supplier of food, clothing and equipment to both sides. A vertiginous industrial boom was accompanied by a fierce inflation, which reached its height in 1916. It was in response to the consequently deteriorating social conditions that the PSOE and its union organisation, the UGT (Unión General de Trabajadores), became involved in the nationwide reform movement of 1917. Even when, in rather complex circumstances, this led to the UGT's becoming involved in a national general strike in August of that year, the maximum aims of the Socialists were the establishment of a provisional republican government, the calling of elections to a constituent Cortes and vigorous action to deal with inflation.[8] The strike was defeated with relative ease by the government at the cost of a savage repression in Asturias and the Basque country, two of the Socialists' major strongholds – the other being Madrid.

The repression of 1917 had a twofold effect on the Spanish Socialist movement. On the one hand, the leadership, and particularly the syndical bureaucracy, was traumatised. On the other, those who had opposed the party line on the world war began to adopt more revolutionary positions. The consequent polarisation became increasingly apparent in the following years. Between 1918 and 1923 there was considerable revolutionary activity (mainly in the rural south and in industrial Barcelona),[9] to which the Socialist leadership maintained an attitude of studied indifference. Yet the continuing inflation and the rising unemployment of the post-war depression had created, in the wake of the bolshevik revolution, a climate of opinion within the Socialist movement, particularly in Asturias and the Basque country, in favour of a revolutionary orientation. Their view was expressed in the journal *Nuestra Palabra*, which under the direction of Ramón Lamoneda and Mariano García Cortés adopted the view that events in

Russia and the failure of the 1917 reform movement in Spain pointed to the irrelevance of the bourgeois democratic stage on the road to socialism. This brought them into conflict with the syndical bureaucracy and especially Trifón Gómez, Manuel Llaneza and Francisco Largo Caballero, who were determined not to repeat what they saw as the senseless adventurism of 1917.[10]

There followed a lengthy debate over what was to be the attitude of the PSOE and the UGT to the Russian revolution and to the Third International. The pro-bolshevik tendency was defeated in a series of party congresses between 1919 and 1921 after a closely fought struggle in which the leadership won the day by being able to rely on the votes of the strong union bureaucracy of paid permanent officials.[11] The defeated Left departed to form the Spanish Communist Party. Numerically, the Communist schism was not a serious blow, but it accentuated the Socialists' ideological weakness at a time of grave economic and social crisis. The party's fundamental moderation was strengthened and there remained a certain moral depression.[12] In the aftermath of the defeat of 1917, the 1921 split left the Socialists without a clear sense of direction and somehow remote from the burning issues of the day. The syndical battles which raged elsewhere attracted less Socialist attention than the parliamentary campaign against the Moroccan war and the King's alleged responsibility for the great defeat of Annual.

The defensiveness and ideological conservatism of the Socialists became patently apparent with the coming of the military dictatorship of General Primo de Rivera on 13 September 1923. His seizure of power was largely a response to the social agitation of the previous six years. Yet the Socialists neither foresaw the coup nor showed great concern when it came, despite the fact that the new regime soon began to persecute other workers' organisations. Beyond a manifesto advocating passive resistance,[13] they did nothing to impede the establishment of the regime and were soon to be found collaborating with it. This reflected the extent to which the leadership had come out of the crisis of 1917 convinced of the need to stick to a legalist tactic, never again to risk the existence of the unions in direct clashes with the state, and to guard at all costs the achievements of existing social legislation.[14]

Years later, the collaboration with the Dictator was to become a moral burden to the Socialists. It is possible that some of the rhetorical extremism shown during the Republic was the symptom of a desire to expunge the egoistic reformism of the Dictadura period. Certainly several Socialist apologists went to some trouble to justify the failure of either the PSOE or the UGT to resist the coup. They claimed that it would have been absurd to risk the workers movement to save the degenerate system of the Restoration monarchy.[15] This was a somewhat specious argument, since there was more at stake than Primo's overthrow of the old politicians, as was shown by the persecution suffered by other parties.[16] Moreover, critics on the Left felt that a general strike would have forestalled the coup and placed the Socialists in a dominant position within national politics.[17] More significantly, there were others within the PSOE itself who were shocked by the opportunism shown by the leadership. They accepted that strike action against the army would have been sentimental and infantile heroics, but could not admit that this justified close collaboration with it. They were disappointed that the party merely shrugged its shoulders instead of taking a strong stand on principle, which might have become a rallying point for later opposition to the Dictator.[18]

As it was, the Socialists took no significant part in the varied resistance movements to the Dictadura, at least until its later stages. This 'discretion' was to lead to division within the Socialist ranks, although left-wing Socialists were later to defend it as a refusal to play the game of the oligarchy.[19] As the Dictator's popularity fell, the Socialist movement in general began to dissociate itself from the regime, but in the early days only a small group was in favour of outright opposition. These were the followers of Indalecio Prieto, who had a certain amount of support in Bilbao and Asturias, and Fernando de los Ríos, whose supporters were to be found in Granada. Although the rest of the Socialist leadership was in favour of collaboration, it was not entirely for the same reasons. Indeed, the collaborationists were in practice equally reformist – as, for that matter, were Prieto and De los Ríos. In theory, however, two distinct factions could be discerned : the practical trade unionists led by Francisco Largo Caballero, and those trade unionists who followed the Marxist revisionist Julián Besteiro. Their differences became apparent only very gradually, and even then they were far from clear to the rank-and-file. Nevertheless, they were to lead to the bitter polemics of the 1930s and to split the movement, owing to the wide personal following which each of the front-rank leaders commanded.

After Pablo Iglesias, the founder of Spanish socialism, Julián Besteiro was the PSOE's most significant figure and one of its very few theoreticians. When Iglesias died in December 1925, Besteiro became president of both the party and the UGT. His theoretical position was analogous to that of Kautsky, of whom he was an open admirer.[20] With Kautsky, he shared an orthodox Marxist analysis of the inevitable progress of society through a bourgeois democratic revolution towards socialism, and he derived from this a pacific and gradualist praxis. Like Kautsky, he rejected the notion of the dictatorship of the proletariat, regarding much of the bolshelvik experience as irrelevant to Spanish conditions.[21] Besteiro, like Iglesias, looked far more towards the British

Labour Party and the Fabians for examples. Accordingly, he was in favour of the Spanish socialists' taking advantage of the opportunities offered by Primo de Rivera in order to defend their material interests.[22]

Those trade unionists within the movement who were not followers of Besteiro tended to be supporters of Largo Caballero, although Prieto also had his adherents, particularly in the north. Largo's attitude to the Dictatorship was similar to Besteiro's, although he lacked the latter's theoretical foundation for it. Largo was essentially a pragmatic trade unionist, who always claimed that he owed his prominence in the movement to his assiduous performance of syndical duties and his close attention to the everyday round of organisational chores. Largo had once written that the workers' movement was the product of their unchanging need to improve their moral and material conditions within the capitalist system.[23] Not unnaturally, he was hostile to any enterprise which might endanger that movement, particularly after the disaster of 1917. When the Dictatorship came, he and his followers reasoned that, although the political struggle was suspended, the syndical struggle had to go on. An economic recovery was being staged after the post-war crisis and they felt that the first task of the UGT was to use any means possible to protect the material interests of their members in the factories and workshops.[24] In practice, this meant going beyond simple pragmatism to a narrow opportunism based on a desire to steal an advantage over the anarcho-syndicalists.[25] This sectarian egoism was to meet considerable rank-and-file opposition, particularly in Asturias, but also among the agrarian sectors of the UGT.

The formal initiative for the collaboration came from the Dictator himself, who could be confident of a sympathetic response in view of the Socialist passivity during his coup. A joint communiqué of the PSOE and UGT had ordered the Socialist movement not to follow the example of the Bilbao workers who had declared a general strike.[26] The approach came in a manifesto to the workers on 29 September 1923 in which Primo thanked the working class for its attitude during his seizure of power. The manifesto was clearly directed at the Socialists. On the one hand favouring social legislation, so dear to the reformists of the UGT, it then called upon the workers to leave those organisations which led them 'along paths of ruin'. This reference to the revolutionary CNT (Confederación Nacional del Trabajo) and PCE (the Spanish Communist Party) was a scarcely veiled offer to the UGT that it could become the exclusive working-class organisation and, in return for collaborating with the regime, eliminate its anarchist and Communist rivals.[27] It struck the chord of the longstanding Socialist hostility to the CNT. Soon after, Pablo Iglesias was gleefully and in similar terms predicting the downfall of the CNT, implying that the workers in its ranks had found themselves there either by mistake or because they were forced. Two days after his manifesto, Primo made a direct offer to Manuel Llaneza, President of the Asturian Miners' Union (SMA : Sindicato Minero Asturiano), to join a committee to examine the problems of the mining industry. Getting the erroneous impression that the SMA would thereby be able to defend its achieve-ments in the way of wages and hours, on the following day Llaneza enthusiastically addressed an already favourably predisposed meeting of the joint national executives of the PSOE and UGT.[28] The meeting decided to support the collaboration begun by Llaneza, although there were three votes against this resolution, including those of Prieto and De los Ríos.

Llaneza was leader of the SMA during the strike of 1917 and, having witnessed its brutal repression, was one of the Socialists most shaken by the events of that year. It was fear of the consequences of another clash with the army which was the basis of his collaborationism. His attitude was opposed even at that early stage by Teodomiro Menéndez, another of the 1917 leaders, and a staunch follower of Prieto.[29] This was symptomatic of nascent division between the UGT rank-and-file and the reformist leadership. The SMA, besides constituting one of the UGT's most substantial sections, was also one of its most militant, and even after the 1921 schism had cordial relations with local Com-munists.[30] For the moment, however, the opposition to the executive's tactic was expressed only by De los Ríos and Prieto, who wrote to Besteiro at the end of 1923 protesting against it. Meeting on 9 January 1924, the National Committee of the PSOE ratified the collaborationist line adopted so far. Nevertheless, it made a small but significant con-cession to Prieto. This was a declaration that no government positions would be accepted without their recipients' being designated by the Socialist organism concerned.[31]

Nevertheless, the integration of the national leadership into the new regime was considerable and the UGT had representation on several state committees.[32] The Socialist 'Casas del Pueblo' remained open and most UGT sections were allowed to continue functioning, while anarchists and Communists suffered a total clamp-down on their activities. The first indication of the military Directory's price for the privileged position accorded the Socialists came in March 1924, when workers' demonstrations were prohibited, prior to the planned May Day celebrations.[33] In return for the workers' docility, the UGT was offered its greatest prize yet, a seat on the Council of State. On 2 June 1924 the Instituto de Reformas Sociales was replaced by a Labour Council, the UGT delegation passing in its entirety from one body to the other. Then, on 13 September, a royal decree allowed for one workers' and one employers' representative from the new council to join the Council of State. The UGT representatives chose Largo Caballero. Within the UGT itself this had no unfavourable repercussions – Besteiro was vice-president and Largo himself secretary-general. However, there was protest within the PSOE.

Prieto and De los Ríos both wrote letters to the PSOE executive denouncing the opportunism of Largo's acceptance of the position and warning that it would be exploited by the Dictator for its propaganda value. In fact, Primo did cite Largo's presence on the Council of State as a reason for not re-establishing democracy.[34] The executive met on 17 October to consider the complaints and decided that the PSOE should not interfere with something concerning the UGT. This was not entirely honest, since the same individuals made up the executive committees of both bodies and it was normal practice to hold joint deliberations on important national issues. As a result of this Prieto resigned.[35] The issue was placed before a plenum of the PSOE national committee on 10 December and Largo's acceptance was ratified by fourteen votes to five. De los Ríos called for a referendum among the rank-and-file, but his proposal was defeated.[36] This division within the party was to have repercussions right up to the Civil War, if only for the personal enmities created. In fact, faced by rumours of schism within the party, Prieto declared publicly that the tactical discrepancies had in no way affected the cordiality and unity among the party's leaders. Nevertheless, it is clear that, both at the time and later, Largo Caballero harboured tremendous personal rancour against Prieto.[37]

The collaboration was to continue and increase despite evidence from Asturias that such a tactic was doing little to protect the workers' interests. The mine-owners provoked a strike in November 1924 by demanding a reduction in wages. While Llaneza hurried to Madrid to see Primo, the owners struck a pre-emptive blow by sacking 350 workers. When the strike came, it was no more than defensive and barely managed to maintain wages at their previous level. This gave rise to criticism, by elements to the left of the Socialists, that collaboration meant handing over the miners bound and gagged to the owners.[38] In no way dismayed, the UGT maintained its pacific attitude, refusing to join movements of resistance to the Dictatorship. Citing the Asturian industrial action as a triumph resulting from collaboration with the regime, Pablo Iglesias claimed that, despite censorship and limits on meetings and strikes, both the UGT and the PSOE were growing under the Dictatorship. In fact, 1926 was to see the most substantial co-operation yet by the UGT. Largo Caballero, speaking at the Madrid Casa del Pueblo, roundly condemned industrial sabotage, go-slows and strikes as likely to provoke lock-outs. He declared that opposition to the regime could prove disastrous for the working-class organisation.[39]

In November 1926, Primo's Minister of Labour, Eduardo Aunós, set up the National Corporative Organisation. Largely the result of a study-tour that he had made in Italy, and incorporating much existing social legislation, its long-term aim was to replace parties of Right and Left and to eliminate the class struggle.[40] Its most practical manifestation was the creation of arbitration committees, *comités paritarios*. The UGT decided to accept the regime's invitation, on the grounds that there were immediate material benefits to be obtained. They reasoned that, if the best conditions for the workers were to be negotiated through the committees, and workers' representation were exclusively in the hands of the UGT, then non-Socialist workers would flock to its ranks. The main activities of the committees consisted of negotiating wages and working conditions (*bases de trabajo*) and arranging compensation for unfair dismissals. It was the belief of the trade-union bureaucracy that the committees prevented many strikes and unnecessary sacrifices for the working class.[41] Years after, when the UGT was criticised for its opportunism in accepting them, it was claimed that UGT orators used them as a front for propaganda against the Dictatorship.[42] There is little evidence for this and, if it happened, it was probably after the tide of popular opinion had turned against the Dictator and the UGT was trying to dissociate itself from the regime.

In any case, it is difficult to calculate how many strikes were avoided by the work of the *comités paritarios*. Certainly by 1927 the economic boom which had so favoured the Dictatorship at first was beginning to come to an end and there was growing evidence of syndical unrest and significant increases in unemployment.[43] Besides affecting the stability of the regime, this was to have major repercussions within the Socialist movement, since it suggested the existence of a rift between the militancy of the rank-and-file and the timid conservatism of the UGT leadership. Nowhere was this more apparent than in Asturias. In the autumn of 1927 the mine-owners tried to increase working hours and decrease piece-work rates. Llaneza was against strike action because he feared that the army would be sent against the miners. The SMA overruled him and went ahead with the strike, which was successful. The effect of this in national terms was that the Asturian leaders began to favour abandonment of the UGT's collaborationist line. They had little choice since members were drifting away from the SMA at an alarming rate, membership dropping from 20,000 in 1921 to 3,000 in 1929.[44]

Opposition to the leadership was not confined to the Asturian miners, but also affected the UGT's rural sections. Agricultural workers were the most numerous occupational group within the UGT and alarm at the drop in their numbers indicated that their importance was being recognised within the Socialist movement.[45] They constituted, moreover, the section which had derived least benefit from UGT co-operation with the Dictadura. Rural *comités paritarios* were never established and Aunós's half-hearted attempts to help rural labourers were instrumental in uniting the landowners of the south against Primo.[46] A significant reflection of feeling within the agrarian section of the movement came from Gabriel Morón, a veteran leader from Córdoba and an important voice within the party. In a devastating critique of the leadership's failure to make a stand against the Dictadura, he claimed that the UGT's egoistic attitude was dividing the workers movement, and complained that nothing was being done to prepare the masses for the end of the regime. He demanded that official posts be relinquished, on the grounds that their retention signified exchanging the party's historical prestige for short-term official patronage.[47]

The discontent now emerging seemed to vindicate the stand taken four years previously by Prieto and De los Ríos. Moreover, it seemed as though their position was gaining adherents, particularly within the PSOE. In September 1927 Primo offered six Socialists seats in his new National Assembly, which was to deliberate on a possible constitutional reform. All six – Largo Caballero, Núñez Tomás, Llaneza, De los Ríos, Santiago Pérez Infante and Lucio Martínez Gil – rejected the offer. Extraordinary congresses of the UGT and the PSOE were called for 7 and 8 October respectively. The rejection was ratified – a clear victory for the anti-collaborationists. Indeed, the PSOE issued a statement demanding the re-establishment of liberty and democracy. Nevertheless, the followers of Besteiro clung to the collaborationist tactic. Besteiro himself was ill, but two of his most loyal supporters, Trifón Gómez of the railway workers' union and Andrés Saborit of the printers' federation, proposed that Primo's offer be accepted if the Socialists could choose their own representatives. The polemic raised was so bitter that it was decided to shelve the issue.[48]

The debate over the National Assembly showed that the intensification of social conflict was having a gradual but significant effect on the configuration of forces within the Socialist movement. Of the three tendencies within the movement – the social-democrats following Prieto, the 'Kautskyism' of Besteiro and the pragmatic trade unionism of Largo Caballero – it was the last that was most noticeably affected by the changing mood of the Socialist working masses. In 1924 Largo had opted for co-operation with the Dictatorship for no more theoretical reason than that he could see substantial material benefits for the UGT in doing so. Thus, in 1927 he began to change his mind in the face of growing evidence that such a tactic was having a deleterious effect on UGT membership. Collaboration had already earned the Socialists the opprobrium of others on the Left.[49] The loss of prestige could be justified only if it were compensated by an increase in numbers. Yet there was little indication that the UGT's virtual monopoly within the state industrial arbitration machinery had a significant effect on recruitment. Indeed, two of the UGT's strongest sections, the Asturian miners and the rural labourers, had suffered appreciable losses during the Dictatorship.[50] The material welfare of the UGT was always to mean more to Largo Caballero than any theory and he was therefore always responsive to shifts in rank-and-file feeling. This goes some way towards explaining some of his otherwise inexplicable changes of tactics during the Republic, when again it was the Asturians and the landworkers who were in the forefront of militancy.

The extent to which opposition to the Dictatorship was growing within the Socialist movement was shown clearly at the Twelfth Congress of the PSOE, which was held from 29 June to 4 July 1928. De los Ríos was in South America, but Prieto and Teodomiro Menéndez defended a line of clear opposition. And it was soon apparent that they were no longer alone. A special committee was created to examine the party's tactics. The tactic of collaboration was rejected by this committee by six votes to four. The majority included Morón from Cordoba and Teodomiro Menéndez from Asturias, who also, in the main Congress, made a resounding speech against collaboration.[51] For censorship reasons, the discussions of the committee on tactics were given no publicity. However, involving as they did the defeat of supporters of Largo Caballero, they seem to have had an effect on his views regarding the Socialist role in the Dictadura. But for the moment, despite the increasingly vocal opposition in favour of a stand for liberty and democracy, the majority view remained pro-collaborationist. This was reflected in the elections for party offices at the Twelfth Congress, and for posts in the UGT at the Sixteenth UGT Congress, held from 10 to 15 September. Besteiro was elected president of both the PSOE and the UGT, and all senior offices went to followers of him or of Largo Caballero.[52]

Nevertheless, conflict between the workers movement and the regime was increasing. After a strike in Seville had been crushed by the forces of order, Socialists of the south retained little faith in the efficacy of co-operation.[53] In Asturias, the inability of the *comités paritarios* to resolve the problems of the mines was ever more apparent. The mines were inefficient and their coal not of high quality. In 1928 the coal industry began to suffer badly from the dumping of cheap British coal. 4000 miners were laid off. Negotiation was impossible and reformist solutions irrelevant. The miners called for nationalisation of the mines; the owners for wage-cuts and redundancies. Primo clearly could never accept attack on the structure of property. When Llaneza complained to him that many miners could get work for only two weeks in any month, the Dictator replied, 'you people panic too easily; it's better to work two weeks than not at all'. The miners were already being pushed towards the radicalisation which was to become a major issue during the Republic.[54]

It was becoming increasingly difficult for the Socialist leadership to maintain that collaboration was for the benefit of the working class, yet in January 1929 Largo Caballero was still arguing against direct action and in favour of government legislation.[55] Nevertheless, he was pulling away from close commitment to the regime. He had little choice, since it was obviously foundering. The universities were in an uproar. Intellectuals, republicans and monarchist politicians protested against the abuse of the law and even prepared resistance movements. In this they were increasingly able to count on support from the army, which had been alienated by Primo's high-handed treatment of the artillery. The bourgeoisie was alarmed to see the peseta falling, and, as 1929 advanced, the first effects of the world depression began to impinge on the Spanish economy. The Socialists were gradually being isolated as the Dictator's only supporters outside his own Unión Patriótica.

Fear of being left behind by the changing circumstances and of losing rank-and-file support finally began to have its effect on the collaborationist majority within the Socialist leadership. On 26 July 1929, Primo offered the UGT the chance to choose five representatives for his National Assembly. His original offer of September 1927 had been rejected only because the Socialists had not been allowed to choose their own delegates. On 11 August the National Committees of the PSOE and the UGT held a joint meeting to discuss the offer. Two main proposals were presented. The first, from Largo Caballero, called for rejection of the offer on the grounds that acceptance would be a contravention of the agreements made in the UGT's extraordinary congress of 7 October 1927. This, apart from bending the truth somewhat, represented a significant change of position by Largo. He had clearly decided that the Dictatorship was discredited and that further association with it would be counter-productive for the Socialist movement. The other proposal, by Besteiro, was in favour of accepting Primo's offer.

The debates in the meeting showed the extent to which the trade union leaders had realised the danger of losing their hold over the Socialist masses. Only Enrique Santiago and Wenceslao Carrillo supported Besteiro's proposal. Yet the change of mind was executed only with the greatest reluctance and because of the pressure of the rank-and-file. Andrés Saborit, Besteiro's most loyal follower, commented, 'our vote was based on the examination of the political circumstances. Really it was a case of rectifying a correct policy out of pure opportunism.'[56] Besteiro had called for an extraordinary congress of the UGT to settle the issue. The objections raised to this proposal showed the extent to which the changing mood of the Socialist masses had begun to influence their leaders. Largo Caballero stated that he was entirely in agreement with Besteiro's reasons for being in favour of collaboration with the regime, but not with the proposal for a congress. It was clear that he did not want to face a revolt from the rank-and-file. Trifón Gómez, leader of the railway workers' union and a Besteirist, said in defence of voting against the president, 'I have no objection whatsoever to supporting what Besteiro says in his declaration, but I am taking into account the sentiments of the organised working class. I believe it useless and damaging to call a congress, because the delegates will come to vote in a majority against participating in the National Assembly.' In the final vote, only Santiago voted with Besteiro, since Carrillo was also convinced that the delegates to any congress would vote against the executive.[57]

Even Besteiro was affected by the circumstances, albeit with greater theoretical consistency. If he was driven now to criticise the Dictadura, it was for reasons of an intellectual reformism and not owing to the practical considerations which swayed the trade-union bureaucracy. The National Assembly to which the UGT had been invited was to discuss a project of constitutional reform which effectively would have blocked any return to 'democratic' normality. Besteiro had been in favour of accepting the invitation in order to contest the project in the Assembly. In fact, the rest of the Socialist leadership was in basic agreement with him, except for the Prieto group, but preferred to make a major gesture to rank-and-file sentiment. With the Dictator's invitation rejected, Besteiro drew up a manifesto containing his thoughts on the projected constitutional reform. Signed by Besteiro and Saborit for the PSOE and by Besteiro and Largo Caballero for the UGT, this manifesto was issued on 13 August 1929. It was refused publication by the censorship apparatus and printed clandestinely and distributed by hand.[58]

The text of the manifesto represented an ample demonstration of Besteiro's thought concerning the political crisis and the role of the Socialist movement therein. It represented no inconsistency with his position regarding collaboration with the regime. On the long road to the establishment of socialism, Besteiro felt that it was legitimate to use all legal means to maintain or improve the situation of the Socialist movement. Seeing the Dictatorship as a transitional stage in the decomposition of the monarchical regime, it seemed logical to him to accept the privileges offered by the Dictator. This was because, according to his rigidly orthodox Marxist analysis, the monarchy had to be overthrown by a bourgeois revolution and therefore the job of the Socialists was to keep their organisation intact until their day should come. In 1929, Primo's project for constitutional reform seemed an attempt to legitimise, and make permanent, the transitional nature of the Dictatorship. Besteiro saw the road to socialism as a legal one and now Primo's scheme was trying to close the legal possibilities. His first reaction was to contest the project legally within the Assembly. When the movement decided against this, he drew up the manifesto. His criticisms of the project were of two sorts. The more immediate and short-term criticisms were based on the fact that the project made only the vaguest promises of social reform and declared an intention to restrict the right to strike. More important were his criticisms of the long-term effects of the project if it were ever put into practice. The powers to be given to the King would make it impossible for the parliament ever to introduce reforms which undermined the interests of the oligarchy. Accordingly, Besteiro reached the conclusion that the precondition for the democratic road to socialism was 'a republican state of liberty and democracy within which we might reach the political power which corresponds to our growing social power'. If Primo destroyed the possibility of establishing the necessary political conditions for the development of socialism, then neither the UGT nor the PSOE could be responsible for the actions to which this might drive them.[59]

This forthright statement did not, however, signify the union of all three tendencies within the Socialist movement. It might have been thought, for instance, that Besteiro's rejection of the Dictatorship would bring him nearer the position of Prieto and De los Ríos, but the coincidence was only accidental. Not being Marxists in any committed way, they were always more concerned with liberty and democratic rights as ends in themselves. Besteiro was also a committed democrat, but he felt that the establishment of basic liberties was the role of the bourgeoisie. Hence, while Prieto and De los Ríos were in favour of Socialist co-operation with middle-class republicans against the monarchy, Besteiro was afraid that the working class could be used to achieve bourgeois goals and lose sight of its own long-term objectives. Largo Caballero's position was different again. Pragmatic and opportunist, he was concerned always with two things : the material interests of the Socialist movement as against any other group and the maintenance of the Socialist bureaucracy's control over the rank-and-file. This pragmatism made Largo's position subject to more sudden and inconsistent shifts than were either of the other two tendencies.

Largo was already moving towards the Prieto position of collaboration with the republicans, although still within a context of profound reformism. Nevertheless, it was a shift and it soon became apparent that it was an adjustment to the wishes of the base militants. On 16 September 1929 he made a speech to the Santander branch of the printing-workers' union (Federación Gráfica Española). He declared that the Socialists could no longer confine their attention to exclusively union matters, 'because, *against our wishes*, circumstances are forcing us to play a part in all kinds of national problems'. He made it clear that he was looking ahead to the end of the Dictadura and was altering tactics accordingly :

> I, who have been accused of rightist tendencies, am one of those who believe that, as long as the working class can act within a legal context which allows it to develop its organisation, it would be madness to leave that context. However, I also believe that if eyes are closed to the desires of the country and if possibilities are closed whereby the country might have developed towards progress, then the working class will know how to do its duty.[60]

This new militancy was perhaps not unconnected with the fact that Santander had seen major clashes between local Socialists and the Dictatorship. Largo was moving away from Besteiro's position towards that of Prieto. On 12 January 1930 he declared that on the road to socialism it would be necessary to pass through a long period of transition, in which Socialists could collaborate in republican bourgeois governments and even become the 'administrators of capitalism'.[61] When, in 1933, that position too proved damaging to the workers movement, Largo just as easily abandoned it in favour of greater radicalisation.

Even though it is possible to distinguish three main tendencies within the PSOE, they were partly masked by some coincidences of political analysis. As befitted a party which had rejected bolshevism, all three tendencies shared an essentially reformist approach. This was made abundantly clear after the decision not to join the Third International. It was further underlined in early 1924, when all sections of the party were to be found rejoicing over the establishment, in January, of the first Labour cabinet in Britain. Pablo Iglesias commented in fulsome terms that it was an event which would repair the damage done to world socialism by the tactics of the Russian Communists. Largo Caballero called it 'the most important event in the entire history of international socialism'.[62] Luis Araquistain, later to be one of Largo's radical advisers, emphasised the importance of following the British road to socialism.[63] Besteiro, of course, was already something of a Fabian and a close follower and admirer of British socialism.[64] De los Ríos was also delighted with the Labour victory and saw it as proof that the class struggle could be avoided.[65] In fact, for many reasons, a gradualist road to socialism in Spain was to prove impossible. The realisation of this was to affect each of the three tendencies of the PSOE in different ways. It was these differing responses that exaggerated the divisions apparent in the 1920s and that formed the basis of the savage polemics which rent the Spanish socialists in the 1930s.

For the moment, however, this was far from apparent. The Dictator resigned on 28 January 1930, and in the subsequent euphoria the Socialists seemed less divided than at any time since 1923. Moreoever, they were in a better position than at any time in their history. The old Liberal and Conservative parties, separated for so long from the old mechanisms of electoral falsification and demoralised by the King's espousal of a dictatorship, were in complete disarray. New republican parties were still in their most embryonic form. Accordingly, at the beginning of 1930 the PSOE was the only properly organised political party in Spain. The situation of the UGT was even more favourable, given the difficulties under which the anarchists and Communists had been forced to operate. Inevitably, the growing opposition to the monarchy looked to the Socialists for support. They were sure of a favourable response from Prieto and his democratic-socialist followers. And, as the crisis sharpened and the rank-and-file grew increasingly militant, Largo Caballero moved ever more quickly towards Prieto's position. Only Besteiro was hostile, believing that it was up to the bourgeois republicans to make their own revolution and determined that the Socialist masses should not be exploited as cannon-fodder. Yet even he adopted something of a passive attitude.

At first, Besteiro threw himself into his academic life as Professor of Logic in Madrid University.[66] It seemed as though he wished to avoid the issues to be faced. He drew up the joint UGT–PSOE manifesto which greeted the government of Primo's successor, General Dámaso Berenguer. Expressing doubts about Berenguer's pledge to re-establish the basic liberties, the manifesto condemned his regime as illegitimate and without a popular mandate. Yet, critical as it was, Besteiro's text contained no hint of active opposition to Berenguer or of any interest in trying to force a change of regime. Indeed, it stated that, if political liberties were re-established, the Socialist movement would resume its participation in normal political life.[67] Not surprisingly, Berenguer was confident that he need expect no trouble from the Socialists. On 29 January 1930, the day he assumed power, he received a report drawn up by the Director-General of Security, General Bazán, on the political and social situation of the country. The report praised the Socialist leaders for keeping the rank-and-file out of political agitation. Its conclusion was that the Socialists, far from constituting a danger to the established order, could be seen as a guarantee of it.[68] Bazán's successor, General Emilio Mola, was also confident that the trade union bureaucracy could be relied on to try to keep the rank-and-file out of militant action,[69] although he was worried about their ability to do so.

It was not long before the Socialists were subjected to mounting pressure by republican forces to add their weight to the movement against the monarchy. Besteiro was firmly against any such Socialist collaboration and spoke out several times, insisting that the republicans show themselves to be united and make clear their programme before requesting Socialist support.[70] Prieto remained as strongly tied to the cause of republicanism as he had been during the Dictatorship, and was playing an ever more important role. One by one, the most significant politicians in the country were declaring themselves against the King. On 20 February 1930, Miguel Maura, son of the great Conservative prime minister Antonio Maura, announced his newly adopted republicanism. On 27 February, another great Conservative, José Sánchez Guerra, declared his lack of faith in Alfonso XIII. They were followed by other significant monarchists, Angel Ossorio y Gallardo and Niceto Alcalá Zamora. But the speech which had the greatest popular effect came from Prieto on 25 April in the Madrid Ateneo. To the chagrin of both Besteiro's group and Largo Caballero, Prieto advocated a revolutionary movement against the monarchy with the participation of the Socialist masses.[71]

Before the summer of 1930 was out, however, Largo Caballero was showing as much enthusiasm as Prieto for Socialist collaboration in the republican movement. There was no theoretical consistency in his attitude. He was acting, as he had done throughout the 1920s, out of an opportunism based on what he calculated to be in the immediate material interests of the UGT. Two things in particular impelled Largo to his change of tactics. They were the increasingly evident economic crisis and its effect on the day-to-day militancy of the Socialist rank-and-file, and, above all, the rapid gains being made by the anarchist CNT, and, on a smaller scale, the Communist Party.

As in the late 1920s, the contraction of the economy was particularly apparent in the mining and agricultural sectors. The militant tendencies of the Asturian miners had been held in check by Llaneza at the cost of falling numbers, but he died in January 1930. Thereafter, the influence of Prieto became ever more powerful. In March, under the leadership of a Prietist, Ramón González Peña, the SMA successfully fought for a 7 per cent wage increase. And, despite orders from the executive committee of the PSOE not to make pacts with republican groups, the Asturian Socialist Federation was soon following a Prietista policy of making alliances in the battle against the monarchy.[72]

On a national level, labour militancy was increasing at a vertiginous rate. 1930 saw, in comparison with 1929, four times as many strikes, involving five times as many strikers, with the loss of ten times as many working days.[73] The UGT leadership seemed unaware of the scope of the economic crisis and was far from prominent in the labour troubles of the spring. Indeed, General Mola even considered proposing an agreement between the UGT and the government-sponsored 'yellow' unions, the Sindicatos Libres, in an effort to combat anarchist and Communist agitation.[74] The CNT had been legalised in April and recovered its old strength at astonishing speed. By June, strikes were breaking out in Catalonia, the Levante, Aragón and Andalusia. The Communists did not attain the same influence, but they had substantial and militant support in the Basque country and in Seville, where the conclusion of Primo's extravagant works programme left a mass of unemployed construction workers.[75]

The wave of strikes made it clear that the UGT rank-and-file was considerably more militant than its leaders. Mola was convinced that what he called the CNT's 'revolutionary gymnastics' was gradually forcing the UGT leadership to follow suit for fear of losing members. A jealous vigilance of other organisations had always been a characteristic of the Socialist trade union bureaucracy and it seems to have had a crucial influence upon the syndical leaders in mid 1930. To go along with the rank-and-file clearly clashed with the economic interests of the leadership. Mola confided in their reformism because of the stipends the Socialist bureaucracy received for running the *comités paritarios*. They had a vested interest in making the wage-arbitration machinery work.[76] It is all the more significant, then, to note the opinion of a member of the UGT bureaucracy renowned for his multiple posts in the state machinery, Manuel Cordero.[77] Explaining how the UGT came to join the movement against the monarchy in 1930, he says 'our revolutionary optimism had hardly been excited at all. It was just obvious that we were faced with an imminent revolution, which would take place with us or without us or even against us.'[78]

Police information led the Director-General of Security to believe that CNT prominence in strikes was damaging the UGT's membership figures, particularly among the young. The main consequence of this, above all in the south, was that the UGT passed gradually, in the summer of 1930, from a secondary role in anarchist-led strikes to a more independent and dynamic one. With the exception of the Basque country, where Prieto had considerable support, the initiative for Socialist participation in the republican movement came from the masses, with the Besteiro and Largo Caballero dominated leadership trailing behind. During the summer, the greatest labour agitation took place in the south, with general strikes in Seville, Granada and Málaga. By September, this had spread to the industrial north. Galicia, Asturias and the Basque country were also becoming active. Moreover, if at first the strikes tended to have limited economic aims, it was not long before they manifested a clearly political orientation, beginning with protests against the repressive measures of the government and finally developing into demands for a change of regime. In October, for instance, a one-day strike called by the UGT in Bilbao on the 4th was met by the Civil Guard. The strike was then extended in protest for another four days. Then on 23 October, the Basque PSOE and UGT decided in favour of joining the republican movement. In mid November, a construction accident in Madrid killed four workers; the UGT, seconded by the CNT, called a general strike, and this too saw clashes between workers and the forces of order. It was becoming increasingly clear that the spontaneous tendency of the Socialist masses was towards the line of action advocated by Prieto and away from that of the syndical bureaucracy. Indeed, one of the Besteirist executive committee of the UGT, Manuel Muiño, told Mola that the leadership could not oppose the general trend within the UGT.[79]

It is not without significance that UGT participation in strikes increased after the foundation in April 1930 of the Socialist Landworkers' Federation (FNTT : Federación Nacional de Trabajadores de la Tierra). Founded with 157 sections, embracing 27,340 members, within two months the FNTT was able to boast 275 sections and 36,639 members. This was the beginning of a rapid expansion which was to take the UGT to over 1 million members by 1932. The importance of the FNTT within the UGT was soon apparent, since the UGT as a whole registered relatively smaller increases than the FNTT on its own. In December 1929 the UGT had 1511 sections, with 228,507 members. One year later it had grown to 1734 sections, with 277,011 members.[80] Such figures are, of course, not definitive, since they are based on subscription payments. Many workers, particularly in the rural south, might obey UGT instructions regarding a strike without being able to afford the membership dues. Nevertheless, the disproportionate growth of the FNTT clearly reflects its growing influence within the Socialist movement. Moreover, the figures suggest that Mola was right when he said that the CNT was making inroads into UGT membership, since the 1930 increases represent virtually all rural workers. In industrial areas, UGT membership can hardly have been better than static.

A large proportion of the wave of strikes which broke out in the second half of 1930 took place in the south. If this was partly a result of frenetic anarchist and Communist agitation, it was above all a response to the intense crisis which was affecting Andalusian agriculture. Storms in the spring had ruined the olive crop. Not only did this deprive the landless labourers of the greater part of their yearly income, normally earned during the mid November to mid January olive harvest, but in addition it limited the amount of work available in the intervening period. Jaén, two-thirds of whose agricultural production consisted of olives, was the worst-hit province, followed by

Córdoba and Seville. The spring storms were then followed by a summer drought so severe that in November the Sierra Nevada was without snow. This seriously damaged the cereal crop. The resulting unemployment ranged from 12 per cent in Cádiz, 13 per cent in Huelva and Córdoba, and 16 per cent in Granada to 50 per cent in Jaén and Seville.[81] The consequent economic hardship of the braceros was clearly reflected in the increase of strikes in the south.

The FNTT was led by a Besteirist, Lucio Martínez Gil – that is to say, a member of the group which opposed any form of collaboration with the republicans.' Nevertheless, there was a growing feeling amongst the working class in general and the landless southern labourers in particular that only a republic could solve Spain's economic and social problems. The growth of the popular notion of the republic as a panacea centred on the prospects of a fundamental agrarian reform.[82] It seems that this attitude and evidence of rising militancy had some influence on Largo Caballero. Certainly, the alacrity with which, when in April 1931 he became Minister of Labour, he introduced decrees favouring the southern labourers demonstrated considerable sensitivity to these workers' problems. And, in general terms it is clear that the increase of labour agitation was accompanied by a parallel increase in his interest in Prieto's links with the republican movement.

Prieto and De los Ríos attended a meeting of republican leaders in San Sebastián on 17 August. From this meeting emerged the so-called Pact of San Sebastián, the republican revolutionary committee and the future republican provisional government. Immediately afterwards, De los Ríos went to Madrid to inform the PSOE executive committee. Besteiro did not take the republican requests for Socialist collaboration very seriously. Nevertheless, after a meeting between Besteiro, Saborit and Cordero, and Prieto, De los Ríos and the republican Alvaro de Albornoz, it was decided to call a full meeting of the National Committee of the PSOE. This was held on 16 September and saw a direct clash between the Besteirists and De los Ríos. Neither group had changed since the Dictatorship. While Prieto and De los Rios, in supporting the coming of a republic, did so for reasons of democratic-socialist ethics, Saborit, for the Besteiro group, adhered to the rigid Marxist line that it was for the bourgeoisie to make the necessary bourgeois revolution. Significantly, Largo Caballero was not present. The outcome of the meeting was a non-committal declaration that no agreement with the republicans had been reached.[83]

Largo had been in Brussels for an international congress, but he was back in Spain in time to hear, in the second week of October, of the revolutionary committee's offer to the PSOE of two ministries in a future republican government. The National Committees of the UGT and the PSOE met on 16 and 18 October (respectively) to discuss this offer and the price asked : the support of the Socialists in a *coup d'état* by means of a general strike. The positions of the Besteirists and the Prietists remained as before. The balance was swung by Largo Caballero. So long in agreement with the Besteirist union bureaucracy, he suddenly began to support the Prieto line, declaring that the PSOE should be one more party in the republican movement. This shift was the result of that same opportunism which had inspired his early collaboration with, and later opposition to, the Dictatorship. He said himself at the time, 'this was not a question of principles but of tactics'. It was decided that the UGT would support the military insurrection in return for assurances that the republic when established would take action to redistribute property, introduce workers' control in industry, and establish the mixed-jury system of arbitration machinery. The republican committee then extended its original offer to three ministries. When the executive committee of the PSOE met to examine the offer, it was accepted by eight votes to six, with Prieto, De los Ríos and Largo Caballero being designated as the three Socialist ministers in the provisional government.[84]

As before, there was no theoretical reason for Largo's brusque change of direction. Given his well-known sensitivity to the mood of the UGT rank-and-file, it is not difficult to see in his action a response both to the rise in labour troubles and to the increasingly political character thereof. Moreover, since Largo was throughout his career obsessed by a sense of rivalry with the CNT, he must have been influenced by the anarchist successes of 1930. There is then discernible here a characteristic of Largo's behaviour already visible during the Dictatorship and to become increasingly obvious during the Republic – a tendency to lead from behind. He cannot have been unaware of a growing dissatisfaction at a local level with the line adopted by the Besteirist leadership in Madrid.[85] Largo never permitted himself to be out of step with the rank-and-file.

There was also a personal element in Largo's sudden switch. His bitterness with regard to Prieto is patently evident in his memoirs, and it was evident to Miguel Maura in the meetings of the revolutionary committee.[86] Saborit felt that Largo was irritated by seeing Prieto in the limelight and enjoying the popularity of the workers.[87] It is interesting to note that, soon after his conversion to republicanism, Largo was outdoing Prieto in his enthusiasm.[88] However, the crucial element in his change of mind may be seen in the offer of ministries in the provisional government. Concerned as he was with the material welfare of the UGT, he cannot have been unaware of the advantages to be derived from tenure of the Ministry of Labour. Control of arbitration machinery could be used to the advantage of the UGT as against the

CNT. Members of the UGT bureaucracy could be placed in lucrative posts within the Ministry. And, above all, wide-ranging social legislation could be introduced. All these things were done when the Republic was established. They demonstrate the primacy of the material interests of the UGT in Largo Caballero's mind.

Tending, as he did, to see things in personal terms, Largo soon developed a strong resentment towards the Besteirist faction of the Socialist party.[89] This became immediately apparent during the arrangements for the UGT's participation in the revolutionary movement agreed upon in October and finally, after various delays, scheduled for mid December. It was arranged that the UGT would support a military coup with a strike. Things were complicated somewhat by the precipitancy of Captains Galán and García Hernández, who rose in Jaca (Huesca) on 12 December, three days before the agreed date – an action perhaps motivated by a suspicion that the other conspirators were not to be relied upon. Nevertheless, there was no change of plan, despite the scarcely veiled opposition of the Besteirist leadership in Madrid. Partly at least because of this opposition, the movement planned for 15 December was a total failure. After the execution of Galán and García Hernández on the 14th, the artillery withdrew from the plot. And, although forces under General Queipo de Llano and aviators from the air-base at Cuatro Vientos went ahead, they realised that they were in a hopeless situation when the expected general strike did not take place in Madrid.[90]

Given that within four months a republic was established after municipal elections, the failure of the December movement was not a definitive set-back. Moreover, if the Republic had been brought in by a military coup, this would have considerably altered its character and perhaps its ability to contemplate sweeping reforms. Nevertheless, the failure of the Madrid strike was the object of bitter discussion within the Socialist movement. It was debated at the Thirteenth Congress of the PSOE, in October 1932, and led to the defeat of the Besteirists in the leadership. It is difficult to find the truth among so many personal accusations, but the evidence does suggest that the failure derived from the Besteirists' dragging their feet, if not actually sabotaging the strike, as supporters of Largo Caballero were later to claim.[91]

On 10 December, for instance, Julio Alvarez del Vayo, one of the Socialists involved in the conspiracy, tried to have the revolutionary manifesto for the day of the proposed strike printed at the Gráfica Socialista, the printing works at which the PSOE newspaper, *El Socialista*, was produced. Saborit, the editor, refused point-blank.[92] Moreover, it is significant that Madrid was the only important city where there was no strike, since Madrid was the stronghold of the Besteiro faction of the UGT bureaucracy. General Mola, who was in touch with Manuel Muiño, the president of the Socialist Casa del Pueblo, was confident on the night of the 14th that the UGT would not join in the strike on the following day. He based his certainty on police reports and other 'assurances'.[93] Such assurances are unlikely to have come from sources other than the syndical bureaucracy, since Largo Caballero was actively working for the strike and his dismay when it did not take place seems to have been genuine. Largo's job was to pass on the final instructions for the strike on the night before. This he did, with Muiño as his contact.[94] Yet the defence later put forward by the Besteiro group was that Largo Caballero failed to pass on the necessary information. In any case, Besteiro told the Thirteenth Congress of the PSOE that, having seen planes dropping revolutionary propaganda over Madrid and being pressed by members of the FJS, the Socialist Youth Federation (Federación de Juventudes Socialistas), to take action, he called the strike at mid-day on the 15th. Yet, after he told Muiño to go ahead, nothing was done except that a message threatening a strike if any more executions took place was sent from the Casa del Pueblo to the government. None of the powerful unions controlled by the Besteirist syndical bureaucracy stopped work. This was later attributed to the apathy of the rank-and-file. It is odd that this apathy was not apparent in the preceding months and that in the provinces there was substantial strike action. The UGT was prominent in stoppages throughout Asturias and the Basque country and even in Barcelona.[95]

The debate within the Socialist movement over responsibility for the failure was of considerable importance. It indicated that, although Besteiro was a theoretical Marxist, he represented a strong current of practical reformism, which was centred on the Madrid-based union bureaucracy and was prepared to act against the wishes of sections of the rank-and-file. The debate also indicated the extent to which Largo Caballero, impelled always by a pragmatic assessment of the mood of the grass-roots militants and a keen sense of the practical advantages to be derived by the UGT, had travelled away from the positions he had maintained in the 1920s. The debate also created a reservoir of bitterness which later was to exacerbate internal divisions within the Socialist movement. It was perhaps because of this that Besteiro later admitted that the responsibility for the December 1930 failure was entirely his.[96]

The immediate result of that failure was the defeat of the Besteirists and the acceptance by the Socialist Party and the UGT of a policy of complete co-operation with the republican movement. A joint meeting of the National Committees of the PSOE and UGT took place on 22 February 1931. Besteiro called for the Socialists to leave the revolutionary committee, a proposal which was defeated by thirty-five votes to twelve. Besteiro resigned from the executive, along with Saborit, Trifón Gómez and Lucio Martínez Gil; the remaining members proposed a new set of candidates, all in favour of collaboration, and these were elected by a considerable majority. It was clear that the desire of the rank-and-file for a change of regime, encouraged by the stance adopted by Prieto and Largo Caballero, had finally influenced the entire movement. Only the Agrupación Socialista Madrileña remained as a staunch bulwark of Besteiro.[97]

In fact, the two positions, of collaboration and abstention, had a shared assumption – that the republic about to be established would be a bourgeois democratic republic which would carry out a bourgeois revolution as the first essential step on Spain's road to progress and socialism. Of course, the conclusions that the two sides drew from that assumption were very different. Besteiro felt that the Socialists should leave the bourgeoisie to make their own revolution, for there was a possibility that the Socialists would find themselves in the contradictory position of carrying out bourgeois policies. Prieto felt that the Socialists should collaborate – first because the establishment of democratic rights was a worthy end in itself, and secondly because he was convinced that the bourgeoisie was too weak to carry out its own revolution unassisted. Largo Caballero was also in favour of collaboration, but rather more because of the immediate material benefits which would accrue to the Socialist movement and because of the opportunity to prepare for the future implantation of Socialism. The fact that the assumption on which these conclusions were based was erroneous was to lead to even wider divisions in the Socialist movement as each sector reacted in its different way to the realisation that the hopes placed in the Republic were not being fulfilled.

The Socialist belief that the old Spain was about to suffer a transformation into a modern bourgeois society was based on two mistaken notions. The first mistake was simply to regard the republican politicians of the revolutionary committee and the provisional government as the 'bourgeoisie' about to undertake the historical role of the English bourgeoisie in the seventeenth century and the French in the eighteenth. In fact, the republican politicians were merely members of the urban petty-bourgeois intelligentsia. The economically powerful oligarchy was not, as the Left supposed, a feudal structure, but had already integrated sections of the bourgeoisie.[98]

This was the second error of analysis. The moment when the Spanish 'bourgeoisie' might have tried to sweep away the outmoded structure of the *ancien régime* had long since passed. The progressive impulse of the bourgeoisie had been sufficiently weak to preclude any major change in the structure of political and economic power. In the first two major periods of pressure, 1833–43 and 1854–6, the bourgeoisie had been virtually bought off by the disentailment of Church lands and release of common lands onto the open market. This process saw much urban mercantile capital invested on the land and the consolidation of the system of large latifundia estates. The class that the Socialists expected to be progressive was already tied to the old oligarchy. Henceforth the *latifundios* were part of the capitalist system and not, as the Socialists thought, feudal vestiges. Part of the process of integration of the urban bourgeoisie with the land-holding oligarchy was a certain penetration of the financial oligarchy by aristocratic and ecclesiastical capital.[99] The second two major periods of bourgeois impulse, 1868–74 and 1916–17, emphasised more than ever the weakness of the bourgeoisie as a revolutionary force. On both occasions, the conjunction of worker and peasant agitation was enough to induce the urban oligarchy to accentuate its ties with the rural.[100] Once the Catalan industrialists had withdrawn from the alliance of progressive forces in 1917 and accepted participation in the 1918 coalition government, the possibility of a bourgeois revolution as the PSOE leaders conceived it was no longer viable.[101]

To a large extent, the development of the Socialist movement during the 1930s was influenced by the importance of an essentially incorrect historical analysis of what was happening in Spain. The calculations of all three sectors of the PSOE were based on the certainty that a bourgeois-directed progressive revolution was about to take place. When it became apparent, by 1933, that this was not happening, each sector reacted according to the norms of behaviour it had established during the pre-Republican period. Besteiro made a quietist withdrawal into his theory; Prieto tried in every way he could to reinforce the Republic and to help it fulfil its historical tasks; and Largo Caballero began opportunistically to channel the discontent of the most vocal sections of the embittered rank-and-file.

2 Building Barricades Against Reform: The Legalist Right, 1931–3

The victory of republican and Socialist candidates in the big towns in the municipal elections of 12 April 1931 generated considerable apprehension among many members of the middle and upper classes. The subsequent decision of Alfonso XIII to leave Spain, and the coming of the Republic on 14 April, signified for them rather more than a simple change of regime. The monarchy symbolised in their minds a hierarchical concept of society, with education controlled by the Church and the social order jealously guarded against change. Hitherto, growing popular resentment of harsh industrial conditions and a manifestly unjust distribution of land had been kept in check by the Civil Guard and, in moments of greater tension, the army. Until 1923, albeit with increasing difficulty, the monarchy's parliamentary system was so managed by means of electoral falsification that universal suffrage never seriously challenged the monopoly of power enjoyed by the great oligarchical parties, the Liberals and the Conservatives. However, in that year, the parties had been supplanted by the Dictatorship. Those of the old politicians who did not throw in their lot with the Dictator never forgave the King for his unceremonious destruction of the constitutional system. Now the Dictator had gone and the King too in his wake. In the changed situation, the upper classes were caught momentarily without the necessary political formations to defend themselves from the threat implicit in the implantation of a popular republic. Even if the great bourgeois revolution anticipated by the Socialists was not to be, a republic supported by the Socialist movement clearly implied some kind of reform, however mild, and some adjustment of political and social privilege.

The privileged classes were not entirely helpless. The peaceful way in which the Republic had been established had left their social and economic power intact. Moreover, there existed organisations of the Right which had been endeavouring to combat the rising power of the urban and rural working class for the previous twenty years. Prominent among them were the ACNP (Asociación Católica Nacional de Propagandistas) and the CNCA (Confederación Nacional Católico-Agraria), both of which were in a position to mobilise mass support against any progressive tendencies in the Republic.[1] So successful did they prove that they shattered completely the hopes that the Socialists had placed in the Republic.

Before the ACNP and CNCA achieved their success, however, it was somewhat more combative groups which tried to take up the cudgels on behalf of the old order. In Burgos, one eccentric monarchist unsuccessfully tried to recruit an army of 'legionaries' to combat the revolution. In Madrid, others, headed by the ACNP member Eugenio Vegas Latapié, tried to found a counter-revolutionary journal and were soon plotting the violent destruction of the Republic. Before the elections, the ex-ministers of Primo de Rivera had founded the UMN (Unión Monárquica Nacional), to strengthen the monarchy with the authoritarian ideas of the Dictator. The UMN had undertaken a large provincial propaganda campaign to fight against republicanism in the elections. The tone of the campaign showed the party's awareness of the issues at stake in a possible change of regime. In a meeting at Santander, a young Catholic lawyer, José María Gil Robles, also a member of the ACNP, told his audience that, 'by defending the monarchy, you defend the basic principles of society'. The point was underlined elsewhere by Antonio Goicoechea, one-time minister of the King: 'the monarchist candidacy does not only mean the permanency of fundamental institutions, it also means order, religion, family, property, work'.[2]

Electoral defeat, and the King's recognition of the futility of defending his throne by force, had caught conservatives by surprise. While the Left had prepared for success, the Right had barely conceived of such resounding failure. However, for all its apparent disarray, the Right was quick to produce a response to the new regime. This took two forms. The first, that of the Carlists and the more ultraist supporters of Alfonso XIII, was a determination to overthrow the Republic by violence.[3] The other, that of the ACNP, was less dramatic and more immediately realistic: an acceptance of the democratic game in an attempt to take over the Republic and draw its teeth. This response grew out of an awareness of the political weakness of the Right and of the tactical insight that its interests could best be defended within the law. This legalistic tactic, known as 'accidentalism', was, in terms of the development of the Republic, far more important than violence. Admittedly, the 'catastrophists' were behind the military rising of 1936 which eventually destroyed the regime. Nevertheless, until that moment most of their activities were external to the mainstream of

Republican politics. The accidentalists, on the other hand, built up a mass right-wing party, used it to block the reformist path of the Republic and thereby completely altered the Socialists' perception of the possibilities of bourgeois democracy. This accelerated the polarisation of Republican politics and created the context which gave a spurious relevance to the activities of the catastrophist conspirators.

The theory behind accidentalism was that forms of government were accidental, of secondary importance, and that the essential issue was the 'content' or socio-economic orientation of a regime. It was propounded by the leader of the ACNP, Angel Herrera, editor of the militantly Catholic, and, hitherto, monarchist, daily *El Debate*. Deriving from the encyclicals of Leo XIII and the writings of the traditionalist thinker Balmes, accidentalism implied no surrender of fundamental objectives, but, rather, a prudent tactical adjustment to unfavourable circumstances, unhindered by any need to defend lost causes. It was more convenient to fight for one's objectives within the established system, especially when its overthrow was patently beyond one's means. The accidentalism of *El Debate* was clearly this, a politic accommodation to an unpleasant situation. On the morning of 14 April *El Debate*'s editorial had said, 'the Spanish monarchy, after fifteen centuries of life, cannot end like this'. On election day it had proclaimed the need for a grand monarchist affirmation, to protect 'the basic principles of society' against 'negative barbarism' as represented by the Republic. Even as the election results came in, the editorial board was meeting to find a formula to get the King to stay. Yet on 15 April *El Debate* proclaimed the need to respect the new, *de facto* regime. Republicans of all shades had reason to believe that this sudden abandonment of yesterday's ardent monarchism was not entirely sincere. It was seen rather as an example of that 'sacristy cleverness' which enabled *El Debate* to be always on the winning side.[4] The other editorial printed on 15 April was entitled 'Our Homage to King Alfonso XIII'. Indeed, the accidentalists' handbook gave a retrospective indication of their attitude to the advent of the Republic : 'the rabble, always irresponsible, took over the resorts of government . . . the sewers opened their sluice gates and the dregs of society inundated the streets and squares'.[5] In fact, it was only after Alfonso's decision to leave became final that it was decided to 'continue the struggle in the only terrain possible : within Republican legality'.[6]

Angel Herrera maintained this combative tone when he addressed members of the ACNP on only the second day of the Republic's existence. He urged them to throw themselves into the defensive battle against 'the avalanche which was overwhelming the bases of the Church'. Their objectives were to be the reorganisation of dispersed forces, the provision of a common ideology to the Spanish Right, and, within legality, 'the reconquest of everything that has been lost'.[7] As Gil Robles, the *El Debate* writer who had taken part in the monarchist election campaign and who was to become leader of the accidentalists, put it, 'with the conservative parties liquidated, the reaction of the dispersed monarchist elements rendered impossible, there was an urgent necessity to establish a strong nucleus of resistance'. The 'resistance' was to be directed against any threat of change in the religious, social or economic order. The propagandists went all over Spain and began a zealous campaign to 'group together the *non-republican* forces, destroyed and badly damaged'.[8]

The unrolling of the campaign revealed something of the political interests for which the 'struggle' was to be undertaken. On 21 April *El Debate* addressed itself to 'all the elements of order not tied before or now to the triumphant revolution', and called upon them to join in a single organisation. Since the 'triumphant revolution' had done nothing to change any aspect of Spanish life except the form of government, the appeal could be seen to be to those who nurtured a prior hostility to the Republic, and whose objective the Left could not but suspect was, if not the rapid return of the King, at least the limitation of the nascent regime to a form indistinguishable from the monarchy. The slogan under which the 'anti-revolutionary' forces were to unite was 'Religion, Fatherland, Order, Family and Property'. The reflective republican could hardly have failed to see the resemblance to the slogans used by the Unión Monárquica Nacional less than a fortnight before. The connection was in any case underlined by the same *El Debate* appeal, which said, 'perhaps someone misses from our slogan an element – a word affirming the monarchy. We omit it deliberately despite our well-known and sincere monarchist sentiments.'

As clear as the tie with the monarchy was the connection with the Vatican. The ACNP and *El Debate* had a tradition of submission to the wishes of the Church hierarchy and throughout the Republic Angel Herrera scrupulously followed instructions from Rome, which he received through the Papal Nuncio, Monsignor Tedeschini.[9] Not surprisingly, *El Debate*'s editorial line and the tactics adopted by the ACNP closely followed the instructions telegrammed by Cardinal Pacelli, the Secretary of State to the Papacy, to Cardinal Vidal i Barraquer. Pacelli recommended that Spanish Catholics follow the Bavarian example of 1918 and unite against the communist menace.[10] Vidal responded immediately with a pastoral letter, framed in similar terms, that virtually enjoined adherence to the organisation that Angel Herrera was founding. Catholics were instructed to vote, in the forthcoming elections for the Constituent Cortes, for those candidates who would protect the rights of the Church and defend the social order.[11]

In mid-May, the Pope issued the anti-socialist and anti-liberal encyclical *Quadragesimo Anno*.

Close ties with the Church hierarchy merely underlined the extent to which the new group's omission of overt monarchism from its slogan was manifest opportunism. Alfonso XIII had always been identified with militant clericalism.[12] Moreover, taking sides in religion involved a clear social alignment, since it was the middle and upper classes whose piety was to be outraged by the Republic's laicism. A close bond with the Church had increasingly become limited to the aristocracy, the large landowners of the south and the conservative smallholders of Castile, Levante and the Basque–Navarrese provinces. Consequently, the nascent accidentalist organisation was to characterised by a blend of religion and reaction : 'We must all defend Spain and ourselves and our material and spiritual goods, our convictions . . . , the conservation of property, hierarchy in society and in work'.[13] This hardly suggested open-mindedness on questions of social reform and it was the corollary of active clericalism. The Church was still the living symbol of the old Spain which the republicans hoped to modernise, and was, on a par with the monarchy, a central pivot of the conservative world. Besides, religion was an issue which could be used to mobilise mass peasant support behind the interests of the oligarchy. Having lost their political hegemony in April 1931, the ruling classes clung all the more to the Church as one of the key redoubts of their social and economic dominance. Equally, the Church hierarchy, as a major landowner, had a somewhat similar view of the value of an alliance with the new political formation being created to defend oligarchical agrarian interests.[14] Not surprisingly, throughout the Republic, the clergy used both pulpit and confessional to defend the existing socio-economic order and to make electoral propaganda for Acción Nacional.

The growth of accidentalism received a considerable boost on 10 May. Followers of Alfonso XIII had tried publicly to regroup as the Círculo Monárquico Independiente (CMI). Their provocative stance created a fervent popular reaction which formed the background to the notorious church burnings of 10–12 May. The origins of the incendiarism remain obscure, although Miguel Maura, the Minister of the Interior, was convinced that the fires were the work of provocateurs drawn from the scab union, the Sindicatos Libres, aiming to discredit the new regime. Other eyewitness reports tend to support Maura's view. Whether the burnings be attributed to left-wing extremists or to right-wing *agents provocateurs*, one thing is clear : the response of the crowds showed how strongly the Church was identified with monarchism.[15] And the intensity of the popular reaction to an open demonstration of monarchist sentiment highlighted the great advantage of accidentalism. It had already been decided on 26 April to form a group, to be known as Acción Nacional, to unite the 'elements of order' for the forthcoming elections. While propagandists began the work of preliminary organisation in the provinces, Herrara held a meeting with other right-wing leaders for the formation of a circumstantial coalition for electoral campaigning. Particularly after the lesson of 10 May, conservatives of all kinds, including the most extreme monarchists, flocked into the organisation.[16]

Prospective members were not asked for any profession of republican faith. Indeed, in León, Acción Nacional was founded in the offices of the monarchist youth.[17] Even the rabidly anti-republican Carlists were anxious to join.[18] In Madrid, a giant task of issuing circulars and making file indexes of voters was undertaken by volunteers. One of them wrote later, 'into Acción Nacional came the first collaborations, the first important sums of money and almost all the hopes of those who could never come to terms with, let alone recognise, the new order. . . . All those who came were monarchists. I didn't meet a single republican in the considerable time I was there writing cards and checking electoral lists.'[19] It followed then that the interim president of the organisation should be Antonio Goicoechea. Other prominent Alfonsists, who were simultaneously plotting the armed overthrow of the Republic, also held important positions in Acción Nacional.

The conservative, not to say reactionary, nature of the new group was even more marked in the provinces. In Cáceres, 'all the people of substance of the province, the great landowners, the politically significant and persons of social influence' met under a monarchist president to found the local section. In Córdoba, the local eleven-man committee included four landowners, two factory directors, and four engineers. In Jerez, the dominance of big-wigs was even more marked.[20] Less spectacularly rightist but equally conservative, and much more plentiful, was the kind of support found in Old Castile and Salamanca. There Acción Nacional inherited the influence of the CNCA. Founded by the Palencian landowner Antonio Monedero-Martín, and largely financed by donations from big landlords and subscriptions organised by *El Debate*, the CNCA claimed to have 500,000 members by 1919. It is certain that the organisation had built up a large following among the conservative smallholders of northern and central Spain by providing a series of services. Rural savings banks, agrarian credit entities, co-operatives for selling crops and bulk-buying, insurance facilities and the hiring-out of machinery all contributed to the mitigation of social conditions in the Castilian plain. The various facilities were available only to peasants who made clear their conservative and religious sentiments. Its main inspiration was traditonalism; its main enemies the 'pagan principle of liberalism' and socialism. The CNCA affirmed 'the principles of religion, family and property as the bases of the social order against the negations of socialism'. The CNCA had a marked counter-revolutionary orientation and occasionally organised strike-breaking. Before his abdication, Alfonso XIII was president of one of its most important branches.[21]

The immediate heir to this body of ultra-conservative peasants was Acción Castellana, based in Salamanca, one of the principal component organisations of Acción Nacional. The development of Acción Castellana showed the extent to which the Catholic organisations were prepared to throw the weight of their peasant masses behind the local territorial oligarchy. Some of the more reactionary local landlords, such as the Carlist Lamamié de Clairac and Cándido Casanueva, were prominent in the leadership. The branch organisations of Acción Nacional in this area consistently defended the interests of the agrarian elite throughout the Republic. This commitment was always skilfully generalised in their propaganda, largely for the consumption of the poorly educated middle-size farmers who made up the basis of their support, into a patriotic concern for 'agrarian interests'. Often poverty-stricken and scraping a bare living from their holdings by working also as day-labourers on the big estates, these peasants still considered themselves to be 'landowners'. Since they occasionally employed casual labour themselves at harvest time, the right-wing press had little difficulty in persuading them that the rural-labour legislation and Socialist trade unions hit them in the same way as they did the bigger owners. This was skilfully achieved by the use of words like *labrador* and *agricultor* to describe all landowners, large and small alike. *Labrador* (ploughman) and *agricultor* (husbandman) implied at once someone who worked the land and someone who was a respectable man of substance. Thus, the conservative and Catholic smallholder of Castile, already imbued by his parish priest with a deep distrust for democracy, readily felt an identification of interest with the local oligarchy, sharing with it a commitment to the monarchy and the Church as the twin pillars of the social order.

On joining Acción Nacional, a statement was issued by Acción Castellana to the effect that it would have preferred to give battle to 'the enemies of the social order' while still in the shadow of the monarchy, but that, since it no longer existed, the fight would go on without it. An inflexible attitude to social reform was revealed in the declaration that any alteration in the landholding structure would be communism and make the land owner a slave. Salamanca was to provide some of the most belligerent support for Acción Nacional during the Republic, but it was not atypical. The orange-growers who formed the basis of its branch in Valencia, the Derecha Regional Valenciana, had more progressive, social Catholic leaders, but they were also the first accidentalists to take up arms in 1936. Unión Castellana Agraria of Palencia was probably nearer the norm in its simple aim of defending the interests of 'conservative social forces.'[22]

Accion Castellana's unwilling tactical acceptance of the Republic was typical of the national body. As early as 21 April, *El Debate* showed why it was adopting accidentalism : 'without certainty of success, and in fact with certainty of failure, we have no right to destroy Spain with civil and fratricidal strife'. So the 'moderate' Right was eschewing violence not out of conviction but out of a recognition of weakness. Herrera felt that it would be easier to render the Republic innocuous by working within it than by attacking it.

The strictly limited nature of even this kind of acceptance of the Republic was shown by the bellicosity of Accion Nacional's campaign for the June 1931 elections. Its candidates included several ex-leaders of the UMN, and its manifesto set the tone of ill-masked hostility to the Republic. The keynote was the battle against Soviet communism, with which the Republic was taken to be consubstantial – a demagogic exaggeration, to say the least. The manifesto described the Republic as 'the rabble that denies God and, therefore, the principles of Christian morality; which proclaims instead of the sanctity of the family the inconstancy of free love; which substitutes individual property, the basis of individual well-being and collective wealth, for a universal proletariat at the orders of the state'. Given the fact that this sort of propaganda was launched at semi-illiterate, politically immature rural audiences, at a time when the government could be characterised by its timidity in social questions, it can be seen only as deliberately or irresponsibly provocative. In fact, the manifesto was openly couched in terms of a declaration of social war 'to decide the triumph or extermination of imperishable principles. This will not be resolved in a single combat; it is a war, and a long one, which is being unleashed in Spain.'[23]

The first electoral meeting confirmed the impression given by the manifesto. Held at Ávila, it was opened by Bermejo de la Rica with a call for intransigence : 'only the lack of masculinity of the aristocracy and bourgeoisie has allowed the rise of the lowest and vilest rabble'. Another speaker, Pérez Laborda, later to become leader of Acción National's youth movement, equated the Republic with bolshevism and appealed to his audience of local farmers either to stand back and see the Republic murder 2 million people or to defend the principles of Acción Nacional. Others speakers, including Angel Herrera, openly admitted their monarchist convictions and that they silenced them only out of expediency. Herrera said that it had been decided not to raise the standard of the monarchy, despite the monarchism of the majority of the movement's members. The example to be followed was that of Hindenburg. This all derived from the insight that nothing could more effectively consolidate the Republic than frontal attacks – the lesson of 10 May.[24]

Characteristic of the campaign was the constant linking of religion with social conservatism. It was stated at the Ávila meeting that the social order had been based on two principles, the monarchy and the Church, and that with one gone, defence of the other had to be the more resolute. Gil Robles said at a meeting in Tamames (Salamanca), 'religion is a brake which stops society driving into anarchy . . . we defend property, not its abuses . . . we make no impossible promises of land division or of socialisation, projects which led to disaster in Russia'. Posters were issued which stated simply 'Landowners! Acción Nacional will be the great safeguard of property in the Constituent Cortes!'[25] The election results were, nevertheless, disappointing. The campaign produced twenty-four deputies from the two Castiles and León; they became known as the Agrarian Minority. Acción Nacional had been founded to organise propaganda for the elections. Now, precisely because the 'revolutionary threat' had been confirmed by the left-wing victory, it was decided to maintain the organisation as a means of defending rightist interests within the legal political arena.[26]

The first task of the Minority was to make its mark on the fashioning of the new Constitution. The sort of mandate they held was indicated by a series of meetings against agrarian reform held by landowners' federations all over the country, but especially in the south. *El Debate* reported the meetings sympathetically and took up their complaints in its editorials.[27] Inevitably, the clauses in the Constitution which most interested the deputies of the Agrarian Minority were those which had implications regarding the position of organised religion in society and the possibility of agrarian reform. Effectively this meant that their opposition to the Constitution crystallised around two main points, articles 26 and 44. The first of these concerned the cutting off of state financial support for the clergy and religious orders; the dissolution of orders, such as the Jesuits, that swore foreign oaths of allegiance; and the limitation of the Church's right to wealth. The republican attitude to the Church was based on the belief that, if a new Spain was to be built, the stranglehold of the Church on many aspects of society must be broken. Religion was not attacked as such, but the Constitution was to put an end to the government's endorsement of the Church's privileged position. This was presented by the Agrarian Minority in parliament, and by the newspaper network of which *El Debate* was the centre, as virulent anti-clericalism, thereby allowing the opponents of any kind of reform to hitch their reactionism to the cause of religion. Article 44 stated that 'Property of all kinds can be the object of expropriation with adequate compensation for reasons of social utility unless a law to the contrary receives an absolute majority in the Cortes.'

In alliance with the ultra-Catholic Basque–Navarrese minority, the Agrarians put up stout resistance to every progressive clause which implied a change in the prevailing social order. When accused of being monarchists, anti-democratic cavemen, the Agrarians responded with feeble protestations of accidentalism, democratic conviction and a love for the poor. However, when it came to debating the articles concerning regional autonomy, private property, and a more flexible and humane approach to labour relations, they piled amendment upon amendment in an attempt to block the passing of the Constitution.[28] It was difficult to avoid the impression that the existing structure of society as it had been under the monarchy was being defended with the banner of persecuted Catholicism. Yet the cordial relations of prominent republicans such as Manuel Azaña, Luis de Zulueta, Jaume Carner and Luis Nicolau d'Olwer with liberal churchmen such as Cardinal Vidal belied the accidentalist cries that the Church was being mercilessly persecuted.[29]

Despite the efforts of the Agrarians, both articles 26 and 44 were included in the final approved draft of the Constitution. This clinched the opposition of the Right. The accidentalist handbook described the passing of article 26 in terms which revealed the extent of the group's flexibility : 'reason fell, smashed by the hoof of the beast, with all the horrors of the Apocalypse and all its majesty mocked and trampled underfoot'.[30] The Agrarian Minority immediately withdrew from the Cortes and announced the launching of a campaign for the reform of the Constitution. The call for revision now became the rallying cry against the Republic. A huge effort of propaganda, through the press and a nationwide series of meetings, attempted to build up a store of conservative resentment of the Republic. Gil Robles, who during the campaign emerged as a major figure in Acción Nacional, wrote later that the aim was to give the Right a mass following which would be prepared to fight the Left 'for the possession of the street'.[31] The tone of the campaign was belligerent and incendiary and had some considerable success in changing the way in which the Catholic population, particularly in rural areas, perceived the Republic. It opened with an appeal in *El Debate* to all Catholics to 'defend yourselves, and at the same time defend, by all methods and with all resources, the threatened existence of Spain'. Miguel Maura, who, in an attempt to maintain his own credibility on the Right, had himself resigned from the government in protest at its markedly laic tone, had already commented that Gil Robles's language regarding the Constitution was a call for religious warfare and would irreparably harm the Republic.[32]

The Catholic press diffused an intepretation of the Constitution which presented it as a blueprint for the persecution of religion and of the respectable citizen. Hundreds of orators were sent all over Spain to present a deliberately distorted view of the political situation. The Republic's reforming aspirations were portrayed as violent revolutionism; its laicism as a santanic assault on religion. At the first meeting of the campaign, held at Ledesma (Salamanca), Gil Robles said, 'while anarchic forces, gun in hand, spread panic in government circles, the government tramples on defenceless beings like poor nuns'. Acción Nacional of Toledo issued a manifesto which claimed that 'when religion is not respected in a state, greater consideration cannot be expected for property or the family'.[33] The terms of such propaganda were entirely out of proportion with the halting steps to reform taken so far by the Republic. They were phrased to make the unsophisticated and conservative rural smallholder or the urban owners of small businesses, whose interests were not threatened by the Republic, feel that they had everything to fear from the new regime. The wealthy backers of Acción Nacional's expensive press and propaganda drives thereby gained mass support against prospective reforms which threatened *their* interests. By the end of 1931, Acción Nacional had twenty-six affiliated organisations in the provinces and by late 1932 this figure had risen to thirty-six.

In Madrid, in a meeting held under the auspices of Acción Nacional, Goicoechea told a cheering audience that there was to be a battle to death between socialism and the nation, and that it was thus necessary to defend property and strengthen the forces of order. Gil Robles told the rich businessmen of the Circle of the Mercantile Union that all right-wingers, monarchist or republican, should join together. The boisterousness of all this propaganda did not go unnoticed on the Left, and the Socialist Minister of Labour, Largo Caballero, protested about the bitterness of attacks on his party. The campaign was reaching the momentum which was to force the government to ban it. On 8 November there was a great revisionist meeting in Palencia which was addressed by all members of the Agrarian Minority and some traditionalists. Joaquín Beunza, a not-extreme Carlist, thundered to an audience of 22,000 people, 'Are we men or not? Whoever is not prepared to give his all in these moments of shameless persecution does not deserve the name Catholic. It is necessary to be ready to defend oneself by all means, and I don't say legal means, because all means are good for self-defence.' After declaring the Cortes a zoo he said, 'we are governed by a gang of freemasons. And I say that against them all methods are legitimate, legal and illegal ones.' When this was followed within a week by a lecture by the Alfonsist Sáinz Rodríguez attacking parliament and the Socialist Party, the government stopped the campaign as anti-Republican.[34]

In December, Acción Nacional held a deliberative assembly which did nothing to dispel the impression created by outbursts such as Beunza's. While it confirmed that Gil Robles was to take over the presidency from Goicoechea, the assembly nevertheless adopted a programme drawn up by the latter. Minimal and circumstantial, it recognised the freedom of the individual member to defend his own views on forms of government. Drafted in such a way as to allow the extreme Alfonsists to remain within the organisation, the programme made it inevitable that Acción Nacional would be tarred with the brush of its own extremists. It also contained statements of policy unrelated to forms of government. The basic premise was that the nation was threatened by international socialism and extremist separatism. The principle of private property was reaffirmed and a fundamental hostility to agrarian reform expressed. Such reform was dismissed as an attempt to sacrifice individual rights and public wealth to the 'unhealthy convenience' of pandering to the working masses with 'pompous schemes'. Above all, the Constitution was to be revised.[35] The Left could only regard this as a declaration of war on the essence of the Republic.

Meanwhile *El Debate* was speaking of founding a political party. A disturbing glimpse of the intransigence it could bring into Spanish politics was afforded by the manifesto issued on the foundation of the Juventud de Acción Nacional. Closely tied to the parent organisation, this youth movement declared 'we are men of the Right . . . we will respect the legitimate orders of authority, but we will not tolerate the impositions of the irresponsible rabble. We will always have the courage to make ourselves respected. We declare war on communism and freemasonry.'[36] Since these latter concepts were represented in the eyes of the Right by the Socialist Party and the Left Republicans, such outbursts did little for the credibility of Acción Nacional's much-vaunted notion of constructive opposition within Republican legality.

This belligerence seems to have been an accurate reflection of the tone which Gil Robles wished to give his group. Opening a massive recruitment drive, he said at Molina de Segura (Murcia) on 1 January, 'in 1932 we must impose our will with the force of our rightness, and with other forces if this is insufficient. The cowardice of the Right has allowed those who come from the cesspools of iniquity to take control of the destinies of the fatherland.·. . .' There was no doubt on whose behalf this militancy was being drummed up : 'I speak to the powerful, to those who have plenty to lose, and I say to them – if you had sacrificed a small sum at the right moment, you would lose less than you might now, because what you give for the press, the rightist press, which defends the fundamental principles of every society – religion, the family, order, work – is a real insurance policy for your personal fortune.' In similar vein, a journalist in the Acción Nacional orbit wrote that 'the danger which threatens our altars also threatens our pockets'.[37]

To defend these interests, then, a political party was being created. Parliament was accepted as the most convenient battleground. This emerged clearly in meeting after meeting as Gil Robles worked to produce a great mass party of the Right. In Málaga he said, 'the ideal of the Spanish Right . . . is to form a united front to put an end to socialism. We must struggle for the conquest of parliament.'[38] Gil Robles made a superhuman effort of organisation and propaganda, travelling ceaselessly around Spain, trying to give Acción Nacional the mass support necessary for the legal 'conquest' of power. At one point, he made speeches in fifteen villages in less than two days. And on his own admission he was always pushing his audiences towards escalatory conflicts with the authorities. He claimed to be training them to defend their rights in the street. Yet at this time the Republic had taken only the most faltering steps towards a limited agrarian reform. In 1937 and in his memoirs, Gil Robles claimed proudly that the fund of belligerence which he built up made possible the victory of the Right in the Civil War.[39]

The movement grew rapidly, particularly in conservative areas likely to be affected by agrarian reform. In New Castile and Extremadura, organisations such as Acción Popular Agraria de Badajoz, Derecha Regional Agraria de Cáceres, Acción Agraria Manchega and Acción Ciudadana y Agraria de Cuenca affiliated to the parent organisation. Growing numbers highlighted the ambiguity of the movement's programme. The many monarchists within Accion Nacional found outright opposition to the Republic much more congenial than accidentalism. Virulent statements to this effect were made under the aegis of the supposedly legalist organisation. Of course, while recruitment was still a major priority, propaganda tended towards demagogy. In April the movement survived a change of name to Acción Popular, and it continued to grow.[40]

A profitable zone of operations for the agrarian oligarchy and its political representatives was the question of wheat prices and supplies. It was an issue which could advantageously be exploited to foment hostility against the Republic and to do so in such a way as to mobilise the support of the many smallholders who produced wheat. This was possible because wheat was grown mainly in Castile, Aragón and parts of Andalusia; that is to say, in both smallholding and *latifundio* areas. In problems relating to stocks and prices at a national level, it was always relatively easy to create an apparent identification of the interests of all wheat-growers, large and small.

Such was the case with a campaign in the autumn and winter of 1931 to secure an increase in the minimum price for wheat, the *tasa*, which stood at 46 pesetas per metric quintal. Organised by the bigger producers, the campaign enjoyed the support of small farmers, lease-holders and share croppers, for obvious reasons. In reality, however, only the big owners stood to benefit. Their production costs were lower, because of economies of scale, and often because their land enjoyed superior yield. Many substantial producers, even in the Castilian small-holding areas, had sufficient capital and the necessary storage facili-ties to enable them to keep their wheat off the market until the most favourable moment for selling. Clearly this meant that a price increase would widen their already comfortable profit margins and certainly not harm the interests of the smallholders. Nevertheless, the smaller growers did not stand to enjoy any improvement in their pre-carious position. At all times short of ready cash, be it for seed, fertiliser or food for his family, the smallholder was usually at the mercy of the local *acaparador* when it came to disposing of his grain. The *acapara-dor*, sometimes a merchant, sometimes a moneylender or even a land-owner, bought up the crops of the smaller growers, who had neither warehousing nor transport facilities of their own. Irrespective of the official minimum price, the smallholder normally had to sell at the price dictated by the *acaparador*, because either immediate necessity or the need to repay a loan to the *acaparador* himself forced him to sell at times of surplus.

Nevertheless, a campaign to raise prices could rely on the support of all wheat-growers. The owners wanted to increase the price from 46 to 53 pesetas. Their campaign was headed by two deputies from Valladolid, Antonio Royo Villanova and Pedro Martín y Martín, whom the Socialists accused of being an *acaparador* himself.[41] Speaking in the Cortes, Royo claimed that the increases in agricultural wages permitted by Largo Caballero had pushed up the cost of producing wheat by 30 per cent, to 54–5 pesetas per metric quintal. Pedro Martín, by stating that an increase in bread prices could be easily absorbed in the towns, skilfully implied that it was urban workers who kept the smallholder poor. The campaign continued with the support of the Acción Popular press network. When a new Minister of Agriculture, Marcelino Domingo took over in December, he immediately investigated the need to revise the *tasa*. Local information showed that production costs varied from 33·25 pesetas per metric quintal in Salamanca to 41·77 pesetas in Badajoz. In the light of this, because he was not prepared to raise bread prices at a time of high unemployment and wage cuts and because he realised that the *acaparadores* would prevent the small-holders from deriving any benefit, he opted against any increase of the *tasa*.[42]

The Minister was subjected to a virulent press campaign which made his action seem responsible for all the ills of the countryside. Those owners who held stocks and had hoped to benefit from 1931's rather poor harvest now began to hold back supplies. Reports reached Domingo in January 1932 that there was a scarcity and he replied with a somewhat ineffectual decree prohibiting clandestine hoarding. Some stocks were forced out onto the market, but not enough to allay fears of bread-price rises and consequent public-order problems. The press began to talk of the need for lifting restrictions on the import of foreign wheat – a politically sensitive decision given the weakness of the peseta and the fact that high-cost Spanish wheat survived against Argentinian and American competition only by means of rigid protection. On 12 April, Domingo authorised just 50,000 tons to be imported for the neediest provinces and then called for stockists to reveal existing supplies and for growers to estimate the forthcoming harvest. The reports received suggested that a drastic shortage was on the horizon. Domingo authorised more imports : 100,000 tons on 27 April, 100,000 tons on 26 May and 25,000 on 15 June.[43]

The prices continued to rise, reaching their highest figure ever in July, at which point about 250,000 tons miraculously appeared on the market, coinciding with the delivery of foreign shipments. There followed a lengthy period of fine weather and stable labour relations which produced a bumper harvest. Throughout the autumn, wheat prices fell steadily, until they reached their lowest figure since 1924. Approximately 2 million wheat-producers were hit by the fall, which had been caused largely by the speculation of the big owners. Nevertheless, the rightist press immediately went to work to ensure that Domingo's imports were firmly planted in the minds of smallholders as the cause of the disaster. He was accused by the Agrarians of deliberately setting out to destroy Spanish agriculture. The campaign against Domingo had considerable success and was one of the central issues in clinching the electoral support of the smallholders of Castile in the elections of November 1933 for the parties of the right.

In the spring of 1932 the question of how best to oppose the proposed agrarian reform and the Catalan statute, discussion of which began in May, raised the question of how far respect for the Republic should go. The ultra-monarchists of the Acción Española group were actively conspiring against the Republic without seeing any incompatibility between this and their membership of Acción Popular.[44] Gil Robles, on the other hand, believed that there was no immediate possibility of successful solutions by force and that the same objectives could best be achieved by the Right infiltrating the Republic to make it its own.[45] It was purely a tactical point. According to Gil Robles himself, the 'immense majority' of Acción Popular members were monarchists and felt an 'insuperable repugnance' to the idea of accepting the Republic. The same applied to himself : 'In a theoretical sense, I was and am a

monarchist. . . . The same motives which prevented 90 per cent of
the members of Acción Popular from declaring themselves republican
held me back, not least for reasons of good taste.'[46]

The efficacy of the legalist tactic was demonstrated during the
spring and early summer. *El Debate* ran hostile commentaries on both
the agrarian and Catalan projects, while the Agrarian Minority began
an intense campaign of obstruction in the Cortes. Their success was
remarkable. Between May and September 1932, one-third of the debating time in the Cortes was taken up by discussion of the agrarian
reform. Debate was held up while the rightist deputies asked complex
technical questions. Each member of the Agrarian Minority had an
amendment to each clause of the bill. By August, only four out of
twenty-four clauses had been passed.[47]

However, this success was nullified by the first manifestation of the
other, 'catastrophist', tactic. This was the abortive rising of 10 August,
which came to be known as the Sanjurjada. The fiasco of the rising
highlighted the relative efficacy of the parliamentary tactic in stalling
reform. According to Gil Robles, 'the tenacious obstruction of various
projects and the constant criticism of the government's labour not
only prevented the passing of many laws, but also produced enormous
wear and tear in the governments of the Left'.[48] Now the decisive
response of the government to the defeated coup showed that the
'catastrophist' tactic was counter-productive to the material interests
of the Right. The wave of Republican fervour produced allowed both
statutes to be passed without difficulties in September. Moreoever,
there was a general crack-down on the activities of the Right. The
point was proved that frontal attacks could only strengthen the Republic. For all that the Right applauded the motives of 10 August, and
it did fulsomely, in practical terms it was a considerable setback.

Gil Robles was determined that it should not happen again. The
ambiguity of the Acción Popular programme, once an advantage, was
now a liability. An assembly of Acción Popular was called for October
to clear the air after the rising. *El Debate* had said in its first number
after the rising, 'we have been and always will be the paladins of the
legal struggle and of respect for the constituted power. . . . We were
not in the secret of the conspiracy.' This was not entirely true. A series
of meetings of right-wing leaders, including one in Biarritz on 7 August,
had put Gil Robles in the picture. Of course, the Alfonsist members
were clearly implicated, while he had kept his hands publicly clean.
Understandably, he was anxious for his movement not to suffer unnecessarily. The Alfonsists were disillusioned by a manoeuvre aimed
at disowning them, convinced as they were that, had the rising not
been a failure, his attitude would have been different.[49]

The assembly opened in Madrid on 22 October. The debate

illustrated the divergency of views within Acción Popular. Fernández Ruano, from Málaga, said, 'a declaration of republican faith? Never!' to rapturous applause. Fernández Ladreda, from Asturias, declared that within Acción Popular there were those who regarded a republic in Spain not as a regime but as a revolutionary doctrine. Cimas Leal, editor of the *Gaceta Regional* of Salamanca, claimed that 'to obey is to accept' and was greeted by cries of 'No! no! no!' The object of the congress had been announced as being to settle the questions of tactics raised by the events of August. Morena Dávila put the final and successful argument for accidentalism when he said, with an eye on the rapid passage of republican legislation in September, 'what has been lost is because of 10 August; our tactic brought victory and other tactics have lost what had been gained. Let us return to yesterday's tactic.' The assembly voted for the legalist tactic.[50]

This victory was not pushed to its logical conclusion, for fear of alienating strong monarchist groups (for instance, the Asturian section, with nearly 30,000 members) within Acción Popular. However, preparations went forward for the creation of a federal Catholic party. The emphasis was on accidentalism, but, if this excluded the active conspirators of Accion Española, it implied no definite split with monarchism. Indeed, the great majority of Acción Popular's members 'conserved their anti-republican spirit intact'.[51] Obviously, Gil Robles did not break with the Alfonsists because he found their monarchism offensive. If that had been the case, he could have declared himself republican. It was rather that their publicly anti-republican 'catastrophist' tactic was undermining the effectiveness of his 'Trojan horse' policy. This was made abundantly clear when Goicoechea resigned from the Acción Popular executive. Gil Robles's letter of reply declared that any incompatibility between the group and Goicoechea 'is not for reason of ideology or political position regarding forms of government, but for reasons of tactics'.[52] And the members of both groups continued to mix socially, to attend each other's meetings, to read each other's press and even to belong to more than one organisation. Goicoechea remained a member of Acción Popular.

The Left in general and the Socialists in particular were understandably not impressed by the accidentalists' republican credentials. The sort of political ideals that Acción Popular seemed to value were regularly indicated in *El Debate* during late 1932. A growing interest in Italian Fascism was emphasised by the eulogistic editorial of 28 October. Entitled 'Ten Years of Fascism', it was couched in terms which suggested a strong identification with Fascism's fundamental objectives. The great triumph of Mussolini was seen as the replacement of 'daily rioting' with 'authority, discipline, hierarchy, order', which was significant since *El Debate*, in common with other rightist papers, was plac-

ing increasing stress on disorder in Spain.[53] Praise for Fascism was
unstinted : 'the Fascist state may be justly proud of having liberated
Italy from parliamentarism and having thus been able to stimulate its
activities, direct the economy, resist the economic crisis and strengthen
the moral resources of the nation'. The key to this achievement was
the destruction of socialism. The Spanish Socialists were not slow to
draw the conclusion that a similar fate awaited them, if ever the Right
came to power.[54] The tone of *El Debate* editorials hardly admitted
of any other interpretation. A regular theme was the need for right-
wing unity to annihilate socialism.[55] The constant reiteration of such
hostility naturally made the Socialists apprehensive.

Meanwhile, Gil Robles was preparing the ground for the formation
of his political party. In an open letter to the press, he made it clear
that the demands to be made on the consciences of the members would
not be excessive; they would be able to maintain their convictions and
defend them outside the organisation.[56] It was the natural outcome of
the October assembly : only those who insisted on attacking the Republic openly would be excluded. A congress of the various provincial
groups affiliated to Acción Popular took place in Madrid at the end of
February 1933. 500 delegates, representing 735,058 members of forty-
two rightist groups, agreed on the creation of the *Confederación
Española de Derechas Autónomas* (CEDA).[57] The new party's general
aims were 'the defence of the principles of Christian civilisation' and
the revision of the constitution, especially in those clauses which
referred to religion, education and property. In his closing speech, Gil
Robles clarified the ostensibly moderate terminology of the programme :
'when the social order is threatened, Catholics should unite to defend
it and safeguard the principles of Christian civilisation. . . . We will go
united into the struggle, no matter what it costs. . . . We are faced with
a social revolution. In the political panorama of Europe I can see only
the formation of Marxist and anti-Marxist groups. This is what is
happening in Germany and in Spain also. This is the great battle which
we must fight this year.' Having thus aligned himself in the mainstream
of the European Right, it was fitting that, later on the same day, in a
meeting at the Teatro Fuencarral (Madrid), he said that he couldn't
see anything wrong with thinking of fascism to cure the evils of Spain.[58]

The inaugural congress of the CEDA produced much talk of an
advanced social programme. In view of the social forces which the
CEDA represented, the Left was not impressed. *El Socialista* saw the
new party as a mixture of all the regressive tendencies in Spain, the
unification of everything that was old, crumbling and rotten.[59] Besides,
Hitler's rise to power and the Reichstag fire were fresh in the minds of
the Socialists. And they were determined that agrarian and Catholic
elements should not do to the Second Republic what they had done to

Weimar. The CEDA's determination to revise the Constitution was seen as the beginning of the end, as the first provocation : 'how can we trust the spiritual and material allies of Italian fascism, of Hitler, or Horthy?' Intensely aware of what was happening already to Jews, communists, socialists and liberals in Germany, the Spanish Left was highly sensitive to the behaviour of the Right. The persistent harping on disorder by the rightist press was seen as the preparation for a move towards fascism.[60] Above all, the Spanish Socialists were determined not to make the same mistakes as their comrades abroad.[61] Their anxiety was understandable when *El Debate* said of the German situation that Nazism had ideals worthy of encouragement, especially in its reinforcement of 'many concepts indispensable for society'. Gil Robles's attitude to fascism was ambiguous. He was attracted by its modes of social organisation and its ruthless elimination of the class struggle, but he found its reliance on violence distasteful. To the Socialists, this was not a meaningful reservation. Moreover, on the one occasion when Gil Robles spoke against fascism in a public meeting, in Barcelona on 21 March 1933, his followers greeted his words with boos and hisses. He did not repeat the exercise.[62]

Throughout 1933 the CEDA spread discontent with the Republic in agricultural circles. It was hardly surprising that the Left chose to regard declarations of legality as a mere fiction, a tactical device whereby the CEDA could work for anti-Republican aims but with all the convenience of doing so legally.[63] The preoccupations of CEDA revealed its origins. In May, *El Debate* gave a cocktail party for a deputation of landowners and employers from Seville, who had come to complain to the government about growing disorder and rising wages. They saw the problem not in terms of a need for reform, but as the lack of government repression before 'a monstrous, anarchic, anti-social offensive against commerce, industry and agriculture'.[64] At the same time, the CEDA was making its own the demands of the National Cereal Growers Association for an increase in minimum wheat prices and action against existing labour legislation. This referred to the two main reforms introduced by Largo Caballero as Minister of Labour : *jurados mixtos*, or arbitration committees, and the Law of Municipal Boundaries. The latter prevented labourers from outside an area from being hired while there were still local unemployed. It had effectively prevented the import of cheap labour to back wage cuts, and the use of blackleg labour in time of strikes. The Castilian cereal-growers wanted the *jurados mixtos* 'reformed' so that they would not favour worker interests, and they wanted the Law of Municipal Boundaries abolished. It was an attack on much that the Socialists regarded as progressive in the Republic, as well as being a blow at the urban worker, who relied heavily on cheap bread.[65]

El Socialista commented bitterly that the claims of the Seville deputation were equivalent to a demand for a return of the profits made 'in the days when there was no social legislation, when pathetic wages were the norm and all conflicts were settled by calling in the Civil Guard'.[66] The Socialists claimed persuasively that the disorder which was always cited in condemnation of the Republic was provoked by an upper class enraged by the limitation by law of their exploitation of the working classes.[67] Just how far disorder at this time went it is difficult to say. The American ambassador went on regular safari in search of it without finding any : 'we had travelled from one end of Spain to the other in search of the disorders "bordering on anarchy" of which we had heard so much in the drawing rooms of Madrid and found nothing of the sort'. Certainly the Left had nothing to gain from disorder, while the Right could always use it to support demands for more authoritarian government.[68]

During this time the CEDA regularly made a show of social-Catholic ideas, both in the press and in the party's frequent meetings. A typical example was a speech made in Seville in May by Federico Salmón, one of the more liberal of the CEDA leaders. He spoke in the vaguest terms about 'class harmony', the need for Christian charity and the need to work for the elimination of inequalities. It seemed a pious embroidery barely related to the real interests served by the CEDA. Moreoever, any given listener who applauded the announcement of a determination to do away with the abuses of property naturally never imagined the orator's strictures to be directed at himself.[69] The only practical remedy for the agrarian situation which was ever suggested with any regularity was that of an increase in the forces of order and an adoption of the methods used in Italy against anarchy.[70]

Most CEDA declarations were double-meaning, but the social-Catholic aspect was the one that seemed least to correspond to the party's actions. In August there could be seen in the Cortes the familiar sight of the Agrarian Minority obstructing reform. This time it was the draft law on rural leases, a crucial element in the projected agrarian reform. It could have improved the lot of the tenant farmers of northern and central Spain, who had in fact voted for the deputies of the Minority. Two hundred and fifty amendments were tabled as part of a planned technical obstruction. Gil Robles disingenuously explained the amendments as the fruit of his group's concern for the leaseholders. Once given security of tenure, they might lose the land to money-lenders and thereby contribute to the creation of *latifundios*, or else divide it among their heirs and create *minifundios*. The level of boredom created by this evident cant so discouraged attendance at the Cortes that, when the time came to vote, a quorum could never be obtained.[71] The Agrarian opposition in parliament to the leases bill, and the Acción Popular campaign against the Republic's religious legislation, inevitably conditioned the Left's response to the CEDA. This was to be emphasised during the build-up to the November 1933 elections, when the CEDA campaign hinged on opposition to everything which the Left might regard as progressive in the Republic.

The continuing identification of the CEDA and its leader with anti-Republicanism had been underlined during the summer. Always aware that the majority of his followers were monarchists, Gil Robles dreaded that Alfonso XIII would declare membership of the CEDA incompatible with monarchist ideals. Accordingly, in June he went to see the exiled King at Fontainebleau, where, it seems, he had little difficulty in persuading Alfonso that the CEDA was a useful method of building up right-wing sentiment without in any way consolidating the Republic.[72]

Gil Robles was closely tied to the old Spain for family reasons. His father was the famous Carlist theoretician Enrique Gil Robles. The Carlist in José María spoke when he referred later to 'the almost physical repulsion which was caused me by having to work within a system whose defects were so patently obvious to me. My doctrinal training, my family background, my sensibility rebelled daily.' In December 1932 he had declared publicly that only its lack of overt monarchism divided his movement from Traditionalism.[73] It was inevitable that the Left would assume that he was using the legalist tactic as the best means available to defend the socio-economic structure and the cultural-religious values of traditional Spain.

Suspicion of Gil Robles's essential hostility towards democracy was strengthened by the knowledge that he had held an official post under the Dictatorship and had been an editor of *El Debate* when it was one of the most lyrical apologists for Primo's regime. But there were more topical reasons for the Left's growing tendency to see Gil Robles and the CEDA as proto-fascist. In the first place, the similarity between the CEDA and the Catholic Party of Dollfuss in Austria was becoming more marked. Both groups were authoritarian, corporativist, and fiercely anti-Marxist. The coincidences were many: both manifested an implacable hostility towards socialism, both found their mass support among backward rural smallholders who resented the socialist dominance of the capital city, and both had a semi-fascist youth movement.

During the summer of 1933, the Spanish Left was becoming highly sensitive to the danger of fascism. Weimar was persistently cited as a warning.[74] Parallels with the Spanish situation were not difficult to find. The Catholic press applauded the Nazi destruction of the German socialist and communist movements. Nazism was much admired on the Spanish Right because of its emphasis on authority, the fatherland and hierarchy – all three of which were central preoccupations of

CEDA propaganda. Once Von Papen had signed a Concordat with the Vatican, *El Debate*'s enthusiasm, previously restrained by unease at Nazi anti-Catholicism, knew no bounds. The Nazis were aware of this and grateful. When Angel Herrera visited Germany in May 1934, officials of the Wilhelmstrasse were anxious to arrange an interview with Hitler, because of the importance attributed to what was seen as the Herrera-inspired pro-Nazi line.[75]

In justification of the legalistic tactic in Spain, *El Debate* pointed out that Hitler had attained power legally.[76] The parallel was starkly underlined in the most eulogistic editorial of all, on 4 August, when the leader-writer, having praised Hitler and Mussolini for their stand against 'communist levelling', rejoiced that the Spanish middle class now had its own organisation to fulfil that task. At the same time, regular calls were made for the adoption of a corporative economic organisation to bring Spain into line with Italy, Austria, Germany and Portugal. While the Catholic press urged its readers to follow the example of Italy and Germany and organise against the dragon of revolution, the CEDA could hardly wonder why the Left regarded it with trepidation.[77] A brilliant and influential book by a Socialist on the rise of Hitler, published in 1933, neatly pointed the parallel with accidentalism, by showing how 'the enemies of democracy take it up to reach power, and once there bury it with every dishonour'. And, when *El Debate* praised Hitler for renewing Germany's moral and spiritual values, *El Socialista* asked itself if the CEDA, which often proclaimed Spain's need of a similar renovation, intended to use the same methods.[78] The rise of Hitler increased apprehension, especially in the leftwing of the Socialist Party, one of whose most distinguished theoreticians, Luis Araquistain, had been ambassador in Berlin. Nor could it have escaped the notice of this group that *El Debate*'s Berlin correspondent, Antonio Bermudez Cañete, later to be a CEDA deputy, was an ardent sympathiser with early Nazism. He had even translated parts of *Mein Kampf* and was involved in the Conquista del Estado group, one of the earliest attempts to introduce fascism into Spain.[79]

There was thus considerable suspicion surrounding the intentions of the CEDA when the campaigns for the November elections began.[80] The extreme bellicosity of Gil Robles's tone was not reassuring. He had just returned from the Nuremberg rally and appeared to be strongly influenced by what he had seen. He recorded his impressions in the CEDA party bulletin, favourably describing his official visit to the Brown House, to Nazi propaganda offices and to concentration camps, and how he saw Nazi militia drilling. While expressing vague reservations about the pantheistic elements in fascism, he pinpointed those elements most worthy of emulation in Spain : its anti-Marxism and its hatred of liberal and parliamentary democracy. The same issue carried a reprint of a piece called 'Towards a new concept of the state', which he had written in September. This was a eulogistic account of how totalitarianism dealt with 'corrosive liberalism', and in it Gil Robles expressed his readiness to follow the new trends in world politics.[81]

The CEDA's election campaign showed just how well Gil Robles had learned his lessons. The German tour had been made 'to study details of organisation and propaganda',[82] and he had been on a similar visit to Italy in January. The keynote of the campaign was to be anti-socialism. *El Debate*'s announcement of the imminence of elections was combative in the extreme. Appealing to all those of right-wing views to co-operate, the paper stated that 'the miserly now know that for each coin they didn't want to give, they lost ten times its value'.[83] It was made clear that the CEDA was determined to win at any cost. The election committee decided for a single anti-Marxist counter-revolutionary front. In other words, the CEDA had no qualms about going to the elections in coalition with groups such as Renovación Española and the Carlists, who were conspiring to destroy the Republic by force of arms. It was an acknowledgement that the Right's material interests could best be defended within parliament, irrespective of how a majority was obtained. The manifesto of the CEDA youth movement, JAP (Juventud de Acción Popular), stated that it expected nothing from the obsolete parliamentary system but that it accepted the Cortes merely as the battleground for the moment.[84]

The climax of Gil Robles's campaign came in a speech given on 15 October in the Monumental Cinema of Madrid. His tone could only make the Left wonder what a CEDA victory would mean for them : 'We must reconquer Spain. . . . We must give Spain a true unity, a new spirit, a totalitarian polity. . . . For me there is only one tactic today : to form an anti-Marxist front and the wider the better. It is necessary now to defeat socialism inexorably.' At this point, Goicoechea, who was present, was made to stand and he received a tumultous ovation. Gil Robles continued with language indistinguishable from that of the extreme conspiratorial Right : 'We must found a new state, purge the fatherland of judaising freemasons. . . . We must proceed to a new state and this imposes duties and sacrifices. What does it matter if we have to shed blood ! . . . We need full power and that is what we demand. . . . To realise this ideal we are not going to waste time with archaic forms. *Democracy is not an end but a means to the conquest of the new state. When the time comes, either parliament submits or we will eliminate it.*'[85] This speech, described by *El Socialista* as an 'authentic fascist harangue', was regarded by the Left as the most crystalline expression of CEDA orthodoxy.[86] Certainly every sentence was greeted by ecstatic applause. There was something ominous about the way Gil Robles ended a plea for financial assistance by threatening 'a black list of bad patriots' who did not contribute. The tenor of the speech was carried over to election posters, which emphasised the need to save Spain from 'Marxists, Masons, Separatists and Jews'.[87]

A vast amount of cash was spent on a campaign technically reminiscent of Nazi procedure. Millions of leaflets were printed and scattered on villages from the air. 200,000 coloured posters were printed. Lorries drove around the streets of the bigger towns carrying screens on which were projected films of Gil Robles's speech. Twenty times a day there were radio spots exhorting listeners to 'Vote for the Right!' or to 'Vote against Marxism!'[88] The election fund was gigantic and based on generous donations from the well-to-do, particularly Juan March, the millionaire enemy of the Republic, and the Conde de Romanones, the ex-confidant of Alfonso XIII. Apart from radio, full use was made of modern transport and neon signs to carry CEDA propaganda to every part of Spain. Throughout November, it was made clear that if the CEDA won an outright victory then it would proceed to the establishment of an authoritarian regime of semi-fascist character along Austrian lines.[89]

The basic minimum programme which held the CEDA in coalition with its monarchist running mates could hardly have been more extreme. Its three points were (1) the revision of the laic and socialising legislation of the Republic, (2) a defence of the economic interests of the country, especially agriculture, and (3) an amnesty. This was an open challenge to the republicans. Religious legislation was widely regarded on the Left as the only blow so far against the *ancien régime*. Social legislation, in the form of the *jurados mixtos* and the boundaries law, was the only practical reform in favour of the landless peasantry. 'Defence of economic interests' meant, in the jargon of the Right, protection of land and industry against the demands of the workers. An amnesty would apply to the collaborators of General Primo de Rivera and those who had been implicated in the 10 August rising. For these latter it was a virtual invitation to continue their plotting, as indeed they did. Alliance with monarchist groups known to be violently hostile to the Republic irrevocably associated the CEDA with them in the eyes of the Left. Statements that the coalition was merely circumstantial could not dispel an impression of coincidence of purpose and method. There was little difference in tone between the speeches of Gil Robles and the pieces sent from abroad by José Calvo Sotelo, the extremist leader-in-exile of the monarchist Renovación Española. At a meeting in Valladolid at the beginning of November, Gil Robles made a menacing reference to 'a strong movement against democracy, parliamentarism and liberalism taking place in Italy, Germany and other countries. The Cortes about to be elected can be the decisive trial for democracy in Spain.'[90]

In addition to the national right-wing coalition, the CEDA made a number of alliances at local level before the first round of the elections. These local alliances took place in areas where the anti-Marxist coalition was relatively weak and there existed some other substantial conservative force in the area. Thus, in Asturias, a deal was made with the Reformist Party of Melquíades Alvarez; in Alicante, with Joaquín Chapaprieta, a monarchist turned conservative republican; in the Balearic Islands, with Juan March; in Guadalajara, with the Conde de Romanones. In Badajoz, Cáceres, Ceuta, Granada, Jaén and Zamora, an arrangement was made with the local Radicals. The elections were held on 19 November. Despite the various alliances and the fact that, in rural areas especially, the Right disposed of quite considerable pressure over the unemployed, the results were disappointing. Out of 378 deputies elected in the first round, there were sixty-seven Cedistas (members of the CEDA) and seventy-eight Radicals. It was an appreciable gain, but far from remarkable in view of the previous year's vast investment in propaganda. So Gil Robles, anxious to take advantage of the fact that the electoral law favoured coalitions, decided to widen his alliances even further. He now clinched local deals with Radicals in the south, the great masters of electoral falsification. This involved going back on previous commitments and created considerable bitterness on the Right. In Córdoba, for instance, the monarchist José Tomás Valverde had only with difficulty been persuaded to run in the first round. Now he was unceremoniously dropped to make way for a local Radical, to the annoyance of the local monarchists. Nevertheless, the tactic paid off. After the second round, the Cedistas numbered 115 and the Radicals 104.[91] The fact that the local alliances had been made at the expense of rightist allies proved nothing to the Left if not that Gil Robles was prepared to do anything and compromise any principles to get a parliamentary majority and deform the Republic from within.[92]

3 Social Democracy and Social Conflict: The PSOE in Power, 1931–3

Unaware of just how successfully the Right would be able to organise its opposition to reform, the Socialist leadership saw the coming of the Republic with great optimism. Two weeks before the municipal elections which were to convince the King that he no longer enjoyed 'the love of my people', Largo Caballero spoke at an electoral meeting in Madrid and expressed the hopes which he and many others placed in a change of regime. Declaring that, because he was a Socialist, he was also necessarily a republican, he claimed that only the overthrow of the monarchy could remedy the hunger in Andalusia and change a situation in which the social order had to be defended by the Civil Guard. At a similar function in Granada, Fernando de los Ríos said that the Socialists were about to help the middle classes make their democratic revolution.[1] In so far as they analysed the situation at all, the majority of the Socialist leadership were convinced that a classic bourgeois revolution was imminent. If they differed over the tactics to be followed – Besteiro counselling that the bourgeoisie be left to get on with its own task, Prieto convinced that without Socialist help the bourgeoisie would be too weak to do so, and Largo keen to participate in the hope of benefit for the party and the UGT – they were all united in the conviction that progress was inevitable. In fact, the 'bourgeoisie' was not about to make an assault on feudalism. The commercial middle class had long since been integrated into the old landed oligarchy, and the one-time feudal ruling class had adopted capitalist modes of exploiting the land and had varied interests in industry and commerce. The adoption of democratic forms, far from being a stage in the advance of capitalism in Spain, was accepted by the economically dominant classes with great reluctance and only because of the demonstration of the monarchy's bankruptcy. That they accepted the change in political form did not signify that they would welcome any change in the social and economic structure of the country. Had the Socialists realised this, their bitterness on eventually realising the strength of the opposition to their timid attempts at reform would perhaps have been less.

Accordingly, the King's departure on 14 April and the establishment of a parliamentary regime constituted far less of a change than was thought either by the joyful crowds in the streets or by many Socialist leaders. Believing that a period of classic bourgeois democracy must now be lived through before socialism could be established, the PSOE hierarchy assumed that the new Republic would allow the improvement of social conditions within the existing economic order. What they failed to realise was that the brutal conditions of the southern day-labourers (jornaleros) or the Asturian miners could hardly be improved by half-measures. The great mine-owners and landlords, unaccustomed to making concessions, would regard attempts at reform as an aggressive challenge to the existing balance of social and economic power. And they were right. Thus, the Socialists' hopeful vision of a social-reforming republic was to leave them trapped between an impatient popular clamour for more and faster reform and the determined resistance to change of the possessing classes. Differing responses to the realisation that the attempt to make the Republic socially meaningful involved the party in harmful contradictions were to lead to a stark increase in the divisions which had already become apparent during the 1920s.

For the moment, however, the PSOE was to be publicly committed to the defence and protection of the Republic. As the crowds began to celebrate in the streets, the executive committees of the PSOE and the UGT issued a joint declaration, which ended with the undertaking that, 'if at any time it became necessary to use our strength to safeguard the nascent regime, the Socialist Party and the UGT would carry out their duty without any kind of vacillation'.[2] Elsewhere in Madrid, the Socialist youth prevented the burning of General Mola's house and also linked arms around the royal palace to hold back the crowds and to avoid any unpleasant incidents.[3] This symbolised the role that the Socialists were to find themselves adopting in the early years of the Republic, that of restraining the enthusiasm of their followers in order to give the regime an image acceptable to the middle classes. The conservative republican and Prime Minister, Niceto Alcalá Zamora, gratefully emphasised the point in an article written six weeks after the establishment of the Republic. He saw the Socialist movement as 'a wall of defence against assault and a reassuring strength within the new regime'.[4]

That the Socialists should make sacrifices for a regime that was not their own seemed natural in the euphoric atmosphere of the spring and summer of 1931. But the extent to which the politically unsophisticated masses, particularly in the rural south, associated the coming of the Republic with proletarian emancipation was soon to be a cause of regret for some Socialists, particularly followers of Besteiro. The moderate trade unionist Manuel Cordero regarded the optimism and illusions of the masses as an impediment to the Socialists' need to take advantage of the Republic slowly. Feeling that the day after the Republic was proclaimed all the problems facing the country would be solved, class privileges would disappear and a regime of equality and social justice would be established, they were soon to be disappointed by the slowness of progress towards reform.[5] Largo Caballero did not share this view. In fact, he was sufficiently enthusiastic about the situation to assume that the divisions of the previous year would now automatically heal. He offered Besteiro's lieutenant, Andrés Saborit, a senior post in the Ministry of Labour, an offer which was immediately turned down. The cabinet, in which Largo, Prieto and De los Ríos now sat, also offered Besteiro himself first an attractive job as state delegate to the national petrol monopoly, CAMPSA, and then the post of ambassador to France. He refused both.[6]

It was not just the traditional abstentionist Right of the party which had its doubts about the wisdom of becoming too involved with the Republic. There soon emerged other discordant voices, only this time more radical ones. Although for the moment in a minority, significantly they belonged to party members whose opinions were of some weight with key militant sectors of the Socialist movement. Javier Bueno, who published a book in June 1931, was later to be editor of the Asturian miners' daily *Avance*, which became increasingly radical after its foundation in November 1931. Bueno's book urged his fellow Socialists to seize the opportunity presented by the birth of the new era. Declaring that capitalist society was finished, he rejected the party's evolutionary reformism : 'if the future lies in a social order which liberates mankind, there can be no reason for delaying the moment of breaking the chains'.[7]

In the optimistic atmosphere of 1931, Bueno's views had little impact. Yet before long he was to be a vocal member of a section of the PSOE which came to feel that it was precisely the party's commitment to the Republic which was delaying the breaking of the chains. Perhaps of greater significance were the misgivings of Gabriel Morón, the militant rural leader from Córdoba who had spearheaded the inner-party protest against collaboration with Primo de Rivera. Morón and a group of his friends were concerned that the reformist hopes of a progressive republic were illusions. Arguing that contemporary events suggested that socialism was now the object of a worldwide offensive by the bourgeoisie, they believed that bourgeois democracy and bourgeois liberties had become meaningless concepts. Accordingly, the PSOE tactics of reformism and revisionism were now obsolete. Instead, claimed Morón, the Socialists must learn that a fundamental struggle was coming between the old capitalist order and the new political aspirations of the workers.[8]

What gave added significance to the views of Morón was that it was in the agrarian south that the front line of the battle for a progressive republic was to be found. Moreover, it was there too that a massive influx of recruits into the UGT was taking place. The vertiginous growth of the landworkers' federation, the FNTT, was greatly out of proportion with the overall growth of the UGT. The total union membership grew from 277,011 in December 1930 to 958,451 in December 1931 and to 1,041,539 in June 1932. The FNTT's membership rose from 36,639 in June 1930 to 392,953 in June 1932.[9] The shift in orientation of the UGT as a whole was immense. In mid 1930, as the agrarian crisis got under way, rural labour made up 13 per cent of UGT membership. Two years later, with class bitterness in the southern villages intensifying by the day, the proportion of landworkers in the UGT had risen to 37 per cent. Largo Caballero was delighted just to see his beloved union growing faster than the anarchist CNT : 'our rapid growth cannot frighten us,' he declared, 'nay, must not frighten us.'[10] More cautious members of the syndical bureaucracy were concerned that the illiterate day-labourers now flooding into the movement, brutalised by conditions on the southern estates, would push the UGT into violent conflict with the landowners. They were anxious that the union organisation should face up to the task of moderating the untutored exaltation of the *jornaleros*.[11] If their fears were born of bureaucratic paternalism, they were none the less justified. The change in orientation of the UGT, from a predominantly elite union of the working-class aristocracy to a mass union of unsophisticated workers and peasants, at a time of economic depression and rising unemployment, was to place it at the centre of the major conflict of the Republic, the one between the large landowners and the landless labourers. Each side in that conflict was represented in the national political arena by a mass parliamentary party : the landowners by the Acción Popular–Agrario coalition, the labourers by the PSOE. Thus, the survival of the parliamentary regime depended to a large degree on the successful resolution of the conflict.

In the first days of the Republic, few Socialists were aware of the sombre implications of the recruiting boom in the UGT. Moreover, the three Socialists in the provisional government were involved as early as 15 April 1931 in a solemn undertaking to improve the living conditions of the Spanish peasantry. This took the form of clause 5 of the Juridical Statute of the Republic, a formal declaration in which the provisional government laid out its objectives and circumscribed its powers until such time as a parliament could be elected.[12] Clause 5 declared that private property was guaranteed by law and could be expropriated only for reasons of public utility and with compensation. It went on to recognise the neglect that previous governments had shown of the great mass of peasants and of agriculture in general, and undertook to alter agrarian legislation in such a way as to make it correspond to the social function of the land. At a cabinet meeting on 21 April, the specific application of this commitment was discussed. The three Socialist ministers were prevailed upon to shelve their party's desire for a sweeping redistribution of the land, at least until such time as parliamentary assent were possible. In return for this forbearance, they were to be allowed to issue a series of decrees to deal with some of the immediate causes of hardship in the countryside.[13]

A Ministry of Labour report commissioned in November 1930 and published in early 1931 gave a sombre picture of the misery caused in the south by the drought during the winter.[14] Such was the hunger of the landless labourers that immediate palliatives were urgently needed. The usual solution of increased public works was inadequate. The Republican government had come to power with the biggest budgetary deficit in the history of Spain, thanks to the grandiose projects of General Primo de Rivera. Public-works contractors were owed 300 million pesetas and, in a context of international financial uncertainty, long-term loans were not to be had. Deficit financing was impossible. Thus, an improvement in the conditions of the rural poor could be sought only in some readjustment of the prevailing economic inequalities – that is to say, at the cost of the rural rich. The *latifundio* system of landholding depended to a large extent for its economic viability on the existence of a large reserve of landless labourers paid the minimum wages for the shortest period possible. Increased wages and protection against dismissal for those labourers therefore challenged the basis of the entire system. What may have seemed to the Socialists to be merely limited reformist palliatives were thus to have far-reaching implications.

At a time of economic boom, wage increases might perhaps have been absorbed by higher profits. As it was, the period in which the Socialists were attempting to ameliorate conditions coincided with the years of the great depression. The consequent situation of exacerbated class struggle could not but impel the landless labourers to push for more reforms and the landowners to oppose any reform at all. The depression affected the Spanish countryside in two main ways – by closing the safety valve of emigration and by forcing down agricultural prices. After forty years of high net emigration, averaging at 32,000 per year, 1931 saw a net return of emigrants of 39,582. By the end of 1933, barriers to immigrants in France and Latin America had caused over 100,000 Spaniards to return to Spain, joining a similar number who would normally have emigrated but could not do so. The industrial depression ensured that there would be little relief in terms of internal migration to the towns and that the returning emigrants would be forced to go to the countryside. During the boom of the 1920s there had been a considerable rural exodus, not least provoked by Primo's great building schemes. Unskilled building labourers were now returning to their villages. Since the world downturn was soon to take its toll of Spanish agricultural exports of wine, fruit and olive oil, the great landowners were far from being disposed to find employment for the rural masses. Since 45·5 per cent of the active population, 3·9 million landed or landless peasants, worked the land and 2 million of them were landless day-labourers, the resolution of the conflict of interest between the landowners and the labourers was the central issue facing the provisional government.[15]

This then was the context in which the Minister of Labour, Largo Caballero, and the Minister of Justice, Fernando de los Ríos, began at the end of April 1931 to issue decrees concerning the rural question. Between 28 April and the opening of parliament on 14 July, they passed a series of edicts of crucial importance. Those emanating from the Ministry of Justice concerned rural leases; those from the Ministry of Labour dealt with the working conditions of the *braceros* (day-labourers). A decree of 29 April froze all leases, automatically renewed any which fell due, and prevented eviction other than for failure to pay rent or lack of cultivation. Its object was to prevent hitherto-absentee landlords from taking possession of their land to avoid the consequences of the proposed agrarian reform. As of 11 July, tenants were allowed to petition local courts for reduction of rents. The decrees introduced by Largo Caballero had a more dramatic impact. The most important of them was the decree of municipal boundaries (*términos municipales*), issued on 28 April. It prevented the introduction of outside labour into a municipality while there remained local workers unemployed. On 7 May, agrarian mixed juries (*jurados mixtos*) were introduced, to arbitrate in rural labour disputes. Significantly, General Primo de Rivera had never dared extend his arbitration committees (*comités paritarios*), on which the mixed juries were based, to rural areas, for fear of the owners' reaction. A decree of 1 July established, in theory at least, the eight-hour day in the countryside. Given that labourers were expected to earn their day-wage by working from sunrise to sunset (*de sol a sol*) and that sixteen-hour days were not uncommon, this decree implied a substantial additional income for the *braceros*, either in the form of overtime pay or in terms of more work for more men. To prevent the owners' sabotaging these various measures by simply ceasing to cultivate their land, a supplementary edict of obligatory cultivation (*laboreo forzoso*) was passed by the Ministry of National Economy, on 7 May.[16]

The cumulative effect of these decrees was, on paper, to strike at the heart of the repressive economic relations prevailing in rural Spain, particularly in the areas of the great estates. Yet it seems that, in promulgating them, Fernando de los Ríos and Francisco Largo Caballero were not aiming at revolutionary objectives. They meant their edicts rather as a palliative to the conditions of acute misery in which Andalusia found itself in the spring of 1931. Apart from the Ministry of Labour report on the agrarian crisis, the cabinet also had at its disposal a number of alarming warnings. General Sanjurjo, head of the Civil Guard, reported to the Minister of War, Manuel Azaña, that agitation was on the increase. On 21 July all the mayors of the towns and villages of the province of Jaén, one of the worst hit, came to beg the government for help. They claimed that, just to prevent widespread starvation and an insurrection, subsidies of 2 million pesetas per day would be necessary for at least three months.[17] Projects for public works were drawn up with the limited funds available but the initial grant for the entire south was only 10 million pesetas.[18] In such circumstances, it was not surprising that the government began to think that the employers should contribute towards alleviating the crisis.

However limited the intentions of the ministers involved, the implicit threat to the hitherto dominant position of the owners remained. The law of municipal boundaries effectively curtailed the introduction of blackleg labour to break strikes and keep wages down. The mixed juries recognised that the labourers also had legal rights and were not simply subject to the economic necessities of the owners. The eighthour day would increase costs in a depressed market. The decree of obligatory cultivation introduced a notion of social utility which limited the owners' right to dispose of their land as they willed, and did so in such a way as to neutralise one of their principal weapons of social domination. The big landowners began to mobilise to meet the threat. Various employers' federations – the Agrupación de Propietarios de Fincas Rústicas, the Confederación Española Patronal Agraria, stockbreeders' associations, olive-growers' associations, and so on – were either founded or revitalised.[19] Much of the success of the Acción Nacional recruiting campaign of the summer of 1931 can be attributed to the resentment generated by these first decrees and to fear of more thoroughgoing measures to come. The press and propaganda network of the ACNP (Asociación Católica Nacional de Propagandistas) was soon at work attacking the decrees. It had considerable success on this issue, as on others, in creating the appearance that the interests of smallholders were the same as those of large landowners. This was relatively easy to do, since many of the decrees' consequences affected any employer of labour, large or small.

Some of the rightist criticisms were, from the owners' point of view, justified, but others were part of a campaign of denigration which skilfully distorted the real details and functions of the decrees. The decree of municipal boundaries, for instance, deprived migrant workers of labour and also hit the inhabitants of smaller, 'satellite' villages near to, but outside, the boundaries of a bigger village. However, that such was the case was not so much a criticism of the decree as proof of the need for fundamental changes in Spain's agrarian structure. It is also likely that local workers used their new-found job security to drag jobs out longer and so guarantee their exiguous wages for a few days longer. That, however, was not sufficient to justify Gil Robles's charge, on a visit to the Ministry of Labour at the end of November, that the decree benefited none but 'professional layabouts' (*vagos profesionales*). There is evidence to suggest that the Socialist municipal councillors in charge of applying the decrees showed little restraint in taking advantage of the shift in the legal balance of power. In some cases, for instance, they used the decree of obligatory cultivation to plough pasture. That is hardly surprising, since the owners had equally not hesitated to derive all the economic benefit possible from the previous situation. The Socialist *alcaldes* (mayors) and councillors did not have it all their own way, however. The machinery to enforce the decrees was almost non-existent. Yet the problem was immense. While thousands of *braceros* were on the point of starvation, vast areas of land lay uncultivated. In Andalusia and Extremadura, between 40 and 60 per cent of all useful land was uncultivated.[20] Nevertheless, fines for infringements of the decree of *laboreo forzoso* did not exceed 500 pesetas and were usually much less. In fact, Largo Caballero complained bitterly of the way in which senior officials, such as the civil governors of several provinces, sabotaged the application of the various decrees by rulings which were contrary to their spirit. Moreover, in remote villages particularly, the power of the Civil Guard remained untouched. Even General Sanjurjo commented to Azaña that the Civil Guard's social commitment was to the rural upper classes and against the Socialist and anarchist *alcaldes* and councillors, whom not so long ago they had been putting in jail. Above all, the power consequent upon being the exclusive providers of work remained to the owners.[21]

The propaganda campaign carried out by the Catholic press merely inflamed the determination of the southern landowners not to abide by the provisions of the decrees. The belief was created that one of the consequences of the law of municipal boundaries was that unemployed barbers, cobblers, school-teachers and other unsuitable unskilled workers were being used for highly specialised tasks to the detriment of the nation's agriculture. Yet, by a supplementary ruling of 6 August, the importation of necessary specialised labour was permitted. By another, of 30 September, it was laid down that the list of workers from a given municipality who had to be employed before the introduction of outsiders could be permitted was to be composed only of agricultural labourers. The rightist press also complained that valuable crops were lost because the law's rigidity prevented the hiring of essential extra labour. In fact, once all the labourers in a village had been hired, there was nothing to prevent the introduction of outsiders. Moreover, the law was suspended altogether on 15 October for the duration of the orange harvest, and on 29 October for the duration of the olive harvest, in the provinces concerned. The various original decrees required some adaptation when put into practice. Nevertheless, it was the theoretical rigidity and not the practical flexibility which attracted the attention of the rightist press.[22]

Less directly offensive to the big landowners, but no less irritating to them, were the decrees passed by Fernando de los Ríos to improve the situation of the hard-pressed leaseholders. Besides the traditional smallholding areas of the north and centre of Spain, there was an increasing amount of land cultivated in small leaseholdings in the predominantly *latifundio* areas. Given the acute land-hunger and consequent competition for plots, leases were accepted by tenants on economically ruinous terms and for periods as short as one year. De los Ríos's decrees mitigated some of the worst results of the disastrous 1930–1 harvest by making eviction almost impossible and preventing rent rises at a time of falling prices. This was seen as an intolerable infringement on property rights by many large landowners. However, the real battle over this issue did not come until 1935, when the liberal CEDA Minister of Agriculture took up the defence of the smallholder. There is little evidence to suggest whether the reason for the delay was that the political formations which protected the big owners' interests were too concerned to gain the support of the small farmers to risk taking up the issue, or whether it was simply a question of priorities.

Indeed, by the end of 1931, it was obvious that the owners' initial resentment to the decrees concerning the working conditions of the *jornaleros* was maturing into a determination to destroy them by means of a virtual rural lock-out. However, in the early summer this future conflict was not foreseen by most of the PSOE leaders. Besteiro's abstentionist faction remained doubtful, but others tended to see the raised expectations of the rural workers and their consequent influx into the UGT as an indication of the possibilities of a reforming bourgeois democracy. In the elections of 28 June for the Constituent Cortes, the PSOE had gained 116 seats. This triumph raised the question of the role to be played by the Socialists within the Republic. Accordingly, an extraordinary congress of the party was called for 10 July, four days before the Cortes was due to open, to debate the policy to be followed by the PSOE deputies. An indication of rank-and-file enthusiasm for collaboration came in the voting for delegates to the congress. In the hitherto strongly pro-Besteiro Agrupación Socialista de Madrid, the abstentionist Andrés Saborit was surprisingly not elected.[23]

The main question at the congress was whether or not the three Socialists in the provisional government should continue to participate. The sub-committee delegated to examine the question was dominated by Besteiro but included a Prietist, Teodomiro Menéndez, and Largo's adviser, Luis Araquistain. The central recommendation of its report was that the three ministers should remain in the government for the period during the elaboration of the Constitution. Prieto then proposed an amendment of its text. This amendment stated that

1. In this historic moment, the fundamental obligation of the PSOE is to defend the Republic and contribute by all means to its definitive consolidation.

2. Since the task entrusted to the provisional government is unfinished, the party will continue to be represented in the government until the Constitution is approved and the supreme organ of power is elected.

3. The parliamentary group, although directly responsible for its activities to the congresses of the party, in cases of exceptional importance in which its attitude could have a decisive effect on the direction of Spanish politics, will appeal to the Executive Committee of the party for a decision.

4. After the Constitution is approved and the supreme organ of power is elected, if the party is requested to continue in the government and the request comes at a time when an extraordinary congress cannot be called, the parliamentary group and the Executive Committee will decide together. If they do not agree, the National Committee will decide.

5. As a general norm, the party declares in principle against participation in power. However, faithful to article 1 of this declaration, and in defence of the Republic, the party would accept such participation if it felt that not to do so would lead to rightist policies contrary to the profoundly radical aspirations revealed by the country on 12 April and confirmed on 28 June and contrary also to the vehement desire for a rigid administrative austerity and a break with the traditional political vices. The party would also accept power if it felt that lack of cohesion between the Republican groups deprived the government of indispensable solidarity.

Prieto's text implied that participation was a necessary sacrifice on the part of the PSOE. Nevertheless, it opened the way to a full collaboration and clearly implicated the PSOE in the success or failure of the Republic. Besteiro opposed it on the grounds that the party would be doing the bourgeoisie's job and consequently lose contact with its own followers, but Prieto's text was accepted by the congress by 10,607 votes to 8362. For the rest, the congress was concerned with elaborating Socialist objectives in the Constituent Cortes. These were basically reformist, but were none the less ambitious, including as they did the establishment of civil rights, the nationalisation of railways, banks, mines and forests, the solution of the agrarian problem, the introduction of divorce, the construction of a laic educational system, and the declaration of the religious independence of the state.[24]

The full implications of the Socialist commitment to the defence of the bourgeois Republic were soon apparent and tended to justify Besteiro's worst fears. Despite the Socialists' readiness to postpone their more amibitious reforms, the upper classes were not satisfied. The peseta began to fall as large sums of capital were spirited out of the country – to such an extent, indeed, that the old adviser of the King, the Conde de Romanones, declared that if he were in power he would shoot the pessimists.[25] At the same time as the upper classes thus expressed their hostility to the Republic, the working class began to reveal its own impatient expectations by a number of strikes throughout 1931. It was an awkward situation for a working-class party in a bourgeois government. To prevent industrial and agrarian unrest from discrediting the Republic, the Socialist ministers acquiesced in the often-violent suppression of strikes involving anarchists and Communists, while the UGT trade-union bureaucracy worked hard to curtail the militancy of its own members. Given the traditional rivalry with the CNT, few tears were shed for the repression of the anarchists. However, the rank-and-file did not always share the egoistic vision of the paid bureaucrats and felt a more basic class solidarity. This was particularly the case in rural areas. Although the Socialist press referred to anarchist unrest,[26] there was little to choose between anarchists and FNTT members. In many villages, the local organisation of *braceros* was, naïvely, affiliated to the UGT, the CNT *and* the Communist Party. Elsewhere, the fact that illiterate day-labourers joined the FNTT did not make them sophisticated Marxists overnight and there was little difference in political maturity or aspirations between them and members of the CNT. In the mines too, the essential harshness of conditions created a solidarity which rose above the rivalries of the various political factions. Not surprisingly then, the acute criticisms of class collaboration and reformism made against the Socialist leadership could not fail to have an effect on the UGT base militants. Significantly, it was precisely those Socialist leaders who were nearest to the problems of the workers – Largo Caballero; Luis Araquistain, his second-in-command at the Ministry of Labour; and Carlos de Baraibar, his Director-General of Labour – who were eventually to reject reformism as worse than useless.[27]

The basic cause of the Socialists' discomfort was the fact that the anarchists regarded the bourgeois Republic as little different from the monarchy and were little disposed to listen to PSOE pleas for patience. At the end of May there was a strike of port workers in Pasajes (San Sebastián). The Minister of the Interior, Miguel Maura, sent in the Civil Guard, and eight workers were killed and many more wounded. The Pasajes incident had an immediate repercussion in Asturias. There, the UGT-affiliated SMA was coming under increasing pressure from the far more militant Sindicato Único, jointly controlled by anarchists and Communists. Since the death of the great reformist Manuel Llaneza, the SMA had been led by Prietists such as Teodomiro Menéndez and Ramón González Peña, strong believers in the party line which was to prevail at the extraordinary congress. They condemned the proposed solidarity strike as reactionary irresponsibility designed to discredit the Republic. Nevertheless, rank-and-file sympathy with anarchist claims that the SMA leadership was acting as the ally of the hated mine-owners eventually forced SMA participation in the general strike which began on 1 June. The Socialists then used all their influence to bring the strike to a rapid and peaceful end.[28]

Elsewhere, the story was similar. In Andalusia and Extremadura, hungry *braceros* and *yunteros* were attacking the great estates and again the Civil Guard was sent in. The Besteirist leadership of the rapidly swelling FNTT had to use all its powers of persuasion to keep the militancy of its new members within Republican legality. The major conflicts of the summer took place in Madrid, Barcelona, and Seville. The first of these, the great telephone strike which broke out on 6 July, starkly highlighted the dilemma of the Socialists in the government. The telephone monopoly in Spain had been established during the Dictadura by the American ITT Corporation, in the midst of a great scandal. Throughout the late 1920s and up to the coming of the Republic, the Socialists had condemned its irregularities and promised support for the wage-claims of the telephone workers. However, when the strike broke out, the cabinet was frantically trying to create confidence in the regime and was also under considerable pressure from the American ambassador. Accordingly, Miguel Maura, with the agreement of his Socialist cabinet colleagues, mobilised a considerable police apparatus against the strikers, instructions being issued to shoot any worker caught trying to sabotage company property. The

Socialist press denounced the strike as a reactionary provocation and the UGT recommended militants not to co-operate with the strikers. However, it was a popular strike against a multinational corporation and many UGT sections sent messages of solidarity and money to the strikers. The strike failed and left a considerable legacy of bitterness between the Republic and the CNT.[29]

Even more dramatic was the outcome of a period of anarchist agitation in Seville. As the culmination of a series of strikes, the CNT called a general stoppage on 18 July. This was the signal for a number of disorders and gun-battles between the anarchists and the Civil Guard. At the cabinet meeting of 21 July, Largo Caballero demanded that Miguel Maura take action to put an end to the disorders which were damaging the Republic's image. When the Prime Minister, Niceto Alcalá Zamora, asked if everyone was agreed that energetic measures against the CNT were called for, the cabinet assented unanimously and Largo actually produced a draft decree for declaring strikes illegal under certain circumstances. The following day, Maura, who was always rather impulsive, authorised the artillery shelling of an anarchist meeting-place, the Casa Cornelio, in Seville. This ended the strike, but it also provoked a wave of criticism of the Socialists, both in the press and in the Cortes. The point of view of the CNT was put in the Cortes by Catalan deputies who had been elected with anarchist votes. In reply to their accusations that the UGT was using the Socialist presence in the government, Largo Caballero and Manuel Cordero replied that the CNT was prepared to bring down the Republic in order to hurt the UGT and that governmental participation involved nothing but sacrifice for the Socialists.[30]

It was extremely wearing on the Socialists to have to bear the brunt of the defence of the Republic against both Right and Left. Yet in the summer of 1931 it still seemed a worthwhile task. This was emphasised by Luis Araquistain in a series of articles which he published at the time of the Seville strikes and with the telephone strike still under way. In 'The syndicalist Antichrist', he tried to show how the CNT's behaviour was playing into the hands of the Right by allowing a picture of chaos and disorder to be created of the Republic. In the second article of the series, 'Why are there so many strikes?', he suggested that the anarchists were motivated by a desire for revenge against the Socialist collaboration with the Dictadura. In contrast to this egoistic irresponsibility, he praised the 'civic heroism' of the UGT's members, who were hit by the economic depression every bit as much as the anarchists, yet put the health of the Republic before their own interests. In the third and final article, 'Against the abuse of the strike', he claimed that the existing conciliation and arbitration machinery could meet any just complaints without recourse to strikes.[31] This was not true, but the Socialists were intensely anxious to reduce social tension and unrest.

As the summer wore on, the attacks from both sides of the political spectrum began to take their toll of the Socialists. Prieto, who always tended to pessimism, was becoming thoroughly disillusioned about his inability to change the financial structure of the country, and talked of resignation. He also expressed the opinion that, by having a Socialist as Minister of Labour, the PSOE was drawing on itself the popular discontent consequent on the impossibility of solving all social problems at once. Largo remained convinced that, by being in the Ministry, he was helping to improve conditions, but he too expressed concern at the hostility it was provoking among the anarchists and on 7 August talked of resigning. Two days earlier he had stated in the Cortes that the *labradores* of Cádiz, Málaga and Seville were refusing to plant seeds, in an attempt to break the *jurados mixtos*. Both Prieto and Largo were persuaded by their cabinet colleagues to stay on, although the upper-class resistance to reform would probably have been sufficient to remind them that things would certainly deteriorate if the PSOE left the government. Largo's attitude was revealed in his preamble to a draft law on work contracts, in which he described himself as a 'Socialist who for thirty years has collaborated with the capitalist classes in order to take from them, gradually and by legitimate means, their impossible privileges'. Provided reformist policies were making some advances for the working class and particularly the UGT, he would continue to collaborate. However, the experience of his reaction to his frustrated hopes of the Dictadura suggested that a rapid change of tack could be expected in the case of a similar disappointment. Already there were those to the left of the PSOE who were thoroughly disillusioned with the collaboration. Significantly enough, when in 1929 Largo rejected co-operation with the Dictator, his decision was preceded by an acute critique of collaborationism by Gabriel Morón. Now, in a book written in late 1931, Morón denounced participation in the government as pointless, and predicted that, if the Socialists did not withdraw from power and prepare for battle with the bourgeoisie, they would be destroyed when eventually their reforming efforts provoked a reaction from the ruling classes. It was only a matter of time before Largo would arrive at similar conclusions.[32]

However, as a result of the failure of the various strikes, there came a lull in the wave of anarchist agitation. Indeed, besides exhausting the anarchist workers, the strikes were provoking a division within the CNT. This came to a head in August when thirty moderates issued a manifesto against the sporadic violence of the pure anarchists of the Federación Anarquista Ibérica.[33] Unrest was to break out again soon, but this respite allowed the Socialists to concentrate during the autumn on the parliamentary debates concerning the elaboration of the Constitution.

After an earlier draft by the conservative politician Angel Ossorio y Gallardo had been rejected, a new constitutional committee, under the Socialist law professor Luis Jiménez de Asúa, met on 28 July. It had barely three weeks to draw up its draft. In consequence, some of its unsubtle wording was to give rise to three months of acrimonious debate. Presenting the project on 27 August, Jiménez de Asúa described it as a democratic, liberal document with great social content. Fernando de los Ríos, speaking in its favour on 3 September, declared his commitment to liberal democracy and the planned economy. Luis Araquistain chalked up the first Socialist victory when he prevailed on the chamber to vote in favour of a text for article 1 which read 'Spain is a republic of workers of all classes'. However, he also reminded his listeners that a paper constitution did not of itself alter the existing relation of economic forces within the country. Nevertheless, the draft provoked bitter opposition from the Agrarian and other rightist deputies This was particularly so with the clause which probably meant most to the Socialists, number 42 in the draft, 44 in the final text. It stated that all the wealth of the country must be subordinate to the economic interests of the nation and that all property could be expropriated, with compensation, for reasons of social utility. It required a magisterial speech by Besteiro on 6 October before it was approved. Besteiro's speech, like that of De los Ríos a month earlier, expressed a more or less Fabian commitment to a mixed economy. Yet, for the Alfonsist monarchist Pedro Sáinz Rodríguez, the very notion of social utility was 'a sword of Damocles hanging over property'. In the main, however, the Constitution was satisfactory to the Socialists and fulfilled the objectives that they had set themselves in the extraordinary congress. Perhaps only on one major issue did they fail. That was when they were persuaded by a brilliant speech by Azaña not to push for the complete dissolution of the religious orders. That aside, the Constitution finally approved on 9 December 1931 was as democratic, laic and reforming as the Socialists might have wished.[34]

After the approval of the Constitution, there arose the question of whether the Socialists could continue in the government, or, indeed, whether the government should not dissolve the Cortes and call new elections. In fact, throughout the period of debate over the Constitution, there had been some controversy on the subject, both in the press and within the cabinet.[35] De los Ríos and Largo Caballero were enthusiastic about staying on; Prieto, as ever, was ready to resign. At one point, Largo even talked of an entirely Socialist government. With UGT recruiting at an all-time high and with many union bureaucrats enjoying lucrative government posts, Largo was satisfied that the existing arrangement was beneficial to the UGT.[36] Moreover, despite the southern landowners' growing aggressiveness against his reforms, he must have reflected that, with the Socialists out of the government, conditions would have been worse. Nor can he have been unaware that, with the massive political mobilisation being undertaken by Acción Nacional, if the Cortes were dissolved, the Socialists would probably lose a number of seats in the consequent elections. So great was Largo's commitment to the Republic that he had been prominent in elaborating the rather authoritarian Law for the Defence of the Republic and also, in a vain attempt to clinch conservative confidence in the regime, had supported the candidacy of Alcalá Zamora for the post of President of the Republic. Despite Alcalá Zamora's hostility to the Constitution, which had led him to resign as Prime Minister on 14 October, Largo and Prieto, in the meeting held by the parliamentary minority of the PSOE to discuss the candidacies, managed to prevail over Besteiro by fifty-three votes to thirty-eight.[37]

The extent to which the Socialist ministers were prepared to make sacrifices in order to defend the Republic was made particularly clear throughout November, when they helped to avert a major railway strike. The railwaymen's leader, Trifón Gómez, a Besteirist, was hostile to the idea of a strike, but was unable to restrain the militancy of the rank-and-file. At one point, when his men had refused an offer by the government, Trifón made an extraordinarily significant remark to Azaña : 'If there were not three Socialist ministers in the government, the concessions would have been received by the workers with applause and gratitude. However, since there are Socialist ministers, they think the railways should be handed over to them lock, stock, and barrel.' Apart from what this revealed about the paternalistic attitudes of the syndical bureaucracy, it emphasised the dilemma faced by the ministers, and in particular Largo Caballero. Azaña underlined the anomaly of their situation when he asked himself in his diary, 'if the presence of three Socialist ministers in the government cannot prevent a strike, what use is it?' Eventually, by dint of frantic persuasion, Trifón Gómez managed to prevail at the congress of railwaymen called to debate the proposed strike.[38]

The railway dispute typified the way in which the Socialists were prepared to sacrifice their popularity by restraining the militancy of their followers. Nowhere was this more true than in Asturias, where the UGT found itself in a cross-fire between the employers and the militants of the Sindicato Único. On 6 December the SMA managed to end a miners' strike in Mieres, declaring that 'surprise stoppages, without a premeditated study of their possible consequences, inevitably fail'. When the anarchists started a general strike in Gijón, during which at least four workers were killed by the Civil Guard, the Asturian UGT condemned it as leading only to hunger and misery for the workers. The union of gas and electricity workers, the SMA and the provincial Federation of Building Workers issued specific instructions that their members were not to go on strike.[39] This constituted a considerable risk, since, at a time of acute economic crisis, particularly in the mining sector, there was a growing rank-and-file sympathy for militant action. Moreover, while accusations of class betrayal from anarchists and Communists abounded, the UGT's moderation did nothing to abate the hostility of the Right. Under such circumstances, continued sacrifices on behalf of the Republic could be justified only by uninterrupted social progress.

The recognition of this became increasingly apparent in the Socialist press towards the end of 1931. Disinterested enthusiasm for the Republic began to give way to a somewhat harder line. It was recalled that the Socialists were in the government to secure social reforms. If the spirit of the Constitution were not carried over into the auxiliary laws which were to put it into practice, this would be a challenge to the Socialists to resort to revolutionary tactics. As *El Socialista* warned, it was time that 'the bourgeois elements realised that the people had not surrendered their revolutionary weapons but simply held them in readiness'. Nevertheless, there was still a reserve of optimism that Azaña's government, having seen the Constitution through the Cortes, would be able to fill its framework with a socially progressive content.[40]

The test for social progress had inevitably to be the most backward sector of Spanish society, the rural south. There, despite promises of agrarian reform and the improvements introduced by the early decrees of Largo Caballero, where they could be enforced, conditions remained brutal. All over the south, many owners had declared war on the republican–Socialist coalition by refusing to plant crops. The Socialist deputies from Badajoz, Jaén, Málaga and Huelva denounced such cases in the Cortes. In Jaén, for instance, the provincial Sociedad de Labradores had called on its members to cease cultivating their lands, in order to combat the various decrees which defended the *bracero*.[41] With the exception of the olive harvest, during which the law of municipal boundaries was suspended, there was, thereafter, massive agrarian unemployment in the province. In Badajoz the story was the same. The governor of the province and the colonel in charge of the province's Civil Guard connived with the local *caciques* against the existing labour legislation. Eventually, on 21 December 1931, the local section of the FNTT resolved to call a general strike in order to get both of them transferred. In the most dramatic way imaginable, this strike was to force the Socialists to face the question of whether social reform was possible without revolutionary change.

The Badajoz strike took place on 30 and 31 December. It was in the main a peaceful strike, in accordance with the instructions of its organisers. In an isolated village called Castilblanco, however, there was bloodshed. Castilblanco is in that most arid and inhospitable part of Extremadura known as *Siberia extremeña*. Its inhabitants lived in the most crushing poverty and misery. The village's common lands had been taken from it in the nineteenth century by legal subterfuge. It was now controlled by the local *latifundista*, and the *alcalde* was his nominee. Castilblanco was not untypical of hundreds of villages in southern Spain. When the strike was called, the workers of Castilblanco had already spent the winter without work. They were all members of the FNTT. On 30 December they held a peaceful and disciplined demonstration, which they intended to repeat on the following day. They did so and were dispersing to their homes when the *alcalde*, frightened that their display of discipline heralded a change in the village's power structure, instructed the Civil Guard to break up the crowd. Some women were pushed, protests were heard and one guard opened fire, killing one man and wounding two others. At that moment, the villagers, in a frenzy of fear, anger and panic, fell upon the four guards and beat them to death with stones and knives.[42]

The consequent uproar starkly revealed the gulf which existed between those who defended and those who hoped to change the prevailing social order. The Right accused the Socialists of inciting the *braceros* against the *Benemérita*, the eulogistic term used for the Civil Guard by its devotees. The Socialists believed the real criminal of Castilblanco to have been the repressive land system and reflected ruefully that workers were regularly killed by the Civil Guard without a flicker of interest by the rightist press.[43] It was a great blow to Azaña's new republican–Socialist coalition, which had been formed with some difficulty, as recently as mid December, Prieto had not wanted to continue in the cabinet and only a sharp reminder by Largo Caballero of party discipline had brought him around. In fact, although the Socialist parliamentary group was in favour of continued participation, among the rank-and-file there was a growing tide of opinion against it.[44] Castilblanco thus came as an unwelcome warning of the obstacles still to be faced on the road to reform. Even before the cabinet had had time to come to terms with it, there occurred an equally disturbing tragedy, in which the Civil Guard's hostility to the working class yet again played a leading part.

Arnedo is a village in the northern Castilian province of Logroño. One of its main sources of employment was a shoe factory, and towards the end of 1931 several of its workers were sacked for belonging to the UGT. The case was put before the local *jurado mixto*, which declared in favour of the workers, but still the owner refused to give them back their jobs. A public protest meeting was held before the town hall.

Without apparent motive, the Civil Guard opened fire, killing four women, a child, and a worker, besides wounding at least thirty more. The incident had all the appearance of an act of revenge for Castil-blanco, particularly in the light of remarks made by General Sanjurjo after the killings there. As more of the wounded died, the Socialist press expressed its indignation. The Civil Guard's action seemed to justify the accusation that it was a repressive force at the service of the ruling classes. Luis Araquistain declared that it had been created by a despotic regime in order to keep the people down with terror, and that, although the monarchist regime was no more, those who had benefited from it still used the Civil Guard as a weapon against the reforming spirit of the Republic. Two weeks later, at a Traditionalist meeting in Bilbao, two Socialists and two Republicans were killed by rightist gunmen. The Civil Guard was nowhere to be seen.[45] That such a situation existed made it all the more difficult for the UGT to justify appeals for union discipline by claims that the Republic was putting an end to the injustices of the old regime.

Nevertheless, there was a strong body of feeling in the UGT that hundreds of years of oppression could not be rectified overnight. Long committed to gradualism, the union officials were determined that the democratic regime should be allowed to establish itself. Accordingly, when the CNT called a national general strike in the fourth week of January 1932, the condemnation from UGT leaders was unanimous. On a national level, the UGT's official note declared against any actions of solidarity. In Asturias the SMA denounced the terrible waste of workers' energies. Even the FNTT, under its Besteirist leader, Lucio Martínez Gil, called for discipline. Not surprisingly, the reformist hierarchy was not prepared to leave the Republic 'at the mercy of extremists'. The general feeling was that anarchist activities played into the hands of reactionaries and 'erected barriers to the serene march of the proletariat towards emancipation'.[46] After all, some visible progress was being made, despite the hostility of the Right and the economic depression. This was particularly true in the field of labour legislation, but in education too great strides were being made. Between 1908 and 1930, the monarchy had built 11,128 schools, an average of 505 per year. In its first year alone, the Republic had built 7000.[47]

Yet, despite this evidence that the Republic was worth defending, there was still a perceptible slackening of enthusiasm for continued participation in the government. This was revealed at a meeting of the UGT National Committee on 1 February 1932, only a week after the anarchist strike had been put down, with considerable severity, especially in the Bajo Llobregat in Catalonia. The UGT leadership had little sympathy for CNT adventurism. Nevertheless, it was impossible to ignore the invidious position of a government containing Socialists apparently reserving its greatest energies for the repression of strikes. The rank-and-file did not always take the long-term view. Antonio Muñoz, one of the leaders of the Federation of Printing Workers, expressed concern that the presence of Socialists in the government was damaging relations between the PSOE and the UGT masses. This was understandable, since the government was responsible, in theory at least, for whatever the Civil Guard did. Muñoz also said that, because the hopes raised by the coming of the Republic had been so great, disappointment at the slowness of reform was all the more acute. Alleging that much of this disappointment stemmed from the fact that the Socialist ministers were helping to consolidate the bourgeois economy, he appealed for them to withdraw. When the issue was debated, however, persuasive speeches by Largo Caballero and De los Ríos caused the meeting to pass a resolution of solidarity with the ministers.[48]

For the moment, the union bureaucracy was committed to the continuation of its policy of restraining militancy. Other advantages of the Republic aside, there was one positive consequence of Largo's tenure of the Ministry of Labour which could not but influence union officials – the UGT recruiting boom. In the first months of 1932, new members were flocking in at the rate of 4000–5000 per week. However, 2000–3000 of these were joining the FNTT.[49] If discipline were to be maintained, progress would have to be made on the agrarian problem. Yet in all sectors of the economy the depression was beginning to bite, and the rank-and-file workers were being impelled to militancy by the actions of the employers. The devaluation of the pound sterling lowered the return on Spanish agricultural exports and made British coal more competitive. This provided the excuse for an offensive against the unions by both landlords and mine-owners. Perhaps the most remarkable feature of the spring of 1932 was the restraint shown by both the FNTT and the SMA in the face of intense hostility.

The theme of the UGT's May Day manifesto for 1932 could hardly have been more reformist : 'For democracy and the forty-hour week !' It typified the mood of the entire movement. The FNTT, for instance, was under intense pressure, yet did not waver in its counsels of moderation. At the beginning of the year, with the olive harvest over, there was massive unemployment in Andalusia. In addition, landowners were systematically ignoring the law concerning obligatory cultivation and were not undertaking essential agricultural tasks. In places where the authorities sent workers into estates to do the jobs, the owners refused to pay them.[50] Throughout La Mancha, members of the FNTT were being refused work because they were trade unionists. The union stood firm and ordered its members not to be provoked. In the second week of February, 200 delegates, representing 80,000 members of the union from Andalusia and Extremadura, met at Montilla in Córdoba for a congress. They resolved to avoid all extremism and to meet attacks with the tactics advised by the UGT nationally. Moreover, at a time when its members were becoming impatient at the government's failure to produce an agrarian reform, the FNTT's newspaper reiterated that reform would take years and warned members not to expect too much.[51]

Considering the provocation to which the *jornaleros* were subject, it was remarkable that the summer did not see even more rural conflict than did in fact break out. On 1 April, in Miguel Esteban (Toledo), the local landowners organised a demonstration of their fixed employees (*pegados*), and during this a worker was shot and the Casa del Pueblo stormed. Boulders were dropped down a well in which it was believed that the local UGT president was working.[52] This and similar incidents led to a demand in the Cortes for the disarming of the *caciques*. The howl of protest from the rightist press was revealing of the attitudes of the large landowners. If their guns were taken away, it was claimed, they would be forced to use less dignified weapons, such as clubs and knives, and with greater frequency.[53] In this context, the FNTT continued to advocate moderation, despite pressure for action from the local rank-and-file organisations. Violence and extremism were condemned, especially in the case of a Communist-inspired rising at Villa Don Fadrique (Toledo) on 8 July, in which three workers were killed.[54] However, the owners' campaign against the Republic's social legislation was making the rural masses, already impatient for agrarian reform, even more desperate. Yet the nearest that the FNTT leadership got to militant action was in protesting to the government about the owners' refusal to abide by the labour laws, and about the slow passage of the agrarian statute. In fact, 83 per cent of all the infractions of labour edicts in 1932 were committed by employers, according to Ministry of Labour statistics.[55] While the rightist press inveighed against the agrarian reform and praised the existing land system, the Agrarian deputies in the Cortes orgaised a systematic obstruction of the bill's passage. Given the conservative tone of the bill, the FNTT press could not but reflect on the intransigence of the possessing classes.[56] The rank-and-file increasingly took matters into their own hands, joining anarchist workers in machine-breaking and strike action throughout the summer.

A similarly conflictive situation was developing in Asturias. The Republic had opened up to the miners the possibility of essential reforms in the application of safety regulations, accident legislation, working conditions and pensions. However, the mine-owners were unwilling to accept the increase in costs which these reforms involved. Profits were falling as the industrial depression hit demand. Imported British coal was 12 pesetas cheaper per ton than the inferior Asturian variety. Thus, mild reforms like the introduction of the seven-hour day became challenges to the existing system. The owners were determined to reduce wages, increase hours and lay workers off. The SMA's initial response to this crisis was to condemn strikes, since it feared that a stoppage would result in temporary coal imports, allowing the owners to build up stocks, and, when the strike was over, begin sackings. In its May Day manifesto the SMA declared that its first priority had always been to obtain social concessions from the coal-owners without violent conflicts or unnecessary cost to the workers. Yet moderation was becoming increasingly difficult. After the *jurado mixto* for the mines introduced improved working conditions, the miners began to experience delay in receiving their wages. Despite the miners' declared readiness to accept work-sharing schemes, the owners began to close down some pits. The SMA claimed that the mines could be made profitable if properly run, and called for nationalisation. Union officials were convinced that the owners' actions were designed simply to break the new work agreements. With great reluctance, they called a total stoppage for 15 May, appealing to the government to prevent the monarchist coal-owners from sabotaging the Republic. For the moment at least, the strike was successful in holding back most of the threatened closures.[57]

The difficulty of the Socialist position can be easily imagined. In order to justify appeals for rank-and-file patience and to counter Communist accusations of 'social fascism', some visible reforms were essential. Yet the economic situation and the hostility of the employers made it almost impossible to translate paper reform into practice. Nevertheless, the Socialist movement still stuck to its self-appointed task of watchdog of the Republic, albeit with growing inner doubts. On 24 June the UGT issued a manifesto underlining the absurdity of strikes at a time of high unemployment: 'Even if they are carried out peacefully, the final balance of strikes originating in the unemployment crisis can be no other than the loss of wages for those fortunate enough to have work. Our comrades should see that all the strikes called in protest against unemployment have failed . . . and, in many cases, the number of unemployed has increased rather than diminished.' Instead of striking, the manifesto urged, the workers should devote their energies to forcing employers to fulfil work contracts and to apply the existing legislation. How this was to be done without recourse to strike action was not specified. Indeed, strikes were condemned yet again as playing into the hands of the extremists of Right and Left.[58]

If anything, opposition to the reforming intentions of the government tended to confirm to the Socialist ministers that their participation was essential. There remained less now of that conviction that, by collaborating with the Republic, they would be helping the bourgeoisie to carry out its historic role of destroying feudalism. The rise of fascism abroad and the determined resistance to reform of both the urban and rural bourgeoisie at home indicated the erroneous nature of the party's analysis of Spain's development. However, the conclusion drawn from this was that, if progress to reform was less and slower than had been hoped, without the Socialists in the government it would have been virtually non-existent. This was illustrated in July by the Socialist reaction to a speech by Lerroux in Zaragoza, in which he advocated their departure from the government. There was, in fact, growing animosity between Lerroux and the Socialists. Not without reason, they regarded him as corrupt and power-hungry.[59] They were also disturbed that, in his quest for power, he had moved considerably to the Right, accepting into his party many monarchist landowners from the south.[60] Lerroux, in his turn, saw the Socialists as an obstacle to the power which he, as the senior republican, felt was his by right.

Lerroux was in touch with Sanjurjo and other generals who were plotting a rising. In his speech, therefore, he said that the country was under the threat of a military dictatorship because of injuries done by the Republic to the Church and the army. If the Socialists left the government, all would be well. At best, it was a clumsy attempt at intimidation. Largo Caballero was furious and inspired a joint PSOE–UGT manifesto on 16 July. Not only did the manifesto state the Socialist movement's determination to meet any threat of a coup with resolute action, but it also rejected in unmistakable terms Lerroux's attempted blackmail. On 20 July, Prieto rose in the Cortes to clarify the manifesto in rather more measured and statesmanlike language. Reiterating the Socialist determination to stay in the government until the passing of the auxiliary laws to the Constitution, he exposed the fatuity of Lerroux's arguments. He pointed out that the measures which had provoked the enmity of the generals were not the work of the Socialists. If the Socialist presence in the government was being attacked by the Republic's enemies, then, according to Prieto, that proved how it strengthened the regime. It was not without significance that· *El Debate* had printed an editorial praising Lerroux's speech as evidence of the success of the great rightist propaganda campaign against the Constitution. Lerroux was forced to back down.[61]

General Sanjurjo's rising took place as planned on 10 August. It was a fiasco. Confident that the government could deal with it, the UGT ordered its militants not to leave their work. In a sense, this attack on the Republic by one of the heroes of the old regime, a monarchist general, benefited the government, by generating a wave of pro-Republican fervour. It was this which made possible, on 9 September, the passing of the agrarian reform bill, which had been delayed for so long in parliament. Mild and contradictory as the reform was, the anarchists denounced it as a farce. Although the FNTT had already warned its members not to expect too much, the disappointment felt in its ranks could not be hidden. The second congress of the Federation was held almost immediately after the passing of the reform bill. Besteiro, addressing the congress, condemned the excessively legalistic language in which the bill was couched. On 1 October the FNTT issued a manifesto expressing its disappointment at the unwieldy and bureaucratic structure of the Instituto de Reforma Agraria. The fact that the workers' representation in the Institute was far outnumbered by agronomists, technicians and others (including even a mortgage-bank representative) was seen as confirmation that the reform would not be far-reaching.[62]

Although the reform was limited, it provoked the landowners into a declaration of all-out war on the Republic. A determination to break the reforming legislation passed by the republican–Socialist coalition had long been apparent, but never before had the Right expressed itself so openly. The Bloque Agrario of Salamanca spearheaded a campaign to get owners not to cultivate their lands. Claiming that the wages decreed by the provincial *jurado mixto* were ruinously high, the Bloque circularised the landowners, large and small, of the province, asking them to sign a pledge not to cultivate their lands. The provincial governor had the governing body of the Bloque arrested.[63] Immediately, the political representatives of the Bloque, Gil Robles, Cándido Casanueva and Lamamié de Clairac, went into action to carry the dispute beyond the narrow confines of the province. According to Gil Robles, the absurdly high wages being paid to day-labourers did not make it economically viable to sow crops. Although he claimed to be thereby representing the interests of the smallholders, who were in fact badly hit by the increase in wages, he did not acknowledge that the Bloque's tactic could be carried out only by those large landlords who could turn their land over to pasture. In a vehement Cortes speech, in which he defended the call for rural lock-out, he produced a number of contentious figures, purporting to show that day-labourers were earning 15 pesetas per day. In reality, the day-wage decreed in the mixed jury's *bases de trabajo* (work conditions) was 5 pesetas.[64]

These figures become more meaningful when examined in context. To begin with, Gil Robles's figure can be discarded, since it is inconceivable that some of the most anti-Republican landowners in Spain would pay three times more than the officially decreed wage. It must also be remembered that these were harvest wages, from which the *braceros* had to save for the six to eight months of unemployment which faced them. Moreoever, not all the *braceros* could find work even at harvest-time.[65] Yet Gil Robles had stated in the Cortes that 'previously there existed a regime of oppression in the countryside, but things have now gone radically to the other extreme'. What did 5 pesetas per day mean in 1932? Taking no account of the need to save for the months without work or to repay credit advanced by the village shopkeeper, an average three-child family needed more than 35 pesetas per week in order to attain the most meagre subsistence diet. Such a diet never contained more than secondary sources of protein, since meat, fish and eggs were beyond the means of the day-labourer.[66] It is not without significance that at this time there were growing numbers of thefts of acorns and other livestock fodder from large estates. The Right did not hesitate to brand the FNTT's members as common thieves, without pausing to reflect that hunger rather than perversity drives men to steal acorns. If, as Gil Robles claimed, the *labradores* could not plant crops unless wages were drastically reduced, then he was admitting that the existing economic system depended for its survival on the rural labourers' accepting starvation wages.[67]

The improvements in working conditions introduced by the Republic constituted an economic challenge to all landowners. The hardest-hit were naturally the smallholders. However, while securing the votes of farmers for Acción Popular, the rightist campaign against (allegedly) inflated rural wages ignored the extent to which much of the hardship suffered by leaseholders and sharecroppers was a consequence of the unfavourable leasing arrangements imposed upon them by their land-lords. The limits of Acción Popular's concern for the smallholders were to be revealed unequivocally by the group's unremitting opposition to any attempts to introduce leasehold reform. There is little doubt that, in the 1932 protest over rural wages, the propaganda value among the small farmers was considerable, but their interests were really marginal. The call for the abandonment of cultivation had more directly political ends than a determination to improve the cash-flow of the smallholders. The central issue of the autumn 1932 rural lock-out was the existence of the agrarian legislation introduced by the Republic.

Even taking into account the profit squeeze caused by the decrees of Largo Caballero, many *latifundios* were far from the economic ruin depicted by Gil Robles. In wheat-growing areas, for instance, profits made by the larger farmers were quite substantial.[68] In other areas growing export crops, that was, of course, not the case. Nevertheless, the owners' refusal to plant crops was not motivated entirely by the economic problems of the day. The FNTT response to the lock-out showed that there was more at stake than just economic self-defence. If it is not worth the owners' effort to cultivate their land, declared *El Obrero de la Tierra* on 8 October, let the land be turned over to the FNTT's members, who will cultivate it collectively and scrape from it a far better living than under the present system. However, armed guards prevented the labourers from entering the estates and there were increasing clashes throughout the following year.

The determination of the big owners to put an end to the Republican legislation seemed to be justified by the fact that there were many owners who fell in between the categories of *latifundista* and subsistence smallholder. Their sympathies were not unnaturally with the big landlords. They were Catholics, read the local rightist press and were *labradores*, like their more powerful neighbours. And, above all, the attempt to end starvation wages for the *jornaleros* was costing them money. In a period of prosperity, the almost irreconcilable conflict of interest on the land would certainly have been softened by a reduction of surplus labour, drawn off to the industrial towns, and by an increase in productivity, stimulated by irrigation and fertilisers. However, the economic depression merely exaggerated the fundamental dichotomy highlighted unconsciously by Gil Robles : either there existed starving labourers or there had to be a transfer of wealth away from the large owners, with many of the middle and small farmers suffering in the process. A collective solution incorporating the smallholders would perhaps have been a viable answer. But the purpose of the lockout was not to hasten a future agrarian solution which benefited the greatest number but to force a return to the pre-1931 situation.

It was thus becoming increasingly difficult for the Besteirist leadership of the FNTT to contain the militancy of its followers. The visible improvements which had hitherto been the best justification for discipline were now being eroded by the employers' offensive. Another sector of the UGT which was being pushed towards militancy yet managed to retain its faith in the government was the SMA. More mines were closing down and the miners were being asked to accept short-time working, reduced wages and even to accept payment in kind. In the context of this crisis, it infuriated miners and pit-owners alike that the total production of Spanish mines was still 2 million tons less than the nation's coal consumption. The SMA called an extraordinary congress to debate strike action. Held on 11 September, the congress called on the government to solve the coal crisis and resolved on a general strike to start on the 19th if nothing were done. In fact, the government was frantically trying to find a solution. The Minister for the Navy was examining the possibility of Asturian coal being used in warships. Railway chiefs were being pressured to use Spanish coal too. Undertakings were made that the existing legislation on coal imports would be tightened up. In the light of this, the SMA called off the strike. 'Never has a government taken so much interest in our problems', said its declaration. To go ahead with the strike was felt to be simply counter-productive intransigence.[69]

The whole question of whether or not the Republic represented a positive benefit for the workers was thus foremost in the minds of delegates to the PSOE and UGT congresses held in Madrid in October 1932. The Thirteenth Congress of the PSOE opened on 6 October. Since the previous year's extraordinary congress, the Besteirist faction, as hostile as ever to Socialist participation in the government, had regained control of the Agrupación Socialista Madrileña. Besteiro himself, however, had considerably modified his position. Prieto put forward a motion in favour of continued ministerial participation. Speaking effectively in its favour Besteiro said, 'if the Socialist ministers leave the government, the political equilibrium of the Republic will be broken, the life of the Cortes will be considerably shortened and premature elections could be too dangerous an adventure'. Prieto's proposal was passed by 23,718 votes to 6356. The main issue debated in the congress was the failed strike of December 1930. Largo considered that the party had been betrayed by the machinations of the Besteirists Saborit and Muiño. Apart from this desire to settle an old score, however, the issue, concerning as it did the party's role in bringing the Republic, had some relevance for the question of continued collaboration in the government. After a vitriolic struggle between Largo and Saborit, the debate had to be cut short lest it lead to a schism in the party. The activities of those who had been in favour of a strike – that is to say, Largo, Prieto, De los Ríos and much of the rank-and-file – were approved. Largo Caballero was also voted president of the PSOE by 15,817 votes to Besteiro's 14,261. Besteiro had not stood for the post. However, it is difficult to say whether the high number of votes that he received reflected anything more than veneration for a respected and senior member of the party. His apparent approval of ministerial participation may also have had some effect on the voting.[70] Whatever the case, the Thirteenth PSOE Congress represented the last major Socialist vote of confidence in the efficacy of governmental collaboration.

The PSOE congress ended on 13 October. On the following day, the Seventeenth Congress of the UGT began. The contrast in mood between the two assemblies was remarkable. The UGT congress was a major triumph for Besteiro. This was not entirely surprising, given the way in which UGT congresses were organised. Each national section of the UGT – railwaymen, printers, bakers, building-workers, miners, land-workers, and so on – was represented by its own union officials and enjoyed a voting strength corresponding to its overall membership. This meant that the votes of a given federation at the congress represented the views of that federation's syndical bureaucracy, and not necessarily of its rank-and-file.[71] This put Largo Caballero at a considerable disadvantage, since, although he enjoyed immense popularity among the workers in general, he did not control the votes of a specific

union. The Besteirists, on the other hand, did enjoy such control –
through Saborit (printers), Trifón Gómez (railwaymen), and Lucio
Martínez Gil (FNTT).

An illness, which was probably no more than diplomatic, kept Largo
away from the congress. Yet again the strike of December 1930 was
discussed, and this time the behaviour of the executive committee of
the UGT, which had been hostile to the strike, was approved. A new
executive was elected, with Besteiro as president, and all his senior
followers in key positions. Largo was in fact elected as secretary of the
UGT. However, he immediately sent a letter of resignation, claiming
that the congress's vindication of the 1930 executive constituted a dis-
avowal of his own activities in December of that year. The other
Caballerists elected, Rafael Henche and Pascual Tomás, also resigned,
leaving the UGT executive entirely in Besteirist hands. Largo complained that the block votes of Lucio Martínez Gil's FNTT and Trifón
Gomez's Sindicato Nacional Ferroviario went against the spirit of the
congress.[72] That was possible but difficult to prove, then or now.

In fact, rightist oposition to reform and the growth of fascism abroad
were soon to be undermining Largo Caballero's faith in the efficacy
of governmental collaboration with the left Republicans. Nevertheless,
this change, when it came, would not bridge the gulf between him and
the Besteirists. They might all have been reformists but they were
reformists of radically different kinds. The union officials who followed
Besteiro felt it their duty to stand back and let the bourgeoisie get on
with its historic task. In the meanwhile, they would get on with defending the working class within the existing economic system as they had
done under the monarchy. Largo's views were more pragmatic. He was
aware that his participation in the government had led to great
advances in the living conditions of the Spanish working class and to
a massive increase in UGT recruiting. Since both of these achievements
had been his life-long ambitions, he would do everything in his power
to prevent a return to pre-1931 conditions. Now in late 1932, the Right
was mounting a challenge to his reforms and to the UGT masses'
expectation of continued reform. If to the Besteirists this was proof
that collaboration was dangerous to the working class, to Largo
Caballero it could only be a stimulus to defend his work so far.

Thus, 1932 saw the beginnings of the radicalisation of Largo
Caballero. Above all, this was a response to the mood of the rank-and-
file, rendered impatient by the slowness of reform and by the success
of right-wing obstruction of its application. However, it was also
strongly influenced by a growing awareness of the spread of fascism.
Largo's closest advisers, Carlos de Baraibar, Luis Araquistain and
Antonio Ramos Oliveira, kept him informed of the failure of social
democratic reformism around Europe.[73] The belief was emerging with-

in the PSOE that a fascist role might be played in Spain by Gil Robles. Accordingly, the rightist resistance to reform was taken by Largo as proof that, far from retreating along Besteirist lines into classical reformism, the Socialists should perhaps advance to some more radical form of social organisation. However, this conviction was a long time in gestation, and it was not until he was being forced out of the government in the summer of 1933, that he began the process of public radicalisation. Even then, given his fundamental moderation in practice, it never went beyond rhetoric.

Two factors during the winter of 1932–3 made Largo begin to reflect on the inadequacies of reformism as a means of changing economic structures at a time of depression. The first was the employers' offensive, which put great strain on the discipline of UGT militants. The second was the obstruction of all government legislation by the Radical Party. In both cases, the section of the UGT most directly hit was the FNTT. At a national level, with Besteirists controlling the executive, the FNTT remained committed to moderation and gradual reformism. The reports which it had sent to both the PSOE and UGT congresses had laid special stress on the need for stricter enforcement of existing legislation.[74] At a local level, however, rank-and-file militancy was becoming impatient with the ineffectiveness of that legislation. In Salamanca, for instance, the success of the employers in evading the rulings of the mixed jury was creating intense bitterness among the local federation of landworkers. Thousands of workers had not been paid their harvest wages and yet not one landowner had been fined. The local leaders felt that, by obeying UGT discipline and submitting to the mixed jury, the workers were worse off. Largo Caballero was held 'morally and materially responsible'.[75] It was no longer possible to restrain the militancy of the local workers, who had exhausted every legal means of protecting their rights. There was talk of seceding from the UGT. This almost certainly had a considerable effect on Largo Caballero. He had, after all, been intensely anxious about 'what the workers would say' if he wore tails at the President's inauguration.[76] His sudden change of tactic at the end of the Dictadura was the result of his realisation that the workers were leaving the UGT in protest at the policy of collaboration. He was unlikely to react differently now.

In protest at the landowners' failure to pay the wages that they owed and at the inadequate functioning of rural social legislation, the Salamanca Federation of Socialist Workers called a general strike on 10 December. The strike was almost total and paralysed the province for ten days. A certain amount of violence broke out, but it was quickly repressed by the forces of order. From Madrid, the UGT executive called for a rapid end to a senseless strike. Not only was the call ignored, but it was regarded as evidence of the betrayal of the rank-

and-file by the bureaucracy. Given the determined intransigence of the Salamanca owners, it is difficult to see what the strike could have gained. Equally, with the unemployed driven to desperation by the lock-out, appeals for patience and discipline were bound to fall on deaf ears and, indeed, provoke bitterness against the Socialists in the government. The strike finally ended in a stalemate, with prisoners being freed, the Casas del Pueblo reopened, and promises made, but not kept, to solve the problem of unemployment.[77]

Growing rank-and-file militancy was creating divisions between the central UGT hierarchy, the government and the local union leadership. So as not to lose their members to more extreme groups, local leaders were increasingly being forced to acquiesce in strike action. In Asturias, for instance, after simmering since September, a general strike was called for mid November. The SMA leaders, Amador Fernández, Ramón González Peña and Teodomiro Menéndez, had little choice. On the one hand, the owners were closing pits, laying off miners and ignoring safety regulations. On the other, the jointly anarchist and Communist Sindicato Único de Obreros Mineros was increasing in both numbers and militancy. If the leaders did not go along with the miners' demands for action, the SMA would risk losing members as it had done during the 1920s. Their demands were not extreme : simply that the government take action to remedy the crisis in the industry. Such action would involve limiting the importation of cheap scrap-iron, which was cutting demand for smelting-coal; obliging government entities to use Spanish coal; and persuading consumers to reduce the immediate surplus by building up their stocks. The anarchists in the region called wide solidarity strikes, particularly in Gijón, where they had complete syndical control. The SMA repudiated these strikes as irresponsible. Nevertheless, they represented a growing solidarity at rank-and-file level which would gradually force the moderate UGT leadership to vie with the anarchists and Communists in militancy. The strikes ended with the defeat of the CNT in Gijón, and with government assurances to the SMA that action would be taken to help the mines.[78]

Further evidence of the rift between the union bureaucracy and its base militants was provided in the second half of December when the railway strike which had been narrowly averted in late 1931 threatened finally to break out. Dissidents from the Sindicato Nacional Ferroviario, in opposition to Trifón Gómez's reformist leadership, had created a rival union, the Federación de la Industria Ferroviaria, and were pushing for a revival of the claims left in abeyance the previous year. On 10 December the UGT issued a note, signed by Besteiro and Trifón Gómez, calling upon affiliated federations not to call strikes without first consulting the executive. This increased the risk of losing members, but was typical of the responsible moderation being shown by the reformist leaders. It was particularly galling for the Socialists when the Radicals, always keen to make things difficult for the government, claimed somewhat demagogically that the railwaymen's claim should be met. Prieto exposed the Radical manoeuvre in the Cortes. He adopted a patriotic line and declared that, if the strike did break out, he would not hesitate to sacrifice the interests of his party in order to defend the Republic. This was unmistakably a threat to subject the railwaymen to the same harsh treatment which had, in the main, hitherto been confined to anarchists and Communists. The strike did not take place, but several thousand members of the Sindicato Nacional Ferroviario drifted away from it.[79]

The greatest blow to Largo, and, indeed, to the entire cabinet, came in mid January. The anarchists had organised a rising for 8 January. It was repressed without great difficulty in Catalonia, Zaragoza, Seville and Madrid. However, in the village of Casas Viejas (Cádiz), the most violent events of the rising and its repression took place. Casas Viejas formed part of an area of endemic hunger and unemployment, exacerbated by the employers' boycott of the Republic. It was, if anything, even poorer than Castilblanco. The dwellings of the *braceros* consisted of a cavity in the ground, mud walls built up for about three feet, and a covering of branches. The fact that some of the best land around the village was given over to the breeding of fighting bulls only added to a situation in which, according to one observer, 'the poor were maddened with hunger and the rich were maddened with fear'. When the FAI (Federación Anarquista Ibérica) declaration of libertarian communism reached the local *Centro Obrero*, the villagers hesitantly followed instructions from Barcelona. Assuming that their strike would be linked to others in Jerez and Cádiz, they did not expect bloodshed. They were surprised by the resistance encountered at the local Civil Guard post. Many fled to the fields and some took refuge in the hut of the septuagenarian Curro Cruz, known as Seisdedos. Reinforcements were brought in and, after a night-long siege, the Civil and Assault Guards set fire to Seisdedos's house. Inside were Seisdedos, his son-in-law, his two sons, his cousin, his daughter, his daughter-in-law and his two grandchildren. Those who tried to escape were shot down. Another twelve people were also shot in cold blood.[80]

The immediate reaction of the rightist press was relatively favourable, since it had long been calling for harsh measures of law and order in the countryside.[81] However, when the enemies of the government realised what political capital could be made out of the incident, a great cry of indignation went up. The anarchists were naturally incensed, but rightist groups which normally applauded such actions by the Civil Guard also added their voices to the campaign. Before the full details were known, all three Socialist ministers, especially Prieto, expressed to Azaña their satisfaction at the repression of the anarchist rising. Fernando de los Ríos said that what had happened at Casas Viejas was necessary, given the anarchist antecedents of the province of Cádiz. Largo Caballero advised vigorous measures as long as the unrest continued.[82] However, despite their hostility to the anarchists, the Socialists could not approve of the gratuitous brutality displayed by the forces of order. They were angered, moreover, by the attempts of the Right and especially, the Radicals to prove that the savage reprisals taken at Casas Viejas were the result of specific government orders.[83] That seems most unlikely in the light of the efforts made by the government to investigate the affair. Nevertheless, the smear campaign took its toll of the government's time and morale. Efforts to clear the government virtually absorbed its entire efforts for the first three months of 1933. Since the campaign was linked to a systematic obstruction of attempts to pass legislation through the Cortes, it demoralised the cabinet considerably.[84]

Casas Viejas and its repercussions brought home graphically to the Socialists the cost of collaboration in the government. It emphasised more than ever that, in order to defend a bourgeois Republic, they were sacrificing their credibility with the Socialist masses. That sacrifice may have seemed worthwhile in 1931, when the new regime's reforms were visibly benefiting the working class. In 1933, however, with legislation paralysed in the Cortes by the Radicals and the Agrarios and in the rural areas by the employers' boycott, only the conviction that things would be worse if they left persuaded the Socialists to stay on in the government. The cabinet was convinced that government by Lerroux would be disastrous for reform, as well as being corrupt and inefficient.[85] Paradoxically, it was the Radical opposition which convinced the reluctant PSOE Cortes deputies to continue supporting Socialist participation in the cabinet.[86]

In the spring and summer of 1933, the Socialist presence in the government increasingly assumed a defensive stance, designed largely to exclude the Radicals. Not only did this mean that little was done in the field of new legislation, but also that the component groups of the republican-Socialist coalition were under increasing strain as the opposition widened. The Radicals, anxious for power, were drawing nearer to the rightist groups; while the Radical-Socialists were dividing into three factions, one of which opposed the government from a rightist position, another from the left. The two motives used to justify opposition were Casas Viejas and the municipal election of April 1933. Approximately 10 per cent of Spain's voters were going to choose new municipal councillors to replace those who had been returned unopposed in April 1931. Catalonia was not taking part and the elections were largely carried out in the conservative provinces of the north and Old Castile. Of the 16,000 councillors elected, approximately 10,000 were Republicans of one kind or another. Of these, 1826 were Socialists, 3222 were left republicans supporting groups represented in the government, 2479 were Radicals and the remainder other republicans. 4954 were declared rightists. Since the areas in which voting occurred were traditionally rightist and, in the previous elections, many *caciques* had been able to name their own candidates, this was a reasonable showing by the government parties, particularly in the aftermath of Casas Viejas. Yet it did not meet the expectations of either the Socialists or the republicans and was hailed by the Right and the Radicals as a national plebiscite against the government and the Socialists.[87]

The parliamentary obstruction which followed the elections was seen by Besteiro as a good pretext for Socialist withdrawal from the government.[88] Largo did not agree, largely because the growing social conflict which was visible in the rural areas convinced him that his presence was essential to protect the interests of the working class. Considerable bitterness was created by the slowness with which the Instituto de Reforma Agraria was functioning, not least because much of the delay was owing to the hearings of the grandees' claims for exemption from the September 1932 confiscation of aristocratic lands.[89] Marcelino Domingo's extended decree on *laboreo forzoso*, despite infuriating the landowners, did little to mitigate the growing crisis of unemployment in rural areas. If the decree was not respected, an inspector could be called in. He then had a week in which to report to the Central Technical Commmittee of the province, which in its turn had eight days in which to pass sentence. If the sentence went against the employer and he still did not undertake the tasks prescribed in the decree, then the local union was empowered to start the work after twelve days had passed. Even then, there was no mechanism to make the owners pay for the work done.[90] Accordingly, in village after village in the south, every day the unemployed thronged the market places. Violence was accumulating. Some estates were invaded. Hungry *braceros* stole acorns and olives. Bloodshed was not uncommon, as the owners opened fire on workers who were trespassing and stealing their crops, or workers attacked owners who denied them work.[91] The latent violence at a local level was transmitted to national politics, where the mutual hostility of the PSOE and the CEDA was growing rapidly.

This hostility was accentuated by the Socialist conviction that the CEDA was likely to fulfil a fascist role in Spain, a charge only casually denied by the Catholic party, if at all.[92] From this belief two very different conclusions were drawn. Largo was soon to be proclaiming that, if bourgeois democracy was incapable of preventing the rise of fascism, it was up to the working class to seek different political forms with which to defend itself. Besteiro, on the other hand, drew a far more defensive conclusion. Throughout the spring and summer of 1933 he made speeches condemning the collaborationist line and advocating that the Socialist movement withdraw entirely into the syndical sphere. Besteiro was celebrated as the PSOE's most accomplished Marxist. Yet, although his speeches had a veneer of Marxist rhetoric, they totally failed to come to terms with the phenomenon of fascism. The line taken by Largo, although hardly the last word in theoretical sophistication, was to be rather nearer to some of the more advanced Marxist thought on the subject. The differences between the two were greatly to accentuate the existing divisions within the PSOE.

Since Besteiro held the rigidly orthodox Marxist view that Spain must pass through a classic bourgeois revolution and concluded that the working class should not get involved in the bourgeoisie's historic task, he considered his stance to be more revolutionary than that of Largo Caballero. Thus, on 26 March, at the Agrupación Socialista Madrileña's commemoration of the fiftieth anniversary of Marx's death, he condemned the reformism of the collaborationists. Denouncing the insufficiency of reformism at a time of economic crisis, he also pronounced against radicalism. In other words, he was counselling inaction. His apparent revolutionary purity was no more than extremely puritanical reformism. This was confirmed on 2 July when he spoke at the Casa del Pueblo of Mieres in a tribute to Manuel Llaneza, the great Asturian union leader. He reaffirmed his view that the bourgeoisie should be left to carry out its own task and advanced the remarkable view that the Italian and German socialists were suffering fascism as a consequence of having participated in bourgeois governments. The implication of this view was that, if the socialists had not tried to defend the working class with the backing of the state, they would not have provoked the bourgeoisie into turning to fascism. The notion was extended on 26 July in the closing speech to the congress of the Sindicato Nacional Ferroviario. Echoing some of the ideas put forward by Turati during the period in which the Italian socialists were being subjected to the attacks of the *squadristi*, Besteiro claimed that the Spanish Socialists must not risk provoking the vengeance of their enemies.[93]

Largo's position was very different. Believing that the Republic was threatened by fascism, and fully aware of the German and Italian socialists' failure to oppose fascism in time, he advocated not retreat but a seizing of the initiative. Throughout the first half of 1933 the Socialist press had fully registered both its interest in events in Germany and its belief that Gil Robles and his followers intended to follow in the footsteps of Hitler and Mussolini. Now, in the summer, Largo and his advisers became conscious of a united assault by both industrial and agricultural employers on the Republic's social legislation.[94] It was obvious that the days of Socialist presence in the government were numbered, since Alcalá Zamora had already tried to persuade Azaña to form a cabinet without PSOE participation. Thus Largo Caballero set about trying to regain his close contact with the rank-and-file, which had been lost during his tenure of a ministry.

Largo's public revelation of his newly acquired radical views began with a speech, in the Cine Pardiñas in Madrid on 23 July, to the most militant sector of the Socialist Party, its youth movement (the FJS). One of his main reasons for breaking his silence, he said, was the growing hostility against the Socialist movement. His speech was essentially moderate and was primarily concerned with defending ministerial collaboration against the criticisms of Besteiro. However, a hardening of attitude was apparent. He took issue with Besteiro's claims that governmental participation had brought fascism upon the heads of the German and Italian socialists and pointed out that fascism was the bourgeoisie's last resort at a time of capitalist crisis. From this he went on to emphasise that the PSOE and the UGT had a duty to prevent the establishment of fascism in Spain. If this meant seizing power, then the Socialists, albeit with the greatest reluctance, should be prepared to do so. It is conceivable that the principal motive behind the speech was a desire to warn the President and the Radicals of the consequences of forcing the PSOE out of the government. However, the enthusiastic cheers which greeted the more extremist portions of his speech could not but confirm Largo in the validity of his new line.[95]

Clearly the PSOE was dividing as the employers' offensive provoked varying responses in the Socialist movement. This was starkly revealed at the summer school held by the FJS at Torrelodones near Madrid in the first half of August. Besteiro was the first of the faction-leaders to address the young Socialists. His speech was mainly concerned to refute the new line adopted by Largo in the Cine Pardiñas. For him, the aggression of the capitalists was not a reason for going onto the attack, but rather a test of discipline : 'if a general staff sends its army into battle in unfavourable circumstances, then it is fully responsible for the consequent defeat and demoralisation'. Without actually naming him, Besteiro accused Largo of adopting a radical line to gain cheap popularity with the masses and, in doing so, of risking a proletarian defeat. He condemned any talk of Socialist dictatorship to defeat fascism as 'an absurdity and a vain illusion'. 'It is often more revolutionary', he said, 'to resist the collective madness than to allow oneself to be carried along by it.' His speech revealed him to be either unaware of contemporary post-Hitlerian currents of Marxist thinking on fascism or else unsympathetic to them. It was received with some hostility and *El Socialista* refused to publish it.[96]

On the following day, 6 August, Prieto spoke. His language was far more moderate than Besteiro's had been, although he also warned against the dangers of a too-facile radicalism. He defended, as Largo had done, the achievements of the Republic so far. Only someone who had expected the Republic to change Spain's economic structure overnight, he declared, could be dissatisfied, particularly in view of the disastrous economic depression. He did acknowledge that the savagery of the ruling class's attacks on the Republic's legislation and on the Socialists was infuriating. In fact, in the most radical, and inevitably the most applauded, part of his speech, he reflected that it might have been better to have taken some reprisals in 1931 for the years of oppression that had gone before. Nevertheless, he called upon his audience to consider that the strength of the rightist assault threw doubts on the Socialists' capacity to challenge the immense economic power which still remained in the hands of the upper classes. Realism, said Prieto, showed that 'our kingdom is not of this moment'. The advocates of radicalism had compared Spain in 1933 to Russia in 1917 to justify, as the bolsheviks had done, a leap across the bourgeois democratic stage in the revolution. Prieto pointed out that it was not a valid comparison, since the weakness of the ruling classes and their state and military institutions in Russia in 1917 could hardly be said to be reflected in the Spain of 1933. He also warned that, even if a Socialist seizure of power were possible, capitalists in other parts of Europe were unlikely to stand idly by. It was a skilful speech, accepting the moral justification of radicalism, but rejecting the notion that there should be a dramatic change of party policy. Realistic as it was, the speech was not what Prieto's youthful audience wanted to hear. It was received coolly, if not quite so icily as Besteiro's had been, and was not published by *El Socialista*.[97]

Largo Caballero was not at first scheduled to speak at the summer school. However, leaders of the FJS informed him of the disappointment created by the speeches of Besteiro and Prieto. Largo, always proud of his rapport with the masses, was not a man to ignore the feelings of the rank-and-file. During the Dictadura, he had shown ample evidence of what Trotsky called 'tailism', or leading from behind. The enthusiasm of the base militants had turned him into a republican then; now it was apparently turning him into a revolutionary. His speech was on the impossibility of truly socialist legislation within the confines of bourgeois democracy. It was a rather bitter speech, reflecting his dismay at the virulence of rightist attacks. He claimed to have been radicalised by the intransigence of the bourgeoisie : 'We thought before that capitalism was a little more noble, that it would be more accommodating, more open to compromise. No, capitalism in Spain is obdurate [*cerril*], no one can convince it.' Nevertheless, Largo affirmed a continuing commitment to legality, despite talking of a future transition to socialism.[98] The speech delighted the young Socialists because of its implication that the party would soon be adopting a full-scale revolutionary policy.

To a certain extent, Largo Caballero's revolutionary rhetoric was not entirely what it seemed to the youthful radicals. It was not just the result of seeing the Marxist light. An element of personal rivalry with Besteiro, and even perhaps with Prieto, cannot be discounted. It is also possible that, with his new stance, Largo was hoping to warn the President against trying to replace the republican–Socialist coalition with the Radicals. However, Largo's new revolutionism responded above all to a sense of outrage at the mounting aggression of employers against social legislation and the effect that this was having on the UGT. Throughout the summer, evidence had been growing that the mixed juries and the various social laws were just being by-passed. Official labour exchanges were being ignored and work was only offered to those who would renounce membership of the UGT and join patronal unions. Land was being withdrawn from cultivation. There were increasing instances of landowners firing on groups of workers. A lengthy meeting of the National Committee of the UGT, held on 16, 17 and 18 June, discussed the extent to which the Socialists' attempt to maintain worker discipline in the face of provocation was simply losing members for the union.[99] Largo was thus determined to maintain the loyalty of the rank-and-file.

In a sense, it was a terrible dilemma. Since the workers were being forced into increasing militancy by the employers' refusal to compromise with social legislation, Largo was effectively committing himself to ever-escalating verbal radicalism. Not to do so would be to see workers drifting away to the CNT and the Communists and into counter-productive strike action. To do so could only exacerbate the polarisation of Republican politics, as well as providing a justification for rightist extremism.[100] Moreover, even if Largo opted for the harder line called for by a growing number of militants, it was unlikely to solve the problem of employer intransigence without a corresponding advance towards active revolutionary praxis. Prieto had recognised this in his speech, but there clearly were limits to the extent to which a policy of moderation could be imposed on the rank-and-file, who were, after all, in the front line of an increasingly bitter class struggle. It was a dilemma which was greatly to strain Socialist unity and eventually to lead Largo to a half-hearted participation in the insurrection of October 1934.

While the Socialists remained in the government, it was possible to call on the unions for discipline and patience while social reform was carried out. However, that situation was unlikely to pertain for much longer. In June, Alcalá Zamora had used Azaña's need to replace the sick Finance Minister, Jaime Carner, as an excuse to withdraw his confidence from the government. Since no one else could get a majority in the Cortes, the President was obliged to let the government continue through the summer. Conscious of growing opposition to the government, and always on the look-out for a more pliant Prime Minister than Azaña, Alcalá Zamora was anxious for a change, even if it meant elections. The difficulties of remaining in power under such circumstances were underlined in August, when the rightist deputies, with Radical complicity, managed to emasculate Marcelino Domingo's bill on rural leases, thereby belying their much-vaunted concern for the smallholder.[101] In early September, despite a parliamentary vote of confidence for Azaña, the President decided that a conservative victory in the elections for the Tribunal of Constitutional Guarantees justified his asking Lerroux to form a government. He did so on 11 September, but could not face the government without certain defeat. He governed with the Cortes closed. To the delight of the landowners, Largo Caballero's social legislation was virtually abandoned. The law of municipal boundaries was lifted in entire provinces and infractions of the law were not punished.[102]

There had long been a feeling of rage and frustration within the Socialist movement that the mild social reform achieved so far should have given rise to such fierce opposition. Now the speed with which a republican government without the Socialists permitted the evasion of social legislation began seriously to undermine Socialist faith in bourgeois democracy. Interviewed by the FJS newspaper, *Renovación*, on 23 September, Largo Caballero declared that the new government had created grave doubts about the possibility of the workers' attaining even their minimum aspirations within the Republic. For many leftists, the rightist assault on the achievement of reformist socialism was the thin end of the wedge of fascism. It had not been a difficult association of ideas. The landowners had launched the most violent attacks on the Republic's social reforms. Hitler and Mussolini had been quick to dismantle social legislation once they were in power. The press and political representatives of the Spanish landowners never tired of praising Nazi and Fascist achievement. In August, *El Debate* had commented on Spain's need for an organisation like those ruling in Germany and Italy and hinted coyly that Acción Popular was that 'necessary organisation'.[103] Gil Robles may not have been a fascist, but the Spanish Left certainly perceived him to be one.

The working class soon felt the effects of Largo's Caballero's absence from the Ministry of Labour. UGT officials complained to the National

Committee that they would lose members if the executive did not make a stand against the government's abandonment of social legislation.[104] That Largo had already realised this was made clear by a speech to the tram-workers on 1 October. He declared that the first task of the Socialist movement was to protect its gains to date. For Largo, most Socialists and many republicans, the Republic was consubstantial with its reforms; otherwise, it did not differ from the monarchy. Thus, reasoned Largo, since an assault was being made on its reforms, the Republic was in danger. The events of the previous month showed Lerroux to be a saboteur of the regime. He had already collaborated with the monarchists and the Agrarians in blocking reform. Largo went on to reflect that the vehemence of opposition to legislation that merely helped the workers to defend themselves did not bode well for the Socialists' long-term ambitions. Thus, while affirming his commitment to legality, Largo recalled the PSOE's revolutionary commitment to a complete transformation of the economic structure of society. If, he concluded, the government fell into the hands of those who would use legality and the Constitution against the working class and its aspirations, then the Socialists would have to consider leaving legality behind.[105]

It is likely that at this stage Largo was adopting radical positions in part as a warning to the President. However, that was soon to change. Speaking in the Cortes on the following day, Prieto declared that all Socialist commitments to the republicans were at an end. On the day after that, the government fell.[106] Alcalá Zamora asked Diego Martínez Barrio, of the Radicals, to form a government which would hold elections. Marcelino Domingo persuaded Martínez Barrio that such a government should include all republican forces, including the Socialists. Largo Caballero, after consulting the rest of the PSOE parliamentary minority, agreed, which rather confirms the premonitory element of his radicalism. However, just as it was becoming clear that Socialist participation was precluded by a constitutional technicality there arrived news of opposition within the party proper to such a move.[107] Martínez Barrio formed an exclusively republican government on 8 October. Elections were announced for 19 November.

Largo Caballero, the Juventud Socialista and much of the UGT rank-and-file went into the electoral campaign with enthusiasm and optimism. Other party leaders did not share Largo's euphoria and were uneasy about the rashness of going to the polls alone in an electoral system which favoured wide coalitions. De los Ríos confided his doubts to the American ambassador.[108] Prieto, by including Azaña and Domingo in the Socialist list, ensured that in Bilbao there would be no division of the left-wing vote.[109] The Socialists could not match the massive propaganda campaign mounted by the Right and only began their campaign two weeks after their opponents. Largo Caballero dominated the campaign, just as Gil Robles did for the 'anti-marxist front'. He made a tour of the country in the first half of November and his language grew more revolutionary as he travelled. That was a response first to the virulence of the rightist campaign whose leitmotiv was the need to smash socialism and secondly to the unrestrained enthusiasm of the crowds, who cheered his speeches long after they were over.[110]

On 15 October, Gil Robles had expressed his determination to establish the corporative state. Largo's speeches announced the Socialist determination to stop him doing so. On 5 November, in the Jaén bullring, the PSOE president told 12,000 workers that they should prepare to defend the Republic's achievements so far and to take them further along the road to socialism. In Albacete on 12 November, Largo was more explicit. He claimed that the opposition to his mild reforms showed that legal reformist tactics were futile. If social progress were made impossible, as it surely would be in a rightist corporative regime, the Socialists would have to abandon bourgeois democracy and proceed to the revolutionary seizure of power. On 14 November, speaking in Murcia, Largo declared that there could never be real democracy in Spain while glaring economic oppression was still rife. He ackowledged that only the dictatorship of the proletariat could carry out the necessary economic disarmament of the bourgeoisie.[111] Such remarks, of course, much as they delighted his audiences, could not but antagonise the Right and justify its already aggressive stance. Given the strength of the Spanish Right, both economically and politically the line adopted by Prieto at Torrelodones appeared far more realistic than the objectives, understandable but unrealisable, put forward by Largo.

The election results brought bitter disappointment for the Socialists, who gained only fifty-eight seats. A variety of factors contributed to the defeat. The efficacy of the rightist propaganda campaign cannot be underestimated. The Left also claimed that there was considerable rightist pressure, in the form of bribery and intimidation, on potential leftist voters. There appears to have been considerable harassment of peasant voters in the south by Civil Guards and thugs in the pay of local landowners.[112] Many observers believe that the introduction of the female vote worked against the Left. Working-class women voted with their husbands, it is argued, while middle-class wives whose husbands voted republican followed the advice of their confessors.[113] However, the two most potent reasons for the Left's poor showing were its electoral fragmentation and the opposition of the anarchists. Because of the Socialist refusal to ally with republicans, it took twice as many Socialist votes to elect a deputy as it did rightist ones. Leftist orators were greeted with cries of 'Assassin!' and chants of 'Casas Viejas' from anarchists in their audiences. In 1931, despite the CNT's apoliticism, most anarchists had voted for republican candidates. Now they either voted Radical or else abstained. The national average of abstentions was 32 per cent; in areas of anarchist influence it was much higher. In Barcelona, Zaragoza, Huesca and Tarragona it was around 40 per cent, and in Seville, Cádiz and Málaga it was over 45 per cent. The rightist victory was, in fact, not nearly so overwhelming as it appeared. Even with the widest coalitions, including Radicals, they did not get more than 40 per cent of the vote anywhere.[114] All these factors could only serve to increase the Socialists' disillusionment with bourgeois democracy and ease the way to greater radicalisation.

4 The Politics of Reprisal: The CEDA, the PSOE and the Insurrection of 1934

Between 1931 and 1933 the republican–Socialist coalition had endeavoured to create a socially progressive republic. In a context of world depression, it is inconceiveable that their programme of tentative reform could have resolved the highly conflictive social and economic problems inherited from the monarchy. Nevertheless, left republicans and Socialists believed that they had done enough to distinguish the new regime from the old and to set Spain off on its first faltering steps to modernity. They agreed that any step backward from the minimum achieved so far would be disastrous for the majority of the population. The Socialists, however, had been disturbed by the vehemence of opposition to what they regarded as basic humanitarian legislation. In the light of this, a growing sector of the trade-union movement and the FJS, encouraged by rather reckless support from Largo Caballero, were losing faith in the possibility that bourgeois democracy would allow the establishment of even a minimal social justice, let alone full-blown socialism.

A variety of reasons had led many of the Socialist rank-and-file to this conclusion. The immense rightist propaganda campaign against the Republic and its reforming projects had had sufficient success to convince them that the democratic process could be easily manipulated. Considerable disillusionment was created by the inability of a large parliamentary majority to overcome determined minority obstruction of reform. The ease with which employers evaded the provisions of the legislation that had been passed further undermined faith in the equitable nature of the bourgeois regime. Of even more importance was an awareness of the fate of similar regimes abroad. The Spanish Right had not hidden its sympathy for the achievements of Hitler and Mussolini. The CEDA had many of the trappings of a fascist organisation, with its rallies, its uniformed youth movement and its blanket propaganda techniques. During the campaign for the November elections, Gil

Robles had confirmed the worst fears of the Socialists when he had declared his determination to establish a corporative state in Spain. He had declared his preference for doing so legally, just as Hitler and Mussolini had done, although he also declared his readiness to do so by other means if necessary. There was a growing conviction among European socialists that the only way to deal with the fascist threat was to destroy the very capitalist system which, in its moment of crisis, had spawned it. It is not surprising then that a significant sector of the Spanish Socialist movement should start to think along similar lines.[1]

Socialist disappointment with the Republic was a direct consequence of the success of Gil Robles's legalist tactic in frustrating the reforming zeal of the new regime. In fact, the politics of the Republic were increasingly a battle between the PSOE and the CEDA to decide which of the two was to impose its stamp on the regime. Certainly, that was how both groups perceived the situation. For all that violent extremists of Right and Left played a considerable role in the polarisation of Republican politics, they were never the principal targets for the denunciations of the Socialist or the Catholic press. Socialist propaganda singled out the Catholic party rather than the Carlists or the Alfonsist monarchists as the most dangerous enemy on the Right. Equally, the ACNP propaganda machine, despite the revolutionary insurrectionism of the anarchists, consistently pinpointed socialism as the enemy to be destroyed. This is not surprising. Both the PSOE and the CEDA were confident that the repressive apparatus of the state could deal adequately with monarchist conspiracy or anarchist subversion. What each really feared was that the other would come to power legally and give the regime a constitutional and legislative content which damaged the material interests of their supporters. In a democratic regime, the numerical advantage might normally have been expected to lie with a working-class party. Accordingly, in 1931 the Socialists took part in the government with optimism. However, by the end of 1933 Acción Popular had demonstrated that ample financial resources and skilful propaganda could also conjure up popular support.

What particularly disturbed many Socialists and republicans in the winter of 1933 was the probability that the rightist victory in the elections would be used to rescind the reforms achieved so far. The reestablishment of the repressive social relations obtaining under the monarchy would be regarded by them as an assault on everything for which the Republic stood. Nevertheless, CEDA hostility to the republican–Socialist legislative programme had been so marked as to make clear the party's determination to annul it at the first opportunity. Now, victory in the elections made it possible for the CEDA to give legal sanction to the resentment that its financial backers felt against the reforming challenge of the first two years of the regime.

This reversal was about to come at the moment when the unemployment crisis reached its peak. In December 1933 there were 619,000 out of work, 12 per cent of the total work-force. This was considerably less than in Germany and Italy, whose economies were so admired by *El Debate*, but given Spain's lack of social welfare schemes, it still represented immense physical hardship. Without Largo Caballero at the Ministry of Labour to help cushion the blow, the impact on the labour force was even greater. Worsening conditions were the basis of rank-and-file pressure on union officials for militant action. The worst-hit sectors were agriculture, metal industries and construction, all of which were represented by substantial groups within the UGT. In the agrarian south, the number of unemployed was much higher than elsewhere. The worst-hit provinces were Jaén, Badajoz and Córdoba, where the percentage of unemployed was 50 per cent above the national average. Once landowners began to ignore social legislation entirely and to take reprisals for the discomforts of the previous two years, unemployment rose even further. By April 1934 it had reached 703,000.[2] The consequent growth of militancy within the FNTT was soon to lead to the replacement of its Besteirist president, Lucio Martínez Gil, with a follower of Largo Caballero, Ricardo Zabalza. The other two unions badly hit by the crisis were already led by faithful Caballerists. The leader of the metalworkers was Pascual Tomás, and the building labourers were led by Anastasio de Gracia. These three unions represented over half the UGT's total strength of 1,041,539 members – the FNTT accounting for 445,414, the metalworkers 33,287, and the building labourers 83,861. Of the next three most powerful unions – the railway workers with 49,117 members, the miners with 40,635, and the urban-transport workers with 34,435 – two were increasingly adopting a militant line. The railway workers remained under the leadership of the Besteirist Trifón Gómez, but the urban-transport workers were led by Largo's most extremist supporter, Carlos Hernández Zancajo, and the miners, without a change of leadership, were developing a harder line.[3]

Rank-and-file militancy was thus a crucial element in Largo Caballero's adoption of revolutionary rhetoric. There were, however, other factors. The most compelling was, paradoxically, a desire to make good the mistake, made before the elections, of rejecting the alliance with the left republican forces. The Socialists only had themselves to blame for failing to take advantage of the electoral system, but that fact did little to mitigate their bitterness at the results. They were anxious to persuade Alcalá Zamora to call new elections because, in their opinion, the recent ones had no real validity as a popular vote. The Socialists had gained 1,627,472 votes, almost certainly more than any other party running alone could have got. These votes had returned fifty-eight deputies, while the Radicals, with only 806,340 votes, had obtained 104 seats. According to calculations made by the PSOE secretariat, the united Right had gained a total of 3,345,504 votes, as opposed to the disunited Left's 3,375,432, winning 212 seats to the Left's ninety-nine.[4] The results were open to various interpretations. Even if the PSOE's somewhat sophistical calculations were correct, it would not alter the fact that the main factor in determining the results was the party's own tactical error.

However, the Socialists had other reasons for rejecting the validity of the elections. They firmly believed that in the south they had been swindled out of parliamentary seats by electoral malpractice. In villages where one or two men were the sole source of employment, it was relatively easy to get votes by the promise of a job or the threat of dismissal. For many workers on the verge of starvation, the offer of food or a blanket was worth a vote. In Almendralejo (Badajoz), the Marqués de la Encomienda distributed bread, olive oil and *chorizo*. In Granada, Fernando de los Ríos was prevented from speaking by armed thugs.[5] Glass voting urns and the presence of the *caciques'* strong-arm men made a mockery of the secret ballot. The authorities turned a blind eye to malpractice carried on in favour of the Radicals, who were in coalition with the CEDA in much of the south. After the elections, the Minister of Justice, Juan Botella Asensi, resigned, in protest at the level of electoral falsification. The Socialists were also convinced that the cynical way in which the rightists and centre republicans formed electoral coalitions made a mockery of the democratic system. Nowhere was this better illustrated than in Asturias. There it looked as if there was going to be a three-way fight between the Socialists, Acción Popular and the Liberal Democrats of Melquíades Alvarez. The campaign started with the liberal press reserving its most ferocious attacks for the 'cavemen' of Acción Popular. Then, in late October, the Liberal Democrats, the one-time monarchist Reformists, made a pact with Acción Popular and turned their efforts against the Socialists. A contest which the Socialists might reasonably have expected to win resulted in a victory for the Centre–Right coalition, which gained thirteen seats to the PSOE's four. Had the local anarchists not abstained, the Socialists would almost certainly have won the majority.[6]

At the end of 1933, then, the Socialist leaders were faced with a rising tide of rank-and-file militancy, which was a consequence both of the employers' offensive and of a feeling of bitterness at unfairly losing the elections. Largo Caballero was not a man to fly in the face of the base militants. Accordingly, his pronouncements in late 1933 and thereafter resumed that revolutionary tone which he had first adopted in his speeches at the Cine Pardiñas and the Torrelodones summer school.

His rhetoric was not, however, matched by serious revolutionary intentions. No concrete plans for a rising were made, and in December 1933 the Socialists ostentatiously stood aside from the CNT's attempted insurrection. Moreover, the Socialists broadcast their revolutionary aspirations in a manner which was totally inimical to subversive efficacy. It is far more likely that the PSOE's verbal revolutionism was intended merely to satisfy rank-and-file aspirations and, at the same time, to impress upon Alcalá Zamora the need to call new elections. It was a dangerous game, since, if the President did not succumb to such pressure, the Socialists would be left with the choice of stepping up their threats or losing credibility with their own militants. The resulting situation could only be of benefit to the CEDA.

Gil Robles was also faced by the need to play a subtle game. The election results had vindicated his tactics but they were far from constituting the overall victory which would have enabled him to install his 'new state' and a corporative system. Moreover, he realised that his victory was much more precarious than it appeared. Even if asked by the President to form a government, he could not have done so. To try to govern with a right-wing coalition was out of the question, since all the rightist elements in the chamber did not make up an absolute majority. Besides, a government containing the declared enemies of the Republic could only arouse the Republican fervour of the Left, including even the Radicals. With leftist divisions healed, the government would be defeated. There would then be either a coalition government of left and centre republicans or, if that were not possible, new elections. It was inconceivable that the Socialists would make the same tactical error twice. Anxious, therefore, not to have to risk his fragile victory in further elections, Gil Robles sought another solution. He thus turned to the notion of a centre government backed by CEDA votes, since he lacked the force to seize power by violence.

On 19 December, Gil Robles rose in the Cortes to express the CEDA's position and to spell out the sort of politics for which the new Radical government might expect his support. Although the speech was moderate in tone, it could not fail to cause great concern on the Left. If he did not demand power immediately, said Gil Robles, it was because tempers were still too high on the Right after the tensions and frictions of the first two years of the Republic. This altruism merely reflected his awareness of the basic weakness of his position. He claimed that the right-wing victory in the elections showed a national revulsion against the policies of the first *bienio*, and demanded that the new government carry out a policy in accordance with what he saw as the wishes of the electorate. The actual details of the desired policies revealed the narrow interests defended by the CEDA. Gil Robles called for amnesty for those condemned to imprisonment for the military rising of August 1932. He also demanded a revision of the religious legislation of the Constituent Cortes. However, it was with regard to social reforms that his demands were most sweeping. All the decrees which had been most welcomed by the landless peasantry – the law of municipal boundaries, that of obligatory cultivation, and the introduction of mixed juries – were the subject of swingeing attack. Then Gil Robles called for a reduction of the area of land subject to expropriation under the agrarian reform bill, justifying his demand with a condemnation of the socialising concept of settling peasants on the land. Having thus succinctly dismantled the entire social legislation of the Republic as it applied in rural areas, the CEDA leader went on, somewhat cynically, to affirm his party's commitment to social justice. CEDA votes, he claimed, would never 'serve to perpetuate social injustices'. He also called for action against unemployment, suggesting public-works projects and pledging CEDA support for the fiscal reform necessary to finance such schemes.[7] In fact, CEDA votes carried through the abrogation of social legislation, but, when the party supported a mild fiscal reform in 1935, there was an internal revolt.

In reply to Gil Robles, Prieto claimed that Lerroux's collaboration with the CEDA in the dismantling of the work of the Constituent Cortes was a betrayal of the Pact of San Sebastian. He went on to declare that the Socialists would defend the Republic against the dictatorial ambitions of the Right by unleashing the revolution. For the Socialists, that legislation which Gil Robles was determined to overthrow was what made the Republic worth defending.[8] Convinced that the CEDA, with the complicity of Lerroux, was about to destroy the progressive content of the Republic, the Socialists were playing the only card left to them. The threat of revolution was intended to make Lerroux and Gil Robles think twice before proceeding with their plans and to impress upon Alcalá Zamora the need for new elections.

In the context of this kind of opposition to CEDA plans, the tactic of supporting the Radical government from outside was the best available to Gil Robles. Such a government could be controlled without moral compromise and without the risk of provoking the formation of a left-wing coalition. Without any qualms of conscience. Gil Robles abandoned his monarchist electoral allies. Their chagrin can be imagined. On 27 September he had sworn not to accept pacts or deals with anyone until article 26 of the Constitution was revoked. In his great 15 October speech he claimed, 'we will not govern with anybody else'. His erstwhile allies, more perhaps even than his leftist enemies, regarded this as gross cynicism.[9] Apologists for Gil Robles have seen his decision to co-operate with the Radicals as a supreme gesture of self-sacrifice which kept the Republic in existence and was therefore the greatest proof possible of his loyalty to the Republic. Indeed, it has been stated that CEDA and Agrarian benevolence made government possible and perhaps saved the country from immediate civil war.[10] It is difficult, however, not to see more self-interest than idealism in a decision which derived from the double knowledge that the CEDA could only lose its gains in another election and that the Right was not yet ready for a violent showdown with the Left. In other words, it was the obvious and unavoidable tactic.

In any case, a partnership with the Radicals was useless as a gesture of republican faith. The Radicals' lack of a consistent political stance had already done the Republic considerable damage. By supporting the group most likely to win, Lerroux had dangerously exaggerated the pendulum effect built into the electoral system and thereby encouraged the politics of reprisal. The Left regarded the Radicals' brusque move to the right in search of votes as the prime cause of the CEDA's success. It was felt that, despite its reputation as the 'historic' republican party, the Radical Party had been infiltrated by monarchist elements. In August 1931, Lerroux had declared that the Radical Party was basically conservative and opened its arms to ex-monarchists. In many parts of the south, to the horror of the rightist press, many monarchists decided that they could best defend their interests from within a republican party.[11] This merely confirmed the leftist conviction that Lerroux was unprincipled and would always sell his services to the highest bidder. *El Socialista* regularly highlighted Radical corruption, of which there was a long history. Largo Caballero believed that the Radical Party included elements who, 'if they have not been in jail, deserve to have been'.[12] A CEDA deputy commented that 'this Radical minority reminds me of the voyage of a ship : people of all ages and conditions, of the most diverse ideologies, brought together merely to travel'.[13] The Left was also aware of the Radicals' ominous connection with Juan March, the millionaire smuggler and declared enemy of the Republic, who had partly financed the Right's election campaign.[14]

The Radical Party was thus a party without ideas or ideals, united only by a certain loyalty to Lerroux, a nostalgic recollection of the struggle against the monarchy especially in its Valencian sections, and, above all, the prospect of enjoying power. Lerroux himself admitted to Santiago Alba that he understood none of Spain's problems in depth.[15] The Radicals were interested in power as an end in itself, as access to a spoils system. Once in the government, they set up an office to organise the distribution and sale of ministerial prizes in the form of monopolies, commissions, concessions, government orders, licences and letters of introduction.[16] The Socialists feared, understandably, that this was not the party to defend the basic precepts of the Republic against the attacks of the Right. In fact, in return for keeping the

Radicals in power with its votes, CEDA support depended upon the implementation of satisfactory policies by the Radicals. Gil Robles stated clearly, 'today I will facilitate the formation of centre governments; tomorrow when the time comes, I will demand power and I will carry out a reform of the Constitution. If we do not receive power, if events show that a right-wing evolution of politics is not possible, the Republic will pay the consequences. This is not a threat but a warning.'[17]

It was in reply to remarks of that nature that Prieto had referred to Gil Robles's ill-concealed dictatorial ambitions. The Socialists appear to have been extremely anxious about the use to which the Right would put its new power. They were convinced that not only the Republic's legislation but also their own persons were in considerable danger from a possible fascist coup. De los Ríos placed information before the PSOE executive committee which suggested that plans were afoot for a rightist seizure of power and the detention of the Socialist leaders.[18] It was probably no more than a rumour, but the Socialists were genuinely afraid. Ever since the republican–Socialist coalition had left power in September, there had been constant reports of rightists in rural areas adopting increasingly violent and provocative attitudes with the acquiescence of the Civil Guard.[19] With a Radical government dependent on CEDA votes, the situation could only deteriorate. Throughout November and December, the Socialist press broadcast its certainty that Lerroux was serving as a bridge to power for the fascism of Gil Robles. Documents were reprinted which showed that Acción Popular was trying to create a citizen militia to face any revolutionary activity on the part of the working class. Other documents showed that Acción Popular was, with the connivance of the police, trying to build up a massive file on all of Spain's politically active workers. The activities of the uniformed militias of the Juventud de Acción Popular were taken as confirmation that an attempt would soon be made to establish fascism in Spain.[20]

Acción Popular was not in a position to seize power; nor, with a pliant Radical Party in the government, did it need to. Socialist fears were exaggerated, but, in the light of contemporary events in Germany, understandable. There was a deep conviction in the Socialist Youth particularly that the only effective answer to fascism was social revolution. This had been strengthened during the election campaign by an extraordinarily influential speech by Luis Araquistain on 29 October. The speech was reprinted as a pamphlet and distributed by the Federación de Juventudes Socialistas.[21] Araquistain had been Spanish ambassador in Berlin during the first month of Hitler's rule and had been active in trying to organise the escape of Jews and leftists from the Nazi terror.[22] In his view, it had been the passivity of the German

Social-Democratic Party which had facilitated the victory of Nazism. If they needed any encouragement, the Socialist youth were quick to seize on Araquistain's belief that only revolution could meet the fascist threat.

The combination of a newly confident employer class taking advantage of the changing political situation and the fears of fascism had a rapid effect on the Socialist rank-and-file. According to Largo Caballero, delegations of workers' representatives from the provinces came to Madrid to beg the PSOE executive committee to organise a counter-offensive. Accordingly, the Caballerist party executive called upon the Besteirist executive of the UGT to attend a joint meeting at party headquarters on 25 November. De los Ríos, who had just come back from a trip around the province of Granada, addressed the meeting. He painted a sombre picture of the sufferings of the rural proletariat at the hands of the newly confident and vengeful *caciques*. The PSOE executive, convinced that this was only the beginning of a nationwide rightist offensive, was keen to take positive action. The UGT executive was hostile to any kind of adventurism. Besteiro, Saborit and Trifón Gómez all argued that the most prudent thing to do would be to wait on events and keep the organisation together until circumstances improved. Largo was infuriated by their immobilism, which he found incomprehensible. Revealing his own sense of priorities, Largo opposed the UGT executive because 'the workers themselves were calling for rapid and energetic action'. As usual, he was frightened of a rank-and-file drift away to more determinedly revolutionary organisations. Prieto finally agreed with Largo on the need for 'a defensive action'. The meeting issued a declaration urging workers to be ready to rise up and oppose 'reactionary elements in the event that they went beyond the bounds of the Constitution in their public determination to annul the work of the Republic'. On 26 November the PSOE executive submitted its view of the situation to the party's National Committee. The executive's line was approved and a statement issued warning that, with working-class rights threatened by fascism, all party organisations should be ready to oppose the 'sinister fulfilment of the Right's ambitions'. This was a reference to Gil Robles's declared intention of implanting the corporative state in Spain.[23]

The CEDA may not have been a fascist organisation in the terms of post-1945 academic definition. In 1933 the full extent of Nazi horrors was as yet unknown.[24] In the light of what was known of Nazi and Fascist persecution of leftists, the CEDA's broadcast intention to smash socialism, Gil Robles's corporativist ambitions, and CEDA-encouraged employers' attacks on unionised labour were, to most Spanish leftists, indistinguishable from contemporary fascism. With a degree of nervous exaggeration, the Socialists in particular were obsessed with the need to avoid the tactical errors made by their German and Italian comrades. However, behind the consequent revolutionary posturing stood a long tradition of reformism. There can be little doubt that even the most verbally radical of the Socialist leaders viewed with considerable trepidation the prospect of actually organising a revolution. Rather, they hoped that their threats of revolution would serve the same purpose as the real thing, satisfying the demands of the rank-and-file and giving the Right pause. It was a tactic subject to the law of diminishing returns, but understandably grasped at by politicians trapped between their own militant masses and an aggressive Right.

The limits of the Socialists' rhetorical revolutionism were shown two weeks after the firm declaration of the joint PSOE–UGT executives. The anarchists, as a corollary to their electoral abstentionist campaign, had organised an uprising for 8 December. The aim of abstentionism was to ensure the return of an undiluted bourgeois government, in order, thought the anarchists, to let the working class see without confusion that the Republic was as oppressive as the monarchy had been and to help rid the Socialists of their reformist illusions. It was an irresponsibly naïve strategy. Only the traditionally anarchist areas responded to the call for a rising – Aragón, the Rioja, Catalonia, the Levante, parts of Andalusia and Galicia. There was a wave of violent strikes, trains were blown up and Civil Guard posts were assaulted. Within a matter of days, the rising had been suppressed.[25] Nowhere had Socialist militants taken part. Moreoever, a joint PSOE–UGT manifesto announced roundly that the Socialist movement had 'had no participation whatsoever in the rising'. The manifesto did, however, blame the rising on the government, 'which, by its contempt for workers' rights, has diverted the Republic from those paths on which the will of the people set it'. In the Cortes, Prieto condemned 'this damaging movement' (*movimiento perturbador*). Yet, when Goicoechea and Gil Robles offered their enthusiastic support to the government to help crush subversion, Prieto reacted angrily. It disturbed him that the 'enemies of the Republic' only ever supported the regime for enterprises which involved the repression of the working class. By their determination to silence the workers' organisations, declared Prieto, the Right was 'closing all exits to us and inviting us to a bloody conflict'. The Socialists' revolutionary stance was intended to inhibit the Right from going too far. In the previous day's manifesto the joint executives had emphasised this by reaffirming their 'firm decision, when the time comes, to fulfil the duties which our ideals impose upon us'.[26] In other words, the revolutionary threats would be applied if an attempt were made to establish fascism.

The premonitory nature of the revolutionary declarations of leaders like Prieto and Largo Caballero cannot be underestimated. Nevertheless, among the younger union members there was a great surge of irresponsible enthusiasm for revolutionism. This was making the position of the UGT executive committee untenable. On 31 December 1933 the UGT's National Committee met to discuss the political situation and to examine the policies being proposed by the PSOE executive. Amaro del Rosal, the young Caballerist president of the Federación de Trabajadores de Banca y Bolsa (Federation of Bank and Stock-Exchange Workers), proposed a motion for 'the immediate and urgent organisation, in agreement with the Socialist Party, of a national revolutionary movement, to gain political power exclusively for the working class'. The proposal was defeated by twenty-eight votes to seventeen. Apart from the expected votes against the motion from the executive – excepting Besteiro himself, who was ill – and the FNTT and Saborit's printers, two of the more unpredictable 'conservative' votes came from Anastasio de Gracia, the construction workers' leader, and Ramón González Peña of the SMA. This confirms that it was the younger element which was pushing for revolutionary tactics. The voting was reversed for the other motion of the day, presented by the executive committee, which simply reiterated the UGT's total identification with the joint executives' declaration of 25 November, which had threatened revolutionary action only if the Right went beyond the limits of the Constitution.[27]

The strident revolutionary rhetoric of the FJS increased the pressure on the Socialist leadership to adopt an insurrectionary line. The dilemma this created for them was revealed by De los Ríos, who visited Azaña on 2 January 1934 to seek his advice. Azaña's account of the meeting is extremely revealing :

He recounted to me the incredible and cruel persecutions that the political and union organisations of the workers were suffering at the hands of the authorities and the employers. The Civil Guard was daring to do things it had never dared do before. It was impossible to restrain the exasperation of the masses. The Socialist leaders were being overwhelmed. Where would it all end? In a great misfortune, probably. I was not unaware of the barbaric policy followed by the government nor of the conduct of the landowners with the rural labourers, reducing them to hunger. Nor of the retaliations and reprisals which were taking place against other workers. I know the slogan 'let the Republic feed you' [*Comed República*]. But all of this and much more that De los Ríos told me, and the government's measures, and the policy of the Cortes majority, which apparently had no other aim but to undo the work of the Constituent Cortes, did not make it advisable, nor justify, that the Socialist Party and the UGT should throw themselves into a movement of force.[28]

Azaña told De los Ríos in no uncertain terms that it was the duty of leaders to make the masses see sense, even at the risk of their own popularity. Yet, for all that their language was intemperate, it is difficult to see how, given the intransigence of the employers, the Socialist leadership could tell their followers to be patient.

From all over Andalusia and Extremadura came reports of considerable provocation from owners and Civil Guards alike. The law was flouted at every turn. In Real de la Jara (Seville) some workers who had stolen acorns were savagely beaten by the Civil Guard. In Venta de Baul (Granada) the armed guards of the *cacique*, a *Cedista*, beat up local union leaders. In Fuente del Maestre (Badajoz) it was the Civil Guard which did the beating. Members of the FNTT were systematically being refused work and wages had dropped by 60 per cent. The FNTT executive had sent several appeals to the Minister of Labour, Ricardo Samper, for the application of existing social legislation. A delegation went to visit Samper on 8 January. It was to no avail.[29]

This was hardly surprising given the composition of the government and the nature of its parliamentary support. On forming his government, Lerroux had looked for collaboration to the Agrarian Party of José Martínez de Velasco, which represented the wheat oligarchy of Valladolid and Burgos. The inclusion of José María Cid, a monarchist Agrarian, as Minister of Communications, caused a crisis of conscience for Diego Martínez Barrio, the most genuinely republican of the Radicals. The loyalty of the Agrarians to the Republic was little more confidence-inspiring than that of the CEDA. Indeed, when Martínez de Velasco announced his group's decision to adhere to the Republic, eight of his thirty-one deputies left in protest. The Left was convinced that CEDA votes in the Cortes gave the Radicals a licence for corruption in return for the protection of the agrarian oligarchy's material interests. In December a draft law was presented to the Cortes for the expulsion of those peasants who had occupied land in Extremadura the previous year. In January the law of municipal boundaries was provisionally repealed. The CEDA also presented projects for the emasculation of the 1932 agrarian reform, by reducing the amount of land subject to expropriation, and for the return of land confiscated after the 10 August 1932 military rising.[30]

The increase in the 'preventive brutality' of the Civil Guard was a consequence of the government's appointment of conservative provincial governors. In fact, the maintenance of authority became one of the CEDA's greatest preoccupations in the Cortes. On 26 January, Gil Robles and a CEDA deputation visited Lerroux to complain about disorder. Although they admitted its origin in unemployment, they demanded sterner measures from the forces of order. *El Debate* devoted a favourable editorial to Hitler's law for the regimentation of labour.

There was talk that the Ministry of Justice might set up concentration camps for unemployed vagabonds. The Socialists were disturbed by further evidence that the CEDA was building up files on workers in every village, with full details of their 'subversiveness', which was equated with their membership of a union. As clashes between the Civil Guard and the *braceros* increased daily, *El Socialista* commented that 'never, not even in the worst days of the monarchy, did the peasants feel more enslaved and wretched than now'. The President of the Supreme Court called for the application of the principles of social justice in the workings of the mixed juries, now under rightist control. Gil Robles, however, aligned himself openly with the owners when the CEDA tabled a proposition for increased credits for the Civil Guard.[31]

In this context, it was difficult for the Socialist leadership to hold back its followers. Largo Caballero tended to give way to the revolutionary impatience of the masses, although his rhetoric, which they cheered, was unspecific and consisted largely of Marxist platitudes. To make the revolution, he said, it was necessary to control the apparatus of the state. If the working class were to gain power, the people would have to be armed. To gain power, the bourgeoisie would have to be defeated. No concrete relation to the contemporary political scene was ever made in Largo's speeches of early 1934 and no time table for the future revolution was ever given. He did, however, dwell on one thing. That was the lesson of defeated European socialism as expressed by Otto Bauer : that only the destruction of capitalism could remove for ever the threat of fascism. Yet it is likely that Largo hoped to avert that very threat with his own revolutionary threat. In one speech he asked rhetorically if the republicans in the government did not see that by their policies they were giving the working class the idea that the legal struggle was useless. They could only do such a thing, he said, if they did not realise that it was provoking a revolutionary movement.[32]

Since the threats and appeals of Largo Caballero's speeches did little to mitigate the aggression of the rural employers and the Civil Guard, rank-and-file pressure for the radicalisation of the Socialist movement continued throughout January and February. Regular meetings between the party and union executives brought them no nearer to agreement. Besteiro tried several tactics to slow down the process of bolshevisation. First, he claimed that such a change of tactic could not be decided by the National Committee, but must be placed before a full congress of the UGT. Largo's supporters were anxious, not so much that a congress would not approve their line, but rather that a public airing of tactical differences might lead to a schism of the substantial Besteirist group. Largo overcame the obstacle by threatening that the PSOE would act unilaterally. The PSOE actually named a special commission, presided over by Largo and with Enrique de Francisco as secretary, to examine the practical side of organising a revolutionary movement.[33] Largo then insisted that the PSOE's policies be submitted to the UGT's National Committee. This was to meet at the end of January.

In the meanwhile, Besteiro insisted that no further steps towards radicalism could be taken until a revolutionary programme was drawn up. This was probably just a delaying tactic. Prieto and Besteiro met several times to hammer out such a programme, but could never reach agreement. Eventually they each elaborated separate programmes. Prieto produced a ten-point project which proposed (1) the nationalisation of land; (2) the dedication of the biggest proportion possible of the nation's savings to irrigation projects; (3) radical reform of the education system; (4) the dissolution of the religious orders, the seizure of their wealth and the expulsion of those considered dangerous; (5) the dissolution of the army and the immediate organisation of a democratic military body; (6) the dissolution of the Civil Guard and the creation of a popular militia; (7) the reform of the bureaucracy and the removal of anti-Republican elements; (8) an improvement in the working conditions of the industrial working class, but not, for the moment, the socialisation of industry; (9) the reform of the tax system and the introduction of an inheritance tax; and (10) that the previous nine measures be carried out in the form of decrees to be ratified by a freely elected legislative body and that the present President of the Republic be replaced. This relatively mild programme was not published until fifteen months later. In addition, a five-point programme of immediate action was drawn up, apparently by Largo Caballero himself. This called for (1) the organisation of a frankly revolutionary movement; (2) the declaration of such a movement at the right moment, preferably before the enemy could take definitive precautions; (3) contacts to be made between the PSOE and the UGT and any other groups ready to co-operate in the movement; and, in the event of triumph, (4) the PSOE and the UGT with other participants in the revolution to take over political power, and (5) the ten-point programme drawn up by Prieto to be applied. Besteiro's project was somewhat inappropriate. It proposed that a great corporative assembly be called to advise on a massive programme of national economic regeneration and nationalisation over a period of years.[34]

The National Committee of the UGT met on 27 January to discuss the various projects. The executive opposed the PSOE's revolutionary line. Besteiro used some strange arguments against Prieto's project. He claimed that it would involve the Socialists in war on the CNT. He also claimed that the violent seizure of power was contrary to the spirit of Marxism, the weapons of which were science and economic technique. When it was submitted to the vote, the PSOE line was approved by thirty-three members of the committee. Only the Sindicato Ferroviario Nacional and the FNTT voted for the executive, which immediately resigned *en masse*. A new executive was elected, with Anastasio de Gracia as president and Largo Caballero as secretary-general. On the following day, the National Committee of the FNTT met to examine the revolutionary line. An identical situation arose. The entire executive, all Besteirists, resigned, and a new committee of young Caballerists was elected. The organisations of the Socialist movement were falling in quick succession to the extremist youth. A meeting of the Agrupación Socialista Madrileña was packed by young Socialists, who passed a motion of censure against its president, Trifón Gómez, obliging him to resign. He was replaced by a group of the most fervent bolshevisers – Carlos Hernández Zancajo, Santiago Carrillo and Rafael Henche.[35]

The first objective of any revolutionary movement organised by the Socialists would be to prevent the CEDA from taking over the government. Yet, while the young revolutionaries loudly made their threats, Gil Robles was gradually achieving his aim of coming to power legally. CEDA votes in the Cortes ensured that the Radicals carried out a policy acceptable to the Right. Gil Robles backed up his demands on the Radicals with scarcely veiled threats. Addressing the Radical deputies in the Cortes, he announced that, if the Right were unable to achieve its programme in full within the parliament, it would be forced to transfer its field of action elsewhere. He made these remarks in a debate which had largely centred on the Socialist adoption of a revolutionary line. Prieto had stated that the PSOE's stance was a direct consequence of the daily violence being carried out against the working class by Gil Robles's supporters. Gil Robles denied that such was the case, on the rather specious grounds that the CEDA was fulfilling its ambitions legally. That was true, but it was precisely the protection of the law which made possible the violence to which Prieto referred. The debate had started because a number of rightist deputies had demanded that the Minister of the Interior, the liberal Radical Martínez Barrio, take firm action against the 'acts of indiscipline' being committed in rural areas. Such 'acts' included the robbery of acorns and olives by hungry day-labourers. Gil Robles, who regarded Martínez Barrio as too liberal, demanded assurances that the government would take action against such 'criminality' and would also oppose the revolutionary aspirations of the Socialists. To Gil Robles's annoyance, Martínez Barrio replied that it was his job to deal with violence, whether committed by the Right, the Left or the Centre. It was in reply to this that Gil Robles made his threat to go beyond parliament if he did not get his way within it.[36]

What his threats could mean was illustrated by contemporaneous events abroad. At the end of the second week in February, the Austrian government began its repression of the socialist movement in Austria. Reporting the fighting in Linz and Vienna, *El Socialista* drew the obvious analogy when it referred to the 'offensive of clerical fascism against the proletariat'. The reaction of the ACNP press to Dollfuss's bombardment of the Karl Marx Hof was enthusiastic. It was 'a lesson for us all'. The Spanish government was exhorted to follow the examples of Italy, Germany and now Austria in dealing with 'disorder'. The extravagant praise of Dollfuss brought forth a ready response from the Socialists : 'as always the Spanish clericals extend a certificate of good statesmanship to the Austrian chancellor after a ferocious and inhuman repression which easily emulates the cruelty of Italian fascism or the horrors of Hitlerism. . . . For us, the best governor is not one who, like Dollfuss, shoots women and children.' The Socialists heeded the warnings of Otto Bauer and Julius Deutsch, which began to fill their publications. They were determined not to share the fate of their Austrian comrades. Reading the CEDA press, they were confirmed in their conviction that to avoid such annihilation they would have to fight.[37]

Gil Robles's attitude did little to calm the young Socialists. For them, any attack on the Republic as created by the Constituent Cortes was fascism and a prelude to an attack on the Socialist movement. The CEDA leader showed a consistent aversion to declaring his loyalty to the Republic. On 4 January in the Cortes, he sidestepped a direct challenge to shout '¡Viva la República!' His normal device in such cases was to use expressions like 'readiness to work within', 'respect for', 'deference to' the Republic, and then only as sparingly as possible, when under direct pressure, and presumably with mental reservations. Miguel Maura, who was shocked by *El Debate*'s fulsome approval of events in Austria, remarked that, despite Gil Robles's acceptance of the Republic's existence, he was still manifestly in contact with Alfonso XIII.[38] The CEDA leader, however, was not concerned for the moment with the restoration of the monarchy. He was interested in state power, republican if necessary, to carry out concrete objectives. Speaking in Pamplona on 18 February, he admitted as much : 'Are we to govern with the present regime? Why not? A political party has a programme and this can only be carried out from a position of power.' The objectives to be pursued with state power were, as the behaviour of his party from its foundation had made clear, inimical to the work of the Constitutent Cortes. This was emphasised three days later when *El Debate* called for a united front of the employer class to mobilise against socialism.[39]

The CEDA's commitment to the promotion of these class interests was illustrated throughout March. The most disturbing event from the republican point of view was the calculated elimination of the more moderate members of the cabinet at the beginning of the month. Martínez Barrio expressed his discomfort at the government's being forced to carry out the CEDA's policies. Although the Minister of the Interior had acquiesced in the toughening of Civil Guard attitudes and had appointed right-wing provincial governors, it was not enough for Gil Robles. The landowners were unhappy at the idea of having a liberal in such a key position of social control. Martínez Barrio's attempts at fairness were denounced as laxity. Gil Robles thus withdrew his support from the government, proclaiming it 'thoroughly exhausted', and demanded a cabinet which more closely corresponded to the forces in the Cortes. Martínez Barrio and two other moderate Radical ministers, Antonio de Lara y Zarate (Finance) and José Pareja Yébenes (Education), were forced to resign. The reactionary and volatile Rafael Salazar Alonso became Minister of the Interior. This was to lead to the schism of the Radical left-wing, which was to become Unión Republicana. The remainder of the Radical Party was thus left even more a prisoner of the CEDA. It was Gil Robles's first major move in a skilful process of gradually eliminating the Radicals from the CEDA's path to power.[40]

The CEDA's success in subverting the progressive nature of the Republic had been analysed in a monumental speech by Azaña on 11 February. Gil Robles, said the republican leader, was using Lerroux's desire for power to impose a narrow class policy. The counter-revolutionary reversal of the republican–Socialist coalition's modest attempt to improve the living standards of the lower classes was now provoking social war. It was tragic that because of the government's contempt for social justice the Socialists were being forced to adopt a revolutionary stance. Azaña considered that it suited the Right for the Socialists to be provoked into a rising. After the Radicals had used the state's repressive apparatus to smash the proletariat, Gil Robles would demand that he be allowed to govern in order to establish his corporative state.[41] This is largely what was to happen between October 1934 and November 1935, although, in the event, Gil Robles was to miscalculate his final bid for power. In a very real sense, the Socialists were just playing into his hands. Many of them, of course, hoped that it would never be necessary to launch the threatened rising. Speaking in the Pardiñas a week before Azaña, Prieto had made it clear that, for him at any rate, the aim of the revolution would be to defend the work of the Constituent Cortes. Its programme, the same one he had drawn up and presented to the UGT, was not incompatible with the Constitution.[42] The trend of politics in general and the appointment of Salazar Alonzo in particular, however, showed that Prieto's hopes that the government would modify its aggressively right-wing policies were unlikely to be fulfilled.

Moreover, Prieto, for all his reluctant acceptance of a revolutionary line, was still far from being the most extreme of the Socialists. The youth, who had gained control of union after union, including even the printers, a Besteirist stronghold, were set on revolution, not to revive the bourgeois Republic, but to establish socialism.[43] In practice, however, their revolutionism did not go beyond verbal infantile leftism. Their extremist propaganda, not backed by any serious revolutionary preparations, was used to justify an increasingly authoritarian stance by the government. In early March they took the bait offered by the employers' intransigence and launched a series of strikes. Those in the metal and construction industries ended in stalemate, but the most important, that of the printers, ended in a major defeat for the hard-liners.

In fact, it was the printing dispute which revealed to what extent the recent cabinet shuffle marked an abrupt surge to the right. On 7 March, Salazar Alonso declared a state of alarm, closing down the headquarters of the FJS, the Communists and the CNT. The printers' strike had been provoked by the monarchist daily *ABC*'s using non-union labour. The owners of *ABC*, Juan Ignacio Luca de Tena, got Salazar Alonso's assurance that the government would support his attempt to break the strike. Thus, when the workers expressed a willingness to return to work, Luca de Tena refused to readmit the strikers. Salazar Alonso made no attempt to conciliate the two sides. He was determined to defeat a strike which, he said, would have brought 'the triumph of the red tyranny'. The newspapers of the Right took advantage of the minister's support and the unemployment crisis to sack union labour and to create pliant work-forces. The strike ended in defeat for the Socialist printers.[44]

The Right was delighted with Salazar Alonzo. On the day after his declaration of the state of alarm, his energy was applauded by Gil Robles, who declared that, as long as he thus defended the social order and strengthened the principle of authority, the government was assured of CEDA support. What he had in mind was clarified by a series of articles in *El Debate* demanding severe measures against what was called the 'subversion' of workers who protested at wage cuts. The CEDA press demanded the abolition of the right to strike. The government responded with an announcement that strikes would be ruthlessly suppressed if they had any political implications. For the right-wing press and, indeed, for Salazar Alonso, all strikes seemed to fall into this category. On 22 March *El Debate* referred to stoppages by waiters in Seville and by transport workers in Valencia as 'strikes against Spain', and recommended the adoption of anti-strike legislation like that current in Italy, Germany, Portugal and Austria. The government attempted to extend its repressive armoury by increasing the numbers of the Civil Guard and the Assault Guard and by re-establishing the death penalty.[45]

Simultaneously, the religious legislation of 1931–3 was being reversed. It was thus part of an overall trend when the CEDA called on the government to introduce the amnesty for attacks on the Republic which had been one of the Right's election pledges. Its text was drafted by Gil Robles, the Alfonsist Goicoechea, the Agrario Martínez de Velasco, and the Carlist Rodezno. Since the main beneficiaries were to be those associated with the Dictatorship and the 10 August rising, the Socialists and left republicans tried, unsuccessfully, to block the measure. For them it was confirmation if any were needed that the Republic was being taken over by its enemies. Even after the Cortes had passed the amnesty, the President of the Republic withheld his consent for fear of the army's being filled with officers who had clearly manifested their determination to overthrow the regime. He hesitated over the weekend of 20–23 April before finally signing. He also issued a note making public his reservations.[46]

While the President dithered, the CEDA made a sinister gesture in the form of a large rally of its youth movement, the JAP (Juventud de Acción Popular). It had been planned swiftly but thoroughly. Hundreds of meetings were held to drum up support and special trains with subsidised tickets were arranged. At one such meeting, Gil Robles made some illuminating remarks about his political strategy. Parliament was something which was repugnant but was accepted as a necessary sacrifice to achieve the CEDA's goals. The CEDA was further to the right than any other group, yet could defend its parliamentary tactic with its successes so far in repealing the legislation of the first *bienio*. 'We are going to get power, by whatever means', he concluded; 'With the Republic? It doesn't matter. To do things otherwise would be senseless and suicidal.'[47] Such admissions could only convince the Left that Gil Robles was exploiting Republican legality as Hitler had used Weimar. The rally's style owed much to Gil Robles's visit to Germany.

Since the rally itself coincided with the political crisis over the amnesty, it naturally had the appearance of an attempt to put pressure on Alcalá Zamora by a show of force. The choice of Philip II's monastery of El Escorial as venue was an obviously anti-republican gesture. Accordingly, a general strike was called in anticipation of a fascist 'march on Madrid'. Significantly, the lead in organising the strike was taken by the Trotskyist Izquierda Comunista, since the Socialists were reluctant to risk a clash with Salazar Alonso's new strike legislation.[48] The rally did little to allay left-wing fears. A crowd of 20,000 gathered in driving sleet in a close replica of the Nazi rallies. They swore loyalty to 'our supreme chief' and chanted, '*¡Jefe! ¡Jefe! ¡Jefe!*' – the Spanish equivalent of *Duce*. The JAP's nineteen-point programme was recited, with emphasis on point two, 'our leaders never make mistakes', a direct borrowing from the Italian Fascists. The general tone was bellicose. Luciano de la Calzada, CEDA deputy for Valladolid, affirmed that 'Spain has to be defended against Jews, heretics, freemasons, liberals and Marxists'. Ramón Serrano Súñer, CEDA deputy for Zaragoza and later architect of Franco's National-Syndicalist state, fulminated against 'degenerate democracy'.

The high point of the rally was naturally a speech by Gil Robles. His aggresive harangue was greeted by delirious applause and pro-longed chanting of '*¡Jefe!*' 'We are an army of citizens ready to give our lives for God and for Spain', he cried, 'Power will soon be ours. . . . No one can stop us imposing our ideas on the government of Spain.' He was disparaging about foreign examples, but only because he felt that the same authoritarian and corporativist ideas could be found in Spanish tradition.[49] 'I want this Spanish feeling to be exalted to paroxysm', he declared. This tone, together with the parading, saluting and chanting, led the English correspondent Henry Buckley to see it as the trial for the creation of fascist shock troops. It was, in this sense, something of a failure. A turn-out of 50,000 had been expected, but, despite the transport facilities, the giant publicity cam-paign and the large sums spent, fewer than half that number arrived. Besides, as Buckley observed, 'there were too many peasants at El Escorial who told reporters quite cheerfully that they had been sent by the local political boss with fare and expenses paid'.[50]

What might have been the outcome had the rally been more of a success is a matter for speculation. Since all the CEDA's propaganda was left in the hands of the JAP, it is not surprising that the Socialists – and indeed the monarchists – took the fascist posturing of the youth as indicative of the predilections of their elders. This was, after all, taking place in the shadow of the widely publicised events in Germany and Austria. Even José Antonio Primo de Rivera, leader of the Falange, described the El Escorial rally as a 'fascist spectacle'.[51]

The immediate outcome of the crisis was that Lerroux resigned in protest at Alcalá Zamora's delay in signing the amnesty and was re-placed by Ricardo Samper, an ineffective Radical, incapable of inde-pendent policies. Lerroux had never considered the possibility that the President would accept his resignation. However, he gave Samper per-mission to form a government, because he was frightened that, if he did not, the President would dissolve the Cortes and call upon a Socialist to preside over new elections. Cándido Casanueva, the leader of the CEDA parliamentary minority, proposed another solution. This was for the CEDA and the monarchist deputies to join the Radicals in passing a vote of confidence in Lerroux, thereby provoking Alcalá Zamora's resignation. The CEDA's proposed scenario would then be completed by the elevation of Lerroux to the Presidency of the Republic.[52] It was an attempt by Gil Robles to speed his progress to power, since the new President would then have to call on him to form a government. Lerroux was too wily to fall for the manoeuvre. He knew that it was only a matter of time before he would be Prime Minister again. Accordingly, Samper formed a cabinet virtually identical to its predecessor. It continued to pursue a policy agreeable to the CEDA. A decree of 11 February which had evicted thousands of *yunteros* in Extremadura was followed by one on 4 May which annulled the post 10 August expropriations and by one on 28 May which left rural wages to the whim of the owners.[53]

The greatest practical victory for the CEDA's landed backers was the definitive repeal of the law of municipal boundaries. The successful assault on it in the Cortes had been led by the most aggressive of all CEDA deputies, Dimas de Madariaga (Toledo) and Ramón Ruiz Alonso (Granada), both representatives of provinces where the law's application had infuriated the large landowners.[54] Its repeal, on 23 May, just before the harvest was due to start, allowed the owners to bring in Portuguese and Galician labour to the detriment of local workers. The defences of the rural proletariat were falling rapidly before the right-wing onslaught. The last vestige of protection that left-wing workers had for their jobs and their wages was, in the countryside, that afforded them by the Socialist majorities on many town and village councils. Salazar Alonso had already begun to remove most of them, on the flimsiest pretexts. From the moment that he took up office, he issued orders for the removal of *alcaldes* who 'did not inspire confidence in matters of public order' – that is to say, Socialists. This left workers increasingly at the mercy of the *caciques'* retainers and the Civil Guard.[55]

The situation in the countryside was growing critical, as landowners took advantage of official acquiescence to slash wages and discriminate against union labour. Even *El Debate* commented on the harshness of many landlords, but it still continued to advocate that jobs be given only to affiliates of Catholic unions. In Badajoz starving labourers were begging in the streets of the towns. The monarchist expert on agrarian matters, the Vizconde de Eza, said that in May 1934 over 150,000 families lacked even the bare necessities of life. Workers who refused to rip up their union cards were denied work. The owners' boycott of unionised labour and the notorious '*Comed República*' campaign were designed to reassert pre-1931 forms of social control and to ensure that the reformist challenge to the system mounted by the first *bienio* should never be repeated. In many villages, this determination was revealed by physical assaults on the Casa del Pueblo. A typical incident took place at Puebla de Don Fadrique, near Huéscar in the province of Granada. The Socialist *alcalde* was replaced by a retired army officer who was determined to put an end to what he saw as the workers' indiscipline. The Casa del Pueblo was surrounded by a detachment of Civil Guard, and as the workers filed out they were beaten by the Guards and by retainers of the local owners.[56]

The response of the FNTT to this challenge was an illuminating example of how the newly revolutionised Socialists were reacting to increased aggression from the employers. The FNTT newspaper, *El Obrero de la Tierra*, had adopted a revolutionary line after the removal of the Besteirist executive on 28 January. The only solution to the misery of the rural working class, it maintained, was the socialisation of the land. In the meanwhile, however, the new executive adopted practical policies indistinguishable from those of their predecessors. It sent to the Ministers of Labour, Agriculture and the Interior a series of appeals for the application of the law regarding obligatory cultivation, work agreements, strict job rotation and labour exchanges, as well as protests at the systematic closures of the Casas del Pueblo. That was in the third week of March. When no action was taken, and, indeed, the persecution of left-wing workers began to increase prior to the harvest, a polite appeal was sent to Alcalá Zamora – also to no avail. The FNTT declared that thousands were slowly dying of hunger and published interminable lists, with details, of villages where union members were being refused work and physically attacked.[57]

Finally, in a mood of acute exasperation, the FNTT decided on a strike. The decision was not taken lightly. The first announcement of a possible strike was accompanied by an appeal to the authorities to impose respect for the *bases de trabajo* and equitable work-sharing.[58] The UGT executive committee advised the FNTT against calling a general strike of the peasantry and gave several reasons for this advice. In the first place, the harvest was ready at different times in each area, so the selection of a single date for the strike would lead to problems of co-ordination. Secondly, a general strike, as opposed to one limited to large estates, would cause hardship to leaseholders and sharecroppers who needed to hire one or two workers. Thirdly – showing even more strongly than the other two reasons the strength of the UGT's reformist tradition – the provocation offered by the owners and the authorities would be such as to push the peasants into violent confrontations. In a series of meetings between the UGT and the FNTT executives throughout March and April, efforts were made to persuade the peasants' representatives to a narrower strategy of staggered, partial strikes. The UGT pointed out that a general strike would be denounced by the government as revolutionary, that it risked a terrible repression which might in its turn provoke a national general strike, which the UGT was not prepared to call. Largo Caballero told the FNTT leaders not to expect any solidarity strikes from industrial workers. Moreover, the joint PSOE–UGT committee appointed in January to look at the problems of organising a revolutionary movement sent messages to its sections in every province informing them that the peasants' strike had nothing to do with any such movement.[59]

The FNTT executive told the UGT that not to go along with their rank-and-file's demand for action would be to abandon them to hunger wages, political persecution and lock-out. Thus, a strike manifesto announced the beginning of the movement on 5 June. Before resorting to this measure, which was carried through in strict accordance with the law, ten days' notice being given of the strike, the FNTT leaders tried every possible procedure to impel the relevant ministries to apply the remaining social legislation. Yet hundreds of appeals for the payment of the previous year's harvest wages lay unheard at the Ministry of Labour. All over Spain, the work conditions agreed to by the mixed juries were simply being ignored. Protests were met by an intensification of repression. In the province of Badajoz, for instance, there were 20,000 unemployed and 500 workers in prison. In Fuente del Maestre the Civil Guard met a typical hunger march with violence. Four workers were shot dead and several more wounded. A further forty were imprisoned. In the province of Toledo, FNTT affiliates found it almost impossible to get work. Those who did find a job had to accept the most grinding conditions. The *bases de trabajo* had decreed a wage of 4·50 pesetas for an eight-hour day. The owners were in fact paying 2·50 pesetas for *de sol a sol* working. In parts of Salamanca, wages of 75 céntimos were being paid.[60] On 28 April, the FNTT sent an appeal to the Minister of Labour for action to remedy the situation simply by ensuring the fulfilment of the existing law. When nothing was done, the FNTT National Committee met on 11 and 12 May to decide on strike action. Its manifesto pointed out that 'this extreme measure' was the culmination of a series of useless negotiations and that the preparation of the strike was legal and open.[61]

The ten objectives of the strike could hardly be considered revolutionary. They had two basic objectives: to secure an improvement of the brutal conditions being suffered by rural labourers and to protect unionised labour from the apparent determination of the employer class to destroy the rural unions. The ten demands were (1) application of the *bases de trabajo*; (2) strict work rotation without prejudice of political affiliation; (3) limitation on the use of machinery and outside labour, to ensure forty days' work for the labourers of each province; (4) immediate measures against unemployment; (5) temporary take-over by the Institute of Agrarian Reform of lands scheduled for expropriation under the agrarian reform bill, and their collective renting to the unemployed; (6) application of the law of collective leases; (7) recognition of the right of workers benefited by the law of obligatory cultivation to work abandoned land; (8) the settlement before the autumn of those peasants for whom the Institute of Agrarian Reform had land available; (9) the creation of a credit fund to help the collective leaseholdings; and (10) the recovery of the common lands. Before the announcement of the strike, the Minister of Labour, the Radical José Estadella Arnó, had denied that hunger wages existed in the countryside and that Socialist workers were being refused work. Now he recognized that something had to be done. He started to make token gestures, calling on the mixed juries to elaborate work contracts and on government labour delegates to report the employers' abuses of the law. Negotiations were also started with FNTT representatives.[62]

Salazar Alonso, however, was not prepared to lose this chance to strike a deadly blow at the largest section of the UGT. He was, after all, the political representative of the Badajoz landowners and a close collaborator of Gil Robles. Just as compromise negotiations between the FNTT and the Ministers of Agriculture and Labour were beginning to make progress, Salazar Alonso issued a decree making the harvest a national public service and the strike a 'revolutionary conflict'. All meetings, demonstrations and propaganda connected with the strike were declared illegal. A Draconian press censorship was imposed. *El Obrero de la Tierra* was closed down, not to reopen until 1936. In the Cortes debate on Salazar Alonso's tough line, the CEDA votes, along with those of the Radicals and the monarchists, ensured a majority for the Minister of the Interior. Nevertheless, the points raised in the debate were illuminating with regard to the issues at stake.

José Prat García, PSOE deputy for Albacete, opened with a speech pointing out the anti-constitutional nature of Salazar Alonso's measures. He reiterated that the FNTT had followed due legal process in declaring its strike. The application of existing legislation in a spirit of social justice would be more than sufficient to solve the conflict, claimed Prat in a reasoned appeal to the Cortes's sense of justice. Salazar Alonso had, despite the availability of a peaceful solution, simply given the government a free hand for repression. The Minister replied belligerently that, because its objective was to make the government take action, it was a strike against the government. He said that there could be no question about the strike's revolutionary nature, since the executive of the FNTT were followers of Largo Caballero. Interestingly enough, Largo Caballero sprang to his feet to deny that he had ever rejected legality, confirming perhaps that his revolutionary rhetoric was meant to frighten the government and satisfy the impetuous demands of his own militants, without his ever seriously facing the prospect of putting it into practice. Prieto shouted out, 'The fact is that we are seeing an attempt to start a dictatorship'. When Salazar Alonso stated, falsely as it happened, that the government was taking steps against owners who imposed hunger wages, Prat replied that, on the contrary, the Minister had frustrated all attempts at conciliation, by overruling the negotiations between the FNTT and the Ministers of Labour and Agriculture. He concluded by stating that the strike aimed only to protect the rural labourers and to end a situation that in Guadix (Granada) had reduced the workers to eating grass. José Antonio Trabal Sanz, Esquerra deputy for Barcelona, pointed out that Salazar Alonso seemed to regard the interests of the plutocracy and the national interest as synonymous. Cayetano Bolívar, Communist deputy for Málaga, claimed that the government's provocation was closing the doors of legality and pushing the workers to revolution. When he referred to the workers' hunger, a deputy from the majority shouted that they too were hungry and the debate ended.[63]

In fact, Salazar Alonso had long since been making plans, with the head of the Civil Guard and the Director General of Security, for the repression of a possible strike. Conciliation had not, therefore, been uppermost in his mind, even before the strike started. His measures were now swift and ruthless. Liberal and left-wing individuals in the country districts were arrested wholesale. Even four Socialist deputies, along with numerous school-teachers and lawyers, were arrested – in flagrant violation of articles 55 and 56 of the Constitution. Several thousand peasants were loaded at gunpoint onto lorries and deported hundreds of miles away from their homes and then left to make their own way back. Workers' centres were closed down and many town councils, especially in Badajoz and Cáceres, were removed, and replaced by government nominees. The government claimed that the strike call was not obeyed. The number of arrests and the maintenance of censorship for several weeks suggest otherwise. In fact, the stoppage seems to have been almost complete in Jaén, Granada, Ciudad Real, Badajoz and Cáceres, and substantial elsewhere in the south. However, the strikers could not stop the owners bringing in outside labour, with Civil Guard protection, from Portugal, Galicia and elsewhere. The army was brought in to use threshing machines and the harvest was collected without serious interruption. Although most of the labourers arrested were soon released, emergency courts sentenced prominent workers' leaders to four or more years of imprisonment. The Casas del Pueblo were not reopened and the FNTT was effectively crippled until 1936.[64] In an uneven battle, the FNTT had suffered a terrible defeat.

Salazar Alonso had effectively put the clock back to the 1920s. There were no longer any rural unions, social legislation or municipal authorities to challenge the dominance of the *caciques*. The CEDA could not have been more delighted at this further practical demonstration of the advantages of legalism. Speaking in Badajoz, Gil Robles said that 'as long as the Radicals carry out our programme, there is no reason to change our attitude. Could we ask for more?' Two days later, on 2 June, he said that the government had fully realised the CEDA's policy. There could be little other reason for the belligerence of Salazar Alonso's attitude than CEDA pressure, and his own authoritarian predilections, since the strike had so evidently not been a revolutionary bid for power. If it had been planned as such, instead of having limited material objectives, it would have been more ambitious and enjoyed the solidarity of the UGT's industrial workers. By choosing to regard the strike as revolutionary, Salazar Alonso was able to continue his attack on Socialist *ayuntamientos* (municipal councils); by the end of the conflict he had removed 193 of them.[65] By his determined and aggressive action during the peasant strike, the Minister of the Interior had inflicted a terrible blow on the largest union within the UGT. He had called Largo Caballero's revolutionary bluff and thereby significantly altered the balance of political power in favour of the Right.

In fact, the defeats suffered in both the printers' and peasant strikes posed a major dilemma for the Socialists. The belligerent stance of the Minister and the enthusiastic support that he received from Gil Robles confirmed the left-wing conviction that the Radicals were fulfilling the CEDA's authoritarian ambitions. It was the same conviction as had largely fuelled the revolutionary threats of late 1933 and early 1934. In fact, when, by the spring, it had become clear that those threats, far from inhibiting the CEDA and precipitating new elections, were simply justifying a rightwards swing of the government, the revolutionary ardour of Prieto and even of Largo began to cool. The one significant move that the Socialist Left had made in the direction of a revolutionary strategy was to adopt the notion of an 'Alianza Obrera' (workers' alliance). The Alianza was the brainchild of Joaquín Maurín, leader of the quasi-Trotskyist Bloc Obrer i Camperol. Foiled in an attempt to infiltrate the CNT and turn it into a bolshevik vanguard,[66] throughout 1933 he advocated the Alianza Obrera as the only valid working-class response to the great advances of the authoritarian Right in Spain and elsewhere. After the electoral defeat in November, the Socialists began, understandably, to show interest in the notion.

However, from the first it seemed that the Socialists saw the Alianza Obrera as a possible means of dominating the workers' movement in areas where the PSOE and UGT were relatively weak. They viewed the Alianza less as an instrument of rank-and-file working-class unity than as a liaison committee linking existing organisations.[67] In Madrid the Alianza was dominated by the Socialists, who imposed their own policy. Throughout the spring and into the early part of the summer of 1934, they blocked every revolutionary initiative proposed by the representative of the Izquierda Comunista, Manuel Fernández Grandizo, and did so on the grounds that the UGT had to avoid partial actions and save itself for the ultimate struggle against fascism. This was underlined even further by the debates over the peasant strike. Once Salazar Alonso had made it clear that there was to be no conciliation and that his objective was to break the FNTT, the only possibility of success for the Federation was a massive show of solidarity by industrial workers. If such an action had taken place, it would either have brought down the government or have led to a bloody confrontation between the forces of order and the unions. Nevertheless, not to declare industrial solidarity was to condemn the peasants to defeat. Faced with the harsh reality of putting his threats into action, Largo refused to take such a dangerous step. Disgusted with a policy which could only strengthen the Right, the Izquierda Comunista representative ostentatiously withdrew from the Madrid Alianza.[68]

The reasons for Largo's caution were made clear when the UGT National Committee met on 31 July to hold an inquest into the failure of the peasant strike. Ramón Ramírez, the representative of the Federación de Trabajadores de la Enseñanza, the small schoolteachers' union, attacked the UGT executive for its failure to go to the aid of the peasants and virtually accused Largo Caballero of being a reformist. Largo pointed out that he had warned Ricardo Zabalza, the FNTT secretary-general, before the strike that there would be no solidarity action. Zabalza claimed that his own rank-and-file gave him no choice but to go ahead with the strike. When the strike was under way and faced with difficulties, it hardly mattered that the UGT had predicted its defeat. Once Salazar Alonso had forced a major confrontation, the UGT had to face the choice of either watching its most important section broken or risk a major trial of strength with the government and the Right. It was a terrible dilemma. In the event, Largo's reformist background prevailed. He was not prepared, he said, to see a repeat of the defeat of August 1917. He attacked the frivolous extremism of Ramón Ramírez, and, with words applicable to his own behaviour of four months previously, declared that the Socialist movement must abandon its dangerous verbal revolutionism. When Ramírez read some texts of Lenin to the meeting, Largo replied that the UGT was not going to act in every case according to Lenin or any other theorist. With incontrovertible realism, the UGT secretary-general reminded his young comrade that Spain in 1934 was not Russia in 1917. There was no armed proletariat; the bourgeoisie was strong. Under such circumstances, Lenin would not recommend revolutionary adventures. Other interventions at the meeting revealed the strength of reformist pragmatism within the UGT. The only section of the Socialist movement which maintained its flow of shrill revolutionary rhetoric was the Juventud Socialista. Although the younger elements acknowledged Largo as their spiritual leader, he seems to have become increasingly annoyed at their facile extremism, complaining that 'they did just what they felt like'.[69]

That the belligerent tone with which the Socialists had greeted their departure from power had led to no fundamental change of the UGT's tactics came as no surprise to more genuine revolutionaries. Largo Caballero had gone to Barcelona in February 1934 to negotiate the formation of the Alianza Obrera with the Trotskyist Izquierda Comunista and Bloc Obrer i Camperol (Worker and Peasant Block), with the dissident anarcho-syndicalists, the *treintistas*, and with various Catalanist groups, including the Unió Socialista and the Unió de Rabassaires. The CNT refused to join, on the grounds that 'the entire Socialist campaign for insurrection is a demagogic platform'. The anarchists distrusted the PSOE's revolutionism, especially after the lack of solidarity shown during their December 1933 uprising. They were convinced that the Socialists intended no more than to provoke new elections and return to the government in coalition with the republicans. An open CNT appeal to the UGT in mid-February to prove its revolutionary sincerity had not elicited any reply. Even those parties who did join the Alianza soon found themselves in the grip of the UGT's cautious domination. Within a month of the creation of the Alianza, the Unió Socialista de Catalunya left in protest at Largo's tutelage.[70]

The Izquierda Comunista also regarded the Socialists' revolutionism as fraudulent and were later to break with Trotsky partly because of that belief. They believed that Largo Caballero was only playing at revolution, and that his aim in doing so was to maintain·his hold on the militant rank-and-file and to gain control over other revolutionary groups (in other words, they accused him of the classic sin of 'tailism', the social-democrat tactic of verbally outflanking the vanguard in order to neutralise their militancy).[71] When Manuel Fernández Grandizo temporarily withdrew from the Alianza during the peasant strike, he told the other delegates that the UGT's lack of solidarity with the FNTT revealed 'yet again that the Alianza Obrera is not for the Socialists an organism of the revolutionary united front, but merely an instrument with which to frighten the bourgeoisie'. The Izquierda Comunista had only a small following, but contained a team of highly competent Marxist theorists, headed by Andrés Nin.[72] Trotsky recommended that they follow the tactic of 'entrism' – that is, join the PSOE in the hope of accentuating its revolutionary line. All but a handful of the Izquierda Comunista rejected Trotsky's advice, because they were convinced that Largo Caballero's reformist grip could not be broken. They opted instead for a valid Marxist alternative, hoping that the Socialist rank-and-file would eventually see how they had been betrayed and then turn their backs on Largo Caballero.[73]

The Trotskyists did, however, agree sufficiently with Trotsky to remain convinced of the need for a united front against fascism. Accordingly they stayed in the Alianza Obrera, as the only potentially revolutionary instrument in Spain. In Madrid the Alianza was never able to overcome the UGT's irresolution, and in Barcelona it faced the almost insuperable obstacle of the CNT's lack of discipline. The one area where the Alianza was a success, uniting discipline and mass support, was Asturias. There were many reasons for this. The Asturian CNT had a long tradition of support for initiatives of working-class unity. The local CNT leaders, Eleuterio Quintanilla and José María Martínez, were sympathetic to the proposals of the Socialists. The high level of maturity that had been attained by the Asturian proletariat through the great mining strikes ensured a thorough rank-and-file support for unity. The miners, perhaps more even than the peasants, realised how violently capitalism in crisis could react to the challenge of reformism. They had little doubt that a fascist threat existed. The SMA newspaper, *Avance*, directed by Javier Bueno, reiterated that threat daily. With their life of brutal conditions and constant risk of violent death, the miners were not afraid to fight to defend what they had gained through years of gradual struggle. The Asturian Alianza Obrera was clinched on 28 March 1934 with the participation of the Socialists, the anarchists, the Izquierda Comunista and the Bloc Obrer i Camperol, only the Communists remaining outside. It maintained a tight discipline, avoiding all sporadic strike action in order to conserve its strength for the expected fascist assault.[74]

Fascist or not, Gil Robles's strength seemed to be waxing in the summer of 1934. After defeating the peasants, the government felt sufficiently secure to extend its offensive elsewhere. The new area of operations was to be Catalonia, which, because of its autonomous status, was the area of Spain where the attack on the achievements of the republic had been least effective. A crisis over Catalan agriculture was provoked in such a way during the summer as to suggest that the last republican stronghold was now to come under attack. The Generalitat of Catalonia, in the hands of the left republican Esquerra, had passed a law known as the *ley de contratos de cultivo*, a progressive measure which gave tenants some security of tenure and the right to buy land which they had worked for eighteen years. It was bitterly opposed by the landowners who rented them the plots. The Catalan conservative party, the Lliga, representative of the Catalan landlords and industrialists, protested to the central government with the enthusiastic support of the CEDA. This raised complex constitutional issues over the competence of the central government to intervene in Catalonia. The government, under pressure from the CEDA, handed the question to the Tribunal of Constitutional Guarantees, whose membership was predominantly right-wing.[75]

The Left was outraged when the court found in favour of the Lliga and against the Generalitat. Azaña said in parliament in June that 'the government of Catalonia is the only republican power left standing in Spain'. The Generalitat replied to the challenge by passing the law again in mid June, something Azaña considered their 'republican obligation'. The Prime Minister, Samper, was inclined to negotiate, but the CEDA pressed for a harder line. Gil Robles was even opposed to the matter's being discussed in the Cortes. When it was, he made two major speeches calling for the sternest application of the law against the Generalitat's 'act of rebellion'. As Samper vacillated, Gil Robles's support for the government began to waver. Throughout the crisis *El Debate* called for the government to make the Catalans submit. This attitude reflected the traditional centralism of the Castilian Right, although it also derived from the fact that the CEDA's landed backers resented any threat to their privileges.[76]

This was shown clearly on 8 September, when the Catalan landowners' federation, the Instituto Agrícola Catalán de San Isidro, organised an assembly in Madrid. The Socialists reluctantly called a general strike.[77] The Bloque Patronal, the employers' block, which had recently announced its determination to reduce the unions to submission, issued detailed instructions for blacklegging and reprisals to be taken against the strikers. The assembly was attended by representatives of all the major pressure groups of the rural oligarchy – the Asociación General de Ganaderos (stockbreeders), the Agrupación de Propietarios de Fincas Rústicas, the Asociación de Olivareros, the Confederación Española Patronal Agrícola, and many regional organisations. The police prepared for the meeting by closing down the Casa del Pueblo and the UGT offices and by arresting large numbers of Socialists and other leftists. The assembly was indistinguishable from any other held by the agrarian financiers of the CEDA. Its objectives – the limitation of the rights of the unions, the strengthening of the forces of authority and, more specifically, the crushing of the Generalitat's 'rebellion' – were the CEDA's. Addressed by Gil Robles, its tone could be gauged from the frequent ovations for aggressive monarchist leaders like Calvo Sotelo and Goicoechea, as well as for the Catalan Carlist Joaquín Bau.[78]

The Catalan owners' assembly was part of a campaign being orchestrated by Gil Robles to impress upon the President the Right's dissastisfaction with Samper's government and his reluctance to adopt harsher methods. Already, in mid August, Gil Robles had decided to make it clear to Samper that his cabinet was no longer to the CEDA's liking. On 5 September he warned both Samper and Salazar Alonso that at a JAP rally to be held on the 9th he would publicly announce his discontent with the government's unsatisfactory approach to public order. That he would do so had been common knowledge throughout the summer. On 21 August *El Socialista* had reported that Gil Robles intended to withdraw support from Samper and demand participation in the government himself. The site for the JAP rally was to be Covadonga in Asturias, the starting-point for the reconquest of Spain from the Moors – its selection clearly a symbol of belligerence. The rally closely resembled that of El Escorial in organisation and it had a similar purpose, that of mounting a show of strength during a government crisis.

The Asturian Alianza Obrera saw the rally as a fascist provocation by which the CEDA would force its way to power. A general strike was called, roads into the province were blocked, and railway lines were sabotaged. Salazar Alonso arranged two trains with naval personnel and Civil Guard escorts.[79] Thus the rally went on, albeit on a reduced scale. The local CEDA leader, José María Fernández Ladreda, announced threateningly that 'the masses of Acción Popular, irrespective of who stands in the way, will conquer power to begin the reconquest of Spain'. Gil Robles also spoke in warlike terms of the need to deal with the 'separatist rebellion' of the Catalans and the Basque Nationalists, with whom government mishandling had also caused a conflict. The supreme *jefe* of the JAP worked himself up to a frenzy of patriotic rhetoric and demanded that nationalist sentiment be exalted 'with ecstasy, with paroxysms, with anything; I prefer a nation of lunatics to a nation of wretches'. He went on to comment that the CEDA was advancing to power with giant steps.[80]

There was more than a small element of provocation of the Left involved in what was happening. Gil Robles was aware that the Left considered him a fascist. He was also aware that it intended to prevent the CEDA coming to power, something it regarded as synonymous with the establishment of fascism. He was confident that the Left was not in a position to succeed in a revolutionary attempt. Constant police activity had revealed the most desultory preparations for a rising. Arms purchases by the Left had been few and the authorities seem to have been well-informed of them. The most celebrated purchase, by Prieto, imported on the ship *Turquesa*, fell partly into the hands of the police. The remainder was not substantial. The Sunday excursions of the young Socialists to practice military manoeuvres, armed with more enthusiasm than weapons, daunted no one. Indeed, Salazar Alonso had virtually no difficulty in banning these activities.[81] Nevertheless, the Left intended to stop the CEDA coming to power. Gil Robles wanted to enter the government as much because as in spite of the fact that it would have serious consequences. 'Sooner or later', he wrote later, 'we would have to face a revolutionary coup. It would always be preferable to face it from a position of power before the enemy were better prepared.' Lerroux was also aware of this argument, since Salazar Alonso had been broadcasting it in a more blatant form for some time. If the entry of the CEDA into the government was the necessary pretext which would provoke a revolutionary bid from the Left and justify a definite blow against it, then the CEDA must be invited into the government. 'The problem', said Salazar Alonso, 'was no less than that of starting the counter-revolutionary offensive to proceed with a work of decisive government to put an end to the evil.'[82]

Gil Robles admitted even at the time that he shared these provocative intentions. He knew that the Left intended to react violently to what it saw as an attempt to establish a Dollfuss-type regime. He was equally aware that its chances of success were remote. Speaking in the Acción Popular offices in December he said,

I was sure that our arrival in the government would immediately provoke a revolutionary movement . . . and when I considered that blood which was going to be shed, I asked myself this question : 'I can give Spain three months of apparent tranquillity if I do not enter the government. If we enter, will the revolution break out? Better that it do so before it is well prepared, before it defeats us.' This is what Acción Popular did, it precipitated the movement, met it and implacably smashed it from within the government.[83]

The Covadonga meeting suggested that the CEDA was now ready to flex its muscles.

The time was as propitious as it would ever be. According to one informed source, 'previous informal contacts with senior military elements appeared to cover any possibility of revolutionary victory; without explicit pacts, the CEDA felt able to count on the army in case of necessity . . . it was more convenient for the Right that the Left annihilate itself in an autumn offensive.'[84] There was a tremendous air of crisis throughout September. Many on the Left, and not just the Socialists, felt that something had to be done to stop further erosion of the Republic. On 30 September, Martínez Barrio closed the congress of Unión Republicana – the party he had formed with liberal elements from the Radicals – with a speech about the 'disfigured Republic'; 'the regime in Spain is still, legally speaking, a republican one; but in reality, if we are to judge by the political and administrative physiognomy of the towns of Spain, it is no longer a republican regime but a monarchical and dictatorial one'. The Left expected the crisis to be resolved by the calling of elections and the Socialists began to step up their revolutionary rhetoric as part of their attempt to convince Alcalá Zamora of the dangers of letting the CEDA enter the government.[85]

On 26 September the CEDA opened the crisis by announcing that it could no longer support a minority government. In view of the present government's 'weakness' regarding social problems, ran its communiqué, and irrespective of the consequences, a strong government with CEDA participation had to be formed. The resignation of Samper was precipitated, as foreseen, on 1 October. Samper announced to the Cortes that a solution to the Catalan problem was near. Gil Robles responded with an attack on the government's lack of decision and a call for a government which reflected the numerical composition of the chamber. The demand was backed by an unmistakable threat : 'we are conscious of our strength both here and elsewhere'. Alcalá Zamora held the normal consultations on the resolution of the crisis. Moderate republicans, such as Martínez Barrio and Sánchez Román, advised him not to allow the entry of the CEDA into the government. The Socialists consulted, Julián Besteiro and Fernando de los Ríos, counselled the dissolution of the Cortes and the calling of elections. It was a difficult decision. The CEDA was the largest party in the Cortes, but, as Besteiro pointed out, its programme was clearly in opposition to both the spirit and the letter of the Constitution. Gil Robles's determination to establish a corporative state made his party's inclusion in the government a threat to the regime. Alcalá was told that because of the Right's power of electoral pressure, the CEDA's numerical strength in the Cortes was a considerable exaggeration of its popular numerical support. There was, then, a case to be made for a dissolution and elections. The President, however, decided to entrust Lerroux with the task of forming a cabinet, with CEDA participation, hoping that this would be limited to one ministry. Gil Robles insisted on three, despite efforts to persuade him that this was being deliberately provocative. He claimed that the dignity of his party and the need to counteract the 'congenital debility' of the Radicals made three the minimum number acceptable.[86]

The provocation did not end there. The cabinet was announced on 4 October and contained three *Cedistas*, José Oriol Anguera de Sojo (Work), Rafael Aizpún (Justice) and Manuel Giménez Fernández (Agriculture). Anguera de Sojo was a deliberately provocative choice.[87] On the one hand, he had been the public prosecutor responsible for a hundred confiscations and numerous fines suffered by *El Socialista*. Equally, as an extreme ultraist member of the Instituto Agricola Catalan de San Isidro, he was a bitter enemy of the Esquerra, the Catalan republican party ruling in the Generalitat. The choice was consciously offensive, since the Esquerra sent a deputation to see Alcalá

Zamora and plead for his exclusion. Gil Robles refused point-blank the suggestions of the President. Aizpún, CEDA deputy for Pamplona, was anything but a convinced republican, and made no secret of his strong traditionalist convictions. Giménez Fernández was, as it happened, to turn out to be one of the more moderate *Cedistas*. This, however, was an unknown factor and could do nothing to mitigate the Left's unease at the prospect of a CEDA Minister of Agriculture. The harsh policies favoured by the CEDA's landowning supporters were well known and it was felt that a CEDA Minister could only intensify the awful repression that had followed the harvest strike. Moreover, Giménez Fernández, as deputy for Badajoz, would inevitably be assumed to be as faithful a representative of the aggressive·landlords of that province as Salazar Alonso had been. The suppositions about the Minister were wrong; those about the Badajoz landlords right. Because of his relatively liberal policies, he was not accepted as a candidate for Badajoz in the 1936 elections and was forced to run in Segovia.

In the light of the policies followed when the CEDA was not in the government, the Socialists were convinced that the new cabinet would consolidate the trend towards authoritarian and reactionary rule. On 1 August the National Committee of the UGT had issued a detailed denunciation of the political situation which had developed since the Radicals had been in power. It pointed out that 222 of the 315 days of Radical government had seen the country submitted to an official state of alarm, which meant the suspension of constitutional guarantees, and that sixty of the ninety-three days on which there was constitutional normality were during the electoral period of late 1933. Press censorship, fines and seizures of newspapers, limitation of the right of reunion and association, declaration of the illegality of almost all strikes, protection for fascist and monarchist activities, reduction of wages and the removal of freely elected Socialist *ayuntamientos* amounted, for the UGT, to the establishment of a 'regime of white terror'. Yet Gil Robles had denounced these policies as weakness and clearly intended to impose more repressive ones. In late September, while there remained a slight hope of persuading the President to resolve the crisis by calling elections, the Socialist press resorted to desperate threats. Talking as if the revolution was highly prepared, *El Socialista* announced that only loose ends remained to be tied up for the workers' army to be mobilised. 'Next month', it cried, 'could be our October.' It is inconceivable that Zugazagoitia, the director of the PSOE paper, was unaware of the fact that the Socialist movement was anything but ready for a revolutionary confrontation with the state. If his paper's line was not senseless irresponsibility – and Julián Zugazagoitia, a faithful supporter of Prieto, was not an extremist – it can be seen only as a last-ditch threat to the President.[88]

Three days before the new government was announced, De los Ríos issued a last appeal for a change of direction of Republican politics. He pointed out that, at a time when an increasing number of the workers and the middle classes were turning to the Socialist movement, the persecution of its organisations, the imprisonment of its members, the closure of its societies and the removal of its town councils were part of a deliberate strategy to force it into illegality. Alleging that the entry of the CEDA into the government would lead to policies which it had been the purpose of the Republic to avoid, he called on the President to bring the Socialists into the government as a prelude to new elections.[89] These were hardly revolutionary objectives. Far from making the final preparations for the seizure of power, Largo Caballero's revolutionary committee spent the next three days 'anxiously awaiting' news of the composition of the cabinet in Prieto's apartment. Largo himself was convinced that Alcalá Zamora would never hand over power to the CEDA. At 11 p.m. on 3 October, two Socialist journalists, Carlos de Baraibar and José María Aguirre, turned up with the news that a government had been formed with CEDA participation. Although the news was still unofficial several members of the revolutionary committee declared that the time had come to start the movement. Largo, however, stated flatly that 'until I see it in the *Gaceta* [the government bulletin], I won't believe it'. Only the arrival of some soldiers shortly after announcing that the new cabinet had already declared martial law convinced him. Even then, it seems to have been with reluctance that the Socialists prepared for action. However, they felt that they had no choice. 'The die was cast', wrote Largo.[90]

The response of all of Spain's republican forces to the new cabinet was, with the obvious exception of the Radicals, unanimous. They all declared that the entry of the CEDA into the government was a direct assault on the essence of the Republic. The Socialists were not alone in their estimate of the CEDA. Azaña's Izquierda Republicana declared that 'the monstrous fact of handing over the government of the Republic to its enemies is treason' and broke with the institutions of the regime. A similar note from Martínez Barrio's Unión Republicana referred to the falsification of the Republic. One of the most significant notes came from Miguel Maura's Partido Republicano Conservador, which was anything but left-wing and had even entered electoral coalitions with the CEDA in the 1933 elections. It stated that the policy of 'surrendering the Republic to its declared and secret enemies was engendering civil war'. The CEDA's public hostility to the essential postulates to which the regime was committed provoked Maura to declare his 'incompatibility with this disfigured Republic'. It is impossible to exaggerate the importance of this moment. Although political differences were to intensify between October 1934 and the outbreak of the Civil War, the basic polarisation of forces would now go no further. Those parties which opposed the entry of the CEDA into the government were those which resisted the military rising of 1936, and *vice versa*.[91] The division in 1934, as it was to be in 1936, was between those who wanted the Republic to reform the repressive socio-economic structures of the old regime and those who defended those structures.

The determination to defend the concept of the Republic developed between 1931 and 1933 was the motive force behind the events of October 1934. The immediate results of the entry of the CEDA into the cabinet were the existence for ten hours of an independent Catalan Republic; a desultory general strike in Madrid; and the establishment of a workers' commune in Asturias. With the exception of the Asturian revolt, which held out during two weeks of fierce fighting and owed its 'success' to the mountainous terrain and the special skills of the miners, the keynote of the Spanish October was its half heartedness. There is nothing about the events of that month, including those in Asturias, to suggest that the Left had prepared a thorough and well-planned rising.[92] In fact, throughout the crisis, Socialist leaders were to be found restraining the revolutionary zeal of their followers. The movement was essentially defensive. The ideal bases for revolutionary local workers' councils had, in most of Spain, been prevented by the caution of the UGT delegates from developing into potential soviets.

After the beginning of the October events, the Socialists actually rejected the participation of anarchist and Trotskyist groups who offered to help make a revolutionary coup in Madrid. The few arms which they had were not distributed. In Madrid, on 4 October, the UGT leadership gave the government twenty-four hours notice of a pacific general strike, presumably to give the President time to consider changing his mind. In the event, this compromise gesture enabled the government to arrest workers' leaders and take precautions against possible insubordination within the police and the army. Those Socialists not arrested either went into hiding, as did Largo Caballero, or fled into exile, as did Prieto. The masses were left to dissipate their enthusiasm standing on street corners awaiting instructions.[93]

Asturias was a different matter. Yet it is significant that, even in Asturias, the revolutionary movement did not start in the stronghold of the party bureaucracy, at Oviedo, but was imposed upon it by outlying areas – Mieres, Sama de Langreo and Pola de Lena. Throughout the insurrection, the president of the SMA, Amador Fernández, was in Madrid, and on 14 October, without the knowledge of the rank-and-file, he was trying to negotiate a peaceful surrender.[94] Left-wing critics of the PSOE have pointed out that the revolution was strongest where the party bureaucracy was weakest : thus, in the Basque country, for instance, the workers seized power in small towns like

Eibar and Mondragón, but Bilbao, the capital, was relatively quiet.[95] There can be little doubt that it was spontaneous rank-and-file militancy which impelled the local PSOE leaders to proceed with the revolutionary movement. They knew that without the solidarity of the rest of Spain it was condemned to defeat, but, unlike the Madrid leadership, they stayed with their followers. Teodomiro Menéndez, Prieto's lieutenant, opposed the movement as suicidal but stayed in Oviedo, being captured and horribly tortured by the government forces. The miners fought mainly with dynamite, since they had little ammunition for the arms that they captured. They organised transport, hospital facilities, food distribution and even telephones within days. Subject to heavy artillery attacks and bombing raids, they fought on with indomitable courage, thinking it was better to die for the ideal of a workers' republic than down a mine.[96] When four military columns converged on Oviedo, the revolutionary committee decided that the movement had been defeated and fled. Yet the miners decided to fight on. Knowing it was hopeless, the local committee of Mieres, under Manuel Grossi of the Bloc Obrer i Camperol, and the Sama committee, under Belarmino Tomás of the SMA, remained with their men in the hope of negotiating a more favourable surrender.[97]

The defeat of the Asturian commune was inevitable once it became clear that Madrid and Barcelona had not risen. In Catalonia, many of the local Alianza Obrera committees did, in fact, take over their villages. They then waited for instructions from Barcelona, which never came.[98] The initiative in Catalonia remained with the bourgeois politicians of the Esquerra. The anarchists took little part in the revolt. On the one hand, the CNT was opposed to the Alianza Obrera; and, on the other, the anarchists bitterly resented the way in which the Generalitat had followed a repressive policy against them in the previous months. This had been the work of the Generalitat's counsellor for public order, Josep Dencàs, leader of the quasi-fascist, ultra-nationalist party Estat Català. Since the Catalan President, Lluís Companys, had 3500 Assault Guards and as many armed Escamots (the Estat Català militia), the Catalan Alianza Obrera decided that the initiative lay with the Generalitat. Accordingly, Companys declared Catalan independence on 6 October in a heroic gesture to meet popular demand for action against the central government and at the same time forestall revolution. Joan Lluhí, a member of the Catalan cabinet, informed Azaña that the Generalitat intended to use its declaration as a bargaining counter in the agrarian dispute with Madrid.[99] A swift and anticipated surrender followed. Although the Generalitat had far more armed men than the 500 mustered by the Barcelona army garrison, Dencàs refused to mobilise them. Since the working class had also been denied arms, the army was able to trundle artillery through the narrow streets and the Generalitat surrendered in the early hours of the 7th.[100]

The lack of resolution shown by the leaders of the Left was in marked contrast to the behaviour of Gil Robles. Indeed, there was little about his policy, both during and immediately after the October revolt, to dispel the suspicion of deliberate provocation. If the Socialists looked for a compromise on 5 October, they found no spirit of conciliation from the new Radical–CEDA government, but rather that same determination to crush their movement which was the favourite theme of CEDA propaganda. Gil Robles told Lerroux that the Chief of the General Staff, General Masquelet, a known republican, did not inspire his confidence. At his insistence, the repression of the Asturian rising was entrusted to Generals Franco and Goded, both of whom were hostile to the Republic. With CEDA approval, Franco insisted on the use of troops from Africa. It is difficult to exaggerate the significance of this. The nationalist values on which the Right claimed to stand rested on the central symbol of the struggle to reconquer Spain from the Moors. Now they shipped Moorish mercenaries to Asturias, the only part of Spain never dominated by the Crescent, to fight against Spanish workers.[101]

The CEDA insisted on the most severe policy possible against the rebels. On 9 October, Gil Robles rose in the Cortes to express support for the government and to suggest that parliament be closed until the repression was over. Thus, the annihilation of the revolution, which was particularly savage, took place in silence. No questions could be asked in parliament and press censorship was total, although the right-wing press was full of gruesome tales – never substantiated – of leftist barbarism. Of even more interest to the CEDA than the military action were the round-ups all over Spain of workers' leaders. Prisons were full in areas where there had been no revolutionary movement, but where landowners had had problems with their *braceros*. Casas del Pueblo were closed down in towns and villages in every part of the country. Socialist *ayuntamientos* were removed. The Socialist press was banned. In the same session of 9 October, the CEDA voted an increase in the forces of order and the re-establishment of the death penalty.[102]

Apologists for Gil Robles have claimed that his failure to seize power following the successful repression illustrates the basic respect he entertained for the parliamentary system.[103] The Socialists, on the other hand, argued that the relative success of the Asturian rising gave him no choice. Four army columns with artillery and air support were held back by poorly armed miners and were defeated by them on two occasions. The difficulty of pacifying one region did not augur well for an attempt to take over the entire country. On the admission of the Minister of War, if there had been risings elsewhere, the army would have been unable to cope. The army had shown itself sufficiently republican in spirit for African mercenaries to be necessary. At least one senior officer is reported to have ordered his men not to fire on their proletarian brothers.[104] 1934 had been a year in which the PSOE and CEDA leadership had engaged in a war of manoeuvre. Gil Robles had had the stronger position and he had exploited it with skill and patience. The Socialists were forced by their relative weakness to resort to threats of revolution, and even this they did badly. In the event, and although the fact was hardly apparent during the repression of October, it was the militancy of their own rank-and-file that saved the Socialists from the CEDA's inexorable progress to the authoritarian state.

5 Socialism Under Stress: Repression, Radicalisation and the Popular Front

In the widest perspective, the Spanish Left did not view the Asturian rising of 1934 as a defeat. The conviction that Gil Robles had intended to establish fascism in Spain coloured all later leftist judgements of the revolutionary movement. The overall balance, it was felt, had been positive in that Gil Robles had been shown that the peaceful establishment of fascism would not be permitted by the working class. For many on the Left, the words with which Belarmino Tomás had explained the need for surrender to the Asturian miners became symbolic. The surrender was merely 'a halt on the road'.[1] This attitude was adopted by the Trotskyists, the orthodox Communist Party (the PCE) and the FJS. Indeed, the PCE publicly claimed responsibility for Asturias and gained considerable kudos among the proletariat for doing so. The claim was largely false. The Communists had joined the Alianza Obrera in Asturias only at the last minute, deciding to do so on 11 September and actually securing entry into the revolutionary committee on 4 October. Nevertheless, with the PSOE reluctant to accept responsibility, the PCE's network of clandestine press had some success with its claim.[2]

The Socialist movement was, in fact, badly scarred by the events of October. The insurrection may have been an 'objective victory', but it remained an immediate defeat. Most prominent Socialists were either in prison or else in exile in France or Russia. In Asturias a desultory guerrilla struggle carried on until early 1935, but in the rest of Spain the movement was cowed.[3] Police vigilance was stepped up. Torture was used in interrogations. Socialist *ayuntamientos* were replaced by government nominees. The *Casas del Pueblo* were closed. The unions, if not formally dismantled, were unable to carry on their syndical functions. Except for the president, Anastasio de Gracia, and Manuel Lois, the entire UGT executive was in jail. The clandestine life of the UGT was, in fact, directed from prison. The Socialist press was also silenced.[4]

Largo Caballero told the military judge investigating his case that he had taken no part in the organisation of the rising. That was a completely plausible claim in the light of the total failure of the movement in Madrid. Nevertheless, it played directly into the hands of the Communists, who were only too glad to assume the responsibility. José Díaz, the PCE Secretary General, visited Largo Caballero in prison and suggested that the PCE and the PSOE jointly claim to have organised the revolution. Largo refused. It was later claimed that the Socialist leader had denied his participation to prevent an admission of guilt being used by the CEDA to justify carrying through its determination to smash both the PSOE and the UGT.[5]

It may well have been the case that to admit responsibility would have been a futile romantic gesture and would simply have played into the hands of bourgeois justice. However, in the political context of 1935, it was a potentially counter-productive tactic for the Caballerist wing of the Socialist movement. In the first place, it gave credibility to the Communist allegation that the events of October showed that the PSOE was not a revolutionary party and that Largo Caballero was incapable of leading a revolution. Moreover, the denial of participation greatly strengthened the Prieto wing of the party. The only parts of Spain where there had been effective action by the workers in October 1934 – that is to say Asturias and part of Vizcaya – were those where the Socialist movement was dominated by followers of Prieto. This influence was clearly not the only one which dictated the course of events, and indeed, the Prietist leaders had at first been reluctant to proceed to an insurrection. However, once the rank-and-file had shown its determination, Ramón González Peña, Belarmino Tomás and the other SMA leaders had stuck by their men. This contrasted starkly with the pathetic showing made in Madrid by Largo Caballero and the Socialist Youth. There, once it was clear that revolutionary threats had not diverted Alcalá Zamora from bringing the CEDA into the cabinet, the Socialist leaders went to ground. No arms were distributed and the masses were left without instructions. No serious plans for a rising had been made, and the Alianza Obrera had been prevented from forming an armed militia. Amaro del Rosal, one of the more extremist young Socialists and one of the supposed leaders of the projected revolution, denied participation. In a sense, he was telling the truth. When Manuel Fernández Grandizo of the Izquierda Comunista asked Del Rosal on 5 October what the plans of the revolutionary committee were, the Socialist leader is reported to have replied, 'if the masses want arms, they can go and look for them and they can do what they like'.[6] The events of October 1934 were to become the central myth of the Socialist movement and the behaviour of the Caballerists was effectively handing the monopoly of that myth to Prieto.

The reformist faction which followed Besteiro had increasingly less influence within the Socialist movement. At a time when the vindictive policies of the CEDA–Radical coalition were provoking rank-and-file militancy, the Besteirists' known hostility to revolutionary tactics tended to leave them isolated. An indication of the distance separating the right and left wings of the Socialist movement was provided when, during the October events, a group of extremists from the FJS attacked Besteiro's home. Understandably saddened by this, in early 1935 the professor virtually withdrew from the political stage for a time.[7] In fact, renewed attacks on Besteiro's revisionist position and calls for his expulsion from the party finally provoked his followers to take up his defence against the youthful bolshevisers. That was not to be until June 1935, and in the immediate aftermath of the insurrection the crucial division among the Socialists was between Largo Caballero and Prieto.

Although both had adopted a more or less revolutionary stance after the electoral defeat of 1933, it is far from paradoxical that 1935 should have found them locked in a struggle for the legacy of the October rising. Ever since the disastrous general strike of 1917, the various factions of the Socialist movement had usually reverted to certain basic patterns of behaviour at moments of crisis. Besteiro's long-term orthodox Marxist projections consistently resulted in his advocating that the working class abstain from bourgeois politics. Prieto and Largo Caballero had always been more pragmatic, albeit in different ways. Prieto valued democracy as an end in itself and favoured a gradual road to socialism in Spain, given the objective strength of the bourgeoisie. Largo had a much narrower view, favouring always whatever seemed most advantageous to the trades-union movement. Concrete benefits for the UGT had led him to collaborate with Primo de Rivera and a drift of militants away from the union had impelled him to join Prieto in the republican camp. While social advances were possible, there was no more fervent advocate of the Republic than Largo Caballero. Only when the total opposition of the Right began to make reform impossible did Largo's attitude change. He started to adopt a revolutionary stance for two reasons. To begin with, he had hoped to frighten the Right into a more pliant attitude. Then he had discovered that his new line found a sympathetic echo among the masses. Rather than risk losing their support to the CNT or the Communists, he gave them what they wanted to hear. Thus in 1934 he came to coincide with Prieto, who was advocating revolution because he believed that the Republic was threatened by an attempt at dictatorship by Gil Robles.

After the Asturian rising, with the more far-reaching rightist ambitions momentarily checked, Prieto hoped to rebuild the Republic along the lines set down between 1931 and 1933. Largo Caballero, however, for all his vacillations in October, began to manifest an increased commitment to a revolutionary position, in rhetorical terms at least. There were several reasons for this, not least of which was an acute personal resentment of Prieto.[8] Largo is also reputed to have read for the first time many basic Marxist–Leninist texts during his sojourn in prison. If he was influenced by his reading, he was equally impressed by the fact that the aggressive policies being carried out by the Radical–CEDA cabinet had seriously undermined working-class faith in the reforming possibilities of the Republic.

The first initiatives in the struggle within the Socialist movement came from Prieto. He made no secret of his conviction that the immediate goal for the Left had to be a broad coalition to ensure future electoral success. His tentative views on the subject had been confirmed in mid January by Azaña, with whom he had been in correspondence since late November. The notion was already being favourably examined by those members of the executive committee of the PSOE who were not in prison. On 20 March one of them, Juan Simeón Vidarte, wrote to Prieto inviting him to submit his ideas on the subject to the committee.[9] This he did on 23 March. He placed much emphasis on the need for a wide alliance with forces both to the right and to the left of the Socialist movement. Not unnaturally, in the light of the Asturian experience, several militants were enthusiastic about the idea of an entirely proletarian block. Prieto, however, pointed out that it would be difficult to arrive at an agreement with both anarchists and Communists. He also showed that not to include the republicans would result in three-sided contests, which would inevitably involve the loss of parliamentary seats. With the possible exception of anarchist electoral participation as opposed to abstention, the failure to ally with the left republicans would lead to the next elections' being fought in identical conditions to those of 1933. Prieto's letter also revealed a determination not to let the party fall into the hands of the extremist youth, which he discreetly hinted would lead to a non-Socialist, and presumably Communist, preponderance. The Federación de Juventudes Socialistas, he said, would have to be disciplined. Prieto was clearly disturbed by the effect that the Communists' attempt to claim a revolutionary monopoly was having on the youth movement. Instead of following its negative rejection of the Republic Prieto proposed the recovery of the Republic by means of an electoral coalition bound by the ten-point reforming programme which he had elaborated in January 1934 and by an undertaking to introduce an amnesty for political prisoners.[10]

This was a realistic proposition based on an awareness of the strength and ruthlessness of the landed and industrial oligarchies. Its weakness lay in the fact that it had been precisely those mild reformist policies of the first *bienio* which had provoked the belligerence of the Right. Yet, even if that suggested that Spain's structural problems required a revolutionary solution, it did not invalidate Prieto's basic point. Most of the Socialists' problems derived from the tactical error of 1933. Out of the government, they could introduce no change, reformist or revolutionary. October may have served as a defensive movement to check the CEDA's dictatorial ambitions, but it had revealed the Socialists' incapacity to organise a revolution. In the objective circumstances, there were two valid positions open to the Left : the one suggested by Prieto, the return to power and the gradualist road to socialism; and the one advocated by the Trotskyists, which recognised the revolutionary incompetence of both the PSOE and the PCE and aimed at the long-term construction of a genuine bolshevik party. Both of these analyses coincided in the need for a prior electoral victory.[11] Although contradictory, they were both coherent policies and more realistic than the FJS's utopian revolutionism.

Prieto's 23 March letter was duplicated and distributed throughout the Socialist movement. It met a sympathetic response from moderate militants and infuriated the left wing of the party, which began to prepare replies. In the meanwhile, Prieto's follower Vidarte, who in the absence of other leaders, was virtually running the party, issued an important party circular on 30 March.[12] Taking up the theme of Prieto's letter, the circular set out to show how the Republic had signified considerable progress over the monarchy. It also argued that the October rising had been a popular attempt to defend the legislation of the Republic, threatened by the oligarchy. The Socialist Party, said Vidarte, was not 'demagogic, nor rabble-rousing, nor terrorist, nor adventurist'. Since the Right would certainly go into the next elections united, the executive committee of the PSOE recommended that local Socialist organisations maintain good relations with republican and other leftist groups. The circular was an intelligent plea for the use of legal possibilities to defend the Socialists movement and the working class.

Much as it infuriated the Socialist Left, Prieto's line delighted republicans of Left and Centre. Virulent and clumsy attacks by Gil Robles and Lerroux on Azaña had, by March 1935, impelled the non-government republican forces to think about their future survival. By the end of the month, Azaña's Izquierda Republicana, Martínez Barrio's Unión Republicana and the conservative Partido Nacional Republicano of Felipe Sánchez Román had arrived at an agreement. On 12 April, the fourth anniversary of the fall of the monarchy, they issued a joint declaration of the minimum conditions that they regarded as essential for the reconstruction of political coexistence in Spain. The seven conditions were : the prevention of torture of political prisoners; the re-establishment of Constitutional guarantees, especially those concerning personal liberties; the release of prisoners arrested during the events of October; an end to discrimination against liberal and leftist state employees; the readmission to their jobs of workers sacked because of the October 1934 strike; the legal existence of trade unions; and the reinstatement of the freely elected town councils which had been overthrown by the government.[13] This programme was not so ambitious as Prieto's January 1934 plan, but it was none the less acceptable to the Socialist moderates.

Already, on 31 March, Prieto had received a letter from Ramón González Peña, the national hero of October, endorsing his position. Peña condemned the 'infantile' attitude of the FJS and called for a wide anti-fascist front for the next elections.[14] Copies of the letter were circulated throughout the Socialist Party, much to the chagrin of the Caballerists. Confident that he enjoyed the backing of the prestigious Asturian section of the movement, as well as that of the Basque country and of the moderates currently running the PSOE executive, Prieto made public his basic agreement with the manifesto of the Azaña–Sánchez Román–Martínez Barrio alliance. On 14 April both Sánchez Román and Prieto published in Prieto's Bilbao newspaper, *El Liberal*, articles on the need for a wide coalition. Above all, Prieto condemned the suicidal tactic that had been adopted in 1933, when, despite the fact that the electoral law had been specifically designed to derive maximum benefit from Socialist–republican co-operation, the Socialists had gone alone into the elections. In the light of what Gil Robles had done with his exiguous victory, there could be little doubt that another leftist defeat would be the end of democracy in Spain. Even if an electoral union were achieved, victory was far from assured, wrote Prieto, given the Right's massive propaganda apparatus and the fact that the unemployment crisis made it easy for the votes of the hungry to be bought. Quoting from his letter to the PSOE executive, Prieto made an appeal for realism and a wide alliance for the defence of the Republic and the Socialist movement and for the release of thousands of political prisoners.[15]

A few days after Prieto's article, the radical youth launched a major counter-attack. This took the form of a long pamphlet, signed by the FJS president, Carlos Hernández Zancajo, entitled *Octubre–segunda etapa*. In fact, it had been written, in prison, by Hernández, Santiago Carrillo and Amaro del Rosal.[16] The publication had three main objectives : to cover up the fiasco of the FJS's participation in the October events in Madrid, to combat Prieto's interpretation of the Asturian rising as an attempt to defend the Republic, and to eradicate the influence of both Besteiro and Prieto from the Socialist movement as a prelude to its 'bolshevisation'. The first part of the pamphlet consisted of a largely mendacious interpretation of the activities of the Socialists during 1934. It was alleged that strikes like those of the printers, the construction and metalworkers and the peasants had dissipated working-class energies. This was true, but what the pamphlet failed to mention was that the 'union organisation' blamed for these tactical errors was dominated at the time by members of the FJS. The responsibility for the immediate defeat of October was placed firmly on Besteiro's reformists. This was used to justify the 'second stage' announced in the pamphlet's title, the expulsion of the reformists and the 'bolshevisation' of the PSOE. Such a process would involve the adoption of a rigidly centralised command structure and the creation of an illegal apparatus to prepare for an armed insurrection. This never took place, partly because the strength of Prieto's and Besteiro's support prevented it and more so because its advocates had joined the Communist Party before they were in a position to try. Conscious of Asturian backing for Prieto, the FJS did not dare call for his expulsion but did demand the abandonment of his 'centrist' line in favour of a revolutionary one.[17]

Octubre–segunda etapa was not nearly so central to the great Socialist debate of 1935 as has been claimed.[18] Largo Caballero, despite being the subject of rapturous praise in the pamphlet, claimed to have been annoyed by its publication, which had been arranged without his permission, and protested to Santiago Carrillo, then secretary-general of the FJS. Carrillo himself admitted that the youth acted in total independence of the PSOE.[19] Few references were made to the pamphlet during the debate, except to admonish the youth for their temerity in daring to dictate to their elders and, above all, in trying to silence inner-party democracy. Within days of the pamphlet's publication, Manuel Cordero, who had lined up with Prieto, publicly disowned the ideas contained in it. In an interview widely publicised in the republican press, Cordero reaffirmed the PSOE's commitment to democracy. He also stated that there was room in the party for all kinds of doctrinal tendencies and for constant ideological revision and debate, a clear rejection of the kind of narrow exclusivism advocated by the bolshevisers.[20]

Prieto's advocacy of an understanding with the republicans, and the continued Caballerist commitment to revolutionism seemed to be the two main poles of Socialist thought in the spring of 1935. However, at much the same time as the pamphlet on October was being published by the FJS, Besteiro was emerging from his silence. His group had opposed the rising, but they had since tried to help the imprisoned Socialists. Nevertheless, they had been the object of insulting attacks from the FJS's clandestine news-sheet, *UHP*, and the call for their purging from the party was growing more strident.[21] It was largely in reaction to the youth movement's demands for their expulsion that the Besteirists were impelled to found a publication to defend their ideas. Called *Democracia*, it appeared weekly from 15 June to 13 December. Given its moderate line and the fact that it was largely concerned with internal PSOE matters, the Minister of the Interior, Manuel Portela Valladares, permitted its appearance. This was taken by the 'bolshevisers' as proof of the Besteirist treachery to the Socialist cause.[22]

Six weeks before *Democracia*, Besteiro himself had entered the fray. On 28 April he had made his inaugural speech as a member of the Academy of Political and Moral Sciences, taking as his subject 'Marxism and anti-Marxism'. Unfortunately for him, he had been elected to the Academy as the replacement for Gabino Bugallal, one-time head of the old monarchist Conservative Party, who had been renowned for the severity he had brought to bear against the Socialists after 1917. Protocol demanded that Besteiro make a formal eulogy of his predecessor. That eulogy, together with the content of his discourse on Marxism, earned him intensified hostility from the PSOE leftists. That was hardly surprising, since his speech constituted an almost direct critique of the 'bolshevisers'. Besteiro set out to prove that Marxism justified democratic socialism and that Marx had been hostile to the notion of the dictatorship of the proletariat. Although Besteiro was reputed to be the PSOE's most sophisticated theorist, his Marxism did not go much beyond the position of Kautsky. He rejected the thought of Lenin and Trotsky with peremptory haste and his analysis of the phenomenon of fascism was extremely slight. His insinuations that the violence of the Socialist Left was hardly distinguishable from fascism did not endear him to the Caballerists.[23]

A reply was undertaken by Largo's most competent theoretical adviser, Luis Araquistain, in the doctrinal journal *Leviatán*, which had survived the repression of the Socialist media. In a series of three long articles, Araquistain demolished Besteiro's arguments with energetic sarcasm. Besteiro had defended Socialists who had become bourgeois politicians – such as Millerand, Briand, Ramsey MacDonald, Philip Snowden and even Mussolini. This formed part of his gradualist theory of socialism, whereby bourgeois society was 'impregnated'. A successful example of the impregnation of bourgeois society by socialist ideas was Roosevelt's New Deal. Araquistain pointed out that this was Fabianism and that there was little valid Marxism in Besteiro's thought. The fact that Besteiro seemed unaware of the close relationship between bourgeois capitalism and fascism proved to Araquistain that the professor's Marxism was of the flimsiest kind. Largo's adviser reasserted the revolutionary nature of Marxism and the temporary need for the dictatorship of the proletariat, while he rejected the 'pseudo-Marxism' of Bernstein and Kautsky, with whom he associated Besteiro.[24] The two articles written in reply by Besteiro protested at the vehemence of Araquistain's tone, but they did not seriously contest the issues raised in *Leviatán*.[25]

Araquistain's articles were of a notably higher level of theoretical competence than the inflammatory tract produced by the FJS in April. To a great extent, Araquistain's victory confirmed Besteiro's withdrawal from the leadership stakes within the PSOE. Despite the continued existence of *Democracia*, Besteiro was no longer a serious contender for the direction of Spanish socialism. He did not re-emerge as a major figure until his participation in Colonel Casado's attempt to end the Civil War in March 1939, although that did not save him from a harsh death in a Francoist prison. Throughout 1935, Besteiro's lieutenants tended to align with Prieto. Oddly enough, *Leviatán*, although closely associated with the Socialist Left, never really made an all-out attack on Prieto. There were two reasons for that. On the one hand, Araquistain was a rather more responsible figure than the FJS leaders who had produced *Octubre–segunda etapa*. On the other, since the fundamental preoccupation of his journal was the analysis of fascism and the search for a valid leftist response to it, Araquistain could not ignore the basic commonsense of Prieto's appeal for unity.[26]

In fact, just as the polemic between Araquistain and Besteiro was getting under way, Prieto made a highly influential statement of his views. This took the form of five articles published in late May in *El Liberal* of Bilbao, *La Libertad* of Madrid and several other republican newspapers in the provinces. Collectively titled *Posiciones socialistas*, the articles were published shortly afterwards as a book.[27] They were concerned to reaffirm the need to avoid the great tactical error of 1933 and to answer some of the more offensive accusations of *Octubre–segunda etapa*. In the first, he rejected the FJS executive's claim that he should remain silent, and gave as his reasons that the executive had not scrupled to break Socialist ranks with its pamphlet and that there was reason to believe that, in areas like Asturias, it did not enjoy the backing of its rank-and-file. In the second article he showed how the proposed electoral alliance would be mutually beneficial to Socialists and republicans. He also rejected criticisms of the electoral law which favoured such coalitions, and in so doing made a veiled reference to the fact that Largo Caballero had been one of the most fervent advocates of the law when it was first introduced.[28] Finally, Prieto pointed out that, since the Right would be united at the next elections and a workers' coalition would be the victim of anarchist indiscipline, there was no other method of guaranteeing an amnesty for political prisoners. The last three articles set about, in mild yet firm language, to expose some of the more absurd contradictions of *Octubre*. He rejected the right of untried youngsters to call for the expulsion of militants who had dedicated their lives to the PSOE. With some distaste he pointed out that the accusations made against various sections of the Socialist movement by the pamphlet were most applicable to the FJS itself. Above all, he denounced the dictatorial tendencies of the FJS and proposed a party congress to settle the direction that the movement was to take.

This was a condemnation of youthful extremism which contrasted starkly with Gil Robles' complicity with the strident ambitions of the JAP. Not surprisingly, it provoked the indignation of the PSOE Left. *Octubre* was reissued with a reply to Prieto. However, a popular edition of the five articles was distributed in large numbers.[29] As a result, the journalist Carlos de Baraibar, one of Largo Caballero's closest collaborators, rapidly prepared, with Largo's knowledge, a book attacking the 'false socialist positions' of Prieto.[30] From a self-proclaimed position of 'the principles of pure Marxism', Baraibar denounced Prieto's arguments as 'puerile and premature'. His main objections were to the fact that Prieto had broken party discipline in publicising his ideas and had done so in the bourgeois press. This was a somewhat specious argument, since the FJS, whose position was approved by Baraibar, had equally made its views public in its clandestine press and in *Octubre*. Moreover, the papers in which Prieto had written were the most left-wing being published legally. Baraibar's points were laboured in the extreme. He opposed Prieto's advocacy of a wide electoral coalition to secure a political amnesty, and gave two reasons for his opposition. On the one hand he claimed that the CEDA would probably change the electoral law, and on the other he declared that amnesty was a short-sighted objective and that the Socialists' aim should be to destroy the system which took political prisoners.[31]

There was more theoretical consistency than practical realism in Baraibar's book. Already the Left of the PSOE had recognised, particularly in the pages of *Leviatán*, that the Republic was not synonymous with a classic bourgeois revolution. The Spanish bourgeoisie had shown by its reaction to the reforming legislation of 1931–3 that its position was anything but progressive. If the realisation of this had pushed some members of the PSOE into believing that only revolution could change Spain's regressive structures, it had convinced others, like Prieto, that the oligarchy's strength was such as to oblige the Left to seek governmental power through the medium of elections. To the Caballerists, it seemed as if Prieto was uselessly pinning his hopes on a discredited bourgeois democracy. There was much to be said for the validity of the revolutionary analysis. However, that did not undermine the accuracy of Prieto's belief in the need for state power. Moreover, even if the activities of the revolutionists in the PSOE were never to go beyond rhetorical extremism, they were still far more counter-productive than Prieto's modest objectives could ever be.

The fact that the revolutionism of the Caballerists was largely verbal could not alter the fact that, in the upper reaches of the movement at least, Spanish socialism was seriously divided. However, it is extremely difficult to estimate with any numerical accuracy how the division was reflected at rank-and-file level. The repressive policies of the CEDA–Radical government certainly intensified militancy and made the Socialist masses more open to revolutionary propaganda. On the other hand, the memory of the Asturian October, the continued existence of thousands of political prisoners, and the vindictive behaviour of the Right all ensured a sympathetic mass response to Prieto's call for unity and a return to the progressive Republic of the first *bienio*. In August, Azaña wrote to Prieto saying, 'I am sure that you have won the battle, not only in the eyes of the public, but also within the mass of your own party. This is not just my assessment but that of many people, Socialists and non-Socialists.' The polemic continued between *Democracia* and the weekly *Claridad*, which the Caballerists had managed to bring out on 13 July. Azaña believed that, since the majority of the Socialists accepted Prieto's point of view, they saw the polemic only as boring irrelevance, although they were shocked by some of the personal insults used. He had been told that in Madrid the average Socialist was just not bothering to read either of the sides in the polemic.[32] This was, of course, only Azaña's opinion, and he was committed to Prieto. Nevertheless, between May and October, he made a series of speeches to massive audiences, in favour of unity. Among the hundreds of thousands of people who came to hear Azaña call for the 'reconquest' of the Republic were many workers. In Bilbao, in particular, there were cheers for Prieto during Azaña's speech. People came from all over Spain to hear him speaking at Comillas near Madrid. Of the alleged audience of 400,000 a large proportion must have been Socialists.[33]

The Socialist masses almost certainly did not divide over the bolshevisation issue in the way that their leaders did. Mass militancy, which favoured Largo, was balanced by a desire for unity, which favoured Prieto. In any case, Prieto ignored the leftist criticisms to which he was being subjected and continued to work for unity with the republicans. Throughout the summer of 1935, Azaña, Martínez Barrio and Sánchez Román worked on a manifesto. On 27 August, Martínez Barrio announced that the document was being submitted for the approval of the PSOE and was soon to be published. Two days later, an anonymous editorialist, presumably Prieto himself, wrote in *El Liberal* that it would benefit the Right immensely if the PSOE adopted a long-term revolutionary strategy to the exclusion of immediate necessities such as an electoral agreement with the republicans. In mid-September, he met Azaña in Belgium to discuss the programme of the projected coalition.[34]

In the meanwhile, the battle between *Democracia* and *Claridad* grew more heated. Under the direction of Andrés Saborit *Democracia* advocated party unity and showed a reluctance to enter into a polemic. This did not save it from a fierce denunciation in the form of a PSOE executive committee circular signed by Largo Caballero.[35] *Claridad* accepted the FJS call for the expulsion of the Besteirists and the removal of the Prietists from positions of power within the movement. Each side regularly claimed the support of various provincial organisations, but no definite picture of the rank-and-file attitude to the polemic emerged. *Claridad* claimed to be backed by the Socialist Federations of Valencia, Salamanca and Alicante. The Agrupación Socialista de Alicante even expelled Manuel González Ramos, one of its Cortes deputies, for writing in *Democracia*. In its turn, Saborit's weekly printed declarations of support from the Socialist organisations of Asturias, Badajoz and Albacete. For what such declarations were worth, the pro-*Democracia* groups were more important by a considerable margin. Equally, *Claridad* claimed that its circulation was rising dramatically while *Democracia* was losing sales at an alarming rate.[36]

The most telling point made in the pages of *Democracia*, by an anonymous Asturian and in a letter from Amador Fernández, president of the SMA, was that the whole bolshevisation campaign was simply a manoeuvre to divert attention from the fiasco created by the FJS in Madrid in October 1934. The unknown Asturian said that the bolshevisers were in no position to call other party members traitors. Amador Fernández pointed out that, since the Caballerists had had exclusive control of the movement in Madrid, they could not throw the blame for its failure on either the reformists or the centrists of the party. He went on to accuse Baraibar in particular of an action tantamount to betraying the movement to government spies, without actually specifying whether that action had been the result of incompetence or of disloyalty.[37] The fact that *Claridad* could never find a satisfactory answer to criticisms from the proven revolutionaries of Asturias tended to lend credibility to their accusations.

In fact, given the indisputable realism of Prieto's analysis of the Left's electoral needs, it is difficult to see how *Claridad* could have maintained its opposition to his views. As it turned out, the Caballerists were saved from an awkward situation by the Communists. Already, as part of their plans for the bolshevisation of the PSOE, some of the younger revolutionaries were toying with the idea of unity with the PCE. On 2 June 1935 the PCE secretary-general, José Díaz, had made a speech in the Cine Pardiñas in Madrid calling for the creation of a 'Popular anti-fascist concentration'. Then in August, at the Seventh Congress of the Comintern, Dimitrov had launched the call for a united front of the proletariat and a wide popular front of all anti-fascist forces. Soon the Spanish Communists were openly calling for union with the PSOE.[38]

This change of tack by the PCE had a twofold effect on the left-wing of the PSOE. The FJS maximalists were delighted, but Araquistain and Largo Caballero remained suspicious. The FJS representative at the Moscow congress, José Lain Entralgo, reported back enthusiastically that the Communist union, the Confederación General de Trabajo Unitaria, would incorporate with the UGT. He also claimed that the switch of tactics implied that Moscow had now returned sovereignty to the various national parties and that there was therefore no longer any reason why the FJS should not join the Comintern.[39] Santiago Carrillo, already well on the way to becoming a Communist, was trying to arrange the incorporation of the Trotskyist Bloc Obrer i Camperol and the Communist youth into the PSOE as part of the process of bolshevising the party. Neither Largo nor Araquistain shared this enthusiasm, seeming somehow to suspect that the Communists wanted to take over the workers movement, which was, of course, Largo's own ambition. Writing in *Leviatán*, Araquistain suggested that the new Comintern policy simply served the interests of Russian foreign policy. He believed that the fundamental objective behind the Popular Front tactic was the Russians' desire to ensure that liberal and left-wing governments would be in power should war break out with Germany. Far from breaking with the old Comintern habit of dictating the same policy for each country, as the FJS fondly thought, the new tactic confirmed the dictatorial customs of the Third International. While Araquistain accepted the need for proletarian unity, he rejected the notion of alliance with the bourgeois Left.[40] Largo Caballero, while maintaining his enthusiasm for working-class unity, opposed the idea of joining the Comintern. And, like Araquistain, he was not favourable to an electoral coalition with the left republicans.[41]

There was a large degree of personal animosity in Largo's attitude. The fact that Prieto favoured alliance with the bourgeoisie was probably sufficient to guarantee Largo's hostility. He was not of a forgiving nature. Thus, having convinced himself in 1933 that the PSOE had been betrayed by the republicans, he opposed a new alliance with them. Even in that there was an element of personal resentment. One of Azaña's senior lieutenants, Claudio Sánchez Albornoz, was always conscious of Largo's enmity without ever finding out the cause.[42] Above all, anxious to maintain his far-from-warranted reputation as a revolutionary, Largo was frightened to disappoint the militancy of the working masses. On 14 November, Azaña made the PSOE a formal proposal of electoral alliance. Largo's opposition to the idea seriously disturbed the Secretariat of the Comintern. Prieto was hostile to the inclusion of the Communists in the electoral coalition. If they could not count on Largo's support, there was danger of their being left out altogether. Accordingly, in early December the Comintern dispatched Jacques Duclos to Madrid to see Largo and change his mind. A meeting was arranged by Largo's pro-Communist adviser, Julio Alvarez del Vayo. For three days Duclos used subtle arguments and flattery to break down Largo's obstinate opposition to the Popular Front. When he told him that a broad front of workers, peasants and intellectuals in France had successfully combated fascism, Largo quoted Marx and Lenin at him to prove that the working class was the only revolutionary class. Finally, the PSOE leader withdrew his opposition, convinced more by Azaña's impact at Comillas than by the cajolery of Duclos.[43]

The outstanding problem which still remained concerned the programme to be elaborated for the electoral coalition. However, before further progress could be made towards its composition, there occurred a dramatic development in the internal struggle for the control of the PSOE. On 16 December there was a meeting of the party's National Committee; this was attended secretly by Prieto, who had returned clandestinely from exile and was living in hiding. In the simplest terms, what happened at the meeting was that Prieto proposed that the PSOE executive committee take responsibility for the activities of the parliamentary minority, the proposal was approved by nine votes to five with two abstentions, and Largo Caballero, who had been one of the five, resigned as president of the party. It seemed a simple issue and not one to provoke Largo's resignation, especially as the parliamentary group's submission to the executive was one of the objectives of the bolshevisers. The reaction of the Socialist rank-and-file to the consequences of the meeting was one of stupefaction. This was understandable, since the average militant was not familiar with the background to the meeting. In fact, the origins of this clash over an apparent technicality went back to 1 October 1934.

In 1934, Largo had played a double game of verbal extremism and practical moderation or inactivity. As part of his revolutionary image-building, he had attacked Prieto, the *de facto* leader of the PSOE parliamentary minority, for allegedly pursuing an insufficiently revolutionary line. This infuriated Prieto for a variety of reasons. On the one hand, the minority's activities in the Cortes had strictly followed the agreements of the executive, and, on the other, Prieto had done more than Largo to put the PSOE's revolutionary rhetoric into practice. Moreover, Largo's performance in the Cortes had been anything but that of a revolutionary. Accordingly, at the PSOE National Committee meeting of 1 October, Prieto set about calling Largo's bluff. He proposed that the parliamentary minority be subject to the authority of the executive committee, which would then have to stand by its own orders. Largo naturally opposed the proposal, alleging that only a party congress could determine such a matter. When the voting went in favour of Prieto, he resigned. Given the tense political context in which the meeting was taking place, the members of the National Committee were disturbed by the possible consequences of the president's resignation. It was decided to scrub the entire debate from the records and Largo withdrew his resignation.[44]

When the National Committee next met, on 16 December 1935, Prieto immediately tabled the same proposition. His objective was presumably to expose Largo Caballero's tactic of masking his own reformism with the revolutionary criticisms of others, which maintained his popularity with the party youth. Contrary to his own published advocacy of the parliamentary group's submission to the executive, Largo again voted against the proposal, basing his objections on the same technicality from the party's statutes. Of the fourteen members present, nine, including Prieto and Cordero, voted against the president. The vice-president, the veteran Remigio Cabello, was one of two who abstained. Interestingly enough, Prieto's lieutenant, Juan Simeón Vidarte, voted with Caballero. That in itself is sufficient to throw doubt on Largo's contention that the whole thing had been a plot to remove him from the party leadership. In fact, when he resigned, Vidarte tried hard to dissuade him.[45]

Largo Caballero's reasons for resigning illustrated the differences between the two groups. He told Vidarte that the executive should always be unanimous, as the 'homogeneous organ of an iron leadership'. This was entirely consistent with his new bolshevising advocacy of a centralised party hierarchy. There was also an element of personal disgust at Prieto's manoeuvre. The moderates, however, being concerned with party unity, were not out to secure the expulsion of their opponents, but rather to make them see reason. This became very apparent in the immediate aftermath of the president's resignation. The National Committee requested that, in view of the reappearance of *El Socialista* on 18 December, both *Claridad* and *Democracia* should cease publication. Saborit complied, but the Caballerists ignored the call. They began a ferocious campaign against the Prietist leadership of the party, calling for its resignation. Hoping to see the imposition of an entirely Caballerist National Committee, *Claridad* organised an unofficial plebiscite within the party. The new line-up favoured by the leftists was Largo Caballero as president, Julio Alvaraz del Vayo as vice-president, Enrique de Francisco as secretary, Wenceslao Carrillo as vice-secretary, Pascual Tomás as minutes secretary, and Luis Araquistain, Ricardo Zabalza, Carlos Hernández Zancajo, Rodolfo Llopis and two others as ordinary members.[46]

The official leadership mildly condemned this fractional activity and raised the banner of unity, claiming that, with or without Largo, the PSOE was still the same party which had made the October rising. While *Claridad* published declarations of support for Largo Caballero, *El Socialista*, the official party newspaper, edited by Prieto's follower, Julián Zugazagoitia, tried to paper over the cracks. On 4 January, Zugazagoitia published a letter to the party's vice-president, Remigio Cabello, signed by himself, González Peña, Luis Jiménez de Asúa, Juan Negrín and many other prominent Socialists. The letter appealed for party unity and discipline, and pointing out that revolution and reform, or legal and illegal tactics, were not incompatible, presented a more democratic alternative than the Caballerists' monolithic ambitions for the party. Four days later Cabello replied, lamenting the divisive language used so far and declaring his commitment to a broadly based party unity. With his letter were printed declarations of support, mainly from Socialist sections in the north, including those of Guipúzcoa and Teruel. *El Socialista* then began to publish a long series of reports about the events of October 1934, and some spine-chilling, and verifiable, accounts of the repression. These articles have usually been considered as part of the election campaign, but it is more likely that their principal objective was to keep the Prietists in the running with the militant rank-and-file.[47]

It is impossible to state with total precision how support for Prieto and Caballero was divided among the Socialist masses, or even to what extent the polemic was followed by the rank-and-file. There can be no doubt that the bolshevisers made more noise, and it is probably this which has led some writers to assume that the masses were completely convinced of Caballero's position.[48] Since the Caballerists aimed at splitting the party, they had no reason to be inhibited about their language. Given the conflictive policies of the *bienio negro*, the Socialist masses were certainly more susceptible to revolutionary rhetoric, but they were not unaware of the need for unity. As it was, both sides published lists of the sections which supported them, but they were contradictory. A given local executive did not necessarily reflect the views of its rank-and-file. It is almost certain that all local sections contained devotees of both sides. The Agrupación Socialista Madrileña, for instance, was alleged by the Caballerists to have voted by 1,800 votes to 600 in favour of the *Claridad* committee. Equally, the Basque country and Asturias were strongly in favour of Prieto.

The selection of candidates for the February elections by local constituency parties indicated that the bolshevisers enjoyed less support than they claimed. The north was solidly pro-Prieto in its choice.

Vizcaya's two candidates were Prieto and Zugazagoitia. Asturias chose the Prietist heroes of October, Belarmino Tomás, Graciano Antuña and the SMA president, Amador Fernández, among its seven candidates. The Levante was ambiguous. Alicante, for instance, had dropped Manuel González Ramos as a reprisal for his collaboration in *Democracia*. Valencia, on the other hand, chose Manuel Molina Conejero (in the capital) and Pedro García y García (for the province), both of whom had voted against Largo Caballero in the 16 December meeting which had provoked his resignation. The south showed growing support for the party maximalists, but they were still far from in total control. Andrés Saborit did not run for Ciudad Real as he had done in 1933. Córdoba dropped Francisco Azorín, who had voted against Largo on 16 December. Equally, Seville did choose Victor Carretero, who had also voted against Largo. Huelva, with a strong contingent of Socialist miners, was an interesting case. The local section did not choose Ramón González Peña as part of the Popular Front candidacy, but he ran alone and was elected with as many votes as the coalition. Jaén dropped the Besteirist Lucio Martínez Gil, but kept the moderates Jerónimo Bugeda, Juan Lozano and Tomás Alvarez Angulo. Granada retained Fernando de los Ríos. Valladolid, however, seems to have been solidly Caballerist. Manuel Cordero and Eusebio González Suárez, who had both voted against Largo, and Remigio Cabello, who had abstained but shown his hostility to bolshevisation, were all three dropped.[49]

There is evidence to suggest that the Caballerists, as budding Leninists, were extremely active and vocal in local party politics. They seem thereby to have attained a level of dominance of certain local party organisations which was disproportionate to their actual degree of rank-and-file support. This is illustrated by an examination of the two Caballerist strongholds of Madrid and Badajoz. The Agrupación Socialista Madrileña voted a candidacy which included the more significant leftists, who also figured in *Claridad*'s suggested executive committee. However, alongside Largo Caballero, Alvarez del Vayo, Araquistain, Hernández Zancajo and Enrique de Francisco, both Julián Besteiro and Luis Jiménez de Asúa were chosen as candidates. There were 3039 voting members of the Agrupación. As might have been expected, Largo came top of their list, with 2886 votes; Besteiro only just made it, with 1157 votes in the second round. What was surprising was that Jiménez de Asúa, who had lined up with Prieto, came second. Even more of a shock to the Caballerists were the actual election results. There were thirteen Popular Front candidates, including the seven Socialists. Azaña came top, with 224,928 votes, followed by Besteiro, with 224,875. The next highest Socialist was Jiménez de Asúa, in sixth place. Alvarez del Vayo, Araquistain, De Francisco and Hernández Zancajo came respectively eighth, ninth, tenth and eleventh.

Largo Caballero was twelfth, with 220,981 votes, beating only the Communist, José Díaz. The triumph of Besteiro cannot be explained by the claim that he received more middle-class votes. The same working-class districts which voted for Largo gave more votes to Besteiro; the upper-class districts gave few votes to either of them.[50] In fact, there was not that much difference in numerical terms, but the success of Besteiro and Jiménez de Asúa gave the lie to some of *Claridad*'s more extreme claims.

Badajoz also presented a fascinating picture. The local Popular Front candidacy consisted of six Socialists, four republicans and a Communist. The republican representation was disproportionate, since in 1933 the Socialists had gained 139,000 votes to the republicans' 8000. Vidarte, Prieto's lieutenant from Badajoz, felt that two places would be sufficient for the republicans, one each for Izquierda Republicana and Unión Republicana. However, the local Socialist federation had included two more republicans, in order to exclude the two Besteirists, Narciso Vázquez, the pioneer of socialism in Extremadura, and Anselmo Trejo Gallardo, who had, with Vidarte, taken part in the defence of the villagers of Castilblanco. Accordingly, the Socialist candidacy included three Caballerists, Ricardo Zabalza, Margarita Nelken and Nicolás de Pablo, and three Prietists, Vidarte, José Aliseda Olivares and José Sosa Hormigo. The Caballerists seemed to have most strength in the provincial capital, while Vidarte and Aliseda apparently enjoyed loyal support in the country towns, such as Don Benito and Llerena. This was illustrated by the fact that they managed to get their supporters to cast tactical votes for centre candidates, thereby ensuring the defeat of the rightist candidacy, even in the contest for the minority allocation of seats.[51] Although an intelligent move, it would not have been approved by the Caballerists.

Although the PSOE's internal power struggle continued through the selection of candidates for the Popular Front, the very fact of the Caballerists' participation in the coalition was a victory for Prieto and, of course, for Jacques Duclos. The two main conceptions of an electoral alliance, that of Prieto and Azaña, and that of the Comintern, had thus been brought together although not without sacrifices on the part of the working class groups. Negotiations for a joint programme were continued between the representatives of Izquierda Republicana (Amos Salvador), of Unión Republicana, (Bernardo Giner de los Ríos), and of the PSOE (Vidarte and Cordero). In fact, the two Socialists were also representing the Communists, the break-away syndicalists of Angel Pestaña and the POUM (Partido Obrero de Unificación Marxista), as well as the UGT and the FJS. The Republicans had originally attempted to limit their negotiations to the PSOE. Vidarte and Cordero had demanded that the UGT at least be represented. In the end, it was Largo Caballero who reluctantly prevented total deadlock by suggesting that the two PSOE delegates should represent all the working class groups.[52]

There was basic agreement on the need for political amnesty, the restoration of civil liberties and the re-establishment of the social legislation of the Constituent Cortes. The Socialists would have like a programme like that drawn up by Prieto in January 1934, but the Republicans refused to accept workers' control of industry and the nationalisation of land and the banks. In fact, it seems to have been the Communists, already attempting to appeal to the petty bourgeoisie, who overcame Largo Caballero's reluctance to accept these limitations. The PCE was anxious lest Largo's intransigence provoke the departure of one of the Republican groups left in the coalition. Sánchez Román had already refused to participate in an alliance with the Communists. However, the pact signed on 15 January could hardly have been more mildly reformist. Indeed, it infuriated the Trotskyists who had not entered the POUM as much as it appeased Miguel Maura and Manuel Portela Valladares.[53]

Since Prieto had to maintain the fiction of being in exile, the Socialists' election campaign was dominated by Largo Caballero. His two main themes were the need for proletarian unity and for the transformation of capitalist society. Presented with an apparently revolutionary rhetoric, they delighted his working-class audiences all over Spain. At one point, on 11 February, he spoke with José Díaz at a joint PSOE–PCE meeting on the subject of unity. In fact, by unity both orators meant the take-over of the entire working-class movement by their own organisations. Moreover, when Largo declared his commitment to thorough social change, he made it clear that he saw revolution as a thing of the future. Thus, while he emphasised that capitalist society could hardly be fundamentally changed by capitalist democracy, he also underlined that this did not mean immediate revolution but simply pointed the need for the long-term preparation of the working-class for the future revolutionary moment. Although he reiterated that the Socialists did not forgo their determination to introduce radical social change, he also declared that they would stick by their undertaking to support a republican government until the fulfilment of the minimum programme of 15 January.[54]

The Left scored a notable triumph in the elections of 16 February. The way in which the Socialists selected their candidates for the elections, the nature of Largo Caballero's propaganda campaign and the success achieved at the polls suggest some important points about the Socialist movement at the beginning of 1936. Above all, the belligerent and vengeful policies followed by the CEDA–Radical coalition had considerably accelerated the leftward trend of the PSOE. The candidacy for the election showed that, while Besteiro seemed to have retained his tremendous personal popularity in Madrid, his reformist section of the party had dramatically lost support, especially in the rural south. However, even if the most rightist section of the PSOE was in decline, the party seemed to be inconclusively divided between supporters of Prieto and those of Largo Caballero.[55] Indeed, the Socialist rank-and-file gave little indication of being aware of the polemic which was sundering its leadership. The future was thus problematic. Prieto was committed to an attempt at rebuilding the progressive Republic of the first *bienio*. Even Largo had expressed a hope that electoral victory would herald a period of social peace. Whether the militant radicalisation of the Socialist masses could be halted by intelligent and forward-looking policies depended on the reaction of the Right. There was little about their behaviour between 1931 and 1935 to suggest that they would adopt the tolerant stance which might have permitted Largo Caballero to risk losing popularity by preaching moderation to his followers.

6 The Legal Road to the Corporative State: The CEDA in Power 1934–5

For Gil Robles the successful repression of the Asturian insurrection was adequate confirmation of the efficacy of his legalist tactic. When the Socialists had formed part of the republican government, his monarchist allies had tried to destroy the regime with a badly organised military coup. That direct assault had, in fact, strengthened the Republic in the same way that the Kapp putsch strengthened the Weimar Republic. Thus Gil Robles, in the aftermath of the abortive 10 August rising, reinforced Acción Popular's commitment to legal tactics. He was confident that skilful propaganda would bring electoral success and eventually power. It clearly made more sense to carry out his party's ambitions – the defence of the pre-1931 social order and the destruction of the Socialist threat – from the government rather than in opposition to the state's repressive apparatus. Having won an electoral victory in circumstances not likely to be repeated, he had nursed that victory with considerable skill and patience until, in October 1934, three CEDA ministers had joined the government. To his satisfaction, the Socialists had taken the bait and launched a hopeless assault on the state. Now thousands of Socialist cadres were in prison and the Socialist press was silenced – *El Socialista*, like *El Obrero de la Tierra*, was not to reappear for over a year. Nevertheless, it has been pointed out that the Cortes continued to meet after 5 November 1934, that the Socialist unions were not destroyed and that the military victory in Asturias was not used to impose the corporative state.[1] There is ample evidence to show that the CEDA was anxious to do all of these things and was held back only by Gil Robles's sense of realism.

The Cortes met, although there was censorship of debates and for some time the Left was not present. It was a valuable tribune from which to denounce the Left's insurrectionism. It also served as an extremely useful legal rubber stamp. In any case, the continued existence of the parliament revealed nothing about Gil Robles's democratic sincerity. Only the Alfonsist monarchists and the Carlists were publicly hostile to parliamentary democracy. It is likely that a substantial number of CEDA deputies would not object to the closing of the Cortes, if their public pronouncements meant anything; but that still left a considerable majority of Radicals, republicans of various sorts, and Socialists, as well as those CEDA deputies who were democrats, committed to the existence of the Cortes. Parliament could be overthrown only by military action. Consultation with senior generals showed Gil Robles that there could be no question of that.

Attacks were made on the unions. The CEDA youth newspaper, *JAP*, called shrilly for the destruction of both the UGT and the PSOE. Speaking for more moderate sections of the party, *El Debate* demanded a ban on Marxist unions and the strict regulation and control of other unions. On 5 November, Gil Robles told the Cortes that the country could not permit the existence of unions with revolutionary social aims. Already, on 19 October, Acción Popular and various non-Marxist and patronal unions had united to form the Frente Nacional del Trabajo. It was to be become the CEDA's response to left-wing unionism and developed into the Confederación Española de Sindicatos Obreros. This coincided with the directive of the Employers' Block (Bloque Patronal) to its members advising the dismissal of all workers who had taken part in the October strike and their replacement where possible by those who had acted as strike-breakers then. In Asturias plans were introduced whereby miners had to carry identity cards, with details of their work records.[2]

If unions were not abolished, it was because of Acción Popular's need to proceed always within the letter of the law. No proof could be found of the unions' part in the October rising and their legal abolition was difficult. Gil Robles did, nevertheless, advocate their dissolution and call for the confiscation of their funds, to pay for the damage done during the revolutionary events of October. In the following Cortes debate, on 14 November, the militant Dimas de Madariaga declared that 'the power of socialism derives from the cowardice of employers and the government' and it should be destroyed. In practice, the continued legal existence of unions hardly mattered, since the arrest of union leaders had effectively emasculated the syndical organisations, and employers were able to take thorough reprisals against workers. Reprisals took other forms as well. *El Debate* called for a purge of 'unreliable' civil servants and school-teachers, meaning republicans appointed during the previous two years. The Catalans' cherished *ley de cultivos* was abolished by military decree. In response to the demands of the CEDA press, a governor-general to assume the functions of the Generalitat was appointed on 2 January 1935.[3]

Throughout October, Gil Robles manifested his anxiety that nothing should stand in the way of the efficient repression of the revolt. On

23 October he said, 'the horrors of Asturias must be adequately punished'. When the Cortes reopened he demanded the 'inflexible application of the law' and some exemplary bloodshed. On 15 November he called for the chamber to announce its 'moral incompatibility' with the Left, a proposal seen by the Left as the prelude to the outlawing of the Socialist Party. This, and with its accompanying call for the dissolution of unions implicated in the rising, was opposed by the Radicals. A further obstacle to the CEDA's demand for implacable repression of the Left arose over the question of executions. Alcalá Zamora, anxious to avoid unnecessarily embittering the situation, was inclined to mercy, as he had been after 10 August 1932. Gil Robles was totally opposed to any form of conciliation, but he was worried that, if the CEDA ministers were intransigent, the President would resolve the crisis by giving power to a leftist cabinet and dissolving the Cortes.[4]

In such an event, Gil Robles would have liked to turn to the army, but as he wrote afterwards, 'it is doubtful that the armed forces really had the internal unity and necessary force'. Nevertheless, it was quite clear that the firmness of the CEDA position would depend entirely on the extent to which the army was in a position to back it. Since 18 October, Gil Robles had been in touch with Generals Goded and Fanjul through his close friend Cándido Casanueva, CEDA deputy for Salamanca. In fact, he had asked the generals to take the initiative in forcing the President's hand. He wanted them to prevent Alcalá Zamora from replying to CEDA intransigence with a dissolution. It appeared, however, that there was little possibility of relying on military action. After checking with provincial garrisons, the generals asked Gil Robles to compromise in order to prevent the arrival of a government of the Left, since the army was in no position to do so by other means. The much-praised legalism of Gil Robles at this stage was thus the result of the unavailability of an alternative line of action.[5]

With no possibility of taking power by force, Gil Robles now returned to the gradual process of taking it legally. On 16 November, Samper and Diego Hidalgo, the Minister of War, were edged out of the government for alleged 'responsibility' in the preparation of the revolt. The process of eliminating 'liberal' elements and restructuring the government to the CEDA's taste took a further step forward on 21 December. The Minister of Public Instruction, Villalobos, of Melquíades Alvarez's Liberal Democrats, had already upset the CEDA by his zeal in building schools. He now made the mistake of complaining against savage cuts in the education budget and was attacked in debate by the CEDA deputy Jesús Pabón. Villalobos was forced to resign – as Gil Robles put it, 'it was the second crisis that I found myself *forced* to provoke' – and complained bitterly that he owed his departure to his republicanism. Together with the forced schism of the Martínez Barrio group nine months previously, it constituted part of an inexorable process whereby liberals were pushed out of the governmental coalition, leaving those who remained increasingly dependent on the CEDA.[6]

It was at this time that the CEDA was able to put into practice its much vaunted aim of beating the revolution by a programme of social reform. This task fell to Giménez Fernández in the Ministry of Agriculture. Yet his mildly reformist plans were to excite such an outburst of embittered opposition within his own party as to confirm leftist fears that no reform could be expected from Spain's conservative classes except by revolution.

Without attacking the agrarian problem at its root, the series of measures which Giménez Fernández tried to introduce between November 1934 and March 1935 did attempt to mitigate with a spirit of social justice some of its more appalling abuses. But he found no solidarity in the CEDA, many of whose deputies regularly voted against him, and he was the object of vicious personal abuse. For instance, in January he introduced a leases bill which would give tenants the chance to buy land they had worked for twelve consecutive years. Mild as it was, the project provoked a coalition of ultra-rightist deputies, led by a traditionalist, Lamamié de Clairac, and three CEDA deputies, Mateo Azpeitia (Zaragoza province), Cándido Casanueva (Salamanca) and Adolfo Rodríguez Jurado (Madrid).[7] This was hardly surprising. *El Debate* had already responded to Giménez Fernández with caution, affirming in December that agrarian reform should not be 'too rapid or extensive in geographical area'. The paper had, moreover, reported with sympathy the meetings of the Agrupación de Propietarios de Fincas Rústicas, the aristocratic union of rural property-owners, which had expressed virulent hostility to the principle of allowing peasants access to property. It is worthy of note that Rodríguez Jurado was president of the Agrupación.

In session after session, Lamamié and the CEDA ultras stripped Giménez Fernández's work of its progressive features. Minimum leases were reduced from six to four years, access to property was dropped, inspection boards to supervise leasing were abandoned. And clauses were added which permitted a spate of evictions. The Minister had even less success with other measures. Gil Robles claimed to be in total agreement with Giménez Fernández's analysis of the need for reform and even admitted publicly that only concessions made in a Christian spirit could hold back the revolution. Yet he stood back and watched his Minister insulted and defeated by CEDA votes. Giménez Fernández was called a 'white bolshevik' and 'a Marxist in disguise'. Hostility came from more than a small minority of the party. Gil Robles speaks of a 'grave split' in the CEDA. He was clearly influenced by the strength of reaction provoked by attempts at reform. When he next provoked a cabinet crisis Gil Robles quietly dropped Giménez Fernández. That it was a sacrifice to party unity is made obvious by the CEDA leader's remark that 'I did not *dare* let Giménez Fernández occupy the Ministry of Agriculture again'.[8]

The defeat of the small social-Catholic wing of the CEDA at this time was merely one aspect of a general swing to the right by the wealthier supporters of the CEDA, who justified their own inflexibility on the grounds that the 'revolution had to be liquidated'. In industry, many union members found themselves out of work. But it was in the countryside that conditions really grew worse. Many landowners continued to keep land uncultivated out of vindictiveness, and still told workers to let the Republic feed them (*Comed República*). With union leaders in jail, *jurados mixtos*, if they were not suspended, barely functioned and were heavily weighted in favour of the owners.[9] On 14 December 1934 the Catalan statute was suspended indefinitely. Yet for all the general intensification of conflict, the CEDA felt that the Radicals had not been decisive enough in exploiting the defeat of the October revolution.

The CEDA dissatisfaction with the 'pace' of politics was expressed in its most extreme form by the JAP. In November its paper called for a purge of Marxists and freemasons, and in February for a new constitution which banned both. Gil Robles described in its pages his vision of the future state : a stronger executive power, the reduction of popular assemblies to specific legislative functions and the drastic limitation of the right to criticise the work of government. Clearly, Lerroux's essential liberalism left a lot to be desired. For the JAP, the defects of the liberal and parliamentary state could be remedied only by following the example of Germany, Italy, Austria and Portugal on the road to corporativism. The JAP leitmotiv was 'All power to the *Jefe*', varied with 'The *Jefe* is always right'. In his memoirs Gil Robles has made it apparent that he found no fault in the postures of his youthful followers. For him, they represented CEDA ideals untrammelled by compromise with political realities. If he himself had to be more moderate, it was merely a question of tactics.[10]

Other sections of the CEDA, even if they did not express their ambitions with the vehemence of the JAP, were little less direct. In December *El Debate* called for a constitution in tune with the spirit of the times, to reinforce authority, diminish the power of parliament and introduce a corporative system of representation. Gil Robles expressed the same sentiments in a lecture at Acción Popular headquarters, manifesting his dissatisfaction with democracy and his desire for something more 'organic' – Italy and Germany were cited as 'prototypes'.[11]

These desires contrasted with the reality of government in coalition with the Radicals. The cabinet lacked vigorous direction. In fact, Lerroux constantly failed to appear in the Cortes. Gil Robles regularly filled the gap, but he wished to invigorate the government with his ideas on a more formal basis; that is, through greater CEDA representation. Frustrated by the government's lack of decision in the 'liquidation' of the revolution and by Radical inertia in contrast to the CEDA's determination to proceed to an authoritarian state, Gil Robles wrote to Lerroux at the beginning of January calling for a 'change of orientation and of acceleration in the rhythm of government'. On several occasions that month he saw the Prime Minister and recommended to him a 'more intense rhythm of political action', and eventually Lerroux agreed to greater CEDA participation in the government.[12]

What might be signified by a 'more intense rhythm of political action' was suggested by an Acción Popular lecturer who called for the restriction of the right to strike and proclaimed the need to organise all social forces in a corporative organisation as in Italy. This line was echoed by *El Debate* in its Sunday supplement of 20 January, with a feature on the economic triumphs of two years of Nazism in power. And it was taken up again by Gil Robles when he addressed the businessmen of the Circle of the Mercantile Union, on 2 March. The economic problem, he said, was one of authority. Its solution lay in the creation of a corporative council of national economy.[13]

The crisis which was to give the CEDA the increased power with which to push its ideas came out of the question of the execution of Socialists implicated in the October rising. Two of Prieto's followers, Teodomiro Menéndez and Ramón González Peña, were sentenced to death, but Lerroux, to the chagrin of the CEDA, was in favour of clemency. Gil Robles called for firmness and *El Debate* declared that pardons would constitute 'a travesty of the law and a mockery of the innocent victims of the October revolution, an undeniable stimulus for the enemies of the social order'. Gil Robles threatened Lerroux with the break-up of the governing coalition, but the Radical leader was adamant. Accordingly, on 29 March, the three CEDA ministers withdrew from the government, because, said Aizpún, the Minister of Justice, 'clemency represents a revealing symptom of leniency in the repression of the subversive movement of October'.[14] While the CEDA complained of the cabinet's lack of zeal in repressing the Left, the government had taken an interesting initiative in the area of social control. The Spanish ambassador in Berlin had been instructed on 14 March to seek formal co-operation between the Gestapo and the Spanish police in the struggle against communism.[15] Nevertheless, Gil Robles still chose to regard the government as 'soft' (*débil*).

Alcalá Zamora hoped to be able to resolve the crisis with a coalition cabinet which would include republican forces to the left of the Radicals. Gil Robles, of course, indignantly refused to allow CEDA participation in such a scheme, since he had provoked the crisis in order to impose a more rightist, not a more republican, orientation. He wanted six ministries in the new government, including that of the Interior, and the Ministry of War for himself. In this ambition he met the strong hostility of the President, who distrusted the CEDA's flimsy loyalty to the regime. The situation was temporarily resolved by a one-month dissolution of parliament and the formation of a government of personal friends of Lerroux and Alcalá Zamora. Gil Robles could afford to wait. With the present Cortes, no government could be formed without his consent. If he did not yet demand to be Prime Minister himself, it was because he was afraid that the President would respond by giving a decree of dissolution of the Cortes to a left repub-lican cabinet. ˙ or the moment, he was content to increase his power slowly, but inexorably, by increasing his control over the government generally and by himself taking command of the Ministry of War. The latter was vital to his policy of strengthening the repressive power of the government, the crucial element of which he saw to be in the army. In December 1934 he had stated publicly that he saw the army as the bulwark against the masses and their social aspirations. How-ever, he had been disturbed by the manifest military difficulties en-countered in Asturias and by the generals' inability to support him with a coup in October 1934. During the second half of April 1935, Gil Robles pushed his case in a series of meetings with Lerroux, who did not object to some increase in CEDA ministerial power. Gil Robles organised a series of noisy CEDA meetings, the final show of strength taking place on Sunday 28 April, when 197 meetings (at least two in each province) took place. At last, knowing that the CEDA would eventually bring down the government, and reluctant to call elections, since he could do so only twice during his mandate, Alcalá Zamora gave in and allowed Lerroux to form a government on 6 May contain-ing five Cedistas, with Gil Robles as Minister of War.[16]

Gil Robles' anxiety to take over this ministry as opposed to any other must be seen in the light of what Fanjul had said in October 1934 regarding the army's inability to rise at that time. He apparently was disturbed by the presence of republican elements in the forces. Already on two occasions, 15 and 27 February 1935, he had made lengthy speeches in the Cortes on the need to eliminate 'masonic' elements from the army.[17] He claimed that he wanted to make the army 'the adequate instrument of a vigorous national policy'. When the Right said 'national', it normally meant 'right-wing'. And so the army was to be strengthened to face the 'revolution', to fight subversion and to defend the fatherland from external and internal enemies. The political overtones were soon made clear. As soon as he took control, Gil Robles held a meeting with several senior anti-republican generals, Fanjul, Goded and Franco, and virtually placed himself in their hands.[18] Franco was appointed Chief of the General Staff and thereby chosen as keystone of the reorganisation of the armed forces. Gil Robles did this against the advice of Alcalá Zamora, who said that 'young generals aspire to be fascist *caudillos*'. Gil Robles's other appointments were equally significant. As his under-secretary he chose Fanjul, a rabid monarchist who had left the Agrarian Party when it declared itself republican. Fanjul had once said 'all the parliaments of the world are not worth one Spanish soldier'. Goded was named Inspector-General. Like Fanjul, he was involved in the Unión Militar Española, the anti-republican conspiratorial group, was an untiring plotter and was closely linked with the monarchists of Acción Española, who were working for the overthrow of the Republic. Every act and decree issued by Gil Robles while he was at the Ministry was examined by a committee including all three. The American ambassador commented that, in upper-class circles, 'there was open jubilation at the expected shifting of monarchistic or fascist-minded generals to the strategic positions'.[19]

Not surprisingly then, the main preoccupation at the Ministry of War was the purging of 'undesirable elements'. Socialists and Communists were systematically weeded out. Even Alcalá Zamora was shocked by the progressive elimination of liberal and Republican officers and their replacement by fierce nationalists and *Africanistas*. Nor can Gil Robles have been unaware of the spread of conspiratorial juntas of the anti-republican Unión Militar Española throughout the officer corps.[20] A series of practical reforms was made with a view to pleasing the more conservative and militarist sections of the army. Regiments were reorganised; motorisation was begun; the General Military Academy, considered by republicans to be the cradle of reactionary officers, was re-established. Arms factories were to be militarised in the event of a 'conflagration', a clear response to the Asturian workers' takeover of such factories. Manoeuvres were held in Asturias to study means of combating a future rebellion. When Gil Robles was forced to leave the Ministry, a major rearmament had just begun. Without accepting the more extreme leftist accusations, it would seem reasonable to suggest that, not least in his choice of staff, Gil Robles did as much as possible to prepare the army for a potential rising.[21] Indeed, a recent apologist for Gil Robles has claimed that the CEDA leader made possible the 1936 rising.[22]

The circumstances of the proposed rearmament, which were kept scrupulously secret within Spain, are extremely illuminating. The five

CEDA ministers met in San Sebastián in August 1935 to discuss the political situation. They were intensely worried that Moscow's recent adoption of the Popular Front line would lead to Communist collaboration with other left-wing forces in Spain and a revolutionary threat to the government. On the grounds that only the army could meet this alleged revolutionary challenge, which he must have known was beyond the resources of the defeated Left, Gil Robles was anxious to increase military striking power. The Minister of War also justified his desire for arms purchases by claims that the Balearic islands were threatened by Italy during the Abyssinian crisis. Mussolini certainly had designs on the islands and the Spanish Foreign Ministry supported the League of Nations line on sanctions. However, *El Debate*, perhaps under pressure from the Vatican, opposed sanctions against Italy and Gil Robles massed troops on the border with Gibraltar while the British cabinet debated the issue. Whatever his motive, the CEDA leader turned to Germany as a potential supplier. There was a case for importing German manufactured goods, since Spanish fruit and ore exports had produced a favourable trade balance with the Reich. Accordingly, Cándido Casanueva, Gil Robles's second-in-command in the CEDA and Minister of Justice, arranged for an agent of the party, a certain Eduardo de Laiglesia, to make contact with the German Federation of Industry. On 14 September, Laiglesia sent a letter, believed by the Germans to have been drafted by Casanueva, to the German ambassador in Madrid, Count Welczeck. The letter stated that the army could be equipped on the necessary scale only over a period of three years. In order to assure the continued presence of the CEDA in the government, the Germans were asked to make a substantial contribution to party election funds. Efforts were made to force the issue on the other ministers in the government by the provocation of a strike in some Basque ore mines. As part of the same deal, the Germans temporarily banned the import of Basque ore, enabling the CEDA to present the arms purchases as an essential way of securing continued ore sales. Throughout the entire operation, considerable efforts were made to prevent the Radicals from finding out what was going on. Senior military staff, including General Franco, were completely in the secret. The arrangement was going ahead until the German firms began to find Laiglesia's demands for commission rather extravagant. Before alternative arrangements could be made, the government had fallen and new elections were on the horizon.[23]

The attempt to strengthen the army as a force of domestic repression was entirely in keeping with the reactionary tone of the cabinet formed on 6 May. The five *Cedistas* included Rafael Aizpún Santafé, traditionalist vice-president of the CEDA, as Minister of Industry and Commerce. The relatively liberal Manuel Giménez Fernández was dropped, and his arch-opponent, Cándido Casanueva, the CEDA's parliamentary leader, joined the government as Minister of Justice. The cabinet included four ex-members of the old monarchist Liberal Party, including Nicasio Velayos y Velayos, one of the more reactionary Agrarians, as Minister of Agriculture. The social orientation of Velayos was made clear when he allowed a meeting of the Confederación Española Patronal Agrícola, the right-wing rural employers' pressure group, to take place within the Ministry itself. *El Debate* crowed triumphantly that the *agricultores* had finally conquered the Ministry. The pace with which workers were being sacked and wages reduced was now stepped up.[24] After the fall of Giménez Fernández, the landowners' offensive against day-labourers and leaseholders alike reached proportions described by a Francoist historian as 'not only anti-Christian, remembering that Spanish landowners never behaved collectively like Christians either before or after 1935, but of an authentic ferocity'. Clauses were added to Giménez Fernández's reforms which made them means of attacking the small peasants. Evictions arose at an astonishing rate. The persecution of the Left in the countryside continued unabated. In Don Benito, a small town in Badajoz notorious for the bitterness of local class hatred, two Socialists were murdered. The Socialist deputy for Badajoz, Pedro Rubio Heredia, who was particularly hated by local owners and who had been illegally arrested during the 1934 peasant strike, was assassinated in a restaurant in Badajoz itself. The same official government historian comments that 'the behaviour of the Right in the countryside . . . in the second six months of 1935 was one of the principal causes of the hatred in the Civil War, and probably of the Civil War itself'.[25] Giménez Fernández himself claimed years later that Velayos created a thorough counter-reform in opposition to the spirit of everything that he had tried to do in the countryside. The Minister's reform of the existing agrarian reform bill even aroused the hostility of the Falange leader, José Antonio Primo de Rivera.[26]

The new Minister of Labour, Federico Salmón Amorín, was secretary of the CEDA and belonged to the party's social-Catholic wing. He made some attempt to promote housing projects and a show of trying to curb the enormities of the employers. *El Debate* boasted of his efforts, but the picture inadvertently painted by the CEDA organ was one of the Minister buried under a mountain of complaints. Even those complaints could not have come from any but a minority of workers familiar with the necessary procedures and not frightened to complain. *El Debate* was still outraged by the fact that union dues were being collected and that workers affiliated to the CNT could on occasions find work. The *jurados mixtos* had virtually ceased to function, few owners ever being sanctioned for infractions of the law.[27]

When Salmón took over the Ministry of Labour, unemployment was up to 732,034. Although it dropped somewhat during the summer harvest, by the end of November it rose to 806,221. In the light of this situation, the Left regarded Gil Robles's continuing protestations of social concern with some contempt. The much-vaunted plans to beat unemployment with public works were shelved for budgetary reasons, although financial stringency was not allowed to hold up Gil Robles's extensive plans for rearmament.[28] Thus, constant propaganda about the CEDA's 'deep Christian sense of social justice' appeared to be little more than hypocrisy. Gil Robles effectively exposed the shallowness of his own pious posturing when he replied to Juan Antonio Irazusta, a Basque Nationalist who protested in the Cortes against evictions which were contrary to the spirit of the law of rural leases. Although the CEDA leader condemned unjust evictions in generàl terms, he took any sting out of his remarks by defending Nicasio Velayos, the reactionary Agrarian Minister of Agriculture. After his rhetorical denunciation of rural injustice, Gil Robles forestalled any sanction against evictions by stating that the Minister could not be expected to define an 'unjust' case.[29] The overall impression left by the reality of CEDA policy was of untrammelled economic egoism hidden behind a façade of social-Catholic verbiage. This was emphasised by the reform of the agrarian reform, which was passed in July. Among a series of amendments was one which destroyed any possibility of fundamental change. This was the abandonment of the Inventory of Expropriable Property. Henceforth there was nothing to prevent owners from simply declaring their lands to be smaller than the size at which they became eligible for expropriation. Of 900,000 estates marked for reform, 800,000 were removed from the list.[30]

While Gil Robles prepared the army to 'fulfil its mission' and the practical social advances of the Republic were dismantled in the countryside, both the CEDA and the JAP were looking to the future. The gradual break-up of the Radical Party and the CEDA's seemingly inexorable increase in power necessitated preparation for the time when Gil Robles would take over the government. A flurry of meetings elaborated and publicised the details of the 'new state' which would then be installed. The vocabulary with which this was done was as ambiguous as ever, although what caught the attention of the Left was the constant recurrence of fascist terminology. Talk of the growing threat from freemasonry and Judaism was, if anything, more prevalent. At a JAP rally held at Uclés (Cuenca) and organised with the usual flurry of preparatory meetings, special trains and buses, Dimas de Madariaga announced that the 'new state' would not be based on 'decadent liberalism in which there circulates the poison of Marxism and separatism and which is infiltrated by freemasons, Jews and

Judaisers'. At this meeting the JAP leader, Pérez Laborda, demanded all power for Gil Robles.[31]

The wave of CEDA propaganda meetings and rallies coincided with early preparations for the reform of the Constitution. While the CEDA's plans were being discussed by the cabinet and being prepared for parliamentary discussion, monster concentrations of the Right's masses were being staged. On 30 June, Gil Robles addressed 50,000 people at Medina del Campo (Valladolid) in the morning and flew to Valencia to speak to 20,000 more in the afternoon.[32] Below the surface of Gil Robles's apparent respect for democratic norms, there was always the threat of using his power if he did not get what he wanted. At a JAP meeting in Santiago de Compostela he played on the Radicals' fear of a dissolution by proclaiming that, 'if the present Cortes does not want to proceed to constitutional reform, we will make the life of parliament impossible'.[33]

The vehemence of certain CEDA orators was taken to extremes by the JAP. Rather than reform of the existing constitution, the JAP, like most groups of the extreme Right, wanted a new constitution altogether. The 'new state' envisaged by the JAP would see a drastic reduction in the power of parliament. The executive power would be free of parliamentary control, as would the economic council which was to direct the new corporativist economy. The corporativism so insistently held up by all sections of the Spanish Right as the model for the country's political future was not notably different from fascism as both phenomena were perceived at that time.[34] The Left regarded the use of the term 'corporativism' as no more than a pious euphemism for fascism. Even more characteristic of the JAP than its authoritarian ambitions for a 'new state' was the virulence with which it reacted to the existing situation. Gil Robles's tactical notion of slowly but surely exploiting the system to attain concrete objectives met only the impatience of his youth movement. In issue after issue of its newspaper, a welter of provocative slogans announced the need to prepare the CEDA for the great battle which awaited it, the war to clean Marxists and freemasons out of Spain. There was to be no dialogue with the Left: 'either Acción Popular smashes Marxism or Marxism will destroy Spain. With the *Jefe* or against the *Jefe*. There can be no dialogue with anti-Spain. Us and not them. Let us annihilate Marxism, freemasonry and separatism so that Spain may continue her immortal road.' This language was more violent even than that employed by the FJS in 1934. Indeed, it was the same language as was to be used by the Falange during the Civil War, after the majority of the JAP's members had passed to the fascist organisation. With five CEDA ministers in the government, it was bound to frighten the Left and the Centre. Gil Robles was aware that the JAP was undermining his long-term plans and tried to restrain some of its virulence. He prevented the ex-JAP president, José María Valiente, who had been deposed because of his open contacts with Alfonso XIII, from speaking at the great JAP rally at Uclés. Valiente resigned from the CEDA and joined the Carlists. Gil Robles held back the week's issue of the JAP bulletin, 15 June, but the following week it was on sale again, with an unchanged line, declaring enthusiastically that 'the *Jefe* is always right'.[35]

Gil Robles never effectively dissociated himself from the excesses of his youth movement. Inevitably, the Left took the slogans of the JAP to be indicative of what the CEDA was merely too devious to say openly. In fact, when the CEDA discontinued its own party bulletin, it clearly associated itself with the JAP. In its last number, *CEDA* carried an appeal for every member of Acción Popular to transfer his subscription to *JAP*, 'a vibrant publication in which he will find audaciousness, faith, enthusiasm, fearlessness, austerity and discipline'. Since Gil Robles regularly stated at meetings that the CEDA and the JAP were totally identified, the Left assumed him to be implicated in the latter's demands for him to take all power in a dictatorial regime and smash the Left.[36] The fact that Gil Robles aimed to advance slowly and legally to power in no way mitigated what the JAP intended him to do with it once it was acquired.

The reckoning for the CEDA was nearer than even Gil Robles suspected. In June he had concluded the Pact of Salamanca with the Radicals, an act seen, by the Acción Española group at the time and by his apologists since, as evidence of his republican faith. There can be no doubt of the cynicism behind the step. Gil Robles told the crowd at the Valencia meeting on 30 June that, just as they did not question who put money into their businesses when profits were at stake, so too he did not question whom he used for his political ends. J. A. Primo de Rivera commented wryly, 'that is to say, he puts up with the Radicals as undesirable, but for the moment indispensable, partners'.[37] The extent to which the Radicals were the essential vehicle of the CEDA's approach to power was shown when their political effectiveness was shattered by the revelation of their corruption and the legalist tactic could not be followed by the CEDA alone.

In mid September there arose a crisis which was not of Gil Robles's making. Its *dénouement* illustrated the fragility of his plans to use the Radicals to leapfrog his way to power without risking elections. The crisis was provoked in September by the resignation of Antonio Royo Villanova, the Agrarian Minister of the Navy, a fierce centralist who resented the government of Catalonia being ceded control of its roads. He was joined by his fellow Agrarian Velayos. The crisis coincided with impending ministerial changes imposed by a scheme, devised by the Minister of Finance, Joaquín Chapaprieta, for reducing government expenditure. To complicate matters further, the President's decision regarding the resolution of the crisis had to be taken in the knowledge that a giant financial scandal, the Straperlo affair, was about to be exposed, to the detriment of the Radicals. After various consultations, Alcalá Zamora decided to offer the premiership to Chapaprieta, who managed to secure the collaboration of both Gil Robles and Lerroux. Both were prepared to accept the situation because they knew that, if they did not, the President would dissolve the Cortes. Chapaprieta was very much the lesser evil.[38]

Chapaprieta being an advocate of austerity, the cabinet was reduced in size from thirteen to nine, with CEDA participation down to three. This represented no loss of power for Gil Robles. He kept the Ministry of War, Luis Lucia held the combined ministries of Public Works and Communications, and Federico Salmón received the combined port-folios of Labour and Justice. The CEDA had the same number of ministers as the Radicals, and, in fact, controlled five ministries. The composition of the cabinet also represented a minor triumph for Gil Robles, in that the centre republican Minister of the Interior, Manuel Portela Valladares, was replaced by a Radical, Joaquín de Pablo-Blanco. Portela had pursued a fairly hard but neutral law-and-order line. It had not been sufficiently anti-leftist for Gil Robles, who had demanded that the command of the Civil Guard pass from the Ministry of the Interior to that of War. This manifest desire for the monopoly of the state's apparatus of violence had disturbed Gil Robles's cabinet allies and his request had been refused. However, he had successfully pressed for Portela's removal. The CEDA leader remained the govern-ment's dominant figure in the Cortes. Moreover, since he was aware from his vantage point in the Ministry of War that the condition of the army was still such as to give him no viable alternative to following the legalist tactic, he can have been little less than satisfied with the outcome of the crisis. In particular, there was advantage to be derived from the fact that Chapaprieta was something of a nonentity and was willing for Gil Robles virtually to take control of the cabinet. As he himself put it, 'to Señor Gil Robles, for whom I felt a great liking and with whom I was always in agreement, I expressed my desire that we should continue in collaboration in all government business'. In fact, Gil Robles used to arrive at cabinet meetings half an hour before the other ministers for a prior discussion about matters to be raised. Chapaprieta regularly dropped in at the Ministry of War to inform the *Jefe* of any new developments. Moreover, for all his concern with financial austerity, Chapaprieta, who remained as Minister of Finance, gave the Minister of War every assistance in budgeting for his pro-gramme of rearmament.[39]

The Left continued to be uneasy about Gil Robles's intentions. Both

Martínez Barrio and Félix Gordón Ordás, of Unión Republicana, expressed concern in the Cortes regarding rumours of an imminent rightist coup.[40] In fact, a coup was unlikely, since at that time Gil Robles was more concerned about maintaining what power he already had. On 9 October, aware that a scandal was brewing, even if he did not realise its magnitude, he took part in a banquet in honour of Lerroux. In his speech he reaffirmed the CEDA alliance with the Radicals, an alliance which was now the central bulwark against the dissolution of the Cortes, an event that he dreaded. The *Jefe* also declared his opinion that the President could dissolve the Cortes only once in his mandate. The precariousness of the situation was soon revealed. Accusations concerning the Radicals' implication in the Straperlo gambling fraud were placed in the hands of the government, and on 22 October the matter was debated in the Cortes.[41]

Chapaprieta and Gil Robles had visited Lerroux and asked him to resign as Foreign Minister, but he refused to do so until the whole business had been discussed in parliament. It was a difficult situation for Gil Robles. After all, his own party was involved in negotiations with the German government for donations of electoral funds in return for a monopoly of arms sales to Spain. This affair was not only as illegal as the Straperlo roulette swindle, but it also involved national security. Gil Robles managed the crisis with some panache. Determined not to be implicated in the Radicals' downfall, he took a prominent role in demanding that the whole affair be thoroughly examined. When he called for the most energetic sanctions, it looked to the Left in general, and to Gordón Ordás especially, as if Gil Robles, having seen that the Radicals could no longer serve him, aimed to gain the fullest advantage from their destruction. They were, in any case, mortally wounded. J. A. Primo de Rivera declared that they were disqualified from public life. He claimed that the entire Radical Party should suffer as the CEDA had made the whole of the Socialist movement suffer after Asturias. On 29 October, Lerroux and his crony, Juan José Rocha, Minister of Education, resigned. They were replaced by two more Radical men of straw, Luis Bardají López at Education, and Juan Usabiaga Lasquivar at Agriculture. The Agrarian Martínez de Velasco passed from the Ministry of Agriculture to that of Foreign Affairs. Now more than ever, Gil Robles was the effective leader of the government. In their death agony, the Radicals did not even bother to turn up for debates.[42]

All things considered, the CEDA leader had come out of the cabinet crisis very well. He was in a strong position to renew his gradual climb to supreme power. For the moment, however, the main political interest of the day was centred on Chapaprieta's schemes for fiscal reform. He wanted to extend the incidence of death duties, which were the lowest in Europe, and to subject company funds to taxation. Inevitably, this aroused the hostility of the classes who constituted much of the CEDA's, and also the Radicals', financial support.

On Gil Robles's own admission, the most tenacious opponents in parliament to Chapaprieta's reforms were to be found in the CEDA. In fact, Chapaprieta was subjected to violent attacks by the *Cedistas* Casanueva and Azpeitia, who had opposed Giménez Fernández with such success. As before, they used the tactic of overloading bills with amendments. They were seconded in their delaying tactics by other CEDA deputies, who stayed away from the Cortes and thereby prevented the passing of any clauses at all. On 2 November, Chapaprieta announced to the press that he would resign if he could not fulfil his plans in their entirety. Gil Robles assured him CEDA votes, but they never materialised. When Chapaprieta finally raised the matter at a cabinet meeting, Gil Robles informed him that he was impotent to oblige his deputies to vote for the reforms. This seems highly unlikely, given the adulation to which the *Jefe* was subjected by all sections of the CEDA. Moreover, Casanueva was Gil Robles's second-in-command, a loyal collaborator, who had once said publicly that, 'with a chief like Gil Robles, even cleaning out latrines is fun'. What seems more probable, and this was Chapaprieta's view, is that Gil Robles was using the CEDA's sincere opposition to fiscal reform to time the next government crisis. He knew that another scandal on the scale of Straperlo was brewing. Known as the Nombela scandal, it concerned illegal payments made by the Radicals from government funds. The continuance of the Radicals in power would be impossible and so Gil Robles was confident that a crisis would result in his being made Prime Minister. He suggested to Chapaprieta that he drop his reforms from the budget, knowing that it would provoke his resignation. It did. Chapaprieta resigned on 9 December.[43]

Under the circumstances, Alcalá Zamora could only choose between offering the government to Gil Robles and dissolving the Cortes. The CEDA leader had no doubt that he would take the former course and advised him to that effect. However, Alcalá Zamora was not prepared to do so, for he had no faith in Gil Robles's democratic convictions. After all, only some weeks previously, JAP had starkly revealed the aims of the legalist tactic in terms which called to mind the attitude of Goebbels to the 1933 elections in Germany: 'with the weapons of suffrage and democracy, Spain must prepare itself to bury once and for all the rotting corpse of liberalism. The JAP does not believe in parliamentarism, nor in democracy.' Democracy, so much 'vacuous word-play', was to be exploited for its own destruction. Soon afterwards, Gil Robles told cheering *Japistas* that he accepted their programme in its entirety.[44] Alcalá Zamora's existing fears about Gil

Robles's lukewarm republicanism and dictatorial ambitions had been intensified by the *Jefe*'s activities as Minister of War. Chapaprieta had the clear impression that the President feared that Gil Robles was under the influence of the extreme monarchist sections of the officer corps, who were determined to destroy the Republic. Every appointmen made by the Minister seemed to the President to be part of a 'scheme to surrender the army to the enemies of the Republic'. It appeared to Alcalá Zamora that the Ministry of War was being turned into a stronghold, that key posts were going to those officers who were preparing a coup and that his own personal safety was threatened. When he had complained to Gil Robles about the conspiratorial activities of General Fanjul, the Minister had defended him without reservation. The President was actually threatened by Gil Robles's Inspector-General, Goded, who told him that the army would not tolerate the Left's being brought into the government again.[45]

In the present cabinet crisis, while there was considerable pressure on the President to give power to the CEDA, there were also compelling reasons for not doing so. This was the period when Gil Robles and the CEDA press were calling for constitutional reform. Until 9 December 1935, four years after its ratification, the Constitution could be amended only by a two-thirds majority of the Cortes, something Gil Robles could never muster. After that date, a simple one-vote majority would suffice – hence the *Jefe*'s anxiety to avoid elections and to be head of the government when the crucial date arrived. In fact, it appears that Alcalá Zamora had already decided that any solution of the crisis must, for the good of the Republic, include the departure of Gil Robles from the Ministry of War. If this should not prove possible, he would dissolve the Cortes, even though that meant exhausting his prerogative to do so. Needless to say, he did not arrive at his decision lightly. The political disqualification of the Radicals was motive enough for a dissolution. Added to that fact, the defeat of Chapaprieta had convinced Alcalá Zamora that the present Cortes was incapable of legislative achievement. For the moment, however, he was prepared to try any solution rather than what he saw as the dangerous step of giving power to Gil Robles. First of all, he asked the Agrarian leader, Martínez de Velasco, to form a cabinet. Even though the latter did not dare tell Gil Robles of the prior condition concerning his exclusion from the Ministry of War, the CEDA leader, intent on supreme power himself, refused to support his government. Gil Robles was so confident that power was within his grasp that he no longer saw any point in collaborating in the cabinets of others.

It is revealing of the depth of Alcalá Zamora's suspicion of Gil Robles that throughout the crisis he had the Ministry of War surrounded by Civil Guards and the principal garrisons and airports placed under special vigilance. When he spoke with the President on 11 December, Gil Robles learned with rage that he was not being offered the government. He could not believe that he had overplayed his hand. Alcalá Zamora pointed out that the present Cortes was incapable of sustaining stable governments. Gil Robles could hardly reply as he might have done that the instability had been artificially created by himself to speed up his own approach to power and that if he were given power it would not need to happen again. Instead, he made a vehement protest against the possibility of elections being called at a time of economic hardship, since the masses would thus be liable to 'all kinds of excesses' – such as, presumably, voting for candidates of the Left.

The only choice open to Gil Robles was between staging a *coup d'état* and taking some backward step which would enable the CEDA to carry on in the government. He essayed both solutions at once. On the same evening a messenger was sent to Cambó, head of the Catalan Lliga, to ask him to join the CEDA and the Radicals in a government which would preclude the President's needing to dissolve the Cortes. Cambó refused. Meanwhile, in the Ministry of War, Gil Robles was discussing the situation with Fanjul, who said that he and General Varela were prepared to rise with the Madrid garrison to prevent the President from going through with his plans for a dissolution. Gil Robles tried to justify his inclination towards such a proposal by replying that Alcalá Zamora's action in itself constituted a coup.[46] However, he was worried that such a rising might fail, since it would have to face the determined resistance of the Socialist and anarchist masses. Nevertheless, he told Fanjul that, if the army felt that its duty lay in a coup, he would not stand in its way and, indeed, would do all that he could to maintain the continuity of administration while it took place. Only practical doubts disturbed him and so he suggested that Fanjul check the opinion of Franco before making a definite decision. He then passed a sleepless night while Fanjul weighed up the chances of success with Goded, Varela and Franco. They concluded that the army was not yet ready for a coup. So, on 12 December, Gil Robles had to abandon the Ministry of War with 'infinite bitterness'. He had overreached himself. Unable to take power by force, he had also lost his grip on the situation whereby he could edge towards power legally.[47]

Now the legalist tactic would again have to pass the test of elections. After tentative attempts by both Chapaprieta and Miguel Maura to form wide coalition governments, the President gave power on 13 December to Portela Valladares, the grand master of electoral management. He formed a government of the old coalition forces minus the CEDA and hoped to manage the elections so as to create a new party of the Centre which would be the arbiter of the Cortes. This could be done only at the expense of the CEDA and Gil Robles was determined to prevent it. Already the monarchist press was joyfully claiming that the legalist tactic had failed. There existed the strong possibility that the substantial right wing of the CEDA, which had accepted legalism for as long as the party was able to pass on to it the material benefits of power, might now go over to those who proposed less dilatory solutions to their problems. So Gil Robles set about bringing down the Portela government. On 16 December he announced his determination to prevent the parties of the old governmental block from being attracted to Portela by the temptation of electoral success through official manipulation of the elections. On the following day he wrote to Alcalá Zamora to demand that the government extend the present budget only with parliamentary approval. Either Portela would have to appear in the Cortes, where the CEDA would bring him down, or else speed up the calling of elections. While he hesitated the CEDA issued a note, on 28 December, saying that it would make no electoral alliances with any groups in the government. This provoked a distintegration of the cabinet, since all its component groups were aware that to go to the polls in opposition to the CEDA would be to hand electoral victory to the Left. The cabinet resigned on 30 December and was replaced by another made up of Portela's friends, without parliamentary support and aiming only at organising the elections.[48]

On the question of electoral alliances, the CEDA held all the cards as far as the Right was concerned. Coalitions were mutually beneficial, but the CEDA as the largest party still had the most to offer. From the first, Gil Robles made it clear that he aimed to win regardless of what alliances he had to form. As early as 14 December, he had called for the widest possible counter-revolutionary national front. To gain victory, he was prepared to include in that front both Radicals and extreme monarchists. The front's appeal was to be to the 'employer, mercantile and industrialist class'. That political ideals would not be allowed to stand in the way of the protection of these social interests was revealed when Gil Robles overrode pressure from the CEDA liberals Lucia and Giménez Fernández to avoid alliances with the extreme conspiratorial Right and to join only with conservative republicans.[49]

Throughout December and January, negotiations were carried out with all groups. In this, Gil Robles enjoyed the active support of the Church. A delegation of the leaders of the Partido Nacionalista Vasco was in Rome to discuss with the Vatican Church–state relations in the Basque country. Archbishop Pizzardo, Cardinal Pacelli's secretary, told them that they must join Gil Robles's coalition, since a victory for the CEDA was a victory for the Church over Lenin. When the Basques replied that the Church should not pin its future on transitory electoral results, Pizzardo replied that, if they did not sign an undertaking to ally with Gil Robles, they would not be received by either Pacelli or the Pope. José Antonio Aguirre, the Basque Nationalist leader, was confident that all the Cortes seats for the Basque region would go to Catholics of his party and therefore refused to join unnecessarily with what he saw as Gil Robles's extremist right-wing coalition. When the Basques were ostracised by the Pope, presumably on Pacelli's advice, the ACNP press network tried to make political capital out of it.[50] Although agreeing with the Popular Front's aim of political amnesty, the Basques did not want to be instrumental in electing a Communist and they went into the elections alone.

With the exception of the Basques, only the monarchists represented any problem. They demanded a broad maximalist programme which would be binding after the election, and a numerous representation in the joint candidacies. Gil Robles stood firm. He realised that, in the event of victory, a sizable Renovación Española group would be able to do to the CEDA what the CEDA had done to the Radicals. In any case, he felt that a national agreement on the bases of an alliance would be counter-productive, since in many areas either the republican Right or the ulta-monarchists would be repelled by a joint candidacy. Therefore he insisted that alliances be made locally. In areas of considerable left-wing strength, like Badajoz, Jaén, Córdoba and Asturias, where the victory had been very narrow in 1933, the CEDA was willing to ally with anyone who did not belong to the Popular Front. On the other hand, in Salamanca, Navarre and most of Castile, the areas of strongest reactionary sentiment, Gil Robles felt that contact with groups not of extreme rightist character would lose votes. Thus, alliances came to depend on local circumstances, with the CEDA standing on its professed ideals only when it could afford it. In Salamanca the alliance was with Carlists and Agrarians only; in Asturias, with the local Liberal Democrats of Melquíades Alvarez; in Pontevedra, with the Radicals; in Navarre, with the Carlists; in the Balearics, with Juan March. In the great republican strongholds of Catalonia there emerged a highly implausible coalition of the CEDA, the Radicals, the Carlists and the Lliga, united in a 'law-and-order' front.[51]

The intense cynicism of the CEDA's approach to the elections was illustrated by Gil Robles's contacts with Portela Valladares, whom he despised and had tried so hard to have removed as Minister of the Interior during the previous autumn. Faced with the virtual impossibility of creating a Centre party without popular support, Portela had proposed an electoral alliance with the Left. His offer was roundly rejected in most provinces except Lugo and Alicante. In Lugo, Portela's personal machinery of electoral falsification made it virtually impossible for anyone to prevail against him. The special circumstances of Alicante are described below. It was an immensely valuable offer that Portela was making – the government had at its disposal a massive apparatus of electoral influence, the control of town councils, of the forces of order, of the mechanisms of electoral scrutiny. The Left's refusal spoke volumes about its attitude to the democratic process as a means of expressing the popular will. In the light of the refusal, Portela announced on 7 February that candidates sponsored by him would ally with the Right in areas where there was no agreement to be had with the Left. The offer was accepted and in many provinces the Right went to the elections in coalition with Portela's candidates.[52]

In his memoirs Gil Robles describes Portela's men as turncoats and parasites. He professes to have been disgusted by the idea of using the mechanism of corruption : 'my repugnance to the idea of an agreement with the government forces was infinite. But how else could we prevent our defeat in constituencies with high numbers of voters?' It is a penetrating commentary on the sincerity of Gil Robles's democratic convictions. He was interested in the power that an electoral victory might bring and had no concern with the pronouncement being made by the electorate.[53] He had already made publicly clear his agreement with the JAP's contention that democracy should be used to bring about its own destruction. Accordingly, he was not above indulging in electoral manipulation to acquire the necessary results. Because of his party's deal with Portela, the CEDA enjoyed government support in most of Extremadura and Andalusia, areas of left-wing rural strength, where the behaviour of the Civil Guard would be crucial in deciding results. An illuminating example of the Right's electoral morality took place in the province of Alicante. There Portela had begun negotiations with the local Right, but, when they had refused to offer him what he considered a satisfactory number of seats in the coalition, he made a proposition to the Left. He placed the control of the province and most town councils in the hands of republicans and Socialists. Chapaprieta has shown in his memoirs the righteous indignation and disgust with which the province's rightists witnessed this corruption. Nevertheless, the Right's negotiations with Portela continued, and, when Gil Robles made an acceptable offer of seats in the candidacy, the left-wing appointees were unceremoniously thrown out and replaced by rightists. Neither Gil Robles nor Chapaprieta appear to have found this situation, morally identical with the first, in any way reprehensible.[54]

Nothing more clearly demonstrated the CEDA's determination to win the election at any cost than the nature of its campaign. Huge funds were available for propaganda, provided by wealthy backers such as Juan March.[55] Already, in late October, Gil Robles had requested the German ambassador, Count Welczeck, for a complete range of Nazi anti-Marxist propaganda pamphlets and posters, to be used as a model for CEDA publicity material.[56] In practical terms, the Right enjoyed an enormous advantage over the Left. 10,000 posters and 50 million leaflets were printed. They presented the elections in terms of an apocalyptic struggle between good and evil, survival and destruction. CEDA propaganda was often printed with a hammer-and-sickle motif or the letters 'CNT', to capture the attention of working-class voters.[57] The content was as virulent as in the majority of cases it was untrue. In Seville, for instance, pamphlets distributed to women claimed that the Republic intended to take away their children and destroy their families. Another leaflet alleged that, if the Left won the elections, the consequences would be 'the arming of the rabble; burnings of private houses and banks; distribution of private goods and lands; wild looting and the common ownership of women'. Rightist defeat was presented as an awful catastrophe. It was claimed that the Republic signified increased crime, with robbery, arson and murder topping the list.[58] This kind of propaganda was distributed by the ton. Lorries carried it to small villages and aeroplanes dropped it on farms. This saturation propaganda was crucial in the northern countryside. It was thereby able to reach the uneducated rural population, for whom the printed word commanded tremendous respect. In Madrid, half a million leaflets were sent by ordinary post – an indication of the Right's access to ready money. A three-storey-high portrait of Gil Robles dominated the Puerta del Sol. Although there was a ban on radio transmissions, Acción Popular could afford to have a Gil Robles speech broadcast privately on 9 February to twenty-six towns, and on the eve of the election to have one relayed to some 400 places. Also in February, ten theatres were hired in Madrid and a speech by the *Jefe* was relayed to them.[59]

The intensity and malevolence of the CEDA campaign reached its peak in meetings and the press. Indeed, the CEDA press, especially in the provinces, was at least as truculent as that of the monarchists and Carlists who were declared enemies of the Republic. *El Debate* saw the election as an irreconcilable conflict between Spain and anti-Spain, between civilisation and barbarism. JAP, which had control of the CEDA campaign, was more explicit and declared that the battle was between Gil Robles and the triangle (freemasonry – a symbol of republicanism), the sickle, and the solitary star (of David). The JAP conducted the campaign in an atmosphere of frenetic adulation for Gil Robles.[60] Chants of *¡Jefe! ¡Jefe! ¡Jefe!* resounded throughout meetings, often mixed with *vivas* for the army. At one point, after a JAP meeting in Soria, Pérez Laborda was arrested because of the viciousness of his attack on the President of the Republic. Gil Robles was little less vehement. On a tour of Galicia he repeatedly railed against a constitution which, he claimed, united the worst aspects of parliamentarism and the presidential system. In Toledo he attacked the moderation of the President regarding the repression of Asturias. And it was an echo of an earlier Gil Robles speech that sounded in Pérez Laborda's words at the close of a meeting in Madrid : 'Exaltation of Spain! Think of Spain! Work for Spain! Die for Spain! Exaltation of the fatherland with ecstasy, with frenzy!'[61]

The CEDA press all over the country was characterised by a relentless hatred of the Left, which was accordingly much preoccupied with what a rightist victory would mean for it. The belligerence of *El Debate* belied its claims to legalism : 'between the ruin and the salvation of Spain there is no middle way'; 'Spain is threatened in its very being by the Marxist hordes determined to fulfil the promise of red October'; a political amnesty would release 'the murderers, the thieves, the firebugs of socialism, syndicalism and communism'. Detailed graphs were printed to prove that socialism was tantamount to gangsterism.[62] The provincial press was, if anything, more bellicose. In Almería *La Independencia* called on voters to rescue Spain from Jews and freemasons. The choice was between God and anarchy. Crude appeals were made to landowners : 'your property will disappear if they triumph'. The tone of CEDA propaganda contrasted with the moderation of the rival Republican newspaper, *El Diario de Almería*. An even more striking contrast was to be found in Granada, between Acción Popular's strident *Ideal* and the rather more controlled *El Defensor*.[63]

Inevitably, it was upon the utterances of CEDA propagandists and newspapers that the Left based its accusations of fascism. The Left's concern is understandable. JAP summed up the CEDA programme in the event of victory : deposition of the President, full powers to the government, dissolution of the Socialist party, annihilation of the revolution, the silencing of the 'rabble press', a new constitution. These were not just the verbal excesses of youth. Gil Robles himself was still toying with the idea of dictatorship. He knew that, even if the CEDA, which had 178 candidates, scored a rousing victory, it could not count on more than 140 seats in the Cortes. This would mean more coalition governments. On 5 February he announced ominously, 'Spain can no longer put up with a sterile Cortes. There has been enough already.' Many of his followers were urging him towards a civilian dictatorship. He, of course, remembered his consultations with the generals in December. Araquistain, the Socialist theoretician, suggested with some plausibility that Gil Robles was not of the stuff of which dictators are made. But the fact remains that many *Cedistas* took up the idea.[64] The most extreme statement of the possibility came from the JAP in as fascistic a battle-cry as ever emanated from the Spanish Right. After the triumph, there would be energy, the repudiation of liberalism, a young and virile policy. Twenty-seven reasons were given as to why Gil Robles should be given full power, and among these were the need to crush the revolutionary spirit, to limit liberties (seen as 'criminal'), to prohibit the organisations which preach the class struggle, to put an end to laicism, to put an end to the vices of parliamentarism, to strengthen the executive power, to realise an energetic policy of public order, and to create a strong army, navy and air-force.[65]

Just how determined the CEDA was to gain the power which would have made all this possible was shown by the extent to which propaganda and electoral alliances were augmented in the field by all kinds of pressures and the use of force. The evidence for this is necessarily anecdotal, but is, nevertheless, overwhelming. Electoral pressures in the towns were various, but were largely variations on the theme of vote-buying. In both urban and rural areas of unemployment, Acción Popular began to open soup-kitchens and to distribute blankets to the poor. *El Socialista* made accusations of the direct purchase of votes. Economic hardship was sufficient to make it possible to do so quite cheaply. The American ambassador recounts that 'an agent, canvassing the apartment house in which Constancia de la Mora lived . . . , thought that he had bought her Andalusian maid for 25 pesetas, but she promptly reported to her mistress'. The English journalist Henry Buckley goes into more detail :

> I knew of one landlord owning seven houses who warned the *concièrges* of the houses that he would call for them with a car in order to take them and such of their famiiles as had votes to the polling station. This meant, of course, that at the door of the booth he would hand them a voting paper for the Right and watch from the door to make sure that they dropped it into the box. And various women of the Right whom I knew had made arrangements to take their servants to the polling booths with them, just as they had done last time.

In Madrid offices, pressure was put on employees to vote for the Right. Those who wanted to act as scrutineers for the Left were told that they would get trouble if they did. At the same time, rightist employees were given every facility, time off and the train fare to their provincial homes, to help them cast their votes.[66]

The situation in rural areas was much more violent and the Right had far more facilities to influence results. An extreme example of the Right's behaviour was in Granada, where a particularly reactionary landowning class saw a CEDA victory as the only chance of protecting its privileges. The Casas del Pueblo were still closed after the October revolution. The republican press mysteriously disappeared somewhere *en route* between Granada and outlying districts. The CEDA paper *Ideal*, which always got through, set the tone when it said that a few beatings would keep the Left quiet, since all leftists were cowards. Local *caciques* seem to have taken it at its word, for they hired gangs of thugs who, often with the assistance of the Civil Guard, prevented the dissemination of left-wing propaganda. Posters were ripped down at gun-point; republican orators were turned away from villages by road-blocks; rumours were spread that the peasants could not vote unless they had special documentation. Known republicans were illegally arrested and the Left's scrutineers were prevented from exercising their functions. During the actual voting, pressures grew more varied. In some villages, groceries were issued to the unemployed before they voted; in others, with only armed right-wing scrutineers present, glass ballot boxes were used. In Loja, the town council requisitioned all cars, taxis, buses and lorries for the day so that workers could not come in to vote. In Chite, all republicans were kept in jail for the day. In Fonelas, peasants ariving to vote found that the *alcalde* had put his watch forward and closed the voting station an hour and a half before time. Even after all this, the *caciques* had to alter the returns, and they did not scruple to keep up appearances. In twenty villages the Popular Front candidates did not receive a single vote – though this was an area of great left-wing strength.[67]

Granada may have been an extreme case, but it was by no means atypical. In Badajoz, for example, the authorities kept the Casas del Pueblo closed, in direct contravention of government orders. At the same time, the Civil Guard co-operated with local rightists to hinder the electoral preparations of Socialists and republicans. In Huelva, rightist *alcaldes* forbade all Popular Front meetings. The few eye-witness accounts that have been published tell the same story. In Mijas (Málaga) the *cacique* deployed his retainers and the Civil Guard to prevent any leftist propaganda. They also took steps to stop the Left from getting its voters to the polls. In Novés (Toledo) the *cacique*, a *Cedista* who had tried to dominate the local peasantry by refusing to cultivate his lands, received full co-operation from the Civil Guard in his efforts to stop the Popular Front electoral campaign. After the elections the Left made accusations of rightist malpractice in several provinces. There seems to have been evidence of vote-buying in Sala-manca, but it was difficult to establish conclusive proof, and the Right had its counter-accusations. However, if the Left had been prepared to pervert the popular will at any cost, it had only to have accepted Portela's offer of a coalition with the government candidates. Yet it did not; it was the CEDA which availed itself of the machinery of falsification.[68]

The elections held on 16 February resulted in victory for the Popular Front. In fact, the parties of the Right increased their vote by more than three-quarters of a million votes, largely as a result of the disappearance of the Radical Party and the probable transfer of most of its votes to the CEDA.[69] In that sense, Gil Robles's immensely expensive electoral campaign had been a success. However, the parties of the Left increased their vote by about 1 million. Rightist policies during the *bienio negro* had ensured that the two vital conditions of the 1933 election result, leftist division and anarchist abstention, were not repeated. The consequent recriminations from monarchists and the more extreme *Cedistas* were directed at Gil Robles for having wasted valuable time and money on an ultimately unsuccessful legalist tactic. In fact, it was not until the final stages of the Civil War that, almost as an after-thought, the validity of the election results was impugned, as part of an attempt to legitimise the military rising of July 1936.[70]

However, it was precisely because the election results did represent a statement of the popular will that the Right so willingly turned to more violent tactics. Already the propaganda campaign of the anti-Marxist front had described defeat as the beginning of the holocaust. To a large extent, Gil Robles had staked the existence of his legalism on victory in the elections. Inevitably, after the apocalyptic tone of the electoral campaign, the results produced a feeling of despair within the CEDA. The youth movement and many of the movement's wealthy backers were immediately convinced of the necessity of securing by violence what was unobtainable by persuasion. By dint of massive expenditure and helped by leftist tactical folly, the Right had managed to gain victory in the 1933 elections. The vindictive use made of that triumph reunited the Left. Now, in 1936, an even greater amount had been spent on propaganda; thousands of Socialist, Communist and anarchists cadres were in jail; the machinery of electoral falsification had been at the disposal of the Right; every form of economic blandishment and threat had been used against voters. And still the Left had won. The October insurrection had prevented the peaceful establishment of the corporative state and the Popular Front elections postponed the possibility indefinitely. The elections marked the culmination of the CEDA attempt to use democracy against itself. This meant that henceforth the Right would be more concerned with destroying the Republic than with taking it over. In the course of the CEDA's gradual undermining of the regime, sufficient dissatisfaction with bourgeois democracy was spread to ensure that the Socialist movement would not be prepared to sacrifice itself for the Republic as it had done between 1931 and 1933. To that extent, for all its apparent failure, the CEDA had considerably eased the task of its more violent allies.

7 The Abandonment of Legalism: The PSOE, the CEDA and the Coming of War in 1936

The events of October 1934 and the results of the 1936 elections shattered CEDA dreams of being able to impose an authoritarian, corporative state without having to fight a civil war. Two years of aggressive rightist government had left the working masses, especially in the countryside, in a far from conciliatory mood. Having been thwarted once in its reforming ambitions, the Left was now determined to proceed rapidly with meaningful agrarian change, which would directly challenge the economic interests of the CEDA's backers. Having predicted that left-wing electoral success would be the prelude to the most spine-chilling social disasters, the CEDA had undermined its own *raison d'être*, the legal defence of landed and religious interests. The small section of the CEDA leadership, around Manuel Giménez Fernández and Luis Lucia, which believed that the party should now fully accept the Republic was unable to influence policy. It was rather late to attempt to reverse the effects of CEDA propaganda and already the rural and industrial oligarchies were switching their financial support to the conspiratorial Right. Gil Robles seems to have accepted that the legalist tactic had now outlived its usefulness. He did not try to stem the flow of CEDA members to more extremist organisations. At the same time, he played a positive role, in parliament and the press, of creating the atmosphere which made a military rising appear to the middle classes as the only alternative to catastrophe.

This is not to say that Gil Robles would not have preferred to see a socially conservative, corporative state introduced by legal means. However, his readiness to turn to the military in October 1934, December 1935 and February 1936 revealed that the end was more important than the means. Once convinced that the legal road to corporativism was blocked, he did everything possible to help those who were committed to violence. He had already made two crucial contributions to the success of the 1936 rising. The first, of which he was later to boast, was the creation of mass right-wing militancy. The other was the undermining of Socialist faith in the possibilities of bourgeois democracy. The success of the CEDA, both in and out of power, in defending the pre-1931 social structure had diminished the readiness of the PSOE to defend the regime.

In a very real sense, the ambiguity of the Socialist attitude to the Republic was to be the crucial factor of 1936. Prieto remained as convinced as ever of the need for Socialist collaboration in the government, not least because of his awarness of the strength and determination of the Right. However, despite controlling the PSOE executive, Prieto still faced the opposition of Largo Caballero and his revolutionary entourage. A series of factors influenced Largo's attitude – resentment of Prieto, a delight in the flattering attentions of the Communists and the PSOE leftists who hailed him as the 'Spanish Lenin', and, above all, the militancy of the Socialist rank-and-file. A combination of the economic crisis and the vindictive policies of landowners towards labour saw unemployment reach 843,872, or 17 per cent of the working population, by the end of February 1936.[1] The election results signalled an almost immediate return to the rural lock-out of 1933 and a new aggression from urban employers. Largo Caballero was frightened of a drift into the CNT or the PCE if he did not hold out hopes of a revolutionary future to the Socialist masses. Moreover, his most revolutionary proposal, the call for proletarian unity, merely concealed the desire to aggrandise the UGT by taking over both the anarchist and Communist movements. It suited the Communists to indulge his conviction that he was a real revolutionary, since they were confident of being able to dominate the united working class in the event of Largo's achieving a proletarian merger.

The anarchists and the Trotskyists remained distrustful. They believed that, although Largo accepted in theory that the working class had little to hope for from a bourgeois regime, in practice he could never break away from his reformist habits.[2] Thus, as far as they were concerned, Largo was doing no more than mouthing revolutionary platitudes. Their analysis was almost certainly correct, but the counterfeit nature of Largo's revolutionism did nothing to allay the fears of a middle class already terrified by rightist propaganda. Embittered by his experience of co-operation with the bourgeois regime between 1931 and 1933, and dètermined never again to suffer the opprobrium of another Casas Viejas, the UGT president hoped that the republicans would carry out the electoral programme and then make way for an all-Socialist government. Largo talked of getting into power 'by any means', but it seems unlikely that he ever considered insurrectionary action, since he was confident of ultimately being able to introduce sweeping social reform from the government. Thus, he opposed any interim Socialist participation in the government and continued to talk of revolutionary social change as being imminent. In doing so, he fell between two stools. The threat of a right-wing military or fascist coup might have been averted by revolutionary action, although the objective conditions were hardly conducive. Equally, a strong Socialist presence in the government might have curtailed fascist provocation before it created the necessary context for a coup. Largo's policy prevented either.

Apart from preventing the PSOE from joining the government, Largo did nothing to hinder the work of the republican government. However, to stand moderately aside was not enough. The Socialist leadership was fully aware of the rightist determination to prevent the Popular Front from enjoying its victory. Shortly before handing over power to Azaña, on 19 February, Portela Valladares had told the PSOE's acting secretary, Juan Simeón Vidarte, that there had been a serious threat of a military coup. At 3.30 a.m. on the morning of the 17th, as the first results were coming in, Gil Robles had gone to try to persuade Portela not to hand over power to the victorious Left. The CEDA leader told the Prime Minister that the Popular Front triumph meant anarchy, and asked him to declare martial law. At the same time, he sent his private secretary, the Conde de Peña Castillo, to get General Franco, who was still Chief of the General Staff, to urge Portela to bring in the army. When Portela refused, efforts to organise military intervention continued. General Goded tried to bring out the troops of the Montaña barracks in Madrid, but the officers of that and other garrisons refused to rebel without a guarantee that the Civil Guard would not oppose them. Franco sent an emissary to General Pozas, the head of the Civil Guard, asking him to join in a rising. Pozas refused and Franco, from his office in the Ministry of War, tried to get local commanders to declare martial law. A state of war was actually declared in Zaragoza and arrangements were made for such a declaration in Huesca and Granada. However, not enough local commanders responded, not least because Pozas surrounded all suspect garrisons with detachments of the Civil Guard. Had the coup worked, Gil Robles would have been made Prime Minister.[8]

As it was, the main consequence of these incidents was to frighten Portela into wanting to hand over power to Azaña immediately, instead of waiting for the opening of the Cortes in order to resign. To his annoyance, Azaña was forced to accept power prematurely, in the afternoon of 19 February. For the moment, then, the CEDA had no choice but to accept the election results. It was a great blow. Deprived of the benefits of legalism, the Catholic party seemed stunned. Rumours flew around that Gil Robles was about to abandon politics.[4] For a while too, it seemed that defeat had moderated CEDA spirits, that the pre-electoral demagogy was a thing of the past and that the party was ready to take part in an effort to tranquillise the political situation. The impression was illusory. Giménez Fernández visited Azaña on 20 February in a state of some agitation to inform him that the CEDA was prepared to vote for the amnesty of those imprisoned for political reasons since October 1934. It seemed to the Prime Minister that this was merely an attempt to avoid the consequences of the CEDA's aggressive policies during the previous eighteen months. 'If they had won the elections', he wrote bitterly in his diary, 'they would not have bothered about pacifying things and, far from granting an amnesty, they would have thrown into prison those who still had their freedom.'[5]

For the moment, however, moderation was ostensibly the CEDA's order of the day. Gil Robles, in an interview for *Le Petit Parisien*, said that opposition to the government would not be systematically destructive but prudent, intelligent and moderate. The CEDA National Committee met on 4 March to examine its position in the aftermath of the electoral defeat. A statement was issued reaffirming the party's commitment to the legalist tactic and claiming that it did not 'think remotely of solutions of force'. Given that Gil Robles had twice since mid December been involved in attempts to organise a coup, the statement may be seen less as a declaration of intent and more as a defensive ploy to mitigate leftist hostility and suspicion. CEDA support was offered to the government for the maintenance of public order, which, it was claimed, was seriously endangered by the supporters of the Popular Front.[6] Such support was clearly worthless to a government committed to fulfilling the aspirations of the masses, and not to their indiscriminate repression.

The Left was not impressed by Gil Robles's protestations of moderation. During the period of CEDA dominance, over 270,000 gun licences had been issued to rightists. Now, in the first half of March, armed attacks on prominent left-wing and liberal politicians were beginning. The Left did not accept that the action squads were manned only by Falangists and financed by the monarchists of Acción Española. *El Socialista* alleged that the CEDA was also organising motorised machine-gun assault groups. As the spring wore on, increasing numbers of rightist youths arrested for acts of violence were members of the JAP.[7] The Left did not feel that Gil Robles's concern for public order distinguished him from other rightist groups. Rather, it was seen, along with the Falangist provocations, as part of an attempt to discredit the government and prove the need for a dictatorial regime of the Right. The CEDA, Renovación Española, the Carlists and the Falange were regarded by the Left as specialised units of the same army. Only their tactics differed. They shared the same determination to establish a corporative state and to destroy the effective forces of the Left. Leaders of each group addressed the meetings of the others and were usually cheered. Space was regularly available in the CEDA press for favourable reports on the activities of its more violent rivals. Divisions between them never went beyond tactical criticisms of the CEDA's legalism. There is considerable evidence to support this interpretation of the parties of the Right. They were all the servants of the landed and industrial oligarchy in so far as they depended on it for their finance and all their political activities were directed towards the protection of its interests. They rarely broke unity in parliament, at election times or during the Civil War – a stark contrast with the divisions which split the Left, both in peace and in war.

The leftist press consistently warned its readers, albeit with varying success, not to respond to fascist provocation. On 12 March, Falangists tried to kill Luis Jiménez Asúa. Four days later, Largo Caballero's house was fired upon. It thus infuriated the Left when Gil Robles went to see the Minister of the Interior, Amós Salvador, on 17 March to protest about disorder. The CEDA also tabled a debate on the subject in the Cortes. Omitting to mention that the Falange and probably the JAP was implicated in the violence, CEDA protests declared that the government and the Left were responsible.[8] This emphasised the entirely propagandist nature of the CEDA's newfound moderation. Gil Robles was forced to tread delicately. He knew that the army was not yet ready to seize power. Equally, he was aware that an all-out obstruction of Azaña's government could only lead to a completely Socialist government, which would have given short shrift to the extreme Right. Accordingly, he devoted his energies to creating the atmosphere in which the middle classes, terrified by the spectre of disorder, would turn to the army as their only saviour.

On 19 March, Manuel Giménez Fernández called for the CEDA to make its position clear. Faced by his demand for a choice between the monarchy and the Republic, the members of the party's parliamentary minority decided that it was not 'opportune' to modify their position of republican legality. Asked to choose between democracy and fascism, the CEDA deputies expressed a preference for the former, but announced ominously that, if democracy were not possible, the party would be dissolved and each member would join the group nearest to his own ideology. On debating whether or not to remain in parliament, the deputies decided to stay, in order to use the Cortes as a tribune of propaganda. An open declaration of republicanism by the CEDA at this time would have strengthened the regime considerably against extremists of both Right and Left. However, the party's backers, and, indeed, most of its members, were not interested in consolidating the regime.[9] In the Cortes, CEDA deputies provocatively challenged the Socialists to abandon their speechmaking and to make a revolution. At the beginning of April, Largo Caballero revealed a similar provocation. Apparently, the Right was printing leaflets, supposedly issued by the UGT, containing detailed plans for revolution and black lists of the Left's enemies. Without renouncing his long-term objectives, the UGT president declared that the Socialists had no intention of disturbing public order.[10]

The way in which the Right in general, and the CEDA in particular, simply used parliament for its propaganda value was clearly established during the debates held to examine the validity of the recent elections. The Francoist commission set up to prove the illegitimacy of the republican government alleged that the Popular Front used its majority on the committee for examining electoral validity, the *comisión de actas*, to inflate the number of its deputies.[11] This was the reverse of the truth, since the committee acted with a punctilious legalism which, by excluding much evidence of falsification, consistently favoured the Right. In Santander, for instance, allegations of intimidation of republicans were ignored for lack of proofs witnessed by notaries, and the rightist victory was confirmed. Other decisions went in favour of the Right in the provinces of Ciudad Real, Toledo and Avila, for similar reasons. In Zaragoza province, evidence of intimidation aside, the results for seventy-eight villages were simply made up by the civil governor. Nevertheless, the rightist victory was approved because of a lack of legally acceptable documentary proofs. The results in the Balearic Islands, the fief of Juan March, were not even questioned. In Albacete there had been villages where more votes were cast than there were voters. The secret vote had also been transgressed. Yet, because the Left had not been able to afford to have a notary present during the election, insufficient acceptable evidence could be gathered to impugn the Albacete results.[12]

Despite the impartiality with which the *comisión de actas* carried out its functions, the CEDA contrived to cover up its own involvement in electoral malpractice and also to give the impression that it was being persecuted. This was a crucial part of the process whereby right-wing opinion was being convinced that democratic coexistence was no longer possible. Several of the constituencies whose results were being challenged were represented by senior rightist leaders. Gil Robles and Cándido Casanueva in Salamanca, Calvo Sotelo in Orense and Goicoechea in Cuenca were all in danger of losing their seats. If the most flagrantly dishonest elections of all, those of Granada, were invalidated, the CEDA stood to lose five deputies. Accordingly, Giménez Fernández, the CEDA representative on the *comisión de actas*, declared the *comisión* partisan and claimed that it was creating a parliament to be the instrument of a totalitarian regime. He then led a withdrawal of the CEDA deputies from the Cortes after a menacing speech which ended with the words 'we leave the fate of the parliamentary system in your hands'. This simple manoeuvre was designed to allow the CEDA to denounce the composition of parliament as abitrary and undemocratic. *ABC* claimed that the Right had been expelled from parliament.[13]

It was precisely to prevent the Right from being able to discredit the Cortes in this way that Prieto, the chairman of the *comisión*, had been prepared to come to an agreement with the CEDA representatives. They demanded more than he was prepared to concede. When he resigned the chairmanship for other reasons, the Right claimed it as proof that he, as an honest Socialist, was disgusted with the dishonest activities of the *comisión*. Prieto seems to have resigned partly out of a feeling that it would have been politically more prudent not to pursue the expulsion of senior right-wing figures, however justified it might have been. He felt that it was safer to have them in parliament than conspiring elswhere. He is also alleged to have resented pressure from Alcalá Zamora to approve the election of Portela Valladares in Pontevedra. He considered it wrong to ignore evidence of malpractice in Pontevedra and not to do the same in Orense. However, he made it quite clear in the Cortes on 7 April that he had not resigned because he felt that the Right was being swindled out of parliamentary seats.[14]

Prieto was replaced by Jerónimo Gomariz, the Unión Republicana deputy from Alicante. The findings of the *comisión* continued to be along the same lines as before. The results of both Pontevedra and Orense were approved. Those of Cuenca were annulled for two reasons. To begin with, there had been falsification of votes, and, then, once the defective votes were discounted, no candidate reached the minimum 40 per cent of the votes required for election. There was overwhelming proof that in Granada the legal representatives of the Popular Front had been imprisoned during the elections, that armed gangs had controlled voting booths and that people had been forced at gun-point to vote for the Right. Accordingly, the Granada elections were annulled. The situation regarding the Salamanca results was rather more complex. All six of the victorious right-wing candidates, Gil Robles, Cándido Casanueva, Ernesto Castaño and José Cimas Leal of the CEDA, together with two Carlists, Lamamié de Clairac and Ramón Olleros, were implicated in improperly soliciting the votes of the province's wheat-growers by offering to buy up their surplus stocks. Eventually the elections of Lamamié, Castaño and Olleros were declared void and they were replaced as deputies by the candidates with the next highest number of votes.[15]

With his own seat now secure, Gil Robles led the CEDA back into the chamber on 3 April, albeit at a price. Azaña, like Prieto, realised that there was little hope for Spanish democracy if the Right could claim through its massive press network that it was being excluded from the Cortes. Accordingly, in compensation for the CEDA return to parliament, Azaña postponed the municipal elections which were due to have taken place on 14 April. In the current atmosphere, these would almost certainly have led to a massive victory for Popular Front candidates and to the elimination of right-wing *alcaldes* throughout most of Spain. The Left was bitterly disappointed.[16] Gil Robles did little to earn his prize. On 7 April, when Prieto raised the issue of the validity of Alcalá Zamora's dissolution of the previous Cortes as a ploy to provoke his resignation, Gil Robles exploited the opportunity to misrepresent the work of the *comisión de actas*. He claimed that the CEDA had been cheated out of forty seats. He then protested about the electoral malpractice in Granada and Cuenca as if it had been the fault of the Left. Needless to say, the right-wing press, on reporting his speech, did nothing to clarify this cunning confusion of the issues.[17]

Prieto's campaign to depose Alcalá Zamora was to have serious consequences for the Republic. Prieto and Azaña were probably the only two politicians with the skill and popularity to stabilise the tense situation of the spring of 1936. They alone might have been able to keep up the pace of reform to a level which could have satisfied the militant Left, might have shown the determination to crack down on the extreme Right, and might have revealed the statesmanship to have attracted the moderate Right. In view of the fact that the CEDA had shown that it could accept only a Republic committed to social conservatism, it is unlikely that significant numbers of its members would have been converted to Republican loyalty by strong liberal government. However, Prieto and Azaña might have been able to stop the fascist provocations and the leftist responses to them which were preparing the ground for a military coup. As it was, by deposing the President and facilitating his replacement by Azaña, Prieto ensured that neither could lead the cabinet.

It has been claimed that it was the left wing of the Socialist Party which wished to be rid of Alcalá Zamora, and that this was because he was 'the last remaining guarantee of moderation within the Republican system'.[18] The only evidence which supports such an affirmation consists of remarks made by Luis Araquistain, shortly before his death, to Juan Marichal. Araquistain claimed that the Socialist Left neutralised both Azaña and Prieto, by making one President and stopping the other replacing him as Prime Minister, in order to prevent there being a strong figure at the head of the government.[19] This view is not substantiated by the facts. Prieto himself took the initiative in attempting to depose the President, against the advice of Besteiro and Fernando

de los Ríos. Seconded by his lieutenant, Vidarte, he made the successful parliamentary denunciation of the President. More significantly,
when the time came to seek a replacement, Prieto did more than anyone
to ensure that it would be Azaña. He rejected Vidarte's suggestion of
Besteiro, on the grounds that Largo Caballero would never agree. When
Vidarte mentioned de los Ríos, Prieto replied that the republicans
would never agree to a Socialist. Largo told Vidarte that he considered
it ludicrous to remove Azaña from where he was doing an essential job.
The UGT leader favoured Alvaro de Albornoz, but when Vidarte
suggested Albornoz to the PSOE executive Prieto objected and ensured
that the Socialists would not propose a candidate. When the Izquierda
Republicana proposed Azaña, Prieto insisted that the PSOE throw its
weight behind his candidacy.[20] He was gambling on being able to follow
Azaña as Prime Minister. If he failed, there would be no one else
capable of leading the government at a time of intensifying rightist
hostility.

The need for determined government was revealed on 15 April, when
Azaña presented his programme of government to the Cortes. He made
an extremely moderate speech and undertook to fulfil the electoral
programme of the Popular Front. Calvo Sotelo replied belligerently
that any government which relied on PSOE votes was only a step away
from Russian dominance. Gil Robles, speaking with less virulence, took
up Calvo Sotelo's theme that the country was in the grip of left-wing
anarchy and the government impotent. The clear implication was that
only solutions of force remained. Already, he said, his followers were
turning to paths of violence. He claimed that the time was rapidly
approaching when he would have to inform CEDA members that they
had nothing to hope for from legality. Speaking in apocalyptic terms
which hardly corresponded to the contemporary situation and which
completely ignored the rightist contribution to political violence, he
issued a dire warning,

> Half the nation will not resign itself to die. If it cannot defend itself
> by one path, it will defend itself by another. . . . Civil war is being
> brought by those who seek the revolutionary conquest of power and
> it is being sustained and weaned by the apathy of a government
> which does not turn on its supporters . . . when civil war breaks out
> in Spain, let it be known that the weapons have been loaded by the
> negligence of a government which has not been able to fulfil its duty
> towards groups which have stayed within the strictest legality.

This was an extremely partial interpretation of a situation which
had largely been created by the Right during the CEDA's sojourn in
power. Gil Robles's speech ended with a prophetic battle-cry which

closely prefigures what was actually to happen to the CEDA when the military rising took place : 'For the fatherland, whatever is necessary, even our disappearance if great national interests demand it. But it will not be a cowardly disappearance, offering our necks to the enemy. It is better to know how to die in the street than to be trampled on as a coward.' This speech has been interpreted as a sincere plea for order.[21] However, it is clear that the only order acceptable to the Right was one which did not challenge 'national interests'. In the vocabulary of the Right, such interests tended to be identical with those of the oligarchy. Gil Robles was effectively threatening war if the government's commitment to thorough reform of the social and economic structure were not dropped.

It is in this context that the growth of disorder during the spring of 1936 must be seen. That there was disorder is clear, but its scale was immensely exaggerated by the right-wing press and in the parliamentary speeches of Gil Robles and Calvo Sotelo. Moreover, it is impossible to apportion responsibility with the certainty that both sides enjoyed at the time. One factor cannot be ignored. Only two groups stood to benefit, even in theory, from the proliferation of indiscriminate lawlessness – the extreme Left and the 'catastrophist' Right. The Communists were overwhelmingly concerned during 1936 to broaden their support among the middle classes as part of the Popular Front tactic imposed by Moscow. They also hoped to take over much of the Socialist movement through unification with the PSOE Left. They were not concerned to seize power in the midst of a total breakdown of law and order. The anarchists were readier to use random violence, but it was not part of their overall strategy. In the Socialist movement, both *El Socialista* and *Claridad* constantly warned their readers to ignore rightist provocation. Having won the elections, none of the components of the Popular Front had any need to provoke violence in order to take power. The creation of an atmosphere of turmoil and disorder could, on the other hand, justify the resort to force to establish a dictatorship of the Right. Nevertheless, it remains almost impossible to say of street fights between Falangists and Communists or *Japistas* and Socialists what was provocation and what reprisal.

True as that may have been of the individual incident, a wider perspective confirms that it was the Right which benefited from the violence. If any of the main leftist groups hoped to use the breakdown of law and order, it remains to be explained why they consistently urged their followers not to get involved in reprisal/provocation spirals and why they stood by the Republican government as the basis of order.[22] It is significant that wealthy conservatives who had previously financed Gil Robles as the most effective defender of their interests were now switching funds to the Falange and the strike-breakers of the Sindicatos

Libres. At the beginning of March, *ABC* opened a subscription in favour of a little known Federación Española de Trabajadores, behind which could be discerned the figure of Ramón Sales, the self-styled fascist *agent provocateur* who had become famous in the political gangsterism of 1919–23. By the end of April the fund had reached 350,000 pesetas, donated by aristocrats, landowners, industrialists and many anonymous 'fascists' and Falangists. Since the money was never used for syndical purposes and an alarming number of individuals arrested for acts of violence were found to be members of the Sindicatos Libres, the Left had no doubts that this was a fund to finance *agents provocateurs*. Professional gunmen were being hired by the Right and their operations were designed to provoke the widest repercussions.[23]

The attacks on Socialist leaders such as Jiménez de Asúa and Largo Caballero were clearly aimed at provoking reprisals. The most successful operation of this kind was carried out in Granada on 9–10 March. A squad of Falangist gunmen fired on a group of workers and their families, wounding many women and children. The local unions called a general strike in the course of which there was widespread violence. Falange and Acción Popular offices were set on fire, the ACNP newspaper, *Ideal*, was destroyed, and two churches were burned. In Granada and elsewhere, incidents were often caused by strangers who disappeared as quickly as they had appeared. The most vociferous anarchists and Communists in Granada later revealed themselves as Falangists when the Nationalists took power. Given the thorough repression of the Left taking place during the war, it is highly unlikely that they were just turncoats. Throughout Spain, leftist municipal authorities went to considerable trouble to maintain order against possible disturbances. They were not helped by the fact that conservative members of the judiciary sympathised with Falangist activities. Judges who did take a strong line against rightist gunmen were, in their turn, selected as targets.[24]

The rightist press magnified every incident and, by the simple device of grouping on one page, devoted to 'social disorders', all brawls, fights and strikes, however insignificant, painted a picture of overwhelming anarchy. Inflated statistics of the alleged anarchy were then cited in the Cortes by Calvo Sotelo and Gil Robles as justification for a military rising. Calvo Sotelo actually made public invitations to the army to make a coup, but both he and Gil Robles knew that a rising was already being prepared. Falangist violence and the leftist responses to it provided material for speeches which placed the entire responsibility on the Left. Unhindered by censorship and fully reported, these speeches created an atmosphere of terror among large sectors of the middle and upper classes, who increasingly looked to the army for salvation.

Gil Robles's attitude to violence was more ambiguous than that of Calvo Sotelo. In the rightist division of labour, his function seems to have been to persuade more-moderate middle-class opinion that the government was impotent and that the only hope was the army and the Falange. His remarks in the Cortes on 15 April and his assiduous attendance at the funerals of Falangist gunmen strengthened the desired impression that political violence was the exclusive province of the Left. He seems to have been remarkably unpreoccupied by the growing taste for the use of force within the CEDA. Nothing was done to stop the drift of members to the Falange and no recruiting took place to replace those who left. It appeared that, in fulfilment of the decisions taken on 19 March, members were being allowed to join the group they found most congenial. Gil Robles implies in his memoirs that the CEDA was kept in being in order to make propaganda in parliament and to act as a shield for more violent groups. In the celebrated interview which he conceded to *El Defensor de Cuenca*, he virtually announced his approval for those 'who take the path of violence, believing that national problems can be solved in this way', condemning only those who left the CEDA because the party, out of power could no longer provide sinecures.[25] Almost immediately after the elections, the majority of the DRV (Derecha Regional Valenciana) rejected the moderation of their leader, Luis Lucia, in favour of direct action. The DRV was organising its own clandestine militia. Throughout the spring, at least 15,000 members of JAP joined the Falange. Many of those remaining with the CEDA were in active contact with groups committed to violence. Calvo Sotelo enjoyed some sympathy in Acción Popular. And, when the war broke out, thousands of *Cedistas* joined the Carlists.[26]

Even officially, the CEDA's links with the Falange were growing. At the beginning of May there were repeats of the disputed elections of Granada and Cuenca. In Granada the CEDA campaigned in exclusive alliance with the Falange. Local Socialists offered to let the CEDA win three seats if the name of the hated Ramón Ruiz Alonso were withdrawn from the right-wing list. Gil Robles refused and the Popular Front put up candidates for all the Granada seats. After the scandal of the previous elections, the masses were determined that they would not be swindled of their victory again. There appears to have been some harassment of rightist candidates, which, paradoxically, enabled the Right to derive benefit from almost certain defeat. Convinced that they could not win, the rightist candidates declared that they had been prevented from campaigning and simply withdrew from the contest, thereby impugning the validity of the elections.[27] In Cuenca, the rightist candidacy included José Antonio Primo de Rivera and General Franco. The Falange leader was included in order that his parliamentary immunity, in the event of success, would ensure his release from jail. General Franco's inclusion was prompted by the need to effect his transfer from the Canary Islands, where he was stationed, to the mainland, where the military conspiracy required his presence. Since the Cuenca election was technically a rerun, on the grounds that no candidate had obtained 40 per cent of the vote in February, new candidates could not be admitted, much to the chagrin of the CEDA deputies, who argued vainly in favour of the fascist leader.

The CEDA leadership's acquiescence in the growth of right-wing violence was a consequence of the realisation that legal methods could no longer keep inviolate the material interests of the landed oligarchy. The rightist obstruction of reform in the Constituent Cortes and the behaviour of landowners while the CEDA was in power had hardened the Left's determination to secure fast and effective reforms. Soon after Azaña's government was formed, his new Minister of Agriculture, Mariano Ruiz Funes, announced his commitment to rapid agrarian reform. The resurgent Landworkers' Federation intended to make him keep his word. After the harsh rural repression of the previous two years, in 1936, the FNTT began to expand at a vertiginous rate. Its militant leadership was in no mood to tolerate delays from the government or obstruction from the big landowners.

Immediately after the elections, Ricardo Zabalza, the dynamic secretary-general of the FNTT, had written to Ruiz Funes urging him to expedite the return to their lands of the leaseholders evicted in 1935. He also called for the re-establishment of the *jurados mixtos*, as well as the application of the decree on obligatory cultivation. In a letter to the Minister of Labour, Enrique Ramos, Zabalza demanded the introduction of a scheme for placing unemployed workers with landowners. A third letter, to Amós Salvador, Minister of the Interior, called for the disarming of the *caciques*. Seriously alarmed by the quantity of weapons at the disposal of landowners and their retainers, and by the fact that the rural upper classes still enjoyed the sympathy of the Civil Guard, the FNTT soon began to recommend that its members form popular militias, to prevent a repetition of the persecution of 1934 and 1935. Before the Cortes opened in mid March, there were peasant demonstrations all over Spain calling for the implementation of Zabalza's requests.[28] The FNTT's demands were not revolutionary but they still constituted a major challenge to the balance of rural economic power. Moreover, the events of the previous two years had exacerbated class tensions to a point which rendered the pacific application of the desired social legislation highly unlikely. Even leaving aside the bitter class-hatred now prevailing in the countryside, economic circumstances ensured that the reforms, which were essential to alleviate the misery of the landless peasants, could not be absorbed by the owners without a significant redistribution of rural wealth. Constant rain between December 1935 and March 1936 had seriously damaged the grain harvest and reduced the profit margins of growers large and small. This natural disaster simply clinched the reluctance of owners and workers alike to be conciliatory.

Throughout March the FNTT encouraged its members to take the law into their own hands, particularly where they had been the victims of eviction. In Salamanca and Toledo there were small-scale invasions of estates. Only in Badajoz were there mass land-seizures. After the government legalised these land invasions, many landowners either abandoned their estates or else adopted highly belligerent stances. Confrontation did not start on a major scale until after the negotiation of work contracts in April, after which time it became clear that the mixed juries intended to implement the contracts by means of substantial fines.[29] There were attacks on local FNTT sections in Cuenca and Ciudad Real. In Castellón, the owners refused to give work to men during the orange harvest. The *bases de trabajo* were virtually ignored in Badajoz, Córdoba, Ciudad Real, Málaga and Toledo. In Badajoz the owners refused work by day and used machinery to bring in the harvest by night. Faced with a virtual rural lock-out, the FNTT resorted to strike action in Málaga and Badajoz. It was remarkable that the FNTT managed to maintain the discipline of its members, even after an incident reminiscent of Casas Viejas. This took place at Yeste (Albacete). The peasants of the village had lost their livelihood when large tracts of fertile land were taken over to make a reservoir. Out cutting wood on once common, now private, land, they clashed with the Civil Guard. Seventeen peasants were killed, as many wounded, and fifty FNTT members were arrested.[30] Yeste and other clashes could have led to bloodshed on a large scale. However, the FNTT leadership restrained its rank-and-file because of its faith in the advanced agrarian policy being pursued by the government. That policy represented precisely the challenge to their social hegemony which the large landowners had struggled to resist since 1931. No longer able to put their hopes in the CEDA as their first line of defence, they began to look to the military for their protection.

At no time during the Second Republic was there a greater need for strong and determined government than in the spring of 1936. Military conspirators were plotting the overthrow of the regime. The youthful activists of Right and Left were clashing in the streets. Unemployment was rising and social reforms were meeting dogged resistance from the landowners. The problem became particularly acute after the elevation of Azaña to the presidency on 10 May. The new President immediately asked Prieto to form a government. Prieto had already advertised his suitability for the job by an extremely statesmanlike speech in Cuenca on 1 May. In that speech he had exposed the danger of a military rising under the leadership of General Franco, spoken of the need to remedy social injustice, denounced the provocations of those on the Right who rejected the election results, and criticised the revolutionary maximalists who were playing into their hands.[31] When summoned by Azaña on 11 May, he told him of his plans to restore order and accelerate reform. He intended to remove unreliable military commanders, reduce the power of the Civil Guard and disarm the fascist action squads. He also planned to promote massive public-works, irrigation and housing schemes, as well as speeding up agrarian reform. It is possible that such a programme of government, carried through with determination, might have prevented civil war. It was a project which would certainly have infuriated the Right and therefore required the unstinting support of leftist forces. Prieto was doubtful that he could count on the votes of the left wing of the PSOE.[32]

Prieto had good reason to anticipate the hostility of the supporters of Largo Caballero. Determined never again to carry out bourgeois policies in a coalition government with Republicans, Largo was waiting for the fulfilment of the Popular Front programme before pushing for an all-Socialist cabinet. He was in a strong position within the PSOE to impose his views. On 8 March, Caballerists had won all the senior posts in the Agrupación Socialista Madrileña, the strongest section of the PSOE. The Caballerist candidacy – Largo as president, Alvarez del Vayo as vice-president, Enrique de Francisco as secretary, and a committee including Llopis, Araquistain, Hernández Zancajo and Zabalza – was the same as that which hoped to wrest the PSOE executive from the Prietists. The ASM now became the centre of the Caballerist struggle for the party leadership. On 16 March, Largo had been elected as president of the PSOE parliamentary minority. The Caballerist grip on the party appeared unshakable. However, an apparent victory for Largo on 5 April did much to redress the balance. Alvarez del Vayo had arranged with the Comintern agent, Victorio Codovila, the unification of the Socialist and Communist youth movements. This seemed to fulfil part of Largo Caballero's ambition of uniting the working class, but in reality it simply meant the loss of about 40,000 young Socialists to the PCE. The FJS leader, Santiago Carrillo, already attended meetings of the central committee of the Communist Party.[33] Nevertheless, at the time the creation of the JSU (Juventudes Socialistas Unificadas) seemed a triumph for Largo, and Prieto had cause to be unsure of his own position. Apart from any theoretical objection to another republican–Socialist coalition, the Caballerists were furious during the first half of May at the undemocratic way in which Prieto had ensured Socialist support for Azana's candidacy.[34]

On 12 May, Prieto informed the PSOE parliamentary minority that

Azaña had asked him to form a government. He had little hope of receiving assurances of its support. On the previous day the minority had met to discuss the party's reply to the Presidential request for its advice on the formation of a government. Opposition within the PSOE to Prieto's becoming Prime Minister was generated by the *Claridad* group of Araquistain, Baraibar and Amaro del Rosal. It was feared within the group that Prieto might become 'the Noske of the Spanish revolution'. Accordingly, at the 11 May meeting of the parliamentary minority, when Prieto proposed that the PSOE recommend a broad Popular Front government, he was defeated by Alvarez del Vayo's counter-proposal for an all-republican cabinet. After Azaña had consulted all the parties, he made a formal offer to Prieto, who faced the minority again. When Largo Caballero argued against his acceptance, he conceded defeat almost without a fight. He did not defend his proposed government programme nor even reiterate the danger of a military rising and the need for a strong, broadly based administration. Apart from his own fatal tendency towards pessimistic defeatism, there were two possible reasons for Prieto's docile surrender of a possible government. On the one hand, he knew that many of the party Left believed that he exaggerated the dangers of a military coup simply to frighten them into supporting him and, therefore, he did not feel that they would give him the backing he needed. On the other hand, he suspected, probably wrongly, that Azaña did not really want him as Prime Minister. Even after Largo Caballero had carried the hostile vote in the minority meeting, Prieto could probably have still gone ahead. The party executive was solidly behind him and so too was the National Committee. He could count on the support of the republican parties. Vidarte urged him to form his government in the confidence that, when the time came, Largo would not vote against him in the Cortes. Yet, when Vidarte offered to arrange a meeting with the UGT president, Prieto replied bitterly, 'Let Caballero go to hell'.[35]

Azaña's offer to Prieto on 11 May was not the only attempt during the spring to form a strong government. Throughout April and May, desultory negotiations were taking place between Azaña, Miguel Maura, Claudio Sánchez Albornoz, Prieto, Besteiro, Giménez Fernández and Luis Lucia. Gil Robles was aware of Giménez Fernández's involvement in these conversations. He knew that they could have little chance of success. It was inconceivable that Prieto, having failed to get PSOE support for a coalition with the left republicans, would get it for a government including the CEDA. Moreover, since most CEDA deputies opposed Giménez Fernández, they were hardly likely to endorse a link with Prieto. Gil Robles was fully aware of the plans being made for a military rising and was involved in them. He would not have tolerated a government of national concentration which attempted to take action against the army. Thus, as his own account implies, he probably only tolerated Giménez Fernández's negotiations, out of a hope of splitting the Socialist Party.[36]

Azaña was replaced as Prime Minister by the consumptive Santiago Casares Quiroga, who was no match for the problems that he was called upon to solve. The men he chose for key posts symbolised the inadequacy of his cabinet. Neither his Minister of the Interior, Juan Moles, nor his Minister of Labour, Juan Lluhí Vallescá, fully appreciated the seriousness of the crisis. Casares himself consistently refused to believe reliable reports of military conspiracy. Both Casares and Moles failed to take action, despite repeated visits from Prieto and Largo Caballero. Prieto was deeply hurt when Casares, in reply to a warning about the plotters, said, 'I will not tolerate your menopausic outbursts.'[37] The Prime Minister's euphoria was entirely misplaced. The conspiracy, the ramifications of which went back to 1931, had got under way as soon as the election results were known and General Franco's attempt to have martial law declared had failed.

Gil Robles stayed in the background of the preparations for war – as did Calvo Sotelo. The CEDA leader was kept fully informed of the development of the conspiracy. Some of the key liaison officers between the military and civilian elements were *Cedistas*. On 8 March a crucial meeting of Generals Franco, Orgaz, Villegas, Fanjul and Varela took place in the home of the prominent CEDA stockbroker José Delgado. Party members who asked the *Jefe* for instructions were told to place themselves under the orders of the army as soon as the rising began. In a declaration made in 1942, Gil Robles stated that he co-operated in the *movimiento* with advice, 'with moral stimulus, with secret orders for collaboration, and even with economic assistance, taken in appreciable quantities from the party's electoral funds'. This last was a reference to 500,000 pesetas which Gil Robles gave to General Mola, confident that its original donors would have approved of his action.[38]

Throughout June and July, Gil Robles issued instructions to provincial CEDA leaders. On the outbreak of the rising, all party members were to join the military immediately and publicly, party organisations were to offer full collaboration without seeking benefit for the CEDA, youth sections were to join the army and not form separate militias, party members were not to take part in reprisals against the Left, power struggles with other rightist groups were to be avoided, and the maximum financial aid was to be given to the authorities. Only the instruction about reprisals was ignored, and *Cedistas* were prominent in the Nationalist repression in Granada and Valladolid. The first section of the CEDA to join the movimiento was the DRV. When General Mola was finalising civilian participation in June, the DRV secretary-general, José María Costa Serrano, offered 1250 men for the early moments of the rising and promised 10,000 after five hours and 50,000 after five days.[39]

Gil Robles was extremely discreet. Nevertheless, he did several useful services for the conspirators. In early July he accompanied the owner of *ABC*, Juan Ignacio Luca de Tena, on a mission to the Carlist leader, Manuel Fal Conde. They were sent by Mola to persuade Fal Conde to ease his conditions for Carlist participation in the rising.[40] Gil Robles's link with Mola was through the CEDA member, Francisco Herrera, who negotiated financial support for the conspiracy with Juan March. Arrangements for civilian participation were to have been made by Gil Robles, the Carlist Conde de Rodezno and Calvo Sotelo, but were frustrated by the assassination of the monarchist chief on 13 July. Gil Robles was determined not to be publicly compromised. It was through his intermediary, Herrera, that he discussed with Mola his future role in the post-war state. When Mola asked him to attend a meeting of rightist deputies in Burgos on 17 July to declare the government and the Cortes factious, and to make a public appeal for military intervention, he refused. After five years of propounding legalism, he felt that it would be 'indecorous'.[41]

It is in the light of Gil Robles's clandestine activities that his public pronouncements should be seen. Ambiguous speeches, which were ostensibly appeals for moderation, were also justifications of violence. On 19 May the CEDA leader replied in the Cortes to Casares Quiroga's presentation of his programme of government. Trying to drive a wedge between the components of the Popular Front, he claimed that the republican government was the servant, and would soon be the victim, of the Socialists. He also alleged that growing disorder was increasing the relevance of fascist solutions. If he was critical of fascism, it was only because of its foreign origins, its philosophical pantheism and its elements of state socialism. He claimed that people were being forced to turn to fascism because there was no other way for them to defend their interests. In identifying democracy and disorder, he made no mention of the contribution to political violence of the repressive and vindictive policies carried out while he was in power nor of the activities of fascist provocateurs. Indeed, he claimed that the arrest of Falangists was unjust. Declaring that democracy was now dead, he praised the trend to fascism as the result of 'a sense of patriotism . . . profoundly wounded to see that the rhythm of politics is not planned in accord with great national interests, but is controlled by you [turning to the Socialist deputies] with orders from Moscow'. With a provocative challenge to the Left's revolutionary ardour, he made a slighting reference to 'you ferocious revolutionaries who do nothing but talk'.[42] At the end of May the CEDA leader stated, in an interview given to an Argentinian daily, that democracy in Spain led inevitably to anarchy.

He also spoke highly of Italian Fascism, which he said had cured Italy of disorder and restored her international prestige.[43]

The picture painted by Gil Robles and Calvo Sotelo of disorder and impending communist revolution was exaggerated. In fact, the last thing that Moscow or the PCE wanted was revolution in Spain, for fear of unfavourable repercussions on Russian foreign policy.[44] The Socialists too, for all their internal divisions, went to great lengths to maintain order. However, disorder aside, two factors contributed to the credibility of the rightist view of the situation : the continued verbal revolutionism of the Caballerist wing of the PSOE and the high level of strike action, particularly where the CNT was involved, throughout the spring of 1936. Behind both the strikes and Caballero's revolutionary rhetoric was a mounting tide of working-class militancy. This was a consequence, in the first instance, of a backlog of grievances dating from the two years of untrammelled aggression by the employers when strikes had been virtually impossible. The situation was then exacerbated by the employers' refusal, sometimes out of economic necessity and sometimes out of tactical intransigence, to readmit workers who had been jailed after the Asturian rising.

The main strike wave did not, in fact, get under way until late May, long after the Right had begun denouncing industrial and rural anarchy. By then there was evidence of deliberate patronal intransigence in the form of lock-outs and the refusal to accept the decisions of arbitration committees. Many industrialists, either out of panic or knowledge of the imminent military rising, abandoned their enterprises and smuggled their capital abroad. The UGT and the Communists appear to have done everything possible to restrain their own militants and to persuade the CNT to do the same. Socialists came to blows with anarchists in Madrid over the UGT's attempts to end the major construction strike which took place in June and July. Communists also fought with anarchists in Málaga. The Caballerist newspaper, *Claridad*, regularly called upon the government to resolve social conflicts so that the rightist press would not be able to use them to foment middle-class terror. The worst strikes took place in Madrid in June among building workers, central-heating and lift engineers, clothing workers and woodworkers. By the middle of the month there were over 110,000 men on strike. The UGT tried to restrain the strikers and pushed for a rapid return to work after the mixed juries had found in favour of workers demands for wage increases and shorter hours. The tailoring employers refused for several weeks to accept arbitration. The construction-site owners withdrew from the juries, declared a lock-out and later boasted how their attitude had favoured the creation of a suitable atmosphere for a military rising. Throughout the crisis the Socialist and Communist press denounced the conflictive stance of the CNT.

Yet the fact remains that the employers provoked strikes in Barcelona by refusing to return to the forty-four hour week, which had been lost after October 1934, and in Badajoz, Málaga and other southern provinces by rejecting the *bases de trabajo* worked out by the mixed juries. Equally, the workers, embittered by the treatment they had received in 1934 and 1935, and intoxicated by the election victory of the Popular Front, were in a determined and aggressive mood.[45]

It was largely a perennial fear of losing his increasingly militant followers which lay behind Largo Caballero's continued predictions of the impending doom of the capitalist system. It is true that his experience of the rightist obstruction of reform between 1931 and 1933, together with his prison reading in 1935, had convinced him of the futility of reformism. However, between the theory and the practice stood a lifetime of pragmatic gradualism. In 1936 Largo Caballero continued to act very much as he had always done, concerned above all with consolidating the UGT. In speeches about the revolutionary road to socialism, he gave the workers what they wanted to hear. The fact that Largo was not seriously propagating immediate revolution was hardly appreciated by the middle classes who read his speeches. In that sense his attempts to maintain the allegiance of the Socialist rank-and-file were playing into the hands of Gil Robles and Calvo Sotelo.

The anarchists were highly suspicious of Largo Caballero's verbal revolutionism. In fact, the most revolutionary thing that the UGT president proposed was the unification of the proletariat. The anarchists suspected, with good reason, that Largo's proposal aimed simply at the takeover of the CNT masses by the UGT. After all, during the early spring the Socialists had made little secret of their conviction that they should have exclusive control of the revolutionary working class. On 18 April the Agrupación Socialista Madrileña had held a meeting to elaborate a new programme to be presented for discussion at the next PSOE congress. In view of the rising threat of fascism and the increasing radicalisation of the working class, the proposed new programme aimed at the elimination of reformist illusions from Socialist thinking. In the course of the discussion, in which Besteiro and Trifón Gómez defended the existing programme, a militant, Antonio Muñoz Lizcano, suggested the addition of a clause emphasising that the leadership of the revolution was the task of the Alianzas Obreras. Largo argued vehemently that the PSOE could and should do the job itself. He stated that the achievement of syndical unity would eliminate the need for the Alianzas. This was typical of Largo's attitude to working class unity. Throughout 1935, he had prohibited local UGT organizations taking part in joint activities with the Alianzas Obreras. The clear implication was that proletarian unification meant Socialist takeover.

Indeed, in the spring of 1936, Araquistain was involved in a polemic with the Communists over which workers' party should lead the revolution.[46] Accordingly, at the CNT congress held at Zaragoza in early May, the Socialists' bluff was called. The CNT rejected the notion of union with the UGT, but offered instead a revolutionary pact with certain conditions. These included the UGT's public rejection of the existing political and social regime, as well as the libertarian notion that the future organisation of society would be freely decided upon by the working class. Not surprisingly, Largo did not take up the CNT's invitation. Moreover, within a couple of days, he resuscitated the idea of the Alianzas Obreras, as a means of disciplining the CNT.[47] If the use that he made of the Alianzas in 1934 had revealed anything, it was that the domination of the working class movement by the UGT meant far more to Largo Caballero than any future prospect of revolution.

Socialist behaviour throughout 1936 belied the rhetoric even of the Caballerists. All sections of the PSOE were aware that a military rising was being prepared. Casares Quiroga's optimism that it could be crushed at will was not shared by the Socialists, nor by the PCE. Nevertheless, the only weapon at the Left's disposal, the revolutionary general strike, was never used. The spontaneous and unsynchronised character of the working class resistance to the rising in July suggests that there had been little preparation for revolutionary action in the preceding months. Indeed, when serious proposals for revolution were made in April by Joaquín Maurín, one of the leaders of the POUM, there were howls of protest. The recently-formed POUM, based on an alliance between the Bloc Obrer i Camperol and the Izquierda Comunista, was branded by the PCE as a renegade enemy of the Popular Front.[48] Much has been made of the divisions within the PSOE as a symptom of the party's revolutionary drift. Certainly the left wing of the party made regular statements – about the death agony of capitalism and the inevitable triumph of socialism – which Prieto, with some cause, regarded as dangerously provocative. Yet party discipline was maintained in such a way as to contribute to the stability of the republican government. The Caballerists, despite their reservations, joined the Prietists in voting for the nomination of Martínez Barrio as president of the Cortes and for the elevation of Azaña to the Presidency of the Republic. The PSOE consistently supported the government, and often, at the request of Casares Quiroga, held back awkward questions in the Cortes about military conspirators and the provocation of disorder.[49]

The Socialists were caught in a terrible dilemma. Prieto believed that strong reforming government was the only answer to the dangers threatening the Republic. However, there was nothing about the behaviour of the Right at the time to suggest that conspiratorial plans would have been voluntarily abandoned for anything less than policies like those which had been the norm during the *bienio negro*. Largo Caballero was convinced, after the experience of the Constituent Cortes, that a republican-Socialist coalition such as Prieto advocated would be incapable of carrying out adequate measures. The UGT president aimed at an all-Socialist government, in much the same way as he aimed at an all-UGT labour movement. This division of opinion, exacerbated by personal resentments, paralysed the political initiative of the Socialist movement. In fact, Largo Caballero and many of his closest associates – Carlos de Baraibar, Luis Araquistain, Carlos Hernández Zancajo and Wenceslao Carrillo – never favoured the idea of splitting the party. They hoped to impose their more revolutionary programme on the rest of the PSOE by means of a party congress. Initiatives to break up the party as a prelude to the unification of schismatic Socialists with the PCE came from fellow travellers like Alvarez del Vayo, Margarita Nelken and JSU leaders Santiago Carrillo and Federico Melchor.[50] On two occasions, meetings addressed by Prieto and González Peña, at Egea de los Caballeros (Aragon) and Écija (Seville), were disrupted by JSU squads in a way which suggested a deliberate attempt to drive a wedge into the PSOE.[51]

Accordingly, the two main consequences of the Socialist division were the prevention of an attempt at strong government and the worsening of middle-class fears of revolution by the demagogic behaviour of the pro-Communist left-wing of the PSOE. The fact that the Communists, for all their demagogy, did not aim at revolution, and that Largo Caballero's rhetoric was directed primarily at the aggrandisement of the UGT, meant little to the middle classes. After all, leftist demagogy, combined with visible evidence of strikes and politically motivated disorder, simply seemed to verify the exaggerated picture of unmitigated chaos being painted by Calvo Sotelo and Gil Robles. The readiness of the JSU to become involved in street clashes with Falangists, under the misguided impression that they were undertaking revolutionary activities, and the CNT's maintenance of a hard line during the strikes of June and July obscured an important internal development within the PSOE. At the end of June the PSOE executive held elections to cover six vacancies, created by the resignation of Largo Caballero and his lieutenants on 16 December 1935 and the death of the party vice-president, Remigio Cabello, in April 1936. Figures for the voting differed widely in the versions published by *El Socialista* and *Claridad*. Many of the votes claimed by the Caballerists were not from fully-paid-up members of the party, but from JSU militants. The Prietist candidacy was declared to have won. Feeble protests from *Claridad* that the Caballerist line had carried the day in Cádiz, an anarchist stronghold, and Jaén, reinforced the impression that the tide was turning in favour of Prieto.[52]

The victory of the PSOE moderates did not go undisputed within the Socialist movement. In any case, it seems unlikely that the Right would have been sufficiently impressed to have changed its tactics. The army's preparations were well advanced. Strikes and disorder, whatever their origin, had convinced much middle-class opinion that Gil Robles and Calvo Sotelo were right when they asserted that nothing could be expected from the democratic regime. On 16 June, in the Cortes, Gil Robles delivered his last great denunciation of the Popular Front government. Superficially couched as an appeal for moderation, it was more of a lengthy justification of the rising that was under way. The CEDA leader read out a long list of murders, beatings, robberies, church-burnings and strikes, a catalogue of disorder for which he placed the responsibility on the government. Some of it was true, some of it blood-curdling exaggeration. He gave no indication that the Right had had any participation in what he described. Indeed, he protested about the imprisonment of Falangist and JAP terrorists and the imposition of fines on recalcitrant employers. The blame for disorder was put firmly on the fact that the government relied on the votes of Socialists and Communists. As long as that remained the case, thundered Gil Robles, there could never be peace in Spain.[53] Since Gil Robles was far from being the most extreme figure on the Right, his attitude indicated that even a moderate government presided over by Prieto would find little tolerance outside the Popular Front.

By the early spring of 1936, coexistence was impossible unless the Left relinquished its aspirations of structural reform or the Right dropped its opposition to such reform. A republican–Socialist coalition under Prieto would have been committed to a rhythm of social change which had been shown to be intolerable to the rural upper classes. In 1936, after five years of accelerating social misery, the Left looked for reform more advanced than that which had been possible between 1931 and 1933. The legalist Right's obstructionist tactics then, and its social policies when in power, revealed the profound incompatibility between the two views of social organisation which were in conflict. On 1 July the Agrarian José María Cid attacked the situation which had developed in the countryside under the republican Minister of Agriculture, Ruiz Funes.[54] Yet the Left regarded what the Minister was doing as the minimum acceptable. Given the Right's determination not to concede, civil war could have been avoided only if the Left had been prepared to accept the pre-1931 social structure.

Gil Robles's speech on 16 June was an *a priori* attribution of responsibility for the war to the Left. The accusation was repeated after the murder of Calvo Sotelo by Assault Guards in reprisal for the killing of two of their number by rightist gunmen.[55] Two days after the discovery of Calvo Sotelo's body on 13 July, Gil Robles spoke again at a meeting of the permanent deputation. He accused the government of criminal, political and moral responsibility for the assassination. He reiterated that the Left had ensured that nothing could be achieved by democratic methods and that it must take the blame for the growth of a movement of violence in Spain.[56] He did not recall that preparations for a military rising had been under way, with his knowledge, since the February elections.

When war broke out on the night of 17 July, the CEDA rank-and-file joined the rebels wherever they could. Gil Robles himself, determined that no blood should be seen to be on his hands, went to France. Expelled by the Blum government, he proceded to Lisbon, where he helped establish a Nationalist junta which organised supplies, propaganda and financial assistance for the rebel cause.[57] He publicly praised the JAP for their patriotic role in joining the rising.[58] In April 1937, when General Franco forcibly united the various political forces of the Nationalist zone, Gil Robles wrote to him to place the entire organisation of Acción Popular at his disposal for its incorporation in the new single party.[59] The *Jefe* visited rebel Spain on several occasions, notably in August 1936 and May 1937, but met an increasingly hostile reception. In the charged atmosphere of war, his legalist stance had no place. Nevertheless, the Francoist war effort was devoted to achieving many of the goals to which the CEDA had aspired. Throughout the Nationalist zone, and in all of Spain after 1939, a corporative state was established. Trade unions were abolished, the left-wing press was destroyed. Socialist and other leftist cadres who survived the war but could not escape into exile were subjected to long terms of imprisonment, if not executed. The pre-1931 social structure was re-established. The Republic's social legislation disappeared. The rural domination of the *caciques* and the Civil Guard was consolidated.

Despite its use of a radical fascist party, the Falange, to mobilise the population of the Nationalist zone during the war, the Francoist state remained the instrument of the traditional oligarchy. The veneer of anti-oligarchical novelty adopted by Hitler and Mussolini was eschewed by Franco. His corporative state jealously guarded the traditional agrarian structure at least until the mid-1950s. Only during the brief period of dominance of the ex-CEDA deputy Ramón Serrano Súñer, while an Axis victory in the world war seemed likely, did Falangist counsels carry more weight than those of Carlists, orthodox monarchists and *Cedistas*. Francoist links with the old order made the Republic appear as a mere interlude. In that interlude, a challenge had been mounted to the existing balance of social and economic power. The most effective part of that challenge was constituted by the reforming programme of the Socialists, because it had the legal sanction of parliament. The response of the traditional Right was twofold. The resort to violence had little possibility of success in the early years of the Republic and the defence of the old social order was assumed by the legalists. So successful were the tactics of the CEDA and the Agrarians in blocking reform and building up a mass party that the optimistic reformism of the Socialists was hardened into a more aggressive and apparently revolutionary stance. The rising of October 1934 and the election results of 1936 signalled the impossibility of defending traditional structures by means of the legal imposition of a corporative state. Given the apparent determination of the working class to introduce major reforms and of the oligarchy to resist them, the failure of legalist tactics could not but lead to a resurgence of the 'catastrophist' Right and the imposition of a corporative state by force of arms.

Notes

CHAPTER 1

1. Richard A. H. Robinson, *The Origins of Franco's Spain* (Newton Abbot, 1970) p. 12.
2. Salvador de Madariaga, *Spain: A Modern History* (London, 1961) p. 455. A more sophisticated version of the same thesis is to be found in Guillermo Díaz, *Como llegó Falange al poder* (Buenos Aires, 1940) pp. 63–74.
3. Andrés Saborit, *Julián Besteiro* 2nd edition (Buenos Aires, 1967) p. 250; Luis Romero Solano, *Vísperas de la guerra de España* (Mexico, n.d. [1947]) pp. 176–7; Carlos de Baraibar, 'La traición del Stalinismo', *Timón* (Buenos Aires) no. 7 (June 1940); speech of Luis Araquistain in Toulouse on 24 Jan 1947, quoted in Saborit, *Besteiro*, p. 262; and remarks by Araquistain to Juan Marichal in introduction to Manuel Azaña, *Obras completas*, 4 vols (Mexico, 1966–8) vol. III, pp. xxxi–xxxii.
4. This has been noted by critics of both Right and Left. See Ricardo de la Cierva, 'Marxismo en España, hoy', *ABC*, 8 June 1973; Juan Andrade, *La Burocracia reformista en el movimiento obrero* (Madrid, 1935), an acute critique; Fernando Claudín, 'Dos concepciones de la vía española al socialismo', *Horizonte español 1966* (Paris, 1966) vol. II, p. 60.
5. Gerald Brenan, *The Spanish Labyrinth*, 2nd edition (Cambridge 1950) p. 218; Grandizo Munis, *Jalones de derrota, promesa de victoria* (Mexico, 1948) p. 50; Gerald H. Meaker, *The Revolutionary Left in Spain 1914–1923* (Stanford, Calif., 1974) pp. 10–14, 196–7.
6. *El Socialista*, 10 Nov 1917.
7. Juan Pablo Fusi Aizpurua, 'El movimiento obrero en España 1876–1914', *Revista de Occidente* (Madrid) no. 131 (Feb 1974); Meaker, *Revolutionary Left*, p. 4.
8. Juan Antonio Lacomba, *La Crisis española de 1917* (Madrid, 1970); Manuel Tuñón de Lara, *El Movimiento obrero en la historia de España* (Madrid, 1972) ch. 10.
9. Juan Díaz del Moral, *Historia de las agitaciones campesinas andaluzas*, 3rd edition (Madrid, 1973); Alberto Balcells, *El Sindicalismo en Barcelona 1916–1923* (Barcelona, 1965).
10. Juan Pablo Fusi, *Política obrera en al país vasco 1880–1923* (Madrid, 1975) ch. 8. David Ruiz, *El Movimiento obrero en Asturias* (Oviedo,

1968 pp. 162–181, indicates the bitterness of social conflict in the region.

11. Dec 1919, June 1920, Apr 1921. The best accounts are Meaker, *Revolutionary Left*, passim, and Tuñón, *Movimiento obrero*, pp. 681–717.

12. Gabriel Morón, *El Partido Socialista ante la realidad política española* (Madrid, 1929) pp. 109–14.

13. *El Socialista*, 14 Sep 1923, was strongly against resistance.

14. This position is fervently stated in Francisco Largo Caballero, *Presente y futuro de la Unión General de Trabajadores de España* (Madrid, 1925) passim.

15. Luis Araquistain, '¿Qué hacen los socialistas?', *El Socialista*, 1 May 1929; Enrique de Santiago, *La Unión General de Trabajadores ante la revolución* (Madrid, 1932) pp. 21, 22, 25, 44; Manuel Cordero, *Los Socialistas y la revolución* (Madrid, 1932) pp. 43–51, 60–7. Largo Caballero's *Mis recuerdos: cartas a un amigo* (Mexico, 1954) is strangely uniformative on the issue, but is vituperative (see esp. pp. 90–1) against those who opposed the passive tactic adopted by the PSOE and UGT.

16. The anarchists were attacked from the first moment; see José Peirats, *La CNT en la revolución española*, 2nd edition, 3 vols (Paris, 1971) vol. I, pp. 37–8. The Dictator offered to tolerate the Communists if they would undertake to abandon their agitation. When the leadership refused, the arrests began, see José Bullejos, *La Comintern en España* Mexico, 1972) p. 54.

17. Joaquín Maurín, *Los Hombres de la Dictadura* (Madrid, 1930) pp. 153–6.

18. Morón, *Partido Socialista*, pp. 78–85.

19. Antonio Ramos Oliveira, *Politics, Economics and Men of Modern Spain* (London, 1946) p. 205.

20. The thought of Besteiro has received considerable attention of late in Spain. See Alberto Míguez, *El Pensamiento filosófico de Julián Besteiro* (Madrid, 1971); Andrés Saborit, *El Pensamiento político de Julián Besteiro* (Madrid, 1974); and E. Lamo de Espinosa, *Filosofía y política en Julián Besteiro* (Madrid, 1973), which contains a detailed account of the positivism and neo-kantianism which always pervaded Besteiro's Marxism. Besteiro provided the introduction to a translation of Kautsky's *El Programa de Erfurt* (Madrid, 1933).

21. Lamo, *Besteiro*, pp. 302–7.

22. *El Socialista*, 5 Feb and 14 Nov 1924.

23. Largo Caballero, *Mis recuerdos*, p. 37 and *Presente y futuro*, p. 7.

24. Largo Caballero, *Presente y futuro*, pp. 42–3; Santiago, *UGT*, pp. 24–5.

25. This rivalry is apparent in many Socialist writings of the time. See Largo Caballero, *Presente y futuro*, passim; Santiago, *UGT*, p. 44; Cordero, *Socialistas*, p. 64; *Convocatoria y orden del día para el XII congreso ordinario del PSOE* (Madrid, 1927) p. 91. It is expressed most openly by Antonio Ramos Oliveira, who in *Nosotros los marxistas: Lenin contra Marx* (Madrid, 1932) p. 185, accepts the persecution of the anarchists and Communists by the Dictator on the grounds that such groups are incompatible with any regime.

26. *Convocatoria*, p. 89.

27. *ABC*, 29 Sep 1929.

28. *El Socialista*, 2 Oct and 1 Nov 1923; Ruiz, *Asturias*, pp. 188–9.

29. Ruiz, *Asturias*, p. 189.

30. Tuñón, *Movimiento obrero*, p. 721. See ibid., p. 776 for evidence of strike action.

31. *Convocatoria*, p. 96.

32. Largo Caballero and Cordero on the Junta de Abastos, in Santiago, *UGT*, p. 39. Lucio Martínez and other members of the executive were on various other committees; see Tuñón, *Movimiento obrero*, p. 776.

33. *Convocatoria*, pp. 101–2.

34. Manuel Tuñón de Lara, *La España del siglo XX*, 2nd edition (Paris, 1973) p. 151.

35. *Convocatoria*, p. 103.

36. *El Socialista*, 11 Dec 1923; Virgilio Zapatero, *Fernando de los Ríos: los problemas del socialismo democrático* (Madrid, 1974) p. 77.

37. *El Socialista*, 13 Dec 1923; Largo Caballero, *Presente y futuro*, pp. 42–7, and *Mis recuerdos*, pp. 90–2.

38. Ruiz, *Asturias*, pp. 190–1.

39. Vicente Marco Miranda, *Las Conspiraciones contra la Dictadura* Madrid, 1930) p. 61, shows that Besteiro would not authorise a move against the regime unless this involved no risk for the Socialists. Later PSOE apologists were to point out with some justification that most of the resistance movements aimed at restoring the monarchy and therefore offered little benefit to the workers movement (Cordero, *Socialistas*, p. 74; Ramos Oliveira, *Nosotros*, pp. 182–3; *El Socialista* 12 May 1925 and 26 Feb 1926).

40. Eduardo Aunós, *La Política social de la Dictadura* (Madrid, 1944) pp. 46–63.

41. Santiago, *UGT*, pp. 25–7, 32–3.

42. Ibid.; Cordero, *Socialistas*, p. 63; Ramos Oliveira, *Nosotros*, pp. 186, 193. Cf. Maurín, *Hombres de la Dictadura*, p. 189.

43. In 1927 there were 107 recorded strikes, involving 70,616 workers and with 1,311,891 working days lost. In 1928, with approximately the same number of strikes and strikers, only 771,293 days were lost. In 1929, the numbers dropped even further: ninety-six strikes, 55,576 strikers and 313,065 days lost (Tuñón, *Movimiento obrero*, p. 780). This seems to reflect the success of the *comités paritarios* in anaesthetising working-class dissent. In Barcelona, for instance, unemployment almost doubled between early 1927 and late 1929; see Alberto Balcells, *Crisis económica y agitación social en Cataluña* (Barcelona, 1971) p. 34. Moreover, after rising slowly until 1925, wages began to fall steadily thereafter, albeit with great regional and trade variations. Staple working-class foods such as potatoes, bread and olive oil also rose in price. For an analysis of wages and prices, see Tuñón, *Movimiento obrero*, pp. 755–73. Cf. Joaquín Maurín, *La Revolución española* (Madrid, 1932) p. 51.

44. Ruiz, *Asturias*, pp. 191–5.

45. Edward E. Malefakis, *Agrarian Reform and Peasant Revolution in Spain* (New Haven, Conn., 1970) p. 159. *Convocatoria* (pp. 11–2) reprints

demands from Socialist organisations in Asturias, Andalusia and Zaragoza for the PSOE to adopt a more coherent and dynamic agrarian policy.

46. Eduardo Aunós, *Itinerario histórica de la España contemporánea* (Barcelona, 1940) pp. 377–9. Santiago (*UGT*, p. 45) claims that sixty-five rural sections of the UGT, with 15,000 members, were closed down by 1928. By December 1929 the UGT had only 30,000 rural members; in August 1922 there had been 65,405.

47. Morón, *Partido Socialista*, pp. 124–35.

48. Saborit, *Besteiro*, pp. 169–70; *Convocatoria*, p. 121.

49. Maurín, *Hombres de la Dictadura*, pp. 188–9; Andrade, *Burocracia reformista*, passim; Ricardo Sanz, *El Sindicalismo y la política* (Toulouse, 1966) p. 149; Alvaro de Albornoz, prologue to Morón, *Partido Socialista*, p. 25.

50. See above notes 44 and 46. It is difficult to establish UGT gains during the period. Santiago (*UGT*, pp. 44–5) admits the loss of 15,000 rural labourers, but claims in compensation a gain of 17,000 industrial workers by the time of the UGT's Sixteenth Congress, in September 1928. Even in the mining sector, despite the spectacular losses in Asturias, there were some gains. Llaneza managed to secure better wages and conditions for the copper-miners of the British-owned Tharsis mines near Huelva. This success led miners in the area to join the *Federación Minera*; see S. G. Checkland, *The Mines of Tharsis* (London, 1967) pp. 212–4. Overall gains within the UGT were not substantial: 1923, 210,617; 1924, 210,742; 1925, 217,386; 1926, 219,396; 1927, 223,349; 1928, 210,567; 1929, 238,501. (Figures from Tuñón, *Movimiento* obrero, pp. 721, 775, 784; Santiago, UGT, p. 45; Maurín, *Hombres de la Dictadura*, pp. 197–8.) They represent a poor return considering the UGT's privileged position; hardly a greater increase than might have been expected in normal years and certainly not an absorption of CNT rank-and-file. Equally the figures represent dues-paying members and times were hard. At the Sixteenth Congress of the UGT, 10–15 September 1928, the 591 delegates represented only 141,269 affiliates – Renée Lamberet, *Mouvements ouvriers et socialistes: l'Espagne* (Paris, 1953) p. 146 – but probably because some sections just could not afford to send a delegate. The PSOE fared slightly better, increasing from 5395 in 1923 to 12,815 in 1929, according to Maurín, *Hombres de la Dictadura*, p. 199. Tuñón (*Movimiento obrero*, pp. 732, 775) gives figures of 8215 in 1923 rising to 13,181 in 1929. Maurín (*Hombres de la Dictadura*, p. 200) claims that the increase merely represented existing UGT members who had also joined the PSOE. In major industrial centres PSOE membership was extremely low. In Asturias it dropped from 528 in 1923 to 391 in 1929; in the Basque country from 670 to 631.

51. Morón, *Partido Socialista*, pp. 182–5; *El Socialista*, 10 July 1928.

52. PSOE: president, Besteiro; vice-president, Largo Caballero; treasurer, Saborit; secretary, Lucio Martínez Gil; minutes secretary, Wenceslao Carrillo. UGT: president, Besteiro; vice-president, Saborit; secretary-general, Largo Caballero; treasurer, W. Carrillo. (Tuñón, *Movimiento obrero*, p. 784.)

53. Morón, *Partido Socialista*, pp. 189–90. This was the beginning of the 1930 wave of strikes throughout the south; see Lamberet, *Mouvements ouvriers*, pp. 146–7.

54. Ruiz, *Asturias*, pp. 195–7; Gabriel Santullano, 'Las organizaciones obreras asturianas en los comienzos de la segunda República', in M. Tuñón de Lara, *Sociedad, política y cultura en la España de siglos XIX–XX* (Madrid, 1973 p. 257.

55. *El Socialista*, 3 Jan 1929. Santiago (*UGT*, p. 54) points out that, in the latter stages of the Dictadura, following strikes (particularly in Santander and Vigo), 150 UGT sections were dissolved, ninety-three workers' centres were closed down and hundreds of Socialists were arrested.

56. Saborit, *Besteiro*, p. 172.

57. *Boletín de la Unión General de Trabajadores de España* (BUGT), Aug 1929; *El Socialista*, 1 Sep 1929.

58. Santiago, *UGT*, p. 47.

59. The text of Besteiro's manifesto is reprinted in Saborit, *Besteiro*, pp. 175–80.

60. *BUGT*, Sep 1929; *El Sol*, 17 Sep 1929 (Emphasis added.)

61 Hundreds of UGT members had been imprisoned in Santander after a strike by the local metalworkers' union (Sindicato Metalúrgico Montañés). See Santiago, *UGT*, 54; *El Socialista*, 14 Jan 1930.

62. *El Socialista*, 5 and 13 Feb 1924.

63. *El Sol*, 6, 13 and 17 Feb 1924.

64. In 1924 Besteiro spent a long period in England, studying the Workers' Educational Association. It was the culmination of a growing interest in the achievements of the Labour Party and in the English guild movement. See Lamo, *Besteiro*, pp. 57–8, 310–2. At the height of the polemic surrounding the so-called bolshevisation of Spanish socialism, Besteiro published an introduction to a series of essays by English socialists – Stafford Cripps et al., *Problemas de gobierno socialista* Madrid, 1934).

65. Zapatero, *De los Ríos*, p. 71. Fernando de los Ríos, in his *El Sentido humanista del socialismo* (Madrid, 1926), gives an idea of his notion of the pre-eminence of democratic socialism. See also Elías Díaz, 'Fernando de los Rios: socialismo humanista y socialismo marxista', *Sistema* (Madrid) no. 10 (July 1975) 115–25.

66. Lamo, *Besteiro*, p. 70.

67. The complete text is reprinted in Saborit, *Besteiro*, pp. 188–90.

68. Dámaso Berenguer, *De la Dictadura a la República* (Madrid 1946) pp. 51–2.

69. Emilio Mola Vidal, *Obras completas* (Valladolid 1940) pp. 351–3.

70. Lamo, *Besteiro*, pp. 72–3.

71. Miguel Maura, *Así cayo Alfonso XIII* (Barcelona 1966) pp. 50–9; José Sánchez Guerra, *Al servicio de España* (Madrid 1930); Angel Ossorio y Gallardo, *Mis memorias* (Buenos Aires 1946) pp. 165–6. Largo demanded that the PSOE executive censure Prieto for appearing at a banquet with Sánchez Guerra; Gabriel Mario de Coca, *Anti-Caballero*

(Madrid 1936) p. 18; PSOE, *Memoria: Convocatoria y orden del dia para el XIII Congreso ordinario* (Madrid 1932) 68–9.

72. Ruiz, *Asturias*, pp. 214–7.

73. Tuñón, *Movimiento obrero*, p. 790 gives the following figures: (1929) strikes 96, strikers 55,576, days lost 313,065; (1930) strikes 402, strikers 247,460, days lost 3,747,360.

74. Mola, *Obras*, p. 260.

75. Bullejos, *Comintern*, pp. 100–1; José Peirats, *Los Anarquistas en la crisis política española* (Buenos Aires, 1964) pp. 60–4; Mola, *Obras*, p. 353; Tuñón, *Movimiento obrero*, p. 792; Lamberet, *Mouvements ouvriers*, pp. 146–7.

76. Mola, *Obras*, pp. 352–3; Andrade, *Burocracia*, pp. 204–20.

77. Many anarchist, and even Soçialist, militants interviewed by the author recalled with bitterness or amusement the great collection of sinecures accumulated by Cordero. For lists, see Andrade, *Burocracia*, pp. 242, 245; Joaquín del Moral, *Oligarquía y 'enchufismo'* (Madrid, 1933) pp. 80–1.

78. Cordero, *Socialistas*, p. 88.

79. Mola, *Obras*, pp. 353–4, 373, 394, 399, 404, 421, 437–46.

80. *Anuario estadístico de España, 1931* (Madrid, 1931) p. 606; *El Obrero de la Tierra*, 17 Sept 1932. This still did not bring the FNTT back to pre-Dictatorship levels. In August 1922 the UGT had 510 agrarian sections, with 65,405 members – *Anuario estadístico, 1923* (Madrid, 1923) pp 308–9. BUGT, Nov 1931, complained that one section which had 80,000 received subscriptions from only 21,000.

81. Constancio Bernaldo de Quirós, 'Informe acerca del paro de los jornaleros del campo de Andalucía durante el otoño de 1930', in Ministerio de Trabajo y Previsión Social, *La Crisis andaluza de 1930–1* (Madrid, 1931) pp. 8–35.

82. Cordero, *Socialistas*, pp. 93–4.

83. Maura, *Así cayó*, pp. 71–3; Saborit, *Besteiro*, p. 191; Largo Caballero, *Mis recuerdos*, p. 107; Zapatero, *De los Ríos*, pp. 82–3; Lamo, Besteiro, p. 72.

84. Saborit, *Besteiro*, p. 194; Lamo, *Besteiro*, p. 74; Zapatero, *De los Ríos*, pp. 84–5; Mario de Coca, *Anti-Caballero*, p. 11; Largo Caballero, *Mis recuerdos*, p. 108.

85. The *Agrupaciones Socialistas* of Bilbao, Valladolid and San Sebastián had already ignored a National Committee instruction to send councillors to the re-established town councils; see Saborit, *Besteiro*, p. 194.

86. Maura, *Así Cayó*, p. 83.

87. Saborit, *Besteiro*, p. 191.

88. Indalecio Prieto, *Convulsiones de España*, 3 vols (Mexico, 1967–9), vol. I p. 61.

89. Largo Caballero, *Mis recuerdos*, pp. 113–4; Saborit, *Besteiro*, pp. 194–5.

90. Ignacio Hidalgo de Cisneros, *Cambio de rumbo*, 2 vols (Bucharest, 1964) vol. I, pp. 221–4. Hidalgo says that the local tramway workers were extremely enthusiastic regarding the revolutionary movement.

91. *El Socialista*, 8–13 Oct 1932.

92. Julio Alvarez del Vayo, *The Last Optimist* (London, 1950) p. 198. He was already using his position as *Guardian* correspondent to smuggle in small-arms for the revolutionary committee (see ibid., pp. 193–6). Saborit does not mention in his memoirs his lack of co-operation.
93. Mola, *Obras*, p. 543.
94. Largo Caballero, *Mis recuerdos*, pp. 111–2. Saborit (*Besteiro*, p. 196) admits that Largo passed the information to Muiño, then rather disingenuously asks why he did not also speak with Besteiro and Trifón Gómez.
95. The debates are reported in *El Socialista*, 8–9 Oct 1932. See also the excellent Besteirist apologia, Mario de Coca, *Anti-Caballero*, p. 63; Saborit, *Besteiro*, p. 197; Cordero, *Socialistas*, pp. 84–5. A list of places affected by strikes is given in Tuñón, *Siglo XX*, pp. 210–11. See also Maura, *Así cayó*, p. 75; Ruiz, *Asturias*, p. 215.
96. *Diario de sesiones de las Cortes (DSC)* 11 Apr 1934.
97. *El Socialista*, 24 Feb 1931; Saborit, *Besteiro*, pp. 201–2; Santiago, *UGT*, pp. 86–8; Mario de Coca, *Anti-Caballero*, pp. 23–4.
98. This process is similar to the alliance of iron and rye in Germany. See Barrington Moore Jr, *Social Origins of Dictatorship and Democracy* (London, 1967) esp. ch. 8. Cf. Leon Trotski, letter to the editors of *Contra la Corriente*, 13 June 1930, and his pamphlet *The Revolution in Spain* (New York, 1931), reprinted in *Escritos sobre España* (Paris, 1971), where he condemns as pedantic the socialist interpretation of the role of the bourgeoisie.
99. Josep Fontana, 'Transformaciones agrarias y crecimiento económico en la España contemporáneo', *Cambio económico y actitudes políticas en la España del siglo XIX* (Barcelona, 1973); Gonzalo Anes, 'La agricultura española desde comienzos del siglo XIX hasta 1868', in Banco de España, *Ensayos sobre la economía española a mediados del siglo XIX* (Barcelona, 1970); Jordi Nadal, 'Spain 1830–1914' in Carlo M. Cipolla, *The Emergence of Industrial Society*, 2 vols (London, 1973) p. 2; Antonio Miguel Bernal, 'Formación y desarrollo de la burguesía agraria sevillana', in *La Propiedad de la tierra y las luchas agrarias andaluzas* (Barcelona, 1974); Miguel Viñas, 'Franquismo y revolución burguesa', in *Horizonte español 1972*, 3 vols (Paris, 1972) vol. III; Nicolás Sánchez Albornoz, *España hace un siglo* (Barcelona, 1968) p. 190.
100. C. A. M. Hennessy, *The Federal Republic in Spain 1868–74* (Oxford, 1962); Lacomba, *Crisis española*.
101. Jesús Pabón, *Cambó* (Barcelona, 1952) ch. 10.

CHAPTER 2

1. For the ACNP, See A. Sáez Alba, *La Otra 'cosa nostra': la Asociación Católica Nacional de Propagandistas* (Paris, 1974) pp. ix–xxii; for the CNCA, see below.
2. *El Debate*, 7 Apr 1931; *La Epoca*, 6 Apr 1931.
3. The genesis and development of this 'catastrophist' response to the

Republic is described in Martin Blinkhorn, 'Carlism and the Spanish Crisis of the 1930s', and Paul Preston, 'Alfonsist Monarchism and the Coming of the Spanish Civil War', both in *Journal of Contemporary History*, VII, nos. 3 and 4 (1972).

4. Rafael Sánchez Guerra, *Dictadura, indiferencia, República* (Madrid, 1931) p. 137.

5. José Monge Bernal, *Acción Popular* (Madrid, 1936) pp. 114–5, 122.

6. José María Gil Robles, *No fue posible la paz* (Barcelona, 1968) pp. 33–4.

7. Monge, *Acción Popular*, pp. 128–9.

8. Gil Robles, *No fue posible la paz*, p. 35. (Emphasis added.)

9. Javier Tusell, *Historia de la democracia cristiana en España*, 2 vols (Madrid, 1974) vol. I, p. 59; Manuel Azaña, diary entry for 18 Oct 1931, *Obras*, vol. IV, p. 189.

10. Telegram from Pacelli to Vidal, 29 Apr 1931, in Vidal i Barraquer archives, *Esglesia i Estat durant la segona República espanyola*, 2 vols (Monestir de Montserrat, 1971–5) vol. I, pp. 27–9.

11. Ibid., vol. I, pp. 36–7.

12. Cf. Henry Buckley, *Life and Death of the Spanish Republic* (London, 1940) p. 58; Constancia de la Mora, *In Place of Splendour* (London, 1940) p. 32.

13. *El Debate*, 28 Apr 1931.

14. Letter of Cardinal-Archbishop of Seville to Cardinal Vidal i Barraquer, 28 Nov 1931, in Vidal i Barraquer archives, *Esglesia i Estat*, vol. II, p. 169; José R. Montero Gibert, 'La CEDA: el partido contrarrevolucionario hegemónico de la II República', in Manuel Ramírez Jiménez (ed.), *Estudios sobre la II Republica española* (Madrid, 1975) p. 99.

15. Interview with Miguel Maura in Gabriel Jackson, *Historian's Quest* (New York, 1969) pp. 114–5; evidence of witness no. 30 in the Basque Clergy's compilation *El Pueblo vasco frente a la cruzada franquista* (Toulouse, 1966) pp. 23–4. Henry Buckley, an English Catholic journalist who was present, wrote, 'Hence the explosion of rage and violence among the Madrid crowds when they found that even the one limb of the octopus of feudalism which had been cut off was beginning to grow again' (*Life and Death*, p. 64). According to Ricardo de la Cierva, in his *Historia de la guerra civil española*, vol. I (Madrid, 1969) p. 172, Gil Robles was present at the CMI meeting. Gil Robles himself, in an interview with the author, denied this strongly.

16. Monge, *Acción Popular*, pp. 130–2.

17. *El Debate*, 5 and 6 May 1931.

18. *El Siglo Futuro*, 5 May 1931.

19. Julián Cortés Cavanillas, *Gil Robles ¿monárquico?* (Madrid, 1935) p. 91.

20. *El Debate*, 8 May 1931.

21. Antonio Monedero Martín, *La Confederación Nacional Católico-Agraria en 1920: su espíritu, su organización, su porvenir* (Madrid, 1921) pp. 22–33; Juan José Castillo, 'Orígenes y primeros años de la CNCA: planteamientos básicos de análisis del catolicismo social en España', paper read at a conference entitled 'La Societé rurale espagnole depuis

la crise de l'ancien régime jusque à celle des années trentes' held at the University of Pau, 21–22 Mar 1975, reprinted in José Luis García Delgado, *La Cuestión agraria en la España contemporánea* (Madrid, 1976); Jean Bécarud, *La Segunda República española* (Madrid, 1967) pp. 58–63.

22. *El Debate*, 9 and 30 May and 17 June 1931; a series of interviews, held in Madrid during the winter of 1970–1, with the Marqués de Gracia Real, a Salamanca landowner, who was a member of both Acción Nacional and Acción Española.

23. Monge, *Acción Popular*, pp. 136–8. There is a recent trend which sees the essential cause of the Civil War as the failure of the 'moderate' Right to achieve its objectives within the Republic. This view argues that the egoism of the Left forced the Right to abandon legalism and defend its interests by other means. Two notable works from this school are Robinson, *Origins*, and Carlos Seco Serrano, *Epoca contemporánea* (Barcelona, 1971). There is, however, considerable evidence to suggest that the aims of the 'moderate' Right were incompatible with the meaningful existence of the Republic.

24. *El Debate*, 2 June 1931.

25. *El Debate*, 11 and 28 June 1931.

26. Only five were members of Acción Nacional, although the majority owed their election to its campaign. They were all of monarchist origins. (*El Debate*, 8 July 1931.)

27. *El Debate*, 22 and 28 July 1931.

28. *Diario de sesiones de las Cortes Constituyentes DSCC* 8 and 9 Oct 1931; Luis Jiménez de Asúa, *Anécdotas de las Constituyentes* (Buenos Aires, 1942) pp. 61–3; Gil Robles *No fue posible la paz*, pp. 51–5; Robinson, *Origins*, pp. 60–8; Joaquín Arrarás, *Historia de la segunda República española*, 4 vols (Madrid 1956–68) vol. I, pp. 181–203.

29. Exchange of letters between Cardinal Vidal and Luis Nicolau d'Olwer on 22 Nov 1931, between Cardinal Vidal and Manual Azaña on 24 and 25 Nov 1931, and between Cardinal Vidal and Cardinal Pacelli, recounting a conversation with Azaña, on 28 Nov 1931 Vidal i Barraquer archives, *Esglesia i Estat*, vol. II, pp. 48–9, 158–63, 168, 179–80).

30. Monge, *Acción Popular*, p. 436.

31. Gil Robles, *No fue posible la paz*, pp. 64–5.

32. *El Debate*, 18 Oct 1931; *El Sol*, 15 Oct 1931. Maura's attempt to create a democratic Right was doomed to failure because the rightist press would never tolerate his refusal to tie Catholicism to a given social and economic order. Cf. *El Debate*, 27 Oct 1931.

33. *El Debate*, 20 and 23 Oct 1931. It is of interest that an English Catholic in Spain at the time commented, 'I welcomed the Republic as a step towards better social conditions and much as I disliked the mob violence and the burning of churches I felt that the people in Spain who professed most loudly their Catholic faith were the most to blame for the existence of illiterate masses and a threadbare national economy' (Buckley, *Life and Death*, pp. 66–7).

34. *El Debate*, 1, 3, 10 and 12 Nov 1931; *El Socialista*, 2 Nov 1931.

35. For the full text, see Monge, *Acción Popular,* pp. 170–83; *El Debate,* 6 Dec 1931.
36. *La Época,* 24 Feb 1932; Monge, *Acción Popular,* pp. 223–5.
37. *La Época,* 2 Jan 1932; Domingo de Arrese, *Bajo la ley de defensa de la República* (Madrid, 1933) p. 68.
38. *La Época,* 5 Jan 1932.
39. Gil Robles, *No fue posible la paz,* pp. 67–76; letter of 25 Apr 1937 from Gil Robles to Luciano de la Calzada, regarding the dissolution of Acción Popular by Franco and its incorporation into the new one-party state. Gil Robles saw this 'splendid harvest' as the fruit of his propaganda efforts during the Republic. *Sur* (Málaga) 28 Apr 1937; cf. José Gutiérrez Ravé, *Gil Robles, caudillo frustrado* (Madrid, 1967) pp. 198–9.
40. Monge, *Acción Popular,* pp. 941, 953, 965, 991. The change was a response to a government ban on use of the word 'national' by non-state entities (see ibid., p. 183).
41. *El Socialista,* 6 Aug 1931.
42. *DSCC,* 7 Aug and 1 September 1931; *El Debate,* 1 Dec 1931; Marcelino Domingo, *La Experiencia del poder* (Madrid, 1934) pp. 240–2.
43. Domingo, *La Experiencia,* pp. 243–8; Gabriel Jackson, *The Spanish Republic and the Civil War* (Princeton, NJ, 1965) pp. 86–7.
44. Even the so-called social Catholic, Dimas de Madariaga was involved in anti-Republican activities with the monarchist plotter, Ansaldo; see Juan Antonio Ansaldo, *¿Para qué? de Alfonso XIII a Juan III* (Buenos Aires 1951) p. 23. Madariaga also led a riot at the Madrid première of Pérez de Ayala's *AMDG,* Juan Simeón Vidarte, *Las Cortes Constituyentes de 1931–1933* (Barcelona 1976) p. 252–3.
45. Gil Robles, *No fue posible la paz,* p. 79.
46. Ibid., p. 79.
47. Malefakis, *Agrarian Reform,* pp. 197–9.
48. Gil Robles, *No fue posible la paz,* p. 60.
49. *El Debate,* 8 Oct 1932; Cortés Cavanillas, *Gil Robles,* pp. 138, 144–6.
50. *El Debate,* 21, 23 and 25 Oct 1932; Robinson, *Origins,* pp. 107–9; Salvador Canals, *El Bienio estéril* (Madrid, 1936) pp. 12–13.
51. Gil Robles, *No fue posible la paz,* p. 84.
52. *El Debate,* 11 Jan 1933; *ABC,* 11 Jan 1933; Arrarás, *República,* vol. ii, p. 137.
53. This was an attempt to arouse the fears of conservative farmers; see *El Debate,* 1, 9, 10, 15 and 25 Nov 1932. For all the talk of endemic disorder, the harvest was one of the biggest of the century.
54. *El Socialista,* 29 and 30 Oct 1932: 'This isn't the first time that we've pointed out fascistic tendencies in *El Debate.* But never before have we heard such spine-chilling language from the Spanish Right.'
55. *El Debate,* 13 Nov 1932. The paper was manifesting a growing sympathy towards possible fascist solutions to Spain's problems, see the editorial on 16 Dec 1932, 'Towards a fascist democracy', and the article on 17 Jan 1933 on the advantages of a fascist economy.
56. Arrarás, *Republica,* vol. ii, p. 138.
57. Spanish Confederation of Autonomous Right-wing Groups.

58. *El Debate*, 1, 2, 3, 5 and 7 Mar 1933; *CEDA*, 1 May 1933; Arrarás, *República*, vol. II, pp. 144–8.

59. *El Socialista*, 8 Mar 1933.

60. *El Socialista*, 31 Jan, 5, 10 and 11 Feb, 10 Mar, and 2 and 21 Apr 1933

61. *El Socialista*, 1 May 1933; the May Day supplement was entitled 'Lessons of the German counter-revolution', The 4 May issue carried an appeal for the victims of fascism, and the 6 May issue had a full report on Hitler's destruction of the German unions.

62. *El Debate*, 8 and 22 Mar 1933; Gil Robles, *No fue posible la paz*, pp. 205–7.

63. *El Debate*, 1 Jan 1933, had claimed openly that accidentalism as a tactic made it difficult for the authorities to restrict the group's activities.

64. *El Debate*, 9 May 1933. This was a considerable exaggeration; cf. Jackson, *Historian's Quest*, pp. 152–3.

65. *El Debate*, 18 May 1933.

66. *El Socialista*, 10 May 1933. On 20 Aug *El Socialista* pointed out that 50 per cent of the population in the province of Seville went to bed hungry every night. It claimed that the salvation that the upper class had looked to Sanjurjo for on 10 Aug 1932 was salvation from wage-claims and from laws which attacked feudal privilege.

67. *El Socialista*, 20 June 1933; for examples of deliberate provocation by the Right, see *El Socialista*, 23 and 29 June.

68. Claude G. Bowers, *My Mission to Spain* (London, 1954) p. 33.

69. *El Debate*, 16 May 1933. For an account of the CEDA's claims to be socially aware and reform-oriented, see Robinson, *Origins*, pp. 114–6.

70. *El Debate*, 19 and 23 May, 16 June, and 17 and 29 Aug 1933.

71. *El Debate*, 10 Aug 1933; Malefakis, *Agrarian Reform*, pp. 268–73; Robinson, *Origins*, pp. 127–8; Gil Robles, *Discursos parlamentarios* (Madrid, 1971), pp. 263–7.

72. Gil Robles, *No fue posible la paz*, pp. 87–9; Cortés Cavanillas, *Gil Robles*, pp. 143–4, and *Vida, confesiones y muerte de Alfonso XIII* (Madrid, 1956) pp. 426–7.

73. Juan Arrabal, *José María Gil Robles* (Madrid, 1933) pp. 9–13; Monge, *Acción Popular*, p. 378; Gil Robles, *No fue posible la paz*, p. 48; *El Debate*, 27 Dec 1932; Martin Blinkhorn, *Carlism and Crisis in Spain 1931–1939* (Cambridge, 1975) pp. 100–3, 158–62.

74. *El Socialista*, 2, 4, 11, 18 and 21 July 1933.

75. In the event, Neurath said that an interview was impossible; see Angel Viñas, *La Alemania nazi ye el 18 de julio* (Madrid, 1974) p. 149.

76. *El Debate*, 28 June, and 16 and 25 July 1933. *El Socialista*, 21 July and 7 Sep, was scathing about the Church's readiness to overlook persecution in authoritarian regimes.

77. *El Debate*, 4, 17 and 25 Aug 1933; *El Pueblo Católico*, 29 Mar 1933.

78. Antonio Ramos Oliveira, *Alemania ayer y hoy* (Madrid, 1933) p. 257; *El Debate*, 30 June; *El Socialista*, 2 July 1933.

79. Juan Velarde Fuertes, *El Nacional-Sindicalismo cuarenta años después* (Madrid, 1972) pp. 131–4.

80. For the background to the calling of elections, see Jackson, *Republic*, ch 4–6.

81. *CEDA*, 30 Sep 1933; *El Debate*, 2 Sep 1933. Gil Robles told the author in February 1973 that he went to Nuremberg as the guest of Von Papen.

82. *El Debate*, 15 Sep 1933.

83. *El Debate*, 10 Oct 1933.

84. Gil Robles, *No fue posible la paz*, p. 94; *El Debate*, 12 Oct 1933.

85. *El Debate*, 17 Oct 1933. (Emphasis added.)

86. *El Socialista*, 17 Oct 1933. Gil Robles's visit to Germany had not gone unnoticed (see ibid., 14 Oct 1933). Fernando de los Ríos, a moderate Socialist and a distinguished professor of law, pointed out with horror that Gil Robles's call for a purge of Jews and freemasons was a denial of the juridical and political postulates of the regime (ibid., 21 Oct 1933). José Antonio Primo de Rivera, leader of the Falange, which was about to be launched, commented, 'these are fascist principles; he may reject the name but the name is not the thing. By speaking thus, Gil Robles does not express himself as the leader of a Christian Democratic party. . . . This speech has been warm, direct – "fascist". I applaud him for it and am in agreement with him. But what mysterious reason makes him say that he is in disagreement with us?' (La Cierva, *La Guerra civil*, p. 509).

87. *CEDA*, 31 Oct 1933.

88. Gil Robles, *No fue posible la paz*, 100; *El Debate*, 27 Oct, 3, 7, 8, 15, 16 and 18 Nov. 1933.

89. Buckley, *Life and Death of the Spanish Republic*, pp. 115, 120, 125; Bowers, *My Mission*, p. 55. Cf. the letter from Gil Robles to fund-donors in *CEDA*, 30 Dec 1933.

90. *El Debate*, 3 Nov 1933.

91. Bécarud, *La Segunda República*, pp. 120–4; Gil Robles, *No fue posible la paz*, pp. 102–5; Ronald Fraser, *In Hiding* (London, 1972) p. 114; *El Socialista*, 25 Nov 1933.

92. *El Socialista*, 26 and 28 Nov, 1 Dec 1933; José Tomás Valverde, *Memorias de un alcalde* (Madrid, 1961) pp. 139–47.

CHAPTER 3

1. *El Socialista*, 31 Mar 1931; Zapatero, *De los Ríos*, p. 89.

2. Zapatero, *De los Ríos*, p. 90.

3. Largo Caballero, *Mis recuerdos*, p. 117; Vidarte, *Cortes Constituyentes*, p. 22.

4. *El Sol*, 24 May 1931.

5. Mario de Coca, *Anti-Caballero*, p. 31; Cordero, *Socialistas*, pp. 93–6.

6. Mario de Coca, *Anti-Caballero*, pp. 31–2.

7. Javier Bueno, *El Estado socialista: nueva interpretación del comunismo* (Madrid, 1931) pp. 9–13.

8. Gabriel Morón, *La Ruta del socialismo en España* (Madrid, 1932) pp. 24–35.

9. *Memoria y orden del día del XVII Congreso que se celebrará en Madrid los días 14 y siguientes de octubre de 1932* (Madrid, 1932) p. 61; *El Obrero de la Tierra*, 10 and 17 Sep 1932; Malefakis, *Agrarian Reform*, p. 292.

10. Franciso Largo Caballero, *Posibilismo socialista en la democracia* (Madrid, 1933) p. 16.

11. Cordero, *Socialistas*, pp. 342–5; Besteiro, interview in *El Sol*, 3 June 1931.

12. Enrique López Sevilla, *El Partido Socialista Obrero Español en las Cortes Constituyentes de la Segunda República* (Mexico, 1969) pp. 12–4.

13. *El Debate*, 22 Apr 1931.

14. *La Crisis agraria andaluza de 1930–1931* (Madrid, 1931).

15. Ramón Tamames, *La República, la era de Franco* (Madrid, 1973) pp. 56–66; *BUGT*, Dec 1931.

16. Malefakis, *Agrarian Reform*, pp. 166–71; *BUGT*, May and June 1931.

17. Azaña, diary entries for 4 and 21 July 1931, *Obras*, vol. IV, pp. 10, 36.

18. *El Sol*, 30 July 1931.

19. Manuel Ramírez Jiménez, *Los Grupos de presión en la segunda República española* (Madrid, 1969) pp. 118–24; Mercedes Cabrera, 'Organizaciones patronales y cuestión agraria en España 1931–1936', in García-Delgado, *La Cuestión agraria*.

20. Extremely detailed tables are provided by Pascual Carrión, *Los Latifundios en España* (Madrid, 1932) esp. facing p. 324.

21. *El Debate*, 8 May, 3 Oct, and 1 Dec 1931; Azaña, diary entries for 5 Aug and 22 Sept 1931, *Obras*, vol. IV, pp. 63, 140; the speeches by PSOE deputies Antonio Marcos Escudero (Huelva), Antonio García Prieto (Málaga), Tomás Alvarez Angulo (Jaén) and Juan-Simeón Vidarte (Badajoz) in *DSCC*, 11 and 24 Sep, 1 and 23 Oct, and 4 Nov 1931.

22. *El Debate*, 22 July, 23 Sep. and 1 Nov 1931; *El Pueblo Católico* (Jaén) 27 and 28 July 1931; Azaña, diary entry for 28 Oct 1931, *Obras*, vol. IV, p. 203.

23. Mario de Coca, *Anti-Caballero*, p. 44.

24. *El Socialista*, 12 July 1931; PSOE, *XIII Congreso*, pp. 126–35; López Sevilla, *PSOE*, pp. 20–1; Morón, *Ruta del socialismo*, pp. 39–48.

25. Azaña, in his diary entry for 4 Aug 1931 (*Obras*, vol. IV, p. 60) was worried that 400 million pesetas had been with drawn from the Banco Hispano-Americano and that the stock exchange was being artificially maintained. See also *El Liberal*, 2 June 1931.

26. *El Socialista*, 13 June 1931.

27. Cf. Luis Araquistain, 'Los socialistas en el primer bienio', *Leviatán*, no. 18 (Oct–Nov 1935), p. 25, where he emphasises the difficulty they found in putting reforms into practice.

28. Gabriel Santullano, 'Las organizaciones obreras asturianas en los comienzos de la segunda República', in Tuñón de Lara, *Sociedad, política y cultura*, p. 261.

29. *El Socialista*, 9 July 1931; Mario de Coca, *Anti-Caballero*, pp. 41–2; Grandizo Munis, *Jalones*, pp. 73–5.

30. Maura, *Así cayó*, pp. 278–87; Azaña, diary entry for 21 July 1931, *Obras*, vol. IV, p. 37; *DSCC*, 28 and 29 July 1931.

31. 'El Anticristo sindicalista', '¿Porqué hay tantas huelgas?' and 'Contra el abuso de la huelga', in *El Sol*, 18, 21 and 24 July 1931; each reprinted the following day in *El Socialista*.

32. Azaña, diary entries for 4 and 7 Aug, and 22 Sep 1931, *Obras*, vol. IV, pp. 60–2, 68–70, 140–5; Prieto, *Convulsiones*, vol. I, pp. 101–6; Morón, *Ruta del socialismo*, pp. 136–41; Marta Bizcarrondo, 'La crisis socialista en la II República', *Revista del Instituto de Ciencias Sociales*, no. 21 (1973) p. 74; *DSCC*, 5 and 26 Aug. 1931

33. Manuel Buenacasa, *La CNT, los 'treinta' y la FAI* (Barcelona, 1933) pp. 20–32; John Brademas, *Anarco-sindicalismo y revolución en España 1930–1937* (Barcelona, 1974) pp. 70–86.

34. *DSCC*, 27 Aug, 3, 8 and 16 Sep, and 1, 6 13 and 14 Oct 1931; Jiménez de Asúa, *Anécdotas de las Constituyentes*, pp. 30–8.

35. *El Socialista*, 8 Aug, and 18, 19 and 23 Nov 1931; *El Sol*, 8, 12 and 15 Sep 1931.

36. *El Socialista*, 17 Nov 1931; Andrade, *Burocracia*, pp. 244–7; declarations by Largo in *Avance* (Oviedo), the newly-founded SMA daily, 24 Nov 1931.

37. Mario de Coca, *Anti-Caballero*, pp. 52–3; Vidarte, *Cortes Constituyentes*, pp. 235–45.

38. Azaña, diary entries for 30 Oct, 16, 17, 21 and 30 Nov, and 4 Dec 1931, *Obras*, vol. IV, pp. 207, 231–3, 240–2, 251, 260.

39. *Avance*, 6, 8, 10, 15 and 16 Dec 1931.

40. *El Socialista*, 5, 11 and 13 Dec 1931; *Avance*, 25 Nov and 27 Dec 1931.

41. *El Pueblo Católico*, 21 Aug 1931.

42. This account is based on the transcript of the trial of the villagers, Luis Jiménez de Asúa et al., *Castilblanco* (Madrid 1933). See also Vidarte, *Cortes Constituyentes*, 294–308.

43. *El Socialista*, 2 and 5 Jan 1932; *Avance*, 3 and 5 Jan 1932; *ABC*, 3 and 5 Jan 1932; *DSCC*, 5 Jan 1932; Arrarás, *República*, vol. I, pp. 287–9.

44. Azaña, diary entries for 30 Nov and 14 Dec 1931, and 5 Jan 1932, *Obras*, vol. IV, pp. 251, 275, 294–5.

45. Vidarte, *Cortes Constituyentes*, pp. 306, 601; *El Socialista*, 6, 7 and 13 Jan 1932; *Avance* 6, 7, 12, 13 and 19 Jan 1932; *DSCC*, 6 Jan 1932.

46. *El Socialista*, 23 Jan 1932; *Avance* 23, 24 and 26 Jan, and 12 Feb 1932; *El Obrero de la Tierra*, 23 Jan 1932.

47. *Avance*, 5 Apr 1931; Mariano Pérez Galán, *La Enseñanza en la II República española* (Madrid, 1975) pp. 332–3.

48. *BUGT*, Jan 1932.

49. *BUGT*, May 1932.

50. *El Obrero de la Tierra*, 30 Jan 1932; *La Mañana* (Jaén) 1, 6 and 7 Apr 1932.

51. *El Obrero de la Tierra*, 5, 13 and 20 Feb, and 5, 12 and 26 Mar 1932.

52. *El Obrero de la Tierra*, 2 Apr 1932.

53. *La Mañana*, 12 Apr 1932.

54. *La Mañana*, 9 July 1932; *El Socialista*, 15 July 1932; Ramos Oliveira, *Nosotros*, p. 68.

55. *Boletín del Ministerio de Trabajo y Previsión* Social, Apr 1933; Bizcarrondo, in *Revista del Instituto de Ciencias Sociales*, no. 21, p. 63.

56. It would be superfluous to discuss the delays in the elaboration of the agrarian reform, since the subject is fully dealt with in the admirable study by Malefakis (Agrarian Reform, ch. 7). See also *El Obrero de la Tierra*, 11 and 25 June 1932.

57. *Avance*, 6 and 16 Apr, 1, 12 and 13 May, and 12 June 1932.

58. *BUGT*, July 1932.

59. *El Socialista*, 11 Nov 1931 and 15 July 1932.

60. *El Pueblo Católico*, 4 May 1933.

61. Azaña, diary entries for 11, 12, 17 and 20 July, 1932, *Obras*, vol. IV, pp. 435–43; *DSCC*, 20 July 1932.

62. *El Obrero de la Tierra*, 24 Sep and 1 Oct 1932.

63. *El Adelanto* (Salamanca) 1 and 4 Oct 1932.

64. *DSCC*, 18 and 21 Oct 1932; *El Adelanto*, 8 Oct 1932, reprints the full *bases de trabajo* which provoked the Bloque's circular.

65. *El Obrero de la Tierra*, 8 Oct 1932.

66. This estimate of living standards is based on the monthly indexes published throughout the Republic in the *Boletín del Ministerio de Trabajo y Previsión*. Figures are remarkably stable for the entire period; they are not coloured by the presence of a Socialist at the head of the Ministry. The figure of 35 pesetas allows nothing for clothing, housing or household requisites, and is calculated on the basis of just one meal per day.

67. This was the belief of the Bloque Agrario of Jaén; see *La Mañana*, 1 Oct 1932. See also *El Adelanto*, 19 Oct 1932.

68. *DSCC*, 20 Oct 1932; a series of interviews held by the author in Madrid in the winter of 1970–1 with the Marqués de Gracia Real, a landowner from Ledesma (Salamanca).

69. *Avance*, 2, 6, 8, 13, 15, 17 and 18 Sep 1932.

70. *El Socialista*, 8 and 9 Oct 1932; Lamo de Espinosa, *Besteiro*, pp. 86–7; Saborit, *Besteiro*, pp. 227–8; Vidarte, *Cortes Constituyentes*, pp. 485–93.

71. Andrade, *Burocracia*, pp. 102, 159.

72. *El Sol* 23 Oct 1932; *El Socialista*, 23 and 25 Oct 1932; Mario de Coca, *Anti-Caballero*, pp. 66–70; Lamo de Espinosa, *Besteiro*, pp. 87–8; Vidarte, *Cortes Constituyentes*, pp. 495–7; Amaro del Rosal, *Historia de la UGT de España 1901–1939*, 2 vols (Barcelona 1977) I, pp. 350–2.

73. *Avance*, 26 Jan, 27 Feb, 10 Mar, 19 Apr 2, 3 and 7 Aug 1932.

74. *El Obrero de la Tierra*, 15 and 22 Oct 1932.

75. *Tierra y Trabajo* (Salamanca) 30 Nov 1932.

76. Azaña, diary entry for 4 Dec 1931, *Obras*, vol. IV, p. 260.

77. *Tierra y Trabajo*, 9 and 20 Dec 1932; Arrarás, *Republica*, vol. II, p. 76.

78. *Avance*, 11, 14, 18, 19 and 23 Oct, 14, 15 and 20 Nov, and 8, 9, 10, 11, 13, 14, 15 and 16 Dec 1932.

79. Mario de Coca, *Anti-Caballero*, pp. 71–2; Arrarás, *República*, vol. ii, p. 77–8.

80. Ramón Sender, *Viaje a la aldea del crimen* (Madrid, 1934) pp. 33–42, 70–130; Francisco Guerra, *Casas Viejas: apuntes de la tragedia* (Jerez, 1933); Jerome R. Mintz, *The Anarchists of Casas Viejas* (Chicago, 1982) pp. 189–225.

81. *El Debate*, 15 Jan 1932.

82. Azaña, diary entry for 13 Jan 1933, *Memorias íntimas* (Madrid, 1939) p. 208.

83. *DSCC*, 3, 23 and 24 Feb, and 2 and 3 Mar 1933; *El Debate*, 24 Feb 1933.

84. Azaña, diary entries for 19 and 21 Feb, 1 and 3 Mar 1933, in *Memorias*, p. 210; and *Obras*, vol. iv, pp. 447–55.

85. Azaña, diary entry for 6 Mar 1933, *Obras*, vol. iv, p. 460.

86. Azaña, diary entry for 14 Apr 1933, *Obras*, vol. iv, pp. 484–5. It took an energetic speech by Prieto to talk the PSOE executive out of abandoning the cabinet, Vidarte, *Cortes Constituyentes*, pp. 522, 532.

87. There is considerable debate over the interpretation of these figures. See *El Debate*, 25 Apr 1933; *El Socialista*, 26 and 27 Apr 1933; Azaña, diary entry for 30 April 1933, *Obras*, vol. iv, pp. 501–3; *DSCC*, 25, 26 and 28 Apr 1933; Arrarás, *República*, vol. ii, pp. 116–7; Jackson, *Republic*, p. 104.

88. Azaña, diary entry for 16 May 1933, *Obras*, vol. iv, p. 530.

89. *ABC*, 26 Jan 1933; *El Obrero de la Tierra*, 19 Nov 1932, and 14 Jan 1933.

90. *Boletín del Instituto de Reforma Agraria*, Mar 1933; *El Obrero de la Tierra*, 28 Jan 1933.

91. *Región* (Cáceres) 24 Feb 1933; *El Pueblo Católico*, 14 Mar 1933; *ABC*, 26 Mar 1933; *La Mañana,* 21 and 27 Jan, 3 and 18 Feb, 5 Apr 1933; *El Obrero de la Tierra* 14 Jan, 4 Mar 1933; *El Socialista*, 21 Jan, 20 Apr, 1 July 1933.

92. See above, Ch. 2.

93. *El Socialista*, 26 Mar, and 4 July 1933; *La Unión Ferroviaria*, Aug 1933.

94. *El Sol*, 15 and 19 July 1933. Bizcarrondo, in *Revista del Instituto de Ciencias Sociales*, no. 21, pp. 64–5, points out that the high point of the employers' mobilisation was only a few days before Largo publicly demonstrated his adoption of a radical line.

95. *El Socialista*, 25 July 1933.

96. Saborit, *Besteiro*, pp. 237–40; Mario de Coca, *Anti-Caballero*, p. 101.

97. Indalecio Prieto, *Discursos fundamentales* (Madrid, 1975) pp. 160–80, and *Convulsiones*, vol. iii, pp. 160–5.

98. *El Socialista*, 13 Aug. 1933. The complete text was published as *Posibilismo socialista en la democracia*.

99. *BUGT*, Aug–Sep 1933; *El Obrero de la Tierra*, 12 and 20 Aug, and 9 Sep 1933; *El Debate*, 22, 23 and 29 Aug 1933.

100. Cf. the editorial comment on Largo's Torrelodones speech in *El Debate*, 15 Aug 1933.

101. Malefakis, *Agrarian Reform*, pp. 268–73; Madariaga, *Spain*, pp. 418–20.

102. *El Debate*, 19 Sep 1933; *El Obrero de la Tierra*, 16, 23 and 30 Sep 1933; *BUGT*, Nov 1933.

103. *El Debate*, 4, 17 and 25 Aug, 2 and 15 Sep; *El Pueblo Católico*, 29 Mar 1933.

104. *BUGT*, Nov 1933.

105. *El Socialista*, 3 Oct 1933.

106. *DSCC*, 2 and 3 Oct 1933.

107. *El Socialista*, 8 Oct 1933; Marcelino Domingo, *La Revolución de octubre* (Barcelona, 1935) pp. 54–8; Vidarte, *Cortes Constituyentes*, pp. 662–73; Azaña, diary entry for 1 July 1937, *Obras*, vol. IV, 646–8. The technicality hinged on the fact that the Socialists had previously moved a motion of censure against other members of the cabinet, something they felt precluded their joining it.

108. Bowers, *My Mission*, p. 42.

109. Domingo, *La revolución*, p. 9.

110. *El Debate*, 12, 17, 18 and 24 Oct, and 7, 17 and 18 Nov 1933.

111. *El Socialista*, 7, 14 and 15 Nov 1933.

112. *BUGT*, Dec 1933; *El Obrero de la Tierra*, 30 Sep, 7 and 14 Oct, and 2 and 23 Dec 1933; Antonio Ramos Oliveira, *Politics, Economics and Men of Modern Spain* (London, 1946) pp. 490–1; Joaquín Maurín, *Hacia la segunda revolución* (Barcelona, 1935) pp. 32, 52–3; Jean Bécarud, *La Segunda República*, pp. 124–5; Zapatero, *De los Ríos*, p. 105.

113. Prieto, *Discursos*, pp. 168–9; Bécarud, *La Segunda República*, pp. 123–4; Brenan, *Labyrinth*, p. 266.

114. Domingo, *La Revolución*, pp. 95–7; Bécarud, *La Segunda República*, pp. 125–8, 136–7. The composition of the Cortes was as follows: PSOE, fifty-eight; left republicans, thirty-eight; Radicals, 104; Lliga, twenty-four, Basque Nationalists, twelve; conservative republicans, forty-one; CEDA, 115; Agrarians, thirty-two; Carlists, twenty-one; Renovación Española and other monarchists, twenty-three. The distribution of votes is discussed in Ch. 4.

CHAPTER 4

1. In a speech on 14 Jan 1934, Largo Caballero adopted some of the ideas of Otto Bauer; see Largo Caballero, *Discursos a los trabajadores* (Madrid, 1934) p. 144.

2. Unemployment figures up to the end of 1934 are as follows: June 1932, 446,263; Aug 1933, 588,174; Dec 1933, 618,947; Apr 1934, 703,814; Dec 1934, 667,898 (*Boletín del Ministerio de Trabajo*, Jan 1935). See also Malefakis, *Agrarian Reform*, p. 288; Balcells, *Crisis económica*, pp. 52–63.

3. Figures for union membership refer to June 1932 (*BUGT*, July 1932, supplement). The loyalty of the various union presidents has been assessed from their statements at the meetings of the National Committee of the UGT, reported in *BUGT*.

4. Appendix to Largo Caballero, *Discursos*, pp. 163–6.

5. Ramos Oliveira, *Politics*, pp. 489–91; Margarita Nelkin, *Porqué hicimos la revolución* (Barcelona, 1936) pp. 67–9. In some provinces (particularly Badajoz, Málaga and Córdoba, the margin of rightist victory was sufficiently small for electoral malpractice to have affected the results. See *El Debate*, 21 and 22 Nov, and 5 Dec 1933.

6. B. Díaz Nosty, *La Comuna asturiana* (Bilbao, 1974) pp. 52–60.

7. *DSC*, 19 Dec 1933. The Socialist Youth regarded this as a fascist speech; see *Renovación*, 23 Dec 1933.

8. *DSC*, 20 Dec 1933.

9. Cortes Cavanillas, *Gil Robles*, pp. 139–41.

10. Alejandro Lerroux, *La Pequeña historia* (Buenos Aires, 1945) p. 212; Robinson, *Origins*, p. 152; Jesús Pabón, *Cambó*, vol. II, part 2 (Barcelona, 1969) p. 290. This compares strangely with Gil Robles's own open admission of his tactical aims (*No fue posible la paz*, pp. 106–7).

11. *El Debate*, 25 Aug 1931; *El Socialista*, 26 and 28 Nov, and 1 Dec 1933; *El Pueblo Católico*, 4 May 1933. The other rightist daily in Jaén, *La Mañana*, indiscriminately supported the Radicals and the CEDA.

12. *El Socialista*, 11 Nov 1931 and 9 May 1934; José Rodríguez de la Peña, *Los Aventureros de la política: Alejandro Lerroux* (Madrid, n.d. [1916]) passim; Largo Caballero, *Discursos*, pp. 54–5. Largo also recounted (*Mis recuerdos*, p. 121) that, in early 1931, with the majority of the republican revolutionary committee in jail, Lerroux started a public subscription for them, the proceeds from which mysteriously disappeared.

13. Jesús Pabón, *Palabras en la oposición* (Seville, 1935) p. 196.

14. Azaña, diary entry for 12 July 1932, Obras, vol. IV, p. 435.

15. Azaña, diary entry for 29 Jan 1932, *Obras*, vol. IV, p. 318; Pabón, *Cambó*, p. 297.

16. Azaña, diary entry for 28 June 1937, *Obras*, vol. IV, pp. 635–6; Buckley, *Life and Death*, pp. 186–7. The level of venality was eventually to cause some unease within the Radical Party. Cf. the two letters reprinted in César Jalón, *Memorias políticas* (Madrid, 1973) pp. 214–18.

17. *El Debate*, 6, 7 and 22 Dec 1933; *DSC*, 19 Dec 1933.

18. Largo Caballero, *Mis recuerdos*, p. 133. By placing this plot in the home of the exiled Calvo Sotelo, Largo confuses it with one in late 1934. Cf. José Bullejos, *España en la II República* (Mexico, 1967) p. 143.

19. *BUGT*, Dec 1933; *El Obrero de la Tierra*, 23 and 30 Dec 1933, and 6 and 13 Jan 1934; *El Socialista*, 14 and 23 Jan 1934.

20. *El Socialista*, 26, 28 and 30 Nov, 1, 2, 8, 19 and 21 Dec 1933, and 13 and 14 Jan 1934.

21. Luis Araquistain, *El Derrumbamiento del socialismo alemán* (Madrid, 1933).

22. María Teresa León, *Memoria de la melancolía* (Buenos Aires, 1970) p. 266.

23. *BUGT*, Dec 1933 and Jan 1934; Largo Caballero, *Mis recuerdos*, pp. 131–3.

24. A point made by Gil Robles, in an interview with the author in Madrid in February 1973, in defence of his own admiration for fascism.

25. Arrarás, *República*, vol. II, pp. 251–7; Peirats, *CNT*, vol. I, pp. 77–80;

César M. Lorenzo, *Les Anarchistes espagnols et le pouvoir* (Paris, 1969) pp. 79–80.
26. *El Socialista*, 12 Dec 1933; *DSC*, 12 Dec 1933.
27. *BUGT*, Jan 1934.
28. *Azaña*, diary entry for 1 July 1937, in *Obras*, vol. IV, pp. 649–50.
29. *Renovación*, 20 Jan 1934; *El Obrero de la Tierra*, 6, 13 and 20 Jan 1934.
30. *El Debate*, 27 Dec 1933 and 26 Jan 1934; *El Socialista*, 23 and 25 Jan 1934.
31. *El Debate*, 27 Jan, and 8 and 25 Feb 1934; *Renovación*, 6 Jan 1934; *El Socialista*, 26 Jan and 2 Feb 1934; *La Mañana*, 17, 19, and 20 Jan 1934.
32. Largo Caballero, *Discursos*, pp. 134–62.
33. Largo Caballero, *Mis recuerdos*, pp. 134–5; Mario de Coca, *Anti-Caballerro*, p. 133.
34. Dolores Ibarruri et al., *Guerra y revolución en España*, 3 vols (Moscow, 1967–71), vol. I, pp. 52–7 (reprints all three projects in full); Ramos Oliveira, *Politics*, pp. 507–8.
35. *El Socialista*, 28 Jan 1934; *BUGT*, Feb 1934; *El Obrero de la Tierra*, 3 Feb 1934; Mario de Coca, *Anti-Caballero*, pp. 137–42.
36. *DSC*, 7, Feb 1934; *La Mañana*, 16 Jan 1934, had denounced such robberies as 'collective kleptomania'.
37. *El Debate*, 14–17 Feb 1934; *El Socialista*, 13, 18 and 20 Feb, and 4 and 7 Mar 1934; *BUGT*, Feb and Mar 1934; *Leviatán* no. 2 (June 1934), was entirely devoted to contemporary fascism and included articles by Austrian socialist survivors.
38. *DSC*, 4 Jan 1934; Gil Robles, *No fue posible la paz*, pp. 111–12; Alfred Mendizábal, *Aux Origines d'une tragédie* (Paris, n.d. [1937?]) pp. 214–5; *El Socialista*, 2 Jan 1934; *El Sol*, 23 Mar 1934. Cambó complained of Gil Robles's doubtful republicanism; see Pabón, *Cambó*, pp. 307–8.
39. *El Debate*, 20–22 Feb 1934.
40. Lerroux, *Pequeña historia*, pp. 216–38; Gil Robles, *No fue posible la paz*, pp. 116–9; *El Debate*, 2 Mar 1934. Monge, *Acción Popular*, p. 898, shows that it was a deliberate tactic.
41. Azaña, *Obras*, vol. II, pp. 911–44.
42. *El Liberal*, 6 Feb 1934.
43. *Renovación*, 10 and 17 Feb, and 8 Mar 1934. At the Fifth Congress of the FJS, in April, the most energetic revolutionists clinched their hold over the youth movement: Carlos Hernández Zancajo became president, and Santiago Carrillo became secretary, and editor of *Renovación*.
44. *El Debate*, 8 Mar 1934; *El Socialista*, 11 and 13 Mar 1934; Rafael Salazar Alonso, *Bajo el signo de la revolución* (Madrid, 1935) pp. 50–73.
45. *El Debate*, 2, 8, 10, 11, 22 and 27 Mar 1934; *El Socialista*, 29 Mar 1934; *DSC*, 8 Mar 1934; Lerroux, *Pequeña historia*, pp. 235–9.
46. Gil Robles, *No fue posible la paz*, pp. 119–22; Lerroux, *Pequeña historia*, pp. 247–57; *DSC*, 20 Apr 1934; *El Debate*, 12 and 21 Apr 1934; *El*

Socialista, 12 Apr 1934; *Leviatán*, no. 1 (May 1934) saw it as the official glorification of 10 August. The American ambassador thought that the amnesty legalised treason (Bowers, *My Mission*, p. 74).

47. *El Debate*, 3, 10 and 17 Apr 1934; Arrarás, *República*, vol. ii, pp. 305–6.
48. Munis, *Jalones*, p. 114.
49. Cf. Blinkhorn, *Carlism*, p. 158.
50. *El Debate*, 21, 22 and 24 Apr 1934; *El Socialista*, 22 and 24 Apr 1934; Monge, *Acción Popular*, pp. 253–304; Buckley, *Life and Death*, pp. 126–7.
51. Herbert R. Southworth, *Antifalange* (Paris, 1967) p. 78; Gil Robles, *No fue posible la paz*, pp. 190–1; Cortés Cavanillas, *Gil Robles*, pp. 143, 180; José Antonio Primo de Rivera, *Obras*, 4th edition (Madrid, 1966) p. 124.
52. Lerroux, *Pequeña historia*, pp. 256–61.
53. La Cierva, *La Guerra civil*, p. 483.
54. Ruiz Alonso was later to play a key role in the Nationalist repression of Granada. See Ian Gibson, *The Death of Lorca* (London, 1973) passim.
55. *El Debate*, 26 May 1934; *El Socialista*, 24 and 25 May 1934; Salazar Alonso, *Bajo el signo*, pp. 122–7.
56. *El Debate*, 6 and 10 May 1934; *El Obrero de la Tierra*, 17 Feb 1934; Brenan, *Labyrinth*, p. 275.
57. *El Obrero de la Tierra*, 24 Feb, 3, 24 and 31 Mar, and 14 Apr 1934.
58. *El Obrero de la Tierra*, 31 Mar 1934.
59. On 31 July 1934 the National Committee of the UGT met to hold a post-mortem on the defeated strike. The above account derives from the proceedings of the meeting. (*BUGT*, Aug 1934.)
60. *El Socialista*, 6 May 1934; *ABC*, 2 May 1934; *El Sol*, 2 May 1934; *El Obrero de la Tierra*, 21 Apr and 5 May 1934.
61. *El Obrero de la Tierra*, 19 May 1934.
62. *El Obrero de la Tierra*, 26 May 1934.
63. *DSC*, 30 May 1934.
64. *La Mañana*, 6 and 8–12 June 1934, shows the thoroughness of the stoppage. See also *El Socialista*, 31 May and 1, 2, 3, 7, 8, 13, 28, 29 and 30 June 1934; *El Debate*, 30 and 31 May, and 6, 7 and 10 June 1934; *DSC*, 7 and 14 June 1934; Jackson, *Republic*, pp. 134–9. A more critical account of the FNTT is to be found in Malefakis, *Agrarian Reform*, pp. 335–40, and Salazar Alonso, *Bajo el signo*, p. 141ff.
65. Salazar Alonso admired Gil Robles and was enthusiastic about CEDA plans. The admiration was mutual. See Salazar Alonso, *Bajo el signo*, pp. 75–7; Gil Robles, *No fue posible la paz*, pp. 120–3.
66. Francesc Bonamusa, *El Bloc Obrer i Camperol (1930–1932)* (Barcelona, 1974) pp. 275–82, 341–2.
67. *El Socialista*, 29 Dec 1933.
68. Grandizo Munis, 'Hace falta una dirección', *Comunismo*, May 1934; Munis, *Jalones*, pp. 116–24. Socialist hesitance was justified by Largo Caballero in *BUGT*, June–July 1934.
69. *BUGT*, Aug 1934; Largo Caballero, *Mis recuerdos*, p. 141.

70. Peirats, *CNT*, vol. I, pp. 81–9; 'Ignotus' (Manuel Villar), *El Anarquismo en la insurreccion de Asturias* (Valencia, 1935) pp. 23–7; Arrarás, *República*, vol. II, pp. 298–9; *Avance*, 1 May 1934. The Caballerist desire to take over the workers movement through the Alianzas Obreras is evident in Segundo Serrano Poncela, *El Partido Socialista y la conquista del poder* (Barcelona, 1935), as the editorial introduction (pp. xi–xii) points out (see also pp. 149, 193).

71. Leon Trotsky, *The Struggle Against Fascism In Germany* (New York, 1971) p. 56.

72. Pelai Pagès, *El Movimiento trotskista en España (1930–1935)* (Barcelona, 1977) passim.

73. *Comunismo*, Mar and Sep 1934; Leon Trotsky, *La Révolution espagnole 1930–1940*, ed. Pierre Broué (Paris, 1975) pp. 252–9; Munis, *Jalones*, p. 122.

74. 'Ignotus', *Anarquismo*, pp. 31–9; Maurín, *Segunda revolución*, pp. 145–7; Ramón Alvarez, *Eleuterio Quintanilla* (Mexico, 1973) pp. 336–7; *Avance*, 15 May 1934.

75. Joaquín Maurín, 'El problema agrario en Cataluña', *Leviatán*, no. 4 (Aug 1934); Albert Balcells, *El Problema agrari a Catalunya* (Barcelona, 1968) pp. 135–214; Pabón, *Cambó*, pp. 340–75.

76. Azaña, *Obras*, vol. II, pp. 902, 977–98; Gil Robles, *No fue posible la paz*, pp. 124–6; *DSC*, 25 June and 4 July 1934; *El Debate*, 13 and 19 June, and 8 July 1934; *El Socialista*, 2 May, 9, 13 and 17 June, and 3 July 1934.

77. Munis, *Jalones*, p. 129; Serrano Poncela, *El Partido Socialista*, pp. 119–20.

78. *El Debate*, 7–9 Sep 1934; *El Socialista*, 7 Sep 1934.

79. Alejandro Valdés, *¡Asturias!* (Valencia, n.d. [1935?]) pp. 16–17; J. A. Sánchez y García Saúco, *La Revolución de 1934 en Asturias* (Madrid, 1974) pp. 39–40.

80. *El Debate*, 11 Sep 1934; *CEDA*, 15 Sep 1934; *El Socialista*, 11 and 20 Sept 1934; Gil Robles, *No fue posible la paz*, pp. 127–30; Cortés Cavanillas, Gil Robles, p. 180.

81. Díaz Nosty, *La Comuna asturiana*, pp. 105–7; Indalecio Prieto, 'La noche del *Turquesa*', *Convulsiones*, vol. I, pp. 109–11; Manuel Grossi, *L'Insurrection des Asturies*, 2nd edition (Paris, 1972) p. 57; Salazar Alonso, pp. 226–7. Manuel Benavides, *La Revolución fue así* (Barcelona, 1935) pp. 9–20, gives a vivid picture of the earnest naïvety with which the Socialist youth went about their preparations.

82. Gil Robles, *No fue posible la paz*, p. 131; Salazar Alonso, *Bajo el signo*, pp. 319–20; Jackson, *Republic*, p. 146; *El Debate*, 28 Sep 1934.

83. *CEDA*, nos 36–7, Dec 1934.

84. La Cierva, *La Guerra civil*, pp. 302–3, a statement apparently based on researches in restricted military archives.

85. *El Socialista*, 1 Aug and 2 Oct 1934; Buckley, *Life and Death*, p. 133. There is no other convincing explanation for the Socialists' lack of preparation. Genuine revolutionary elements complained bitterly about the way in which the PSOE was unwillingly forced into a defensive

movement. See Munis, *Jalones*, pp. 130–3; Andrade, *Burocracia*, pp. 250–63.

86. *El Debate*, 26, 27 and 28 Sep 1934; *El Socialista*, 3 and 4 Oct 1934; Gil Robles, *Discursos*, pp. 338–43, and *No fue posible la paz*, pp. 134–9.
87. Mario de Coca, *Anti-Caballero*, p. 107, makes the remarkable claim that Anguera's mother was a canonised saint.
88. *El Socialista*, 1 Aug and 27 Sep 1934.
89. Díaz Nosty, *La Comuna asturiana*, p. 136.
90. Largo Caballero, *Mis recuerdos*, p. 136; Rosal, *UGT*, vol. i, pp. 387, 401–2.
91. Antonio Ramos Oliveira, *La Revolución española de octubre* (Madrid, 1935) pp. 55–61.
92. The two accounts by miners confirm this. See Grossi, *L'Insurrection*, pp. 57, 119; José Canel, *Octubre rojo en Asturias* (Madrid, 1935) pp. 31, 43.
93. Munis, *Jalones*, pp. 130–40; Maurín, *Segunda revolución*, pp. 144–67; testimony of Madrid CNT secretary, Miguel González Inestal, to the author; Enrique Castro Delgado, *Hombres made in Moscú* (Barcelona, 1965) pp. 176–83; Andrés Nin, *Los Problemas de la revolución española* (Paris, 1971) pp. 156–7.
94. Benavides, *La Revolución fue así*, p. 372.
95. Munis, *Jalones*, p. 154; 'Ignotus', *Anarquismo*, pp. 176–9.
96. Grossi, *L'Insurrection*, pp. 108, 114ff.; Canel, *Octubre rojo*, p. 33.
97. Grossi, *L'Insurrection*, pp. 155–6; Canel, *Octubre rojo*, pp. 151–7.
98. J. Costa i Deu and Modest Sabaté, *La Veritat del 6 d'Octubre* (Barcelona, 1936), recounts the revolutionary events in Lerida, Gerona and other parts of provincial Catalonia where the Alianza Obrera had influence.
99. Azana, *Obras*, vol. iii, pp. 74–6; Munis, *Jalones*, pp. 140–7.
100. Maurín, *Segunda revolución*, pp. 123–44. It has been claimed that Dencàs was a rightist provocateur; see Brenan, *Labyrinth*, p. 284, and Consuelo Berges, *Explicación de octubre* (Madrid, 1935) p. 121. Cf. Andrés Nin, 'Los acontecimientos de octubre en Barcelona', *Leviatán*, no. 18 (Oct–Nov 1935).
101. Gil Robles, *No fue posible la paz*, p. 140; Joaquín Arrarás, *Franco* Valladolid, 1939) p. 186; Brenan, *Labyrinth*, p. 288. The actual campaign is described, from the army's point of view, in General López Ochoa, *Campaña militar de Asturias en octubre de 1934* (Madrid, 1936) and, from the Civil Guard's point of view, in Colonel F. Aguado Sánchez, *La Revolución de octubre de 1934* (Madrid, 1972) p. 253ff.
102. *DSC*, 9 Oct 1934; *La Mañana*, 7 and 11 Oct 1934. Arrests were made on a large scale. *El Debate*, 11 Oct 1934, reported that in Madrid alone there were already 2000 prisoners. Total figures are difficult to find. The lowest respectable figures are those of Malefakis (*Agrarian Reform*, p. 342), who gives 15,000–20,000. Jackson (*Republic*, p. 161) gives 30,000–40,000, and Buckley (*Life and Death*, p. 166) gives 60,000. The prisoners fate is described in Leah Manning, *What I Saw in Spain*

(London, 1935). See also Ignacio Carral, *Por qué mataron a Luis de Sirval* (Madrid, 1935).
103. Robinson, *Origins*, p. 194; Madariaga, *Spain*, p. 435.
104. Ramos Oliveira, *Octubre*, pp. 161–2; Berges, *Explicación de octubre*, pp. 89–90; Diego Hidalgo, *¿Porqué fuí lanzado del Ministerio de la Guerra?* (Madrid, 1934) pp. 83–9; José Martín Blázquez, *I Helped to Build an Army* (London, 1939) p. 34.

CHAPTER 5

1. Grossi, *L'Insurrection*, p. 224.
2. Dolores Ibárruri, *El Único camino* (Paris, 1965) pp. 181–3.
3. Sánchez Saúco, *La Revolución de 1934*, pp. 149–52; Díaz Nosty, *La Comuna asturiana*, pp. 361–72; Munis, *Jalones*, pp. 167–8.
4. Rosal, *UGT*, vol. I, pp. 409–22.
5. Largo Caballero, *Mis recuerdos*, pp. 138–9; Ibárruri et al., *Guerra*, vol. I, p. 62; Luis Araquistain, 'Largo Caballero ante los jueces' in *Leviatán* no. 20 (Jan 1936).
6. Castro Delgado, *Hombres made in Moscú*, p. 193; Mario de Coca, *Anti-Caballero*, p. 155; Alvarez del Vayo, *Last Optimist*, pp. 264–6; Munis, *Jalones*, pp. 134–40, 153; Eduardo Comin Colomer, *Historia del Partido Comunista de España*, 3 vols (Madrid, 1967) vol. II, pp. 325–7, 341–3; Manuel Tagüeña Lacorte, *Testimonio de dos guerras* (Mexico, 1973) pp. 67–72.
7. Saborit, *Besteiro*, p. 251; Lamo de Espinosa, *Besteiro*, p. 98.
8. Largo Caballero, *Mis recuerdos*, pp. 143, 145.
9. Azaña, letter to Prieto of 16 Jan 1935, *Obras*, vol. III, pp. 591–3; Juan Simeón Vidarte, *Todos fuimos culpables* (Mexico, 1973) p. 25.
10. The text of the letter is reprinted in Carlos de Baraibar, *Las Falsas 'posiciones socialistas' de Indalecio Prieto* (Madrid, 1935) pp. 139–45.
11. Nin, *Problemas*, pp. 155–8; Munis, *Jalones*, p. 183; Pelai Pagès, *Andreu Nin: su evolución política 1911–1937* (Bilbao, 1975) p. 188. Trotsky later denounced as treachery the POUM's participation in the Popular Front; see Trotsky, *Révolution espagnole*, pp. 285–91.
12. *La Libertad*, 30 Mar 1935.
13. *La Libertad*, 13 Apr 1935; Diego Martínez Barrio, *Orígenes del Frente Popular español* (Buenos Aires, 1943) pp. 24–31.
14. The text of the letter is reprinted in Baraibar, *Prieto*, pp. 197–200. Largo Caballero (*Mis recuerdos*, p. 144) claimed to have received a letter from Peña endorsing *his* position. If so, it is strange that, given the no-holds-barred polemic at the time, the text was not published.
15. Indalecio Prieto, 'La coalición de izquierdas', *El Liberal*, 14 Apr 1935.
16. [Carlos Hernández Zancajo], *Octubre–segunda etapa* (no place or date [Madrid, 1935]). There were two editions, of which the cheaper had no cover and smaller print. References given here are to that popular edition. See evidence by Carrillo in María Eugenia Yagüe, *Santiago Carrillo* (Madrid, 1977) p. 26, and by Amaro del Rosal in Marta Biz-

carrondo, *Octubre del 34: reflexiones sobre una revolucion* (Madrid, 1977) p. 50, confirmed personally by Carrillo to the author on 5 Oct 1977.

17. *Octubre*, pp. 26–31, 39–46, 52–5, 94.
18. Comín, *PCE*, vol. II, pp. 459–74; Stanley G. Payne, *The Spanish Revolution* (London, 1970) pp. 164–5; Ricardo de la Cierva, *La Historia perdida del socialismo español* (Madrid, 1972) pp. 189–90.
19. Largo Caballero, *Mis recuerdos*, p. 141; Santiago Carrillo, *Demain l'Espagne* (Paris, 1974) p. 32. Prieto believed otherwise; cf. Vidarte, *Todos fuimos culpables*, p. 30.
20. *La Libertad*, 24 Apr 1935. At first Cordero had been in favour of ignoring the pamphlet; see Vidarte, *Todos fuimos culpables*, p. 30.
21. Saborit, *Besteiro*, pp. 251–7.
22. Serrano Poncela, *El Partido Socialista*, p. 156.
23. Julián Besteiro, *Marxismo y anti-marxismo* (Madrid, 1935). References are to the 4th edition (Madrid, 1967) pp. 16–23, 93–102, 107–13, 130–1.
24. Luis Araquistain, 'El marxismo en la Academia', 'Un marxismo contra Marx', and 'La esencia del marxismo', *Leviatán*, nos. 13–15 (May–July 1935).
25. Julián Besteiro, 'Leviatán: el socialismo mitológico' and 'Mi crítico empieza a razonar', *Democracia*, 15 June and 6 July 1935.
26. This aspect of Araquistain's thought is discussed at length in Paul Preston, introductory essay to *Leviatán: antología* (Madrid, 1976).
27. Indalecio Prieto, 'Mi derecho a opinar', 'La Amnistía, base de la coalición electoral', 'El valor de la acción parlamentaria', 'Los roedores de derrotas' and 'La planta exótica del caudillismo', *El Liberal* and *La Libertad*, 22–26 May 1935.
28. Azaña reminded Prieto of this in a letter of 20 Apr 1935, *Obras*, vol. III, p. 601.
29. Indalecio Prieto, *Posiciones socialistas del momento* (Madrid, n.d. [1935]).
30. Baraibar presented a copy of his *Las Falsas 'posiciones socialistas' de Indalecio Prieto* to Largo Caballero on 30 June 1935 with a dedication which stated 'You know better than anyone – my dear Don Francisco – the moral motives behind this book. Receive with it the affection and the limitless devotion of Carlos de Baraibar' (copy in private collection).
31. Baraibar, *Prieto*, pp. 22–6, 46, 67–9, 113. That many of Baraibar's accusations were false was proved by documents published by Prieto in *El Liberal*, 11 Sep 1935.
32. Azaña, letter to Prieto of 7 Aug 1935, *Obras*, vol. III, pp. 603–4.
33. Buckley, *Life and Death*, p. 183; Azaña, *Obras*, vol. III, pp. 229–93.
34. *El Liberal*, 27 and 29 Aug 1935; *Democracia*, 27 Sep 1935.
35. *Democracia*, 25 Aug 1935; *Claridad*, 20 July 1935.
36. *Democracia*, 13 and 20 Sep, 8 Nov, and 6 Dec 1935; *Claridad*, 29 July, 26 Oct, and 30 Nov 1935.
37. *Democracia*, 13 Sep and 11 Oct 1935.
38. José Díaz, *Tres años de lucha*, 2nd edition (Paris, 1969) pp. 7–30, 33, 57.

39. *Claridad*, 17 Aug, and 12 and 19 Oct 1935.
40. Luis Araquistain, 'La nueva táctica comunista', *Leviatán* no. 16 (Aug. 1935).
41. *Claridad*, 7 and 14 Dec 1935.
42. Claudio Sánchez Albornoz, *De mi anecdotario político* (Buenos Aires, 1972) pp. 105, 116.
43. Jacques Duclos, *Mémoires* (Paris, 1969) pp. 106–10.
44. Largo Caballero, *Mis recuerdos*, pp. 146–7; Mario de Coca, *Anti-Caballero*, pp. 152–4.
45. *El Socialista*, 25 Dec 1935; *Claridad*, 23 Dec 1935; Vidarte, *Todos fuimos culpables*, p. 26; Largo Caballero, *Mis recuerdos*, p. 148; Mario de Coca, *Anti-Caballero*, pp. 193–8.
46. *El Socialista*, 18 and 19 Dec 1935; *Claridad*, 15 Jan 1936.
47. *El Socialista*, 22 Dec 1935, and 4 and 8–16 Jan 1936.
48. Payne, *Revolution*, p. 174; La Cierva, *Socialismo*, pp. 200–1.
49. This account is based on a comparison of candidates in the 1933 and 1936 elections as listed in *El Debate*, 21 Nov and 5 Dec 1933, and 18 Feb 1936.
50. Lamo de Espinosa, *Besteiro*, pp. 101–2, 125–33.
51. Vidarte, *Todos fuimos culpables*, pp. 38–40; *Claridad*, 25 Jan 1936.
52. Letter of Largo Caballero to the UGT executive, 5 Jan 1936, reprinted in Rosal, *UGT*, vol. I, pp. 445–8.
53. *El Socialista*, 16 Jan 1936; Ibárruri et al., *Guerra*, vol. I, pp. 69–78; Largo Caballero, *Mis recuerdos*, pp. 150–1; Munis, *Jalones*, pp. 191–201; Vidarte, *Todos fuimos culpables*, pp. 27–35.
54. *Claridad*, 25 and 30 Jan and 6 Feb 1935; *El Socialista*, 12 Feb 1936.
55. *Claridad*, 18 Jan 1936.

CHAPTER 6

1. Robinson, *Origins*, p. 194; Madariaga, *Spain*, p. 435.
2. *JAP*, 27 Oct 1934; *El Debate*, 9, 17, 21, 24 and 31 Oct, and 4 Nov 1934; *DSC*, 5 Nov 1934; Antonio Elorza, 'El sindicalismo católico en la segunda República', *La Utopía anarquista bajo la segunda República española* (Madrid, 1973) pp. 295–350. For the subsequent activities and fiercely rightist tone of the CESO, see Juan José Castillo, 'El Comité Nacional Circunstancial de la Confederación Española de Sindicatos Obreros 1936–1938', *Revista española de la opinión pública*, no. 38 (Oct 1974).
3. *DSC*, 14 and 15 Nov 1934; *El Debate*, 24 Oct, and 2, 3, 8 and 14 Nov 1934.
4. *El Debate*, 24 Oct, and 16 and 17 Nov 1934; *Leviatán* no. 7 (Nov 1934); *DSC*, 15 Nov 1934; Gil Robles, *No fue posible la paz*, pp. 141–5.
5. Joaquín Arrarás, *Historia de la Cruzada española*, 7 vols (Madrid, 1939–40) vol. II, p. 277; Gil Robles, *No fue posible la paz*, pp. 145–9.
6. Gil Robles, *No fue posible la paz*, pp. 152–3, 157–8; *DSC*, 21 Dec

1934; *El Debate*, 28 Dec 1934; La Cierva, *La Guerra civil*, p. 458; Jackson, *Republic*, p. 170.

7. Lamamié and Casanueva were both deputies for Salamanca, as was Gil Robles. They were all three members of the Bloque Agrario of Salamanca, and in February 1935 were to be found addressing meetings together while Giménez Fernández was under attack.

8. *El Debate*, 24 Nov, and 1, 5, 7, 20 and 21 Dec 1934, and 2 and 6 Feb, and 1 and 19 Mar 1935; Gil Robles, *No fue posible la paz*, pp. 172–88; Malefakis, *Agrarian Reform*, pp. 347–55; Robinson, *Origins*, pp. 200–2; Jackson, *Republic*, p. 169.

9. A graphic picture of a *pueblo* in Toledo is provided by Arturo Barea, *La Forja de un rebelde* (Buenos Aires, 1951) pp. 483–90.

10. *JAP*, 10 and 24 Nov, 8 Dec 1934 and, 2 and 11 Feb, and 16 Mar 1935; Gil Robles, *No fue posible la paz*, p. 203. At a meeting in Santiago de Compostela, Gil Robles said that JAP was the vanguard, CEDA the consolidator (*El Debate*, 3 Sep 1934).

11. *El Debate*, 22 and 23 Dec 1934, and 12 Jan 1935.

12. *El Debate*, 12 Jan 1935; Gil Robles, *No fue posible la paz*, pp. 165–8; Pabón, *Cambó*, p. 299.

13. *El Debate*, 4 and 20 Jan, and 3 Mar 1935; *CEDA*, 1 May 1935.

14. *El Debate*, 10 Feb, and 19 and 27 Mar 1935; Lerroux, *Pequeña historia*, pp. 374–5; Gil Robles, *No fue posible la paz*, pp. 212–7; Jackson, *Republic*, pp. 161–7.

15. Viñas, *La Alemania nazi*, p. 172.

16. *El Debate*, 2, 3, 21, 23, 28 and 30 Apr, and 4 and 7 May 1935; Gil Robles, *No fue posible la paz*, pp. 218–31; Lerroux, *Pequeña historia*, pp. 387–91. The most liberal section of the Radicals, those from Valencia, nearly split off from the party because of Lerroux's acquiescence in Gil Robles's plans. Alcalá Zamora persuaded Samper against this schism. See Martínez Barrio, *Orígenes del Frente Popular*, pp. 66–7.

17. *DSC*, 15 and 27 Feb 1935.

18. *El Debate*, 12 May 1935.

19. *El Debate*, 16 and 18 May, and 27 Aug 1935; Gil Robles, *No fue posible la paz*, pp. 232–44; La Cierva, *La Guerra civil*, pp. 488–90; Arrarás, *Franco*, pp. 191–9; Manuel Goded, *Un 'Faccioso' cien por cien* (Zaragoza, 1939) pp. 23–4; Stanley Payne, *Politics and the Military in Modern Spain* (Stanford, 1967) pp. 304–6.

20. Gil Robles, *No fue posible la paz*, pp. 238–40; Azaña, letter to Prieto of 7 Aug 1935, *Obras*, vol. III, p. 604.

21. Brenan (*Labyrinth*, p. 293), says, 'It was at this time that those concrete trenches were dug in the Sierra de Guadarrama overlooking Madrid that proved so useful to General Mola's levies in the Civil War'. Identical accusations were made in *ABC*, 31 July 1936, and in *Solidaridad Obrera*; see S. Cánovas Cervantes, *Apuntes historicos de Solidaridad Obrera* (Barcelona, 1937) p. 31.

22. Seco Serrano, *Epoca contemporánea*, p. 133.

23. *Documents on German Foreign Policy*, ser. C, vol. IV (London 1964)

documents 303, 330 and 445; Earl of Avon, *Facing the Dictators* (London, 1962) p. 256; Buckley, *Life and Death*, pp. 175–6; *El Debate*, 27 Aug and 15 Sep 1935.

24. *El Debate*, 7 and 16 May 1935; *Arriba*, 13 June 1935; Robinson, *Origins*, pp. 204–5.

25. *El Debate*, 14 May and 14 June 1935; La Cierva, *La Guerra civil*, p. 487.

26. Seco Serrano, *Epoca contemporánea*, p. 138; Primo de Rivera, *Obras*, pp. 631–42.

27. *El Debate*, 21 May, 2 and 21 June, 6 July, and 19 Sep 1935; *Boletín del Ministerio de Trabajo, Sanidad y Previsión*, Aug and Sep 1935.

28. 'Emilio Ruiz' (Juan Andrade), 'La política pre-supuestaria Radical–Cedista', *Leviatán*, no. 15 (July 1935); *Boletín del Ministerio de Trabajo*, June, Oct and Dec 1935, and Jan 1936.

29. *El Debate*, 2 July 1935; *CEDA*, 1 July 1935; *DSC*, 12 July 1935.

30. *El Debate*, 3 July 1935; Malefakis, *Agrarian Reform*, p. 358.

31. *El Debate*, 21 and 28 May 1935; *Arriba*, 13 June 1935 (which graphically illustrated its report of the Uclés meeting with a photograph of pigs jostling for swill); *JAP*, 14 Mar, 27 Apr, and 1 June 1935.

32. *El Debate*, 14, 20 and 23 June, and 2 and 3 July 1935; *JAP*, 1 July 1935.

33. *El Debate*, 3 Sep 1935.

34. *JAP*, 22 June, and 1 and 14 July 1935; La Cierva, *La Guerra civil*, pp. 508–10.

35. *JAP*, 16 Mar, 8 June, 27 July, 31 Aug, and 28 Sep 1935; Gil Robles, *No fue posible la paz*, p. 194.

36. *CEDA*, 30 Nov 1935; *JAP*, 17 Aug, 7 Sep, and 5 October 1935; *El Debate*, 10 Nov 1935. The fascist leader, Ledesma, regarded the CEDA as a 'fascisticised' force; see Ramiro Ledesma Ramos, *¿Fascismo en España?*, 2nd edition (Barcelona, 1968) p. 72.

37. *El Debate*, 25 June 1935; Lerroux, *Pequeña historia*, pp. 392–4; Gil Robles, *No fue posible la paz*, p. 285; Primo de Rivera, *Obras*, p. 609.

38. Joaquín Chapaprieta, *La Paz fue posible* (Barcelona, 1971) pp. 207–33; Gil Robles, *No fue posible la paz*, pp. 286–91; Pabón, *Cambó*, pp. 433–5; *El Debate*, 20 and 24–26 Sep 1935.

39. Mendizábal, *Aux Origines*, pp. 221–2; Chapaprieta, *La Paz fue posible*, pp. 234–5.

40. *DSC*, 2 Oct 1935. Their concern might have been greater had they known that on 11 September the German embassy in Madrid had replied in the affirmative to the government feelers of March regarding a possible collaboration between the Spanish police and the Gestapo in the fight against 'communism'; see Viñas, *La Alemania nazi*, pp. 172-–3.

41. *DSC*, 22 Oct 1935; Chapaprieta, *La Paz fue posible*, pp. 257–62; Gil Robles, *No fue posible la paz*, pp. 292–304; Pabón, *Cambó*, pp. 440–6.

42. Chapaprieta, *La Paz fue posible*, pp. 262–80; Gil Robles, *No fue posible la paz*, pp. 304–12; *DSC*, 28 Oct 1935; Primo de Rivera, *Obras*, pp. 665–8; Lerroux, *Pequeña historia*, pp. 446–55; Pabón, *Cambó*, pp. 446–50; *El Debate* 23, 27, 29 and 30 Oct 1935.

43. Chapaprieta, *La Paz fue posible*, pp. 292–305; Gil Robles, *No fue posible la paz*, pp. 341–58; Cortés Cavanillas, *Gil Robles*, p. 151; Pabón, *Cambó*, pp. 452–8. Samper later alleged that the CEDA leader had turned a blind eye to the Radicals' financial immorality in return for being left to carry out his own plans in the Ministry of War; see Martínez Barrio, *Orígenes*, pp. 82–3.

44. *JAP*, 12 Oct 1935; *El Debate*, 10 Nov 1935.

45. Chapaprieta, *La Paz fue posible*, pp. 318–21.

46. During the Civil War, Gil Robles told a Portuguese journalist that the initiative for a coup was his; see Armando Boaventura, *Madrid–Moscovo – Da Ditadura a República e a Guerra Civil de Espanha* (Lisbon, 1937) pp. 191–2.

47. *El Debate*, 10–14 Dec 1935; Gil Robles, *No fue posible la paz*, pp. 358–67; Chapaprieta, *La Paz fue posible*, pp. 324–32; Pabón, *Cambó*, pp. 459–64; Arrarás, *República*, vol. III, pp. 267–71. It is interesting to note that, while Gil Robles was toying with the idea of a coup, his 'rival', Calvo Sotelo, was in touch with the same set of generals, urging them to rise; see Ansaldo, *¿Para qué?*, p. 111.

48. *El Debate*, 17, 18 and 28 Dec 1935; *La Nación*, 14 Dec 1935; *La Epoca*, 17 and 27 Dec 1935; *ABC*, 17 Dec 1935; Gil Robles, *No fue posible la paz*, pp. 380–403; Chapaprieta, *La Paz fue posible*, pp. 353–77.

49. Gil Robles, *No fue posible la paz*, p. 404; Arrarás, *República*, vol. IV, p. 41.

50. *El Pueblo vasco*, pp. 105–39.

51. Gil Robles, *No fue posible la paz*, pp. 404–30; Javier Tusell, *Las Elecciones del Frente Popular*, 2 vols (Madrid, 1971) vol. I, pp. 42–133; *El Socialista*, 11 and 18 Jan 1936 (which noted this chicanery with grim amusement); Blinkhorn, *Carlism*, p. 204.

52. *El Debate*, 9 Feb 1936; *ABC*, 8 Feb 1936.

53. Gil Robles, *No fue posible la paz*, pp. 431–4.

54. Chapaprieta, *La Paz fue posible*, pp. 390–6.

55. Buckley, *Life and Death*, p. 188; Bowers, *My Mission*, p. 187; *El Socialista* 19 Jan and 13 Feb 1936; Gil Robles, *No fue posible la paz*, p. 472.

56. Viñas, *La Alemania nazi*, p. 147.

57. Buckley, *Life and Death*, p. 189; Tusell, *Elecciones*, vol. I, p. 217; Vidarte, *Todos fuimos culpables*, p. 37.

58. *El Debate*, 2 Feb 1936; Tusell, *Elecciones*, vol. II, Appendix 7.

59. *El Debate*, 10, 11 and 15 Jan, and 9, 11, 14 and 16 Feb 1936; Gil Robles, *No fue posible la paz*, pp. 464–73.

60. *JAP*, 28 Dec 1935. The *JAP* issue for 21 Dec printed *JEFE* 195 times on page 3.

61. *El Sol*, 24 Jan 1936; *El Socialista*, 21 Jan 1936; *El Debate*, 7 Feb 1936; *JAP*, 14 Feb 1936.

62. *El Debate*, 3, 10 and 17 Jan 1936; *El Socialista*, 18 Jan 1936.

63. Tusell, *Elecciones*, vol. I, pp. 211–9, 230–4, 273–85; *El Defensor*, 24 Jan 1936 which made an eloquent and reasoned plea for the Right to

moderate its aggressiveness); Ian Gibson, *La Represión nacionalista de Granada en 1936 y la muerte de Federico García Lorca* (Paris, 1971) pp. 1–24.

64. *JAP*, 11 Jan 1936; Gil Robles, *No fue posible la paz*, pp. 484–5; *Leviatán*, no. 20 (Jan 1936).

65. *JAP*, 4 Jan 1936; *El Debate*, 3 Jan 1936; *El Socialista*, 18 Jan 1936.

66. *El Debate*, 3 Jan 1936; *El Socialista*, 30 Jan 1936; Bowers, *My Mission*, p. 182; Buckley, *Life and Death,* pp. 190–1; De la Mora, *In Place of Splendour*, p. 207.

67. *Ideal*, 14 Feb 1936; *El Defensor* 14, 19 and 28 Jan, 1, 6 and 15–20 Feb, and 5–7 Mar 1936; *El Socialista*, 7 Mar 1936.

68. *El Socialista*, 18 Jan, and 9 Feb 1936; Fraser, *In Hiding*, p. 116; Barea, *Forja*, pp. 522–9; Tusell, *Elecciones*, vol. ii, pp. 123–91; Bécarud, *La Segunda República*, pp. 152–3; Robinson, *Origins*, pp. 255–6, 387–8.

69. There has been endless controversy about the actual results. The most exhaustive study to date is by Tusell, who gives the following figures: Left, 4,654,116; Centre, 526,615; Right, 4,503,505 (*Elecciones*, vol. ii, p. 13. The only other monographic study. José Venegas, *Las Elecciones del Frente Popular* (Buenos Aires, 1942) p. 65, favours the Left rather more: Left, 4,838,449; Centre, 449,320; Right, 3,996,931. The two general accounts which deal with the elections in most detail – Bécarud, *La Segunda República,* p. 156 and Jackson, *Republic*, p. 193 – produce figures similar to those of Venegas.

70. Ministerio de la Gobernación, *Dictamen de la Comisión sobre ilegitimidad de poderes actuantes en 18 de julio de 1936* (Barcelona, 1939) pp. 31–45. The final composition of the Cortes was as follows: PSOE, 102; Azaña's Izquierda Repúblicana, ninety, Martínez Barrio's Unión Repúblicana, thirty-six; Companys's *Esquerra*, thirty-six; PCE, fifteen; Portela Valladares's Centre Party, eighteen; Lliga, twelve; Basque Nationalists, nine; Radicals, four; conservative republicans, seventeen; CEDA, eighty-seven; Agrarians, fifteen; Renovación Española and other extreme monarchists, nineteen; Carlists, nine.

CHAPTER 7

1. *Boletín del Ministerio de Trabajo*, Apr 1936.

2. Munis, *Jalones*, p. 201; Díaz, *Lucha*, p. 149; Peirats, *CNT*, vol. i, p. 120; testimony of Miguel González Inestal to the author.

3. Arrarás, *Cruzada*, vol. ii, pp. 439–40; Gil Robles, *No fue posible la paz*; pp. 492–7; Goded, *Un 'Faccioso' cien por cien*, pp. 26–7; B. Félix Maíz, *Alzamiento en España*, 2nd edition (Pamplona, 1952) p. 37; Vidarte, *Todos fuimos culpables*, pp. 40–55; Azaña, diary entry for 19 Feb 1936, *Obras*, vol. iv, p. 563.

4. Gil Robles, *No fue posible la paz*, pp. 503–7.

5. Azaña, diary entry for 20 Feb 1936, *Obras*, vol. iv, p. 572.

6. *El Debate*, 6 Mar 1936; Gil Robles, *No fue posible la paz*, p. 533.

7. *El Socialista,* 7, 8 and 15 Mar 1936; speech of Rodolfo Llopis, *DSC,* 15 Apr 1936.
8. *El Debate,* 18 and 19 Mar 1936.
9. Gil Robles, *No fue posible la paz,* pp. 575–6; Vidarte, *Todos fuimos culpables,* p. 53.
10. *El Socialista,* 22 Mar 1936; *Claridad,* 6 Apr, and 30 May 1936.
11. Ministerio de la Gobernación, *Comisión sobre ilegitimidad,* pp. 41–3, and Appendix, I, p. 129; Robinson, *Origins,* pp. 255–6; Gil Robles, *No fue posible la paz,* pp. 541–7 (Gil Robles attributes to Madariaga the opinions of Alcalá Zamora).
12. *DSC,* 20, 24 and 31 Mar, and 1 and 2 Apr 1936.
13. *DSC,* 31 Mar 1936; *ABC,* 1 Apr 1936.
14. Vidarte, *Todos fuimos culpables,* p. 71; Venegas, *Elecciones,* pp. 47–8; Gil Robles, *No fue posible la paz,* pp. 548–9. Prieto wanted to annul all the Galician results. Cf. his own version in his prologue to Romero Solano, *Vísperas,* pp. 6–7.
15. *DSC,* 1 and 2 Apr 1936.
16. Vidarte, diary entry for 3 Apr 1936, *Todos fuimos culpables,* p. 71; *El Sol,* 4 Apr 1936.
17. *DSC,* 7 Apr 1936; *El Debate,* 8 Apr 1936; *ABC,* 8 Apr 1936.
18. Payne, *Revolution,* p. 192; La Cierva, *Socialismo,* pp. 202–3, 214.
19. Marichal, introduction to Azaña, *Obras,* vol. III, pp. xxxi–ii.
20. *DSC,* 7 Apr 1936; Vidarte, *Todos fuimos culpables,* pp. 74–80, 96–9; Largo Caballero, *Mis recuerdos,* p. 155; Julián Zugazagoitia, *Guerra y vicisitudes de los Españoles,* 2 vols (Paris, 1968) vol. I, p. 20.
21. *DSC,* 15 Apr 1936; Robinson, *Origins,* pp. 259–60.
22. *El Socialista,* 18 and 19 Apr, and 8 May 1936; *Claridad,* 15, 16 and 18 Apr 1936.
23. *ABC,* 4, 5 and 11 Mar, and 2, 19 and 29 Apr 1936; Ansaldo, *¿Para qué?,* pp. 77–8; De la Mora, *In Place of Splendour,* pp. 214–5; Buckley, *Life and Death,* p. 129; Stanley G. Payne, *Falange: A History of Spanish Fascism* (Stanford, 1961) pp. 98–105.
24. Gibson, *Lorca,* pp. 40–3; *La Mañana,* 14 Mar 1936; *Claridad,* 14 Apr 1936; *El Sol* 4, 11, 15, 21 and 26 Mar, and 6 Apr 1936; Bowers, *My Mission,* pp. 200–8.
25. Gil Robles, *No fue posible la paz,* pp. 573–5.
26. Payne, *Military,* p. 318; *Falange,* pp. 104–5; Blinkhorn, *Carlism,* p. 257; Ramón Serrano Súñer, *Entre Hendaya y Gibraltar* (Madrid, 1947) p. 25.
27. Gil Robles, *No fue posible la paz,* pp. 558–70; Gibson, *Lorca,* pp. 45–6.
28. *El Obrero de la Tierra,* 29 Feb, and 7, 21 and 28 Mar 1936.
29. Malefakis, *Agrarian Reform,* pp. 364–74.
30. *El Obrero de la Tierra,* 18 Apr, 1, 16, 23 and 30 May, and 13, 20 and 27 June 1936; *Claridad,* 6, 9 and 18 June 1936. The events at Yeste on 29 May were debated in the Cortes on 5 June.
31. Prieto, *Discursos,* pp. 255–73.
32. Vidarte, *Todos fuimos culpables,* pp. 115–18.
33. Burnett Bolloten, *The Grand Camouflage,* 2nd edition (London, 1968)

pp. 115–16; *Claridad,* 2 and 6 Apr 1936; Carrillo, *Demain l'Espagne,* pp 48–9; Vidarte, *Todos fuimos culpables,* pp. 56–7.
34. *Claridad,* 7, 8 and 11 May 1936.
35. Rosal, *UGT,* vol. i, p. 479; *Claridad* 12 May 1936; Vidarte, *Todos fuimos culpables,* pp. 100, 115–27; Prieto, *Convulsiones,* vol. i, p. 164; *Convulsiones,* vol. iii, pp. 135–6.
36. Arrarás, *República,* vol. iv, pp. 273–81; Gil Robles, *No fue posible la paz,* pp. 616–27; *El Debate,* 24 Apr 1936; Payne, *Military,* p. 330; Vidarte, *Todos fuimos culpables,* p. 136.
37. Vidarte, *Todos fuimos culpables,* pp. 147, 190–2; Prieto, *Convulsiones,* vol. iii, pp. 143–4; Largo Caballero, *Mis recuerdos,* pp. 161–3; Ibárruri, *El Único camino,* pp. 252–3.
38. Gil Robles, *No fue posible la paz,* pp. 719, 728–30, 798; Cierva, *La Guerra civil,* p. 742.
39. Cierva, *La Guerra civil,* pp. 743–4.
40. Juan Ignacio Luca de Tena, *Mis amigos muertos* (Barcelona, 1971), p. 68; Payne, *Military,* p. 335; Gil Robles, *No fue posible la paz,* p. 733.
41. Gil Robles, *No fue posible la paz,* pp. 730–1, 787–8; Payne, *Military,* p. 339.
42. *DSC,* 19 May 1936.
43. *El Debate,* 31 May 1936.
44. Bolloten, *Camouflage,* passim; David T. Cattell, *Communism and the Spanish Civil War* (Berkeley, Calif., 1955) pp. 39–43.
45. *Claridad* 19 and 30 May, 9, 15, 19 and 24 June, and 8 and 9 July 1936; *El Sol,* 9, 11 and 15 June, and 15 July 1936; Bolloten, *Camouflage,* pp. 22–3; Jackson, *Republic,* pp. 220–2; J. Alvarez del Vayo, *Freedom's Battle* (London, 1940) p. 23.
46. *Claridad,* 20 and 21 Apr 1936; Araquistain, articles in *Leviatán,* nos 22 and 24 (March and May 1936); *Mundo Obrero,* 23–28 Mar 1936; Rosal, *UGT,* vol. i, pp. 423–4.
47. *Claridad* 9 and 11 May 1936; Peirats, *CNT,* vol. i, pp. 119–22; Brademas, *Anarco-sindicalismo,* pp. 168–71.
48. Munis, *Jalones,* pp. 208–13; Payne, *Revolution,* p. 199.
49. Vidarte, *Todos fuimos culpables,* pp. 162–3, 170.
50. Romero Solano, *Vísperas,* pp. 176–7.
51. *Claridad,* 20 May and 1 June 1936; Prieto, *Convulsiones,* vol. iii, pp. 159–60.
52. *Claridad,* 30 June, and 1, 2 and 13 July 1936; *El Socialista,* 1 and 2 July 1936; Vidarte, *Todos fuimos culpables,* pp. 192–6, 205–8; Jackson, *Republic,* pp. 221–2.
53. *DSC,* 16 June 1936.
54. *DSC,* 1 July 1936.
55. Vidarte, *Todos fuimos culpables,* pp. 213–7, contains an account by one of the officers present.
56. Gil Robles, *Discursos,* pp. 613–72.
57. FO371/2057W9964/9549/41, quoted in Glyn A. Stone, 'The Official British Attitude to the Anglo-Portuguese Alliance 1910–1945', *Journal*

of Contemporary History, x, no. 4 (Oct 1975) p. 745; vol. III, 53–5; Arthur Koestler, *Spanish Testament* (London, 1937) pp. 22–5; Gutiérrez Ravé, *Gil Robles*, pp. 198–9.

58. *La Gaceta Regional*, 18 Oct 1936.
59. *Sur* (Málaga) 25 and 28 Apr 1937.

Bibliography

PRIMARY SOURCES

Parliamentary Debates

Diario de sesiones de las Cortes Constituyentes de la República española, comenzaron el 14 de julio de 1931 (DSCC), 25 vols.

Diario de las sesiones de Cortes, Congreso de los Diputados, comenzaron el 8 de diciembre de 1933 (DSC), 17 vols.

Diario de las sesiones de Cortes, Congreso de los Diputados, comenzaron el 16 de marzo de 1936 (DSC), 3 vols.

Trade Union and party bulletins and Congress reports

Boletín de Información de Acción Popular (Madrid), fortnightly, Mar 1932 to May 1933.

Boletín de la Unión General de Trabajadores de España (Madrid), monthly, Aug 1929 to Aug 1934.

CEDA–Organo de la Confederación Española de Derechas Autonomas (Madrid), fortnightly, May 1933 to Nov 1933.

JAP–Organo nacional de las Juventudes de Acción Popular de España (Madrid), fortnightly, Oct 1934–Feb 1936.

PSOE, *Convocatoria y orden del día para el XII Congreso ordinario del Partido Socialista Obrero Español* (Madrid, 1927).

PSOE, *Convocatoria y orden del día para el XIII Congreso ordinario del Partido Socialista Obrero Español* (Madrid, 1932).

Renovación–Organo de la Federación de Juventudes Socialistas de España (Madrid), weekly, Feb 1933 to Sep 1934.

La Unión Ferroviaria–Boletín del Sindicato Nacional Ferroviario (Madrid), monthly, 1933.

Unión General de Trabajadores, *Memoria y orden del día del XVII Congreso, que se celebrará en Madrid los días 14 y siguientes de octubre de 1932* (Madrid, 1932).

Ministerial Bulletins and reports

Boletín del Instituto de Reforma Agraria (Madrid), monthly, Jan 1933 to July 1936.
Boletín del Ministerio de Trabajo y Previsión Social (Madrid), monthly, Jan 1931 to Apr 1936.
Ministerio de la Gobernación, *Dictamen de la Comisión sobre ilegitimidad de poderes actuantes en 18 de julio de 1936* (Barcelona, 1939).
Ministerio de Justicia, *Causa general. La dominación roja en España. Avance de la información instruida por el ministerio público* (Madrid, 1944).
Ministerio de Trabajo y Previsión Social, *La Crisis andaluza de 1930–1931* (Madrid, 1931).

Newspapers and Periodicals

ABC (Madrid), daily, Aug 1923 to Aug 1936.
Acción Española (Madrid), monthly, Dec 1931 to Apr 1936.
Arriba (Madrid), weekly, Mar 1935 to Feb 1936.
Avance (Oviedo), daily, Nov 1931 to Oct 1934.
Claridad (Madrid), weekly (then daily from Apr 1936), July 1935 to July 1936.
Comunismo (Madrid), monthly, May 1931 to Oct 1934.
El Debate (Madrid), daily, Jan 1930 to July 1936.
El Defensor (Granada), daily, Dec 1935 to June 1936.
Democracia (Madrid), weekly, June 1935 to Dec 1935.
La Época (Madrid), daily, Apr 1931 to Apr 1936.
FE (Madrid), weekly, Dec 1933 to July 1934.
Leviatán (Madrid), monthly, May 1934 to July 1936.
El Liberal (Bilbao), daily, Mar 1935 to Mar 1936.
La Mañana (Jaén), daily, Apr 1932 to July 1936.
El Obrero de la Tierra (Madrid), weekly, Jan 1932 to July 1936.
El Pueblo Católico (Jaén), daily, Jan 1931 to May 1933.
El Socialista (Madrid), daily, Aug 1923 to Aug 1936.
El Sol (Madrid), daily, Aug 1923 to July 1936.
Tierra y Trabajo (Salamanca), weekly, Nov 1932 to May 1933.

In addition to the above continuous runs of newspapers and periodicals, many shorter runs and odd copies were also consulted. These included :

El Adelanto (Salamanca).
Campo Libre (Madrid).
La Gaceta Regional (Salamanca).

El Heraldo (Madrid).
Ideal (Granada).
La Libertad (Madrid).
Mundo Obrero (Madrid).
La Nación (Madrid).
Región (Cáceres).
Sur (Málaga).
La Tierra (Madrid).

Printed documents, diaries, letters and speeches

Arnau, Roger, *Marxisme català i qüestió nacional catalana 1930–1936*, 2 vols (Paris, 1974).
Azaña, Manuel, *Obras completas*, 4 vols (Mexico, 1966–8).
Azaña, Manuel, *Memorias íntimas de Azaña* (Madrid, 1939).
Cierva, Ricardo de la, *Los Documentos de la primavera trágica* (Madrid, 1967).
Clero Vasco, El, *El Pueblo vasco frente a la cruzada franquista* (Toulouse, 1966).
Díaz, José, *Tres años de lucha*, 2nd edition (Paris, 1969).
Documents on German Foreign Policy 1918–1945, ser. C, vol. IV, and ser. D, vol. III (London, 1964 and 1951).
Gil Robles, José María, *Discursos parlamentarios* (Madrid, 1971).
Iglesias, Pablo, *Escritos* 2 vols (Madrid, 1975).
Jiménez Asúa (Luis), Vidarte (Juan-Simeón), Rodríguez Sastre (Antonio) and Trejo (Anselmo), *Castilblanco* (Madrid, 1933).
Largo Caballero, Francisco, *Discursos a los trabajadores* (Madrid, 1934).
Largo Caballero, Francisco, *Posibilismo socialista en la democracia* (Madrid, 1933).
López Sevilla, Enrique, *El PSOE en las Cortes Constituyentes de la segunda República* (Mexico, 1969).
Mola Vidal, Emilio, *Obras completas* (Valladolid, 1940).
Pabón, Jesús, *Palabras en la oposición* (Seville, 1935).
Prieto, Indalecio, *Dentro y fuera del Gobierno* (Madrid, 1935).
Prieto, Indalecio, *Discursos fundamentales*, ed. E. E. Malefakis (Madrid, 1975).
Primo de Rivera, José Antonio, *Obras*, 4th edition (Madrid, 1966).
Trotsky, Leon, *La Revolution espagnole 1930–40*, ed. Pierre Broué (Paris, 1975).
Vidal i Barraquer Archives, *Esglesia i Estat durant la segona República espanyola*, 4 vols (Monastir de Montserrat, 1971–5).

Memoirs and theoretical works by protagonists

Alvarez del Vayo, Julio, *Freedom's Battle* (London, 1940).

Alvarez del Vayo, Julio, *The Last Optimist* (London, 1950).

Andrade, Juan, *La Burocracia reformista en el movimiento obrero* (Madrid, 1935).

Ansaldo, Juan Antonio, *¿Para qué? de Alfonso XIII a Juan III* (Buenos Aires, 1951).

Araquistain, Luis, *El Derrumbamiento del socialismo alemán* (Madrid, n.d. [1933]).

Baraibar, Carlos de, *Las Falsas 'posiciones socialistas' de Indalecio Prieto* (Madrid, 1935).

Berenguer, Dámaso, *De la Dictadura a la República* (Madrid, 1946).

Besteiro, Julián, *Marxismo y anti-marxismo* (Madrid, 1935).

Bueno, Javier, *El Estado socialista* (Madrid, 1931).

Bullejos, José, *España en la segunda República* (Mexico, 1967).

Bullejos, José, *La Comintern en España: recuerdos de mi vida* (Mexico, 1972).

Canel, José, *Octubre rojo en Asturias* (Madrid, 1935).

Carrillo, Santiago, *Demain l'Espagne* (Paris, 1974).

Castro Delgado, Enrique, *Hombres made in Moscú* (Barcelona, 1965).

Chapaprieta Torregrosa, Joaquín, *La Paz fue posible: memorias de un político* (Barcelona, 1971).

Cordero, Manuel, *Los Socialistas y la revolución* (Madrid, 1932).

Domingo, Marcelino, *La Experiencia del Poder* (Madrid, 1934).

Domingo, Marcelino, *La Revolución de octubre* (Barcelona, 1935).

Duclos, Jacques, *Mémoires*, vol. II *Aux jours ensoleillés du Front Populaire* (Paris, 1969).

Gil Robles, José María, *No fue posible la paz* (Barcelona, 1968).

Goded, Manuel, *Un 'Faccioso' cien por cien* (Zaragoza, 1939).

Gorkin, Julián, *El Revolucionario profesional: testimonio de un hombre de acción* (Barcelona, 1975).

Grossi, Manuel, *L'Insurrection des Asturies*, 2nd edition (Paris 1972).

[Hernández Zancajo, Carlos], *Octubre–segunda etapa* (no place or date [Madrid, 1935]).

Hidalgo, Diego, *¿Porqué fui lanzado del Ministerio de la Guerra? Diez meses de actuación ministerial* (Madrid, 1934).

Hidalgo de Cisneros, Ignacio, *Cambio de rumbo*, 2 vols (Bucharest, 1964).

Ibárruri, Dolores, *El Único camino* (Paris, 1965).

Jalón, César, *Memorias políticas: periodista, ministro, presidiario* (Madrid, 1973).

Jiménez de Asúa, Luis, *Anécdotas de las Constituyentes* (Buenos Aires, 1942).

Largo Caballero, Francisco, *Mis recuerdos* (Mexico, 1953).

Largo Caballero, Franciso, *Presente y futuro de la Unión General de Trabajadores* (Madrid, 1925).

Ledesma Ramos, Ramiro. *¿Fascismo en España?*, 2nd edition (Barcelona, 1968).

Lerroux, Alejandro, *La Pequeña historia. Apuntes para la Historia grande vividos y redactados por el autor* (Buenos Aires, 1945).

López de Ochoa, General Eduardo, *Campaña militar de Asturias en octubre de 1934* (Madrid, 1936).

Luca de Tena, Juan Ignacio, *Mis amigos muertos* (Barcelona, 1971).

Mario de Coca, Gabriel, *Anti-Caballero: una crítica marxista de la bolchevización del Partido Socialista Obrero Español* (Madrid, 1936).

Martín Blázquez, José, *I Helped to build an Army: Civil War Memoirs of a Spanish Staff Officer* (London, 1939).

Martínez Barrio, Diego, *Orígenes del Frente Popular español* (Buenos Aires, 1943).

Maura, Miguel, *Asi cayó Alfonso XIII*, 2nd edition (Barcelona, 1966).

Maurín, Joaquín, *Hacia la segunda revolución: el fracaso de la Repúblic y la insurrección de octubre* (Barcelona, 1935).

Maurín, Joaquín, *Los Hombres de la Dictadura* (Madrid, 1930).

Maurín Joaquín, *La Revolución española* (Madrid, 1932).

Monedero Martín Antonio, *La Confederación Nacional* Católica *Agraria en 1920: su espíritu, su organización, su porvenir* (Madrid, 1920).

Monge Bernal, José, *Acción Popular (estudios de biología política)* (Madrid, 1936).

Mora, Constancia de la, *In Place of Splendour* (London, 1940).

Moral, Joaquín del, *Oligarquía y 'enchufismo'* (Madrid, 1933).

Morón, Gabriel, *El Partido Socialista ante la realidad política española* (Madrid, 1929).

Morón, Gabriel, *La Ruta del socialismo en España* (Madrid, 1932).

Munis, Grandizo, *Jalones de derrota, promesa de victoria* (Mexico, 1948).

Nelken, Margarita, *Porqué hicimos la revolución* (Barcelona, 1936).

Nin, Andrés, *Los Problemas de la revolución española* (Paris, 1971).

Ossorio y Gallardo, Angel, *Mis memorias* (Buenos Aires, 1946).

Pi Sunyer, Carles, *La República y la guerra: memorias de un político catalán* (Mexico, 1975).

Prieto, Indalecio, *Convulsiones de España*, 3 vols (Mexico, 1967–9).

Prieto, Indalecio, *Del Momento: posiciones socialistas* (Madrid, n.d. [1935]).

Ramos Oliveira, Antonio, *Nosotros los marxistas: Lenin contra Marx* (Madrid, 1932).

Ramos Oliveira, Antonio, *La Revolución española de octubre* (Madrid, 1935).

Ríos, Fernando de los, *El Sentido humanista del socialismo* (Madrid, 1926).

Ríos, Fernando de los, *Escritos sobre democracia y socialismo* (Madrid, 1974).

Romero Solano, Luis, *Vísperas de la guerra de España* (Mexico, n.d. [1947]).

Rosal, Amaro del, *Historia de la UGT de España 1901–1939* 2 vols (Barcelona, 1977).

Ruiz Alonso, Ramón, *Corporativismo* (Salamanca, 1937).

Salazar Alonso, Rafael, *Bajo el signo de la revolución* (Madrid, 1935).

Sánchez Guerra, José, *Al Servicio de España* (Madrid, 1930).

Santiago, Enrique de, *La UGT ante la revolución* (Madrid, 1932).

Sanz, Ricardo, *El Sindicalismo y la política: los 'Solidarios' y 'Nosotros'* (Toulouse, 1966).

Sanz, Ricardo, *El Sindicalismo español antes de la guerra: los hijos del trabajo* (Barcelona, 1975).

Serrano Poncela, Segundo, *El Partido Socialista y la conquista del poder* (Barcelona, 1935).

Serrano Súñer, Ramón, *Entre Hendaya y Gibraltar* (Madrid, 1947).

Tagüeña Lacorte, Manuel, *Testimonio de dos guerras* (Mexico, 1973).

Trotski, Léon, *Escritos sobre España* (Paris, 1971).

Trotsky, Léon, *The Struggle Against Fascism in Germany* (New York, 1971).

Valdés, Alejandro, *¡Asturias! (relato vivido de la insurrección de octubre)* (Valencia, n.d. [1935]).

Valverde, José Tomás, *Memorias de un alcalde* (Madrid, 1961).

Vidarte, Juan-Simeón, *Las Cortes Constituyentes de 1931–1933* (Barcelona, 1976).

Vidarte, Juan-Simeón, *Todos fuimos culpables* (Mexico, 1973).

Villar, Manuel ('Ignotus'), *El Anarquismo en la insurrección de Asturias* (Valencia, 1935).

Zugazagoitia, Julián, *Guerra y vicisitudes de los Españoles*, 2 vols (Paris, 1968).

Contemporary and eye-witness accounts

Arrabal, Juan, *Gil Robles, su vida, su actuación, sus ideas* (Madrid, 1933).

Arrese, Domingo de, *Bajo la ley de defensa de la República* (Madrid, 1933).

Aunós, Eduardo, *La Política social de la Dictadura* (Madrid, 1944).

Avon, Earl of, *Facing the Dictators* (London, 1962).

Azpeitia, Mateo, *La Reforma agraria en España* (Madrid, 1932).

Barea, Arturo, *La Forja de un rebelde* (Buenos Aires, 1951).

Belausteguigoitia, Ramón de, *Reparto de tierras y producción nacional* (Madrid, 1932).

Benavides, Manuel, *El Último pirata del mediterráneo* 2nd edition (Mexico, 1976).

Benavides, Manuel, *La Revolución fue así* (Barcelona, 1935).

Berges, Consuelo, *Explicación de octubre: historia comprimida de cuatro años de República en España* (Madrid, 1935).

Boaventura, Armando, *Madrid–Moscovo: Da Ditadura a República e a Guerra Civil de Espanha* (Lisbon, 1937).

Bowers, Claude G., *My Mission to Spain* (London, 1954).

Buckley, Henry, *Life and Death of the Spanish Republic* (London, 1940).

Buenacasa, Manuel, *La CNT, los 'treinta' y la FAI* (Barcelona, 1933).

Canals, Salvador, *El Bienio estéril: perspectivas electorales* (Madrid, 1936).

Cánovas Cervantes, S., *Apuntes históricos de Solidaridad Obrera* (Barcelona, 1937).

Carral, Ignacio, *Porqué mataron a Luis de Sirval* (Madrid, 1935).

Carrión, Pascual, *Los Latifundios en España* (Madrid, 1932).

Carrión, Pascual, *La Reforma agraria: problemas fundamentales* (Madrid, 1931).

Casares, Francisco, *La CEDA va a gobernar (Notas y glosas de un año de vida pública nacional)* (Madrid, 1934).

Conze, Edward, *Spain Today: Revolution and Counter-Revolution* (London, 1936).

Cortés Cavanillas, Julián, *Gil Robles ¿monárquico?* (Madrid, 1935).

Cortés Cavanillas, Julián, *Vida, confesiones y muerte de Alfonso XIII* (Madrid, 1956).

Costa i Deu, J., and Sabaté, Modest, *La Veritat del 6 d'octubre* (Barcelona, 1936).

Díaz, Guillermo, *Como llegó Falange al Poder: análisis de un proceso contrarrevolucionario* (Buenos Aires, 1940).

Díaz del Moral, Juan, *Historia de las agitaciones campesinas andaluzas*, 3rd edition (Madrid, 1973).

Ehrenburg, Ilya, *España, república de trabajadores* (Madrid, 1976).

Félix Maíz, B., *Alzamiento en España*, 2nd edition (Pamplona, 1952).

García Palacios, Luis, *El Segundo bienio (España en escombros)* (Madrid, 1936).

Guerra, Francisco, *Casas Viejas: apuntes de la tragedia* (Jerez, 1933).

Jellinek, Frank, *The Civil War in Spain* (London, 1938).

Jupin, René, *La Question agraire en Andalusie* (Paris, 1932).

Koestler, Arthur, *Spanish Testament* (London, 1937).

León, María Teresa de, *Memoria de la melancolia* (Buenos Aires, 1970).

Manning, Leah, *What I Saw in Spain* (London, 1935).

Marco Miranda, Vicente, *Las Conspiraciones contra la Dictadura: relato de un testigo* (Madrid, 1930).

Martín-Sánchez Juliá, Fernando, *La Reforma agraria italiana y la futura reforma española* (no place or date [Madrid, 1931]).

Martínez Aguiar, Manuel, *¿A Dónde va el Estado español? Rebelión socialista y separatista de 1934* (Madrid, 1934).

Medina Togores, José. *Un Año de Cortes Constituyentes: impresiones parlamentarias* (Madrid, 1932).

Mendizábal, Alfred, *Aux Origines d'une tragédie: la politique espagnole de 1923 à 1936* (Paris, n.d. [1937?]).

Nicolás, L., *À Travers les révolutions espagnoles* (Paris, 1972).

Ramos Oliveira, Antonio, *Alemania: ayer y hoy* (Madrid, 1933).

Ramos Oliveira, Antonio, *Politics, Economics and Men of Modern Spain* (London, 1946).

Rangil Alonso, Félix, *El Ensayo socialista en la República española* (Buenos Aires, 1934).

Reporteros Reunidos, *Octubre rojo: ocho días que conmovieron a España* (Madrid, n.d. [1935]).

Rivas-Xerif, Cipriano de, *Retrato de un desconocido: vida de Manuel Azaña* (Mexico, 1961).

Rodríguez de la Peña, José, *Los Aventureros de la política: Alejandro Lerroux* (Madrid, n.d. [1916]).

Ruiz del Toro, José, *Octubre: etapas de un período revolucionario en España* (Buenos Aires, 1935).

Saborit, Andrés, *Julián Besteiro* (Buenos Aires, 1967).

Saborit, Andrés, *El Pensamiento político de Julián Besteiro* (Madrid, 1974).

Sánchez Albornoz, Claudio, *De mi anecdotario político* (Buenos Aires, 1972).

Sánchez Guerra, Rafael, *Dictadura, indiferencia, República* (Madrid, 1931).

Sender, Ramón J., *Viaje a la aldea del crimen (documental de Casas Viejas)* (Madrid, 1934).

Tusquets, J., *Orígenes de la revolución española* (Barcelona, 1932).

SECONDARY SOURCES

Monographs and general works published since 1936

Abad de Santillán, Diego, *Contribución a la historia del movimiento obrero español*, 3 vols (Puebla, 1962–71).

Aguado Sánchez, Francisco, *La Revolución de octubre de 1934* (Madrid, 1972).

Alvarez, Ramón, *Eleuterio Quintanilla (vida y obra del maestro): contribución a la historia del sindicalismo revolucionario en Asturias* (Mexico, 1973).

Arrarás, Joaquín, *Franco*, 7th edition (Valladolid, 1939).

Arrarás, Joaquín, *Historia de la cruzada española*, 8 vols (Madrid, 1939–43).

Arrarás, Joaquín, *Historia de la segunda República española*, 4 vols (Madrid, 1956–68).

Aunós, Eduardo, *Itinerario histórico de la España contemporánea* (Barcelona, 1940).

Balcells, Alberto, *Crisis económica y agitación social en Cataluña (1930–1936)* (Barcelona, 1971).

Balcells, Alberto, *El Problema agrari a Catalunya 1890–1936: la qüestió rabassaire* (Barcelona, 1968).

Balcells, Alberto, *El Sindicalismo en Barcelona 1916–1923* (Barcelona, 1965).

Bécarud, Jean, *La Segunda República española* (Madrid, 1967).

Bernal, Antonio Miguel, *La Propiedad de la tierra y las luchas agrarias andaluzas* (Barcelona, 1974).

Bizcarrondo, Marta, *Leviatán y el socialismo de Luis Araquistain* (Glashütten im Taunus, 1974).

Bizcarrondo, Marta (ed.), *Octubre del 34: reflexiones sobre una revolución* (Madrid, 1977).

Blinkhorn, Martin, *Carlism and Crisis in Spain 1931–1939* (Cambridge, 1975).

Bolín, Luis, *Spain: The Vital Years* (New York, 1967).

Bolloten, Burnett, *The Grand Camouflage: The Spanish Civil War and Revolution, 1936–1939*, 2nd edition (London, 1968).

Bonamusa, Francesc, *El Bloc Obrer i Camperol: Els primers anys (1930–1932)* (Barcelona, 1974).

Brademas, John, *Anarco-sindicalismo y revolución en España 1930–1937* (Barcelona, 1974).

Brenan, Gerald, *Personal Record 1920–1972* (London, 1974).

Brenan, Gerald, *The Spanish Labyrinth*, 2nd edition (Cambridge, 1950).

Broué, Pierre, and Témime, Emile, *The Revolution and the Civil War in Spain*, trans. from French (London, 1972).

Bruguera, F. G. *Histoire contemporaine d'Espagne 1789–1950* (Paris, 1953).

Cabanellas, Guillermo, *La Guerra de los mil días: nacimiento, vida y muerte de la segunda República española*, 2 vols (Buenos Aires, 1973).

Calero, Antonio M., *Movimientos sociales en Andalucía 1820–1936* (Madrid, 1976).

Carr, Raymond (ed.), *The Republic and the Civil War in Spain* (London, 1971).

Carr, Raymond, *Spain 1808–1939* (Oxford, 1966).

Castillo, Juan José, *El Sindicalismo amarillo en España* (Madrid, 1977).

Cattell, David, T., *Communism and the Spanish Civil War* (Berkeley, Calif., 1955).

Checkland, S. G., *The Mines of Tharsis* (London, 1967).

Cierva, Ricardo de la, *Bibliografía general sobre la guerra de España (1936–1939) y sus antecedentes históricos* (Madrid and Barcelona, 1968).

Cierva, Ricardo de la, *Historia de la guerra civil española*, vol. I (Madrid, 1969).

Cierva, Ricardo de la, *La Historia perdida del socialismo español* (Madrid, 1972).

Comín Colomer, Eduardo, *Historia del Partido Comunista de España* 3 vols (Madrid, 1967).

Cruells, Manuel, *El 6 d'Octubre a Catalunya* (Barcelona, 1971).

Díaz Nosty, B., *La Comuna asturiana: revolución de octubre de 1934* (Bilbao, 1974).

Elorza, Antonio, *La Utopía anarquista 'bajo la segunda República española* (Madrid, 1973).

Fontana, Josep, *Cambio económico y actitudes políticas en la España del siglo XIX* (Barcelona, 1973).

Fraser, Ronald, *In Hiding: The Life of Manuel Cortes* (London, 1972).

Fusi Aizpurua, Juan Pablo, *Política obrera en el país vasco 1880–1923* (Madrid, 1976).

García Delgado, José Luis (ed.), *La Cuestión agraria en la España contemporánea* (Madrid, 1976).

Gibson, Ian, *La Represión nacionalista de Granada en 1936 y la muerte de Federico García Lorca* (Paris, 1971).

Gibson, Ian, *The Death of Lorca* (London, 1973).

Gutiérrez Ravé, José, *Gil Robles, caudillo frustrado* (Madrid, 1967).

Hennessy, C. A. M., *The Federal Republic in Spain 1868–1874* (Oxford, 1962).

Ibárruri, Dolores, et al., *Guerra y revolución en España 1936–1939*, 3 vols (Moscow, 1967–71).

Jackson, Gabriel, *Costa, Azaña, el Frente Popular y otros ensayos* (Madrid, 1976).

Jackson, Gabriel, *Historian's Quest* (New York, 1969).

Jackson, Gabriel, *The Spanish Republic and the Civil War* (Princeton, NJ, 1965).

Lacomba, Juan Antonio, *La Crisis española de 1917* (Madrid, 1970).

Lamberet, Renée, *Mouvements ouvriers et socialistes: l'Espagne* (Paris, 1953).

Lamo de Espinosa Emilio, *Filosofía y política en Julián Besteiro* (Madrid, 1973).

Lorenzo, César M., *Les Anarchistes espagnols et le pouvoir, 1868–1969* (Paris, 1969).

Madariaga, Salvador de, *Spain: A Modern History* (London, 1961).

Malefakis, Edward E., *Agrarian Reform and Peasant Revolution in Spain* (New Haven, Conn., 1970).

Maurice, Jacques, *La Reforma agraria en España en el siglo XX (1900–1936)* (Madrid, 1975).

Meaker, Gerald H., *The Revolutionary Left in Spain, 1914–1923* (Stanford, Calif., 1974).

Míguez, Alberto, *El Pensamiento filosófico de Julián Besteiro* (Madrid, 1971).

Moore, Barrington, Jr., *Social Origins of Dictatorship and Democracy* (London, 1967).

Pabón, Jesús, *Cambó*, 3 vols (Barcelona, 1952–69).

Pagès, Pelai, *Andreu Nin: su evolución política, 1911–1937* (Bilbao, 1975).

Pagès, Pelai, *El Movimiento trotskista en España 1930–1935* (Barcelona, 1977).

Payne, Stanley G., *Falange: A History of Spanish Fascism* (Stanford, Calif., 1961).

Payne, Stanley G., *Politics and the Military in Modern Spain* (Stanford, Calif., 1967).

Payne, Stanley G., *The Spanish Revolution* (London, 1970).

Peirats, José, *Los Anarquistas en la crisis política española* (Buenos Aires, 1964).

Peirats, José, *La CNT en la revolución española*, 2nd edition, 3 vols (Paris, 1971).

Pérez Galán, Mariano, *La Enseñanza en la segunda República española* (Madrid, 1975).

Preston, Paul (ed.), *Leviatán: antología* (Madrid, 1976).

Ramírez Jiménez, Manuel, *Los Grupos de presión en la segunda República española* (Madrid, 1969).

Ramírez Jiménez, Manuel (ed.), *Estudios sobre la segunda República española* (Madrid, 1975).

Robinson, Richard, A. H., *The Origins of Franco's Spain: The Right, The Republic and Revolution, 1931–1936* (Newton Abbot, 1970).

Ruiz, David, *El Movimiento obrero en Asturias* (Oviedo, 1968).

Sáez Alba, A., *La Otra 'cosa nostra': la Asociación Católica Nacional de Propagandistas* (Paris, 1974).

Sánchez Albornoz, Nicolás, *España hace un siglo* (Barcelona, 1968).

Sánchez y García Saúco, Juan Antonio, *La Revolución de 1934 en Asturias* (Madrid, 1974).

Seco Serrano, Carlos *Epoca contemporánea* (Barcelona, 1971).

Southworth, Herbert R., *Antifalange* (Paris, 1967).

Southworth, Herbert R., *El Mito de la cruzada de Franco* (Paris, 1963).

Tamames, Ramón, *La República, la era de Franco* (Madrid, 1973).

Tuñón de Lara, Manuel, *El Movimiento obrero en la historia de España* (Madrid, 1972).

Tuñón de Lara, Manuel, *La España del siglo XX*, 2nd edition (Paris, 1973).

Tuñón de Lara, Manuel (ed.), *Sociedad, política y cultura en la España de los siglos XIX–XX* (Madrid, 1973).

Tusell, Javier, *Las Elecciones del Frente Popular*, 2 vols (Madrid, 1971).

Tusell, Javier, *Historia de la Democracia Cristiana en España*, 2 vols (Madrid, 1974).

Venegas, José, *Las Elecciones del Frente Popular* (Buenos Aires, 1942).

Velarde Fuertes, Juan, *El Nacional-Sindicalismo cuarenta años después* (Madrid, 1972).

Viñas, Angel, *La Alemania nazi y el 18 de julio* (Madrid, 1974).

Yagüe, María Eugenia, *Santiago Carrillo* (Madrid, 1977).

Zapatero, Virgilio, *Fernando de los Ríos: los problemas del socialismo democrático* (Madrid, 1974).

Articles

Anes, Gonzalo, 'La agricultura española desde comienzos del siglo XIX hasta 1868', in Banco de España, *Ensayos sobre la economía española a mediados del siglo XIX* (Barcelona, 1970).

Baraibar, Carlos de, 'La traición del Stalinismo', *Timón* (Buenos Aires) no. 7, (June 1940).

Bécarud, Jean, 'La acción política de Gil Robles', *Cuadernos de Ruedo Ibérico* (Paris) nos 28–9 (Dec 1970 to Mar 1971).

Bizcarrondo, Marta, 'La crisis socialista en la segunda República', *Revista del Instituto de Ciencias Sociales* (Barcelona) no. 21 (1973).

Bizcarrondo, Marta, 'Julián Besteiro : socialismo y democracia', *Revista de Occidente* (Madrid) no. 94 (Jan 1971).

Blas Guerrero, Andrés de, 'La radicalización de Francisco Largo Caballero, 1933–1934', *Sistema* (Madrid) no. 8 (Jan 1975).

Blinkhorn, Martin, ' "The Basque Ulster" : Navarra and the Basque Autonomy Question under the Spanish Second Republic', *The Historical Journal*, xvii, no. 3 (1974).

Castillo, Juan José, 'El Comité Nacional Circunstancial de la Confederación Española de Sindicatos Obreros', *Revista Española de la Opinión Pública* (Madrid), no. 38 (Oct 1974).

Claudín, Fernando, 'Dos concepciones de la vía española al socialismo', *Horizonte español 1966*, 2 vols (Paris, *Cuadernos de Ruedo Ibérico*, 1966).

Díaz Elías, 'Fernando de los Ríos : socialismo humanista y socialismo marxista', *Sistema* (Madrid) no. 10 (July 1975).

Fusi Aizpurua, Juan Pablo, 'El movimiento obrero en España, 1876–1914', *Revista de Occidente* (Madrid) no. 131 (Feb 1974).

Madden, Marie R., 'The Status of the Church and Catholic Action in Contemporary Spain', *Catholic Historical Review*, xviii (1933).

Malefakis, Edward E., 'Peasants, Politics and Civil War in Spain, 1931–1939', in Bezucha, Robert J., *Modern European Social History* (Boston, Mass, 1972).

Nadal, Jordi, 'Spain, 1830–1914', in Cipolla, Carlo M., *The Emergence of Industrial Society*, 2 vols (London, 1973).

Preston Paul, 'Alfonsist Monarchism and the Coming of the Spanish Civil War', *Journal of Contemporary History*, vii, nos 3–4 (1972).

Preston, Paul, 'El accidentalismo de la CEDA : ¿aceptación o sabotage de la República?', *Cuadernos de Ruedo Ibérico* (Paris) nos 41–2 Feb–May 1973).

Preston, Paul. 'The "Moderate" Right and the Undermining of the Second Spanish Republic, 1931–1933', *European Studies Review*, iii, no. 4 (1973).

Preston, Paul 'Spain's October Revolution and the Rightist Grasp for Power', *Journal of Contemporary History*, x, no. 4 (1975).

Romero Maura, Joaquín, 'El debate historiográfico acerca de la segunda República', *Revista Internacional de Sociología* (Madrid) 2nd ser., nos 3–4 (July–Dec 1972).

Varela Ortega, José, 'Reacción y revolución frente a la reforma', *Revista Internacional de Sociología* (Madrid) 2nd ser., nos 3–4 (July–Dec 1972).

Viñas, Miguel, 'Franquismo y revolución burguesa', *Horizonte español 1972*, 3 vols (Paris, *Cuadernos de Ruedo Ibérico*, 1972).

SUPPLEMENTARY BIBLIOGRAPHY (1983)

A number of important works have appeared since first publication. The following list is a selection of the most outstanding memoirs and scholarly studies.

Ben-Ami, Shlomo, *The Origins of the Second Republic in Spain* (Oxford, 1978).

Carr, Raymond, *The Spanish Tragedy* (London, 1977).

Contreras, Manuel, *El PSOE en la II República: Organización e ideología* (Madrid, 1981).

Espín, Eduardo, *Azaña en el Poder: el Partido de Acción Repúblicana* (Madrid, 1980).

Fraser, Ronald, *Blood of Spain* (London, 1979).

Fusi, Juan Pablo, *El problema vasco en la II República* (Madrid, 1979).

Jiménez Campo, Javier, *El fascismo en la crisis de la II República* (Madrid, 1979).

Juliá, Santos, *La izquierda del PSOE (1935–1936)* (Madrid, 1977).

Juliá, Santos, *Orígenes del Frente Popular en España* (Madrid, 1979).

Márquez Tornero, A. C., *Testimonio de mi tiempo* (Madrid, 1979).

Mintz, Jerome R., *The Anarchists of Casas Viejas* (Chicago, 1982).

Montero, José R., *La CEDA: el catolicismo social y político en la II República*, 2 vols (Madrid, 1977).

Pérez Yruela, Manuel, *La conflictividad campesina en la provincia de Córdoba 1931–1936* (Madrid, 1979).

Rosado, Antonio, *Tierra y libertad* (Barcelona, 1979).

Serrano, Vicente-Alberto, and San Luciano, José María (eds), *Azaña* (Madrid, 1980).

Sevilla Guzmán, Eduardo, *La evolución del campesinado en España* (Barcelona, 1979).

Shubert, Adrian, 'Revolution in self-defence; the radicalization of the Asturian coal miners, 1921–1934', *Social History*, VII, no. 3 (1982).

Tuñón de Lara, Manuel, *Luchas obreras y campesinas en la Andalucía del siglo XX* (Madrid, 1978).

Vidarte, Juan-Simeón, *El bienio negro y la insurreción de Asturias* (Barcelona, 1978).

Index